MEDIEVAL WARFARE

Other books by the author
The Knights Hospitaller (2001)
The Knights Templar: A New History (2001)
Love, War and the Grail: Templars, Hospitallers and Teutonic Knights in Medieval Epic and Romance (2000)
The Military Orders, vol. 2: Welfare and Warfare (editor, 1998)
Chronicle of the Third Crusade: A Translation of the Itinerarium Peregrinorum et Gesta Regis Ricardi (1997)
Templars, Hospitallers and Teutonic Knights: Images of the Military Orders, 1128–1291 (1993)

MEDIEVAL WARFARE

Theory and Practice of War in Europe
300–1500

HELEN NICHOLSON

First published 2004 by
PALGRAVE MACMILLAN
Houndmills, Basingstoke, Hampshire RG21 6XS and
175 Fifth Avenue, New York, N.Y. 10010
Companies and representatives throughout the world

PALGRAVE MACMILLAN is the global academic imprint of the Palgrave
Macmillan division of St. Martin's Press, LLC and of Palgrave Macmillan Ltd.
Macmillan® is a registered trademark in the United States, United Kingdom
and other countries. Palgrave is a registered trademark in the European
Union and other countries.

ISBN 0–333–76330–0 hardback
ISBN 0–333–76331–9 paperback

This book is printed on paper suitable for recycling and made from fully
managed and sustained forest sources.

A catalogue record for this book is available from the British Library.

Library of Congress Cataloging-in-Publication Data

Nicholson, Helen J., 1960–
    Medieval warfare : theory and practice of war in Europe, 300–1500 / Helen
    Nicholson.
        p. cm
    Includes bibliographical references and index.
    ISBN 0–333–76330–0 (cloth) –ISBN 0–333–76331–9 (pbk.)
        1. Military history, Medieval. 2. Europe–History, Military. 3. Military art and
science–History–Medieval, 500–1500. 4. Military weapons–Europe–History–To 1500.
5. Fortification–Europe. I. Title.
U37.N52 2003
355'.0094'0902–dc21

                                                                2003046951

10 9 8 7 6 5 4 3 2 1
13 12 11 10 09 08 07 06 05 04

Printed in China

Contents

Preface

In this study I consider various themes of continuity and discontinuity in warfare and, more broadly, military activity, from the late Roman Empire in the West down to the beginning of the sixteenth century. This period was termed 'the middle ages' (*medium ævum* in Latin – hence 'medieval') by Western scholars of the seventeenth century and later, and that term is used here as a familiar label of convenience.[1] The geographical area of this study is, broadly, the area which modern scholars of the Middle Ages would now call 'Latin Christendom'; but as this term is not familiar to non-experts in the period, it seemed better to use the term 'Europe', despite the fact that the concept of 'Europe' did not exist in the period under consideration.

This book is intended to provide a point of entry to the subject of medieval warfare for students and others with an interest in the subject who are perplexed by the rapidly expanding body of scholarship in this area. It is meant as a synthesis and summary of the present state of knowledge on the themes and debates that are considered here. It should enable readers to trace these themes from the ancient period through the medieval period and from the medieval period forward, and provides an introduction and overview of the whole of the field of medieval warfare. This book is not intended to be a definitive history of the subject, nor is it intended to settle any of the current debates. However, by setting out points in debate, and approaching the subject thematically rather than chronologically, it should help to clarify some of the issues.

My intention in this volume is to provide students with a succinct thematic survey of this important field, avoiding the very detailed chronological approach which, while useful, can be less accessible. As thematic discussions are apt to become vague and over-generalising unless they are firmly tied to actual examples, the chapters on personnel and equipment begin with relatively detailed considerations of certain aspects of the subject in order to introduce the reader to some of the issues before progressing to more general analysis, while the chapter on buildings begins with an overview of categories of building before plunging into a chronological account of development. The chapter on the practice of warfare on land deals with themes in the order in which they might occur in an actual campaign: training of troops, reaching the place of conflict, sieges and battles and the aftermath of the war. I have illustrated points with references to medieval writers and examples which were selected as being particularly striking or memorable. The traditionalist may find that this book departs too far from the usual paths to be palatable, but I hope that it will be a more accessible 'way in' to the subject for the non-specialist.

The subject of medieval warfare and military activity is now so wide that it has not been possible to include all areas of debate here and, in the interests of providing a wide overview, some important issues have had to be dealt with in summary or overlooked. Scholars of medieval warfare have long recognised that the subject is too vast for one individual to have direct command of the whole subject. In his *Crusading Warfare, 1097–1193* (1954), R. C. Smail wrote: 'Since no one scholar can hope to master the sources for the history of so great a subject through a millennium, such works need to be rooted in the more limited researches of specialists.'[2] His words were repeated in 1980 by Philippe Contamine in the introduction to his *La Guerre au moyen âge*, a study covering the period from the fifth to the end of the fifteenth century.[3] However, since 1980 there has been very rapid growth in the number of original sources printed and in the number of secondary studies produced on medieval warfare, so that merely mastering the 'more limited researches of specialists' has become a major undertaking, and detailed consideration of them all in one volume would require a much larger book than is possible here. Even Everett U. Crosby's recent *Medieval Warfare: A Bibliographical Guide* (New York and London, Garland, 2000), which covers 190 pages and includes around 3000 entries, is not fully comprehensive: as the author himself admits (p. xv), there are no entries, for example, on the expanding research into women's roles in medieval warfare. Hence, although in this present work I have attempted to cover the major areas of warfare and military activity, it has been impossible to deal with every aspect of the subject. Many areas of interest to modern historians such as morale, uniforms, commanders, the financing of war, the impact of war on government and the production of weapons have received only cursory treatment. I apologise to readers who do not find what they are seeking here.

Again, due to limitations of space, I have not been able to include detailed consideration of Byzantine or Muslim practice, although this would certainly have been useful for comparison. I have, however, included some examples drawn from Catholic Christian experiences during the Crusades in Syria and Palestine.

Given the vast changes which occurred in warfare during the period covered by this book, some explanation is required as to why the period 300–1500 was chosen. In the Renaissance period (the dating of which is itself the subject of scholarly debate, as it began at different times in different parts of what is now Europe), scholars regarded the period between the fall of the Western Roman Empire and what they regarded as the recovery of classical learning in the West as a period of decline and stagnation between two ages of civilisation and learning. However, modern scholars have stressed the continuity of institutions and learning from the late Western Roman Empire throughout this so-called 'middle age' to the so-called 'renaissance'.[4] In the field of warfare, while there were clear changes in practice, there were also continuities. The most obvious continuity was the significance of the analysis of military matters composed by the Roman bureaucrat Vegetius. This book, written in the late fourth century, was cited as a practical authority on warfare until the sixteenth century. Taking that particular continuity as a basis, this study covers the period from the century in which Vegetius wrote down to the beginning of the sixteenth century. The year 1500, by which time classical learning had been restored and rulers were again maintaining professional standing armies, provides a convenient cut-off point.

Because this study considers a period of over a millennium and adopts a thematic approach to the subject, there is a certain amount of 'leaping about' chronologically in the examples given. These examples are intended to illustrate continuity of practice, or to demonstrate change. As it has not always been possible to illustrate this change smoothly in this brief book, a chronology has been provided to help readers to find their way around the period. A few examples are given from a sixteenth-century biography of the Chevalier Bayart (or Bayard), who died in 1524, after the end of the period covered by this book. Bayart is included here because his career illustrates the continuation of knightly ideals and practice, while also showing how changes in military technology and organisation affected war by the early sixteenth century. His career therefore forms a neat conclusion to the period.

* * *

The notes and 'further reading' here make no attempt to be comprehensive. I have included in the notes works which I have specifically consulted on individual points, while the further reading gives a brief list of well known and, I hope, easily accessible recent works on each area. For the most part the notes are intended to illustrate, not to prove points. The vast majority of the information in this book is not in question and does not require proof. Only where there is debate among scholars or where the subject has not been considered in detail by scholars have I included lengthy lists of references. I apologise to scholars whose works I have inadvertently overlooked. For the convenience of monolinguist English-speaking readers, I have attempted where possible to refer in the notes to modern English translations of the works I have used. In some cases this has not been possible: for instance, there is no complete modern English translation of the work of Jean Froissart,[5] nor of the work of Jean le Bel. Translations in the text are referenced to the translation I have used; if I cite no translated edition then the translation is my own. Readers seeking more detailed listings of secondary works may now refer to Crosby's bibliography.

In rendering medieval names, I have tried to use the most familiar form for English-speaking readers. Where there is none, I have tended to use the form of the name given in the medieval text, unless there is a very obvious English translation which could be used instead.

I have incurred many debts in the writing of this book. It could not have been written without the assistance of the staff of Cardiff University Library, Leicester University Library and the British Library in London. My thanks are due to Professor Jeremy Black for first suggesting that I write on this subject, and to the editors and reader at Palgrave Macmillan for their input and guidance. I am extremely grateful to Professor John France of Swansea University, who read through my initial plan and made constructive suggestions, provided bibliographical material and discussed the subject with me on various occasions. I am also very grateful to my colleagues Professors Peter Coss, Peter Edbury and Denys Pringle, and Dr Bill Aird, Dr Kate Gilliver, Dr Kari Maund, Dr Louis Rawlings and Bill Zajac (now of CADW: Welsh Historic Monuments) for their input and ideas at various stages of the scheme. Some further specific acknowledgements are given in the notes. My husband Nigel and son Gawain have accompanied me around numerous sites in Britain and the Mediterranean. Nigel read this work and pointed out various lapses. Finally, but not least, my students have asked awkward questions and have frequently forced me to rethink my ideas.

Chronology of main events

Southern Europe	Iberian Peninsula	Gaul/Francia	British Isles	Central Europe	Eastern Europe	Middle East
305 Death of Diocletian 312 Conversion of Constantine						
					330 Refounding of Constantinople	
337 Death of Constantine						359 Capture of Amida by Persians
					386–8 Vegetius writes *De re militari*	
410 Sack of Rome 425-55 Valentinian III Emperor of the West 430 Death of Bishop Augustine of Hippo Regius						
	455 Vandals invade Italy					
476 Deposition of last Roman emperor in the West						
		c.481–c.511 Clovis holds power in Gaul				
	507 Visigothic kingdom set up	500s war between Gundobad and Godigisel of Burgundy				
		520 Danish fleet defeated by King Theuderic				
526 Death of Theodoric, Ostrogothic king of Italy						

534 Death of Athalaric; death of Amalasunth 561 Lombards invade Italy from north		531 Siege of Chastel-Marlhac 561 Death of Lothar I 572 Saxons pillage Gaul; Count Mummolus fights Lombards 585 Rebellion of Gundovald 594 Death of Gregory of Tours, historian	539 Battle of Camlann	531 Thuringians and Franks in battle	560s Death of Procopius, historian
					597 Avars besiege Thessaloniki
					636 Arab capture of Jerusalem
	680–7 Visigothic King Ervig's law code 711 Muslims invade peninsula		634 Death of King Osric of Deira 655 Battle on River Winwaed		
		732 Battle of Poitiers 735 Duke Childebrand of Aquitaine besieges Avignon 741 Death of Charles Martel	735 Death of Bede, historian		
747 Pope Zacharias appeals to Pepin III for aid 750 King Aistulf of the Lombards issues regulations on military equipment				750s? Danevirke built	

Southern Europe	Iberian Peninsula	Gaul/Francia	British Isles	Central Europe	Eastern Europe	Middle East
760 Byzantine fleet helps Lombards against Pepin III		760 Pepin III marches to Aquitaine 762 Pepin III besieges Bourges	757–96 Reign of King Offa of Mercia			
768 Death of Pepin (Pippin) III, king of the Franks. Charlemagne takes power in Francia			Late 8th century? Composition of *Beowulf*			
	778 Battle of Roncesvalles					
800 Charlemagne crowned as emperor at Rome 814 Death of Charlemagne						
		830 Rebellion of sons of Louis the Pious 836–8 Louis the Pious pressurises Danish king to arrest pirates 842 Alliance between Charles the Bald and Louis the German				
		845 Viking fleet sails up Seine	851 Vikings sack Dublin			
		861–4 Viking fleets sail up Seine and Loire				
		865–6 Vikings besiege Paris				
		869 Fortified bridge built on Seine	871–99 Reign of King Alfred of Wessex	872 Sea battle of Hafrsfjord		
				876 Death of King Louis the German		
877 Death of Charles the Bald, western emperor						
				880–1 Viking band winters at Nijmegen		
		882 Death of Hincmar, archbishop of Reims	882 Ships of Wessex fight Vikings			

924–5 King Henry 'the Fowler' sets up defence system against Magyars	896 King Alfred builds a fleet	911 Charles *Simplex* establishes Norsemen in Normandy	
	899–924 Edward the Elder king of Wessex		
950s Liudolf rebels against Otto I.		930s? Odo, abbot of Cluny, composes 'The Life of Gerald of Aurillac'	
		947 Siege of Senlis	
		975 First 'peace council', at Le Puy	
		985 Siege of Verdun	
		987 Fulk Nerra becomes count of Anjou	
1000 Sea battle of Svoldr	991 Battle of Maldon	1027 Council of Toulouges inaugurates 'truce of God'	
			1039 First *carroccio* recorded, at Milan
		1040 Death of Fulk Nerra	
1044 Sea battle of Aarhus			1046 Roger Guiscard comes to Italy
		1060 Death of Geoffrey Martel, count of Anjou	1060 Roger Guiscard raids Sicily
1062 Sea battle of Nisaa	1066 Battle of Hastings		1062 First recorded tournament
			1087 Pisan-Genoese fleet sacks Mahdiyyah
		1085 Toledo captured by Alfonso VI of Castile	

Southern Europe	Iberian Peninsula	Gaul/Francia	British Isles	Central Europe	Eastern Europe	Middle East
1090 Death of Bishop Bonizo of Sutri	1090 Rebuilding of walls of Avila 1099 Death of Rodrigo Díaz de Vivar ('El Cid')		1098 Sea battle off Anglesey	1095 Bishop Otbert of Liège besieges Clermont-sur-Meuse		1095–9 First Crusade 1099 Capture of Jerusalem by First Crusade
1106 Death of Emperor Henry IV 1115 Death of Countess Matilda of Tuscany		1106 Battle of Tinchebrai 1120s Composition of *La Chanson de Roland*?		1114 Valenciennes lays down regulations for communal army		1119 Second battle of Tell Danith 1120s Military religious orders set up
1135 Roger II of Sicily captures Jerba	1140 Castle of Amposta given to Hospitallers 1147 Siege of Lisbon	1130 Church council of Clermont bans tournaments 1147–51 Siege of Montreuil-Bellay	1141 Battle of Lincoln; siege of Winchester 1150–5 Wace composes the *Brut* 1159 John of Salisbury composes *Policraticus* 1169 Cymro-Norman invasion of Ireland	1151 Guild set up at Roskilde to stop Wendish pirates 1159 battle of Gotha River	1160 Siege of Zevgminon	1147–8 Second Crusade
1160 Battle of Carcano 1160s: Benjamin of Tudela in Italy						

1177 Peace of Venice	1180–3: 'White Hoods' fight mercenary bands.	1181 Assize of Arms	1183 Peace of Constance	1194 Livonian crusade begins	1177 Battle of Montgisard
	1189 Death of King Henry II of England		1184 Danes use fire ships against Wendish port		c.1184 Death of Archbishop William II of Tyre, historian
	1199 Death of Richard I, king of England	1194 Ban on tournaments in England lifted			1187 Siege of Tiberias; Battle of Hattin
	1209–26 Albigensian Crusades				1189–92 Third Crusade
	1211 Siege of Castelnaudry				1189–91 siege of Acre
	1214 Death of Bertrand de Born	1214–17 Barons' War			1193 Death of Saladin
		1215 Magna Carta			
	1218 Simon de Montfort killed at siege of Toulouse	1217 Sea battle off Sandwich			1217–21 Fifth Crusade
		1219 Death of William Marshal			

Southern Europe	Iberian Peninsula	Gaul/Francia	British Isles	Central Europe	Eastern Europe	Middle East
1237 Emperor Frederick II fighting the north Italian cities	1233 King James I of Aragon attacks Valencia				1230s Teutonic Order begins campaigns in Prussia	
1240 Castel del Monte built		1244 Louis IX of France takes Crusade vow	1240 Death of Llywelyn ap Iorwerth			1248–54 Crusade of King Louis IX of France
1249 Siege of Viterbo				1252 Siege of Cologne by Archbishop Konrad		
1266 Battle of Benevento 1268 Battle of Tagliacozzo 1270s Rusticien de Pise compiles his collection for Edward I of England		1271 Egidio Colonna (Giles of Rome) composes De regimine principum				1271 Crac des Chevaliers falls to Baybars
1275 Earliest surviving sea chart produced in Pisa 1282–1302 War of the Sicilian Vespers 1283 Sea battle at Malta 1284 Sea battle in Bay of Naples	1276 Death of King James I of Aragon		1276–77 Edward I's first Welsh War 1282 Edward I's second Welsh War			1277 Death of Sultan Baybars
	1284 Death of King Alfonso X of Castile 1285 Crusade against Aragon; sea battle at Las Hormigas	1284 Jean de Meun translates Vegetius				

1287 'Battle of the Counts' in Bay of Naples

1302–3 Creation of the Catalan Company

1309 Death of Charles II of Anjou, king of Naples

1326 Guns in a Florentine armoury inventory

1330 Alfonso XI of Castile sets up 'The Order of the Band'

Late 1280s Jean Priorat de Besançon trans. Vegetius

1302 Battle of Courtrai
1303 Battle of Arques
1304 Battle of Mons-en-Pévèle

1314 Death of King Philip IV

1288 Battle of Worringen

1324 Guns used at siege of Metz

1330s Composition of *Perceforest*

1307 Battle of Loudon Hill. Death of King Edward I

1314 Battle of Bannockburn

1327 First Scottish campaign of King Edward III

1332 Battle of Dupplin Moor

1333 Battle of Halidon Hill
1337 English gov. orders archers to practise;
1337–8 1st ref. to shipboard gunpowder weapons

1305 Murder of Roger de Flor

1311 Battle of Kephissos

1291 Loss of Acre: end of Latin kingdom of Jerusalem

1309 Hospital of St John captures Rhodes

Southern Europe	Iberian Peninsula	Gaul/Francia	British Isles	Central Europe	Eastern Europe	Middle East
			1338 French naval attack on Southampton			
		1339 Hundred Years War begins				
		1340 Sea battle off Sluis				
		1346 Capture of Caen; battle of Crécy	1346 Battle of Neville's Cross			
		1347 Siege of Calais				
		1352 King John II of France sets up 'The Order of the Star'				
		1356 Battle of Poitiers. Death of Geoffrey de Charny, knight				
		1361 Pope Innocent VI calls a crusade against the Companies				
	1365 The Great Companies go to Spain	1364 Battle of Cocherel; battle of Auray				
		1368 Death of Jean de Venette, chronicler				
		1370 Battle of Pontvallain				
		1372 English fleet sunk off La Rochelle by Castilians. Fall of La Rochelle to French				

			1403 Marshal Boucicaut raids Syrian-Palestinian coastline
	1386 Conversion of Lithuania		
	1396 Battle of Nicopolis		
	1410 Battle of Tannenberg (Grunwald)		
	1420 First crusade against the Hussites. Battle of Kutná Hora		
	1420–34 Hussite crusades		
1377 Duke Philip the Bold of Burgundy besieges Odruik with cannon			
1380s Invention of the bombard?			
1426 Battle of Bouwershaven			
1377 Death of King Edward III of England			
1378 John Philipot, London Merchant, equips a fleet to destroy pirates			
1380 Death of Bertrand du Guesclin			
1381 'Peasants' Revolt'			
1387 Honoré Bouvet produces *L'Arbre des Batailles*			
1408–9 Christine de Pisan composes *Le livre des faits des armes et de la chevalerie*			
1410: Death of Jean Froissart, chronicler			
1415 Battle of Agincourt			
1421 Death of Boucicaut			
1429 Joan of Arc arrives at Orléans			
1431 Execution of Joan of Arc			
1434 King Duarte of Portugal composes 'On the art of good horsemanship'			

Southern Europe	Iberian Peninsula	Gaul/Francia	British Isles	Central Europe	Eastern Europe	Middle East
		1445 King Charles VII starts a standing army		1441 Duke Philip the Good of Burgundy sends a fleet to the Middle East	1445 Burgundian fleet bombards Giurgevo	
		1453 Battle of Castillon: effective end of the Hundred Years War	1457 Mons Meg given to King James II of Scotland	1467 Duke Charles the Bold of Burgundy attacks Liège		
		1471 Battle of Amiens		1471 Charles the Bold sets up a permanent army 1475 Battle of Neuss 1476 Battle of Murten (Morat) 1477 Death of Charles the Bold Battle of Nancy		1480 First Ottoman siege of Rhodes
			1485 Battle of Bosworth 1489 King Henry VII commissions Caxton to translate Christine de Pisan's *Livre des faits*		1499 Sea battle of Zonchio (Navarino)	
1512 Battle of Brescia; Battle of Ravenna 1524 Death of Chevalier Bayart						

Introduction

It is a truth universally acknowledged that warfare was central to medieval society. The power and authority of kings rested largely on their ability to wage war successfully; social theorists depicted the warriors as forming one of the three divisions of society, with an essential role within it; and those who recorded the history of the period devoted the bulk of their pages to describing war.

Yet exactly what medieval warfare was can be difficult to define. In modern times, 'war' generally refers to a military conflict between states, but this definition is not very helpful for the period before nation-states were established. In the medieval period, military hostilities carried on by the leader of one military band against another could be 'war', waged in a similar manner and even on a similar scale to military hostilities carried on by one king against another. While military theorists in the later Middle Ages made a distinction between 'public' war fought by the ruler and 'private' war fought by individuals, in fact the two sorts of war could not be so easily separated. Individual conflicts could form part of larger conflicts, and large campaigns were made up of small bands under individual leaders, rather than one large army led by one overall general to whom all owed allegiance. There might be little difference between simple banditry and a rebellious lord waging war against a king. In fact, a history of medieval warfare could very easily become a history of medieval violence. In this study 'war' is taken in the broad sense of 'hostile contention by means of armed forces' (to quote the *Oxford English Dictionary*), and means any form of ongoing armed violence between bands of men. It need not be a conflict between kings or states, and this book is as much a history of medieval military activity as of large-scale warfare.

The difficulty of defining warfare is linked to the problem of why warfare was fought during the Middle Ages: in other words, what the long-term strategy of war was. It is clear that those in authority waged war in order to stay in authority. They had to show that they possessed the power to force their subjects to obey them. They needed to win land and booty to reward their followers, and prove to them that it was worthwhile remaining in their service rather than going to serve a different lord. They also had to protect their subjects from enemies – this was one of the duties of Christian lordship inherited from the Christian emperors of the later Roman Empire. In the early and central Middle Ages, the king who could not go on campaign each year and win territory and booty to give to his followers would have difficulty in retaining the services of his followers. The campaigns of Charlemagne (king of the Franks 768–800, emperor of the West 800–14), were of this type: defending his core territories, inherited from his father; and attacking and conquering new territory and booty as a means of rewarding his vassals and the Church. This said, Bernard Bachrach has argued that Charlemagne's grandfather, Charles Martel (d. 741), did not go to war to seek booty, and when possible used diplomacy rather than warfare to maintain control of his nobles. But diplomacy did not always work; and then war was necessary.[1]

As boundaries of kingdoms became more fixed and society more settled, such annual campaigns of acquisition or suppression were possible or necessary only on the frontiers of Christendom, or in territory involving disputed rights, such as France during the Anglo-French war of the fourteenth and fifteenth centuries, otherwise known as 'the Hundred Years War'. Nevertheless, a king must be successful in warfare, and one that was not would have problems in retaining his position as king.

There were also individual reasons for waging war. Individual warriors became involved in war partly because they had no choice: their employer or superior demanded that they fight. On the other hand, they also fought in order to win glory and honour and so raise their prestige in society. They might win wealth (land or money or other property), both from booty taken during war and from gifts from their grateful employer or lord. They would win the admiration of others, and might be able thereby to attract the attention of desirable partners, so increasing the possibility of marriage and leaving children to carry on their line. Brave deeds could be recorded in poetry or in written history, ensuring fame after one's death; likewise, a marriage with many children ensured a different sort of continuation after death.

Christian thinking was ambiguous on the subject of war: on the one hand, some of Christ's words set out in the New Testament seemed to condemn war, but on the other, the Old Testament and other passages in the New Testament seemed to permit it.[2] 'Holy war' was, however, acceptable. In brief, this was war fought to further God's purposes, identified as 'holy' by ecclesiastical or secular authorities.[3] Those taking part in such wars would, they believed, win God's approval, and might also hope to win booty and perhaps territory. The crusades to the Holy Land were holy wars, as were the wars between Christians and Moors in the Iberian Peninsula from the eleventh century to the late fifteenth and between

Christians and pagans in north-eastern Europe from the twelfth century to the late fourteenth. Those engaged in such campaigns typically took part in various penitential and devotional exercises during the campaign, which encouraged group loyalty and raised morale. In 791, Charlemagne set out on a campaign against the pagan Avars on his eastern frontier: before engaging battle, the army prayed and fasted for three days. On 8 July 1099, before the final assault on Jerusalem, the army of the First Crusade processed around the base of the city walls, prayed and fasted.[4]

Not all war was long term or large scale. Much 'warfare' was actually short-term raids with the aim of taking booty (particularly livestock) and slaves or prisoners; the booty was immediate wealth, while prisoners could be ransomed and slaves could be sold, put to work to produce wealth, or retained in the captor's household as a symbol of status. Most of the warfare described by Gregory of Tours (d. 594) was of this type, in which rulers would devastate even their own subjects in order to enforce their authority over an area.[5] Much of early medieval warfare can be characterised as essentially raiding without any long-term aim of permanently acquiring territory or any obvious motivation other than gaining booty and honour. By the eleventh century this sort of warfare was becoming morally questionable in the face of the peace-making efforts of the Catholic Church in western Europe, and John Gillingham has described how the raiding activities of the Irish, Welsh and Scots were depicted by twelfth-century Anglo-Norman writers as barbaric, underpinning their image of these Celtic peoples as barbarians unfit to govern land.[6] Yet such raiding could have a definite strategic purpose: Scottish raids against northern England in the first three decades of the fourteenth century played a fundamental role in undermining the authority of the English king north of the Trent, and contributed to the downfall of King Edward II (1227). Raids could also force the payment of tribute, providing a valuable income for the conqueror. This was one of the aims of Viking raiding in the ninth and tenth centuries, and arguably of the kings of East Francia against the Slavs in the ninth century.[7]

On the frontier between Christian Spain and Moorish al-Andalus in the Iberian Peninsula from the eleventh to the late fifteenth century, the raid against the enemy was the normal means of keeping up hostilities. It was not that the war was pressed continuously. There were truces, diplomatic contacts, occasional conversions, and Christians and Muslims crossed the border for peaceful as well as martial purposes. But the rulers of neither side wanted long-term peace. War ensured security (by reducing the risk of a raid from the other side); war might gain territory, certainly gained booty; war was a means of revenge; war was a means of winning honour. Moorish frontier raiders who were captured by Christian soldiers were dealt with brutally, and the Christian authorities paid a bounty for their heads. For instance, three Moorish frontier raiders captured in January 1435 by three Christians in the Aledo region were beheaded. The three brought the heads to the municipal council of Murcia and asked for a reward: they were paid 300 *maravedíes*, in accordance with an old municipal ordinance.[8] Raiding on this frontier, then, could take two forms: raids into the enemy territory to ravage and take booty and prisoners, and raids throughout one's own territory to catch and destroy enemy raiders.

The campaigns of the military religious Teutonic Order in north-eastern Europe in the thirteenth to fifteenth centuries were called *reisen*, literally 'rides' – that is, raids – but were on a much larger scale than the word suggests. These were essentially hostile campaigns into their opponents' territory.[9] Each year there were two such campaigns, one setting out on the Assumption of the Blessed Virgin Mary (15 August), and one on the Purification of the Blessed Virgin Mary (2 February). These dates were originally chosen because they were the principal feast days of the Order's patron, the Virgin. The campaigns were conducted with cavalry and foot soldiers, and included crusaders who came especially from Germany, Britain and France to take part in the crusade against the unbelievers – although after the conversion of Lithuania in 1386 the war was against Christians. The aim of the campaign was to take booty and prisoners, but also to weaken the enemy so that in the long term Lithuanian territory could be taken under the rule of the Order; given the nature of the terrain (forested or marshy) it was difficult to win long-term gains in any one campaign. It is true, however, as Eric Christiansen has noted, that it was unsuccessful as a war of attrition – while the Order grew stronger, so did the Lithuanians.[10] Travel across country was difficult, so river transport was used to carry supplies, reinforcements, siege machines and horses. Having reached enemy territory and set up a base, the Order's forces conducted raids on a daily basis, moving on to a new area after each raid; and then withdrawing before the enemy's army could arrive to engage them.[11]

This devastation of territory as part of a war of attrition was also a feature of the Hundred Years War. Anne Curry has argued that the devastation, inflicted during a series of *chevauchées* or raids across the kingdom of France, was a deliberate strategy of attrition with the aim of extracting concessions from the enemy. This theory explains why kings of England made a truce and withdrew to England after winning victories in battle: their aim was not to conquer the kingdom of France but to win recognition of their claims to certain territory under the authority of the king of France.[12] After 1356 the French tended to avoid battle, and to concentrate on raiding into the English-dominated areas of the kingdom of France. This weakened their opponents without taking the risk of complete defeat in battle.

The Hundred Years War was ostensibly an inheritance dispute, as Edward III of England (d. 1377) claimed the French throne through his descent from King Philip IV of France (d. 1314). While Curry's arguments indicate that in fact his actual aim was more complex, other wars were certainly fought with the target of claiming an inheritance. The invasion of England in 1066 by William of Normandy, known as 'the Bastard' to his contemporaries, is one of the more famous examples.[13] The rebellion of Gundovald, which will be considered at the beginning of Chapter 2, had as its basis Gundovald's claim to be an heir of King Lothar I (d. 561), king of the Franks.

So warfare was fought for different reasons, and varied in scale and effect. How war was fought also varied from one area to another, depending on geography and tradition; and it changed over time. For many years, historians of medieval warfare doubted that there was such a thing as military planning in the Middle Ages. They regarded medieval warfare as a matter of individuals seeking glory, without discipline or battle tactics and without a wider grasp of strategy. This view was based more on the descriptions of battles in the entertainment literature of the Middle Ages, the epics and romances, than on careful study of battles and sieges. The work of J. F. Verbruggen has now established that there was in fact 'an art of war' in the Middle Ages, and many modern studies have elaborated on this 'art of war' and how it developed.[14]

During the period between the break up of the Roman Empire in the West and the beginning of the sixteenth century, military tactics evolved from an emphasis on infantry to an emphasis on cavalry and back to an emphasis on infantry; artillery changed with the development of improved weaponry for killing at a distance, such as the crossbow and the bombard. The use of fortifications developed from walls defining areas (such as the famous Hadrian's Wall in northern England) and protecting cities (such as Trier in the late Roman period) and temporary refuges such as hill forts, to strongly fortified buildings containing one household and its retainers. These buildings, now called 'castles', differed from the hill fort mainly in that they were intended to withstand sieges for long periods of time, but the older types of fortification continued to be constructed and to be used throughout the period covered by this book. Armies themselves changed in nature from being largely paid professionals employed by the state on a permanent basis to being amateurs bound by personal loyalty to a war leader, and then again to being paid professionals.

Yet despite the changes during this period, certain factors remained constant. The Germanic warriors who were employed by the late Western Roman Empire as auxiliaries believed that they were superior to the Romans who employed them because they had energy and drive in battle, unlike their employers. In the fifth and sixth centuries their leaders were delegated or took over the administrative and military structures of the old Western Empire, but these warriors' organisation and ideology differed somewhat from the Roman army.[15] As is clear from the warriors' own literature and will be set out in greater detail in later chapters, the warriors' ties of loyalty to their leader and their code of honour meant that their warfare was personal and victory or defeat was a matter of concern to every individual, not only to their general. They fought on foot or on horseback, but valued the horse as a status symbol for the warrior. They valued martial skills; and they saw booty as the due reward for their martial exploits. They regarded Christ as a warrior God, fighting against evil; they regarded fighting as the proper activity for an able-bodied man. Ideally, battle should be joined hand-to-hand and attacking one's enemy from a distance with artillery could be regarded as cowardly. Death in battle was glorious, although the amazement and shock expressed by chroniclers and other contemporaries at the deaths in battle of nobles of high status suggest that a well-armed and skilled noble warrior was relatively unlikely to be killed in battle, and if he was, he could be expected to take much of the enemy army with him.[16] Social stratification within the army was important, and those of lower status should not engage those of higher status. The death and suffering of non-combatants, while regrettable, was unavoidable and regarded by the warrior as a natural concomitant of war.[17] These attitudes of mind and expectations were common to the warrior elite throughout the medieval period.

But by the end of the period under consideration here, with the increasing importance of guns, greater professionalism and the effective re-emergence of the standing national army, certain attitudes and expectations were being modified. Improved weaponry meant that even nobles were more likely to be killed on the battlefield; those of lower social status had proven again and again, notably during the Hussite crusades, that they could easily outmanoeuvre and defeat nobles in the field; and, while they were still fighting for their own honour, the honour of their nation (in the case of the Hussites, Bohemia) was of increasing importance for warriors of all classes. This was not 'national identity' in the modern sense, as the nation-state did not exist; but the literature of the later medieval period indicates an awareness of what could be termed 'geographical identity', so that (to give but two examples) in the late eleventh-century or twelfth-century poem glorifying his death the hero Roland was depicted declaring his aim of defending France, indicating that this was a priority also for the audience of French nobles for whom the work was intended, while Thomas Elmham, writing in around 1418 about the Battle of Agincourt (1415), depicted King Henry V of England referring to 'England' as an entity on whose behalf he was fighting.[18] At the same time, as war became more efficient, the demands that non-combatants should not have to suffer at warriors' hands became more strident. Yet the most familiar aspects of medieval warfare were still present in 1500, when this study concludes.

* * *

The greatest hurdle to the study of medieval European warfare over the period 300–1500 is not the vastness of the time scale or the geography, but the sources. Sources for medieval European warfare vary considerably in type and quality. The period from the dissolution of the Western Empire during the fifth and sixth centuries to 750 is under-represented in the sources, so that scholars are less decided about most aspects of warfare than for the period after 750, when Charlemagne's capitularies (ordinances) and chronicle sources begin to give more information. In particular, evidence for seventh-century Francia is sparse, although Roger Collins has noted that the seventh century was 'not a time of warfare' for Merovingian Francia, so that perhaps we may view the lack of sources in a positive light.[19] Evidence for the tenth century is sketchy. Hence histories of medieval warfare tend to emphasise the period after 1100, when surviving sources are more plentiful, and especially after 1330, when writings on warfare, both actual and theoretical, and biographies of great warriors are so readily available and enjoyable to read that the temptation is to start at 1500 and work backwards.

Some sources are much more useful and straightforward than others. Manuals of advice on military methods survive from the whole of this period, but were mostly based on Vegetius's *De re militari* ('On military matters'). While some writers incorporated material from their own times into their reworking of Vegetius, they also retained sections of Vegetius's work – such as how to deal with an attack by elephants – which were already anachronistic in Vegetius's time, and which the medieval translators seem to have included simply to amuse the medieval reader. This means that to a large extent medieval military manuals reflect classical practice rather than medieval practice.

Documentary sources – such as law codes and, later, records of the raising of troops – give very valuable details when they are available. But until the thirteenth century it was not usual to record in writing details such as the captains of units within an army and how many men each commanded, let alone what equipment they had. This sort of information is non-existent for the earlier centuries. Law codes might mention who was expected to fight for their lord and what happened to people who fought illegally. Such evidence is rather piecemeal and has to be compiled patiently by the researcher, and only applies to the period of a particular law code. What was true for England in the tenth century, for instance, would not necessarily apply to Castile in the eleventh.

Religious literature such as saints' lives and sermons gives some insights to warfare, although usually explaining how to avoid violence rather than taking part in it. These insights are distorted by the intention of the writer, which was generally to condemn warfare or its excesses.

The authors of chronicles, annals and histories claimed to recount actual wars of their day. Technically, annals are accounts of events on a year-by-year basis, while chronicles and histories are continuous narratives. A history should concentrate on a specific subject, as did Archbishop Gregory of Tours's history of the Franks, or, for example, recount a specific war. A chronicle is more wide-ranging and contains a mass of

information on the past and on recent events, usually recited uncritically
and in chronological order. The authors of all of these types of writing
emphasised the importance of telling the truth and declared this to be their
main intention.[20] However, the writer was seldom an eyewitness, and
what is recorded could be based on hearsay or on the imagination of the
writer. The writer might include speeches and descriptions of the generals'
intentions, but unless the writer was an eyewitness or quoted a contemporary source, these sorts of details were likely to be inventions of the
writer. Battle accounts were usually distorted by the writer's own
allegiances.[21]

What was more, rather than basing their account of contemporary battles on what actually happened, writers often preferred to base their
account on classical accounts of battles (such as Julius Caesar's campaigns). This practice enabled writers to show off their own classical education and gave their account colour; and also glorified the military
leaders of their own day. As a result, medieval accounts of contemporary
battles can be very unreliable.[22] Medieval writers seldom gave much detail
of the nitty-gritty of how war was waged, tending to give a very brief
account of events, or concentrating on glorious events such as battles and
single combats rather than the organisation of a campaign. What is more,
as the majority of medieval writers of history had little or no military
experience, they did not properly understand what they were describing.[23]

It should also be noted that despite the fact that writers of chronicles,
annals and histories claimed to be writing objective truth, their works
were also intended to be read and enjoyed. They were, to use the description coined by Nancy Partner, 'serious entertainments'.[24] These works
were not composed as text books consisting only of absolute truth, if that
were possible, but were literature, and as such they must be analysed and
subjected to searching criticism like any other sort of literature. The problems of categorising such works as either 'historical fact' or 'fiction' are
well illustrated by the chronicle of Jean Froissart (died *c*.1410), the queen
of England's secretary. Like most medieval chronicles, this is a mixture of
eyewitness material and information derived from other sources that are
not always identified. Like all chronicles, it contains errors, but it is very
wide-ranging and contains much information not available from other
sources. Froissart's own personal viewpoint is of interest in itself, as the
view of a well-travelled, well-educated courtier of the fourteenth century,
and the 'spin' he put on his material gives modern readers an insight into
the expectations of his noble readership. In recent years historians have
become far more critical of those chronicles and historical writing which
earlier generations of historians accepted at face value,[25] and have
reassessed works, such as Froissart's chronicle, which earlier generations
rejected as unreliable.[26]

Epic and romance literature presents a similar problem. The epic
focused on the history of a family; the romance focused on the develop-

ment of an individual. (A 'romance' in the Middle Ages was simply a story written in the vernacular. It did not necessarily involve a love affair.) Both forms of writing provide an attractive overview of medieval warfare for the periods for which they survive, but an exaggerated one. Epic and romance literature was composed for the military classes, those who led and who played a leading role in medieval armies; so it concentrated on members of the military classes and on their deeds, and said very little about the logistics of campaigning, or the role of others in the army. However, because it had to contain a certain level of realism in order to be acceptable to its audience, and because it gives a picture of its intended audience's expectations, epic and romance literature has enormous value to the historian in depicting the thought-world of those who led armies and who played a leading role in them.

In the first place, because epic and romance literature was written in the vernacular, it used the same vocabulary as the warriors used themselves, giving armour, weapons and divisions of the army (for example) their correct terms. J. F. Verbruggen has emphasised the importance of vernacular sources particularly for this reason, and refers frequently to 'fictional' sources as historical evidence.[27] Second, the wide distribution of these works and their impact on medieval culture indicates that they were significant to the society which produced them. Some works of romance literature survive in a great many manuscripts and were clearly widely known among the warrior nobility until at least the early sixteenth century, when they were printed. They affected many aspects of cultural activity, from royal ceremonies to children's names.[28] Such works were authored by both clerics and knights: for instance, the compilation of Arthurian romances put together by Rusticien de Pise in the 1270s was not only compiled by a knight – Rusticien – but intended for a renowned warrior – King Edward I of England – although Rusticien expected not only kings, emperors, dukes, counts and knights to hear his work read but also burgesses in the towns.[29] Clearly, such works reflected the belief system of the warrior nobility to a certain extent; otherwise they would not have won such lasting popularity.

In his magisterial work *Chivalry*, Maurice Keen argued that the value of the epics of Charlemagne and romances of King Arthur lies 'with the mirror that the twelfth- and thirteenth-century versions of them held up to life, with what they had to tell the knightly world about itself, its history and values – in other words, how together they came to constitute its distinctive mythology'. He contended that only through studying the so-called fictional literature of the medieval period can the modern historian discover to any meaningful degree the mentality of the medieval warrior.[30]

This begs the question of how far epic and romance literature are actually 'fiction' – in comparison to, for example, medieval chronicles. Both 'fiction' and chronicles were written for entertainment, and the authors of both claimed to be basing their work on actual events. Epic tales of

Charlemagne and of classical heroes such as Alexander and the heroes of
Troy were regarded in the medieval period as having a sound historical
basis.[31] The Arthurian stories appear to modern readers to be less obviously historical, and during the medieval period were criticised for being
partly fantasy. But, at least from the early thirteenth century, no writing
could venture far into fantasy without incurring the danger of being
accused of heresy.[32] Literature therefore had to reflect reality and be inherently probable. It would be unreasonable for modern scholars to reject
these sources as totally unrepresentative of the society which produced
them, as medieval audiences regarded them as having some veracity.

In short, no such line can be driven between 'factual' and 'fictional'
medieval sources. The chronicles authored by monastic and other ecclesiastical writers, who claimed to be recording only fact, have been shown
by modern historical and literary analysis to be often unreliable. The
details of everyday life in the vernacular epics and romances, such as the
emphasis in romance literature on the beauty of castles, are borne out by
the archaeological evidence. While the so-called fictional sources do not
recount actual events, they give us valuable information about everyday
life that does not appear in ecclesiastical chronicles: such as fashionable
underwear for young noble warriors or the problems that a knight might
encounter getting into his armour.[33] These are the sort of details which
help to bring a period to life in the minds of modern readers, and there is
no reason to doubt that the literary depiction of these detailed matters
accurately reflects the practices of the period in which these works were
written.

Archaeological sources provide material evidence of warfare: for example, examination of fortified buildings, analysis of remains of weapons
and armour, excavation of battlefields – showing the wounds of those who
died – and other evidence of the impact of warfare. Another form of material culture is art: sculpture, painting and tapestry can provide evidence of
what warriors wore and how they fought, with the proviso that (as in the
epic and romance) it is an idealised image that is portrayed here. To some
degree, historical reconstructions can help to establish how medieval siege
machinery actually worked and what its capabilities were (for instance),
or how knights actually fought on horseback, but so much practical
knowledge and experience which would have been commonplace to the
medieval warrior was never written down, and now cannot be recovered,
that it is impossible to reconstruct completely the experience of the
medieval warrior.

The reader will realise that all forms of evidence present problems of
interpretation, so that if I were to analyse every piece of evidence I am
using in this book as my discussion develops, the book would never reach
an end. It is clear that no single piece of evidence can prove anything; only
by combining many pieces of evidence can the modern scholar hope to
construct an approximation of past events and experiences. However, as

many scholars have already combined many forms of evidence and attempted to construct such approximations, I will not attempt to duplicate their work here. This study is largely constructed from their conclusions, and references to primary evidence are simply to illustrate those conclusions – not to attempt to prove them again. The examples from primary sources that I will cite have already, so to speak, been 'vetted' and analysed and found suitable to appear in this book, and I will not try the patience of my readers by analysing each piece of evidence afresh as I cite it.

Yet even following the conclusions of modern scholars is far from straightforward. Because of the uneven quality of the evidence and the problems of interpreting it, and because there was so much geographical variation in the practice of warfare, historians differ on many aspects of medieval warfare, while other aspects remain mysterious. Even at the most basic level, such as the size of the war-horse that gave the mounted warrior status, there has been much debate.[34] Some historians have argued that the medieval use of cavalry has been drastically exaggerated, and that in fact knights very often fought on foot.[35] The problem is that the evidence is so diverse and scattered that it is very difficult to reach a firm conclusion that is accurate for the whole of western Europe for a long period.

In recent years some historians have attempted to reach conclusions about the size, range and abilities of medieval armies in terms of how much food and water each person and each animal would require, exactly how much space they would occupy on the road and in accommodation, the precise length of rampart one man should protect or exactly how much space he would require in the battle line. Such precise calculations rely on descriptions such as Vegetius's *De re militari*, or legal records such as the Burghal Hideage (produced in England in the ninth or tenth century, precise date uncertain). Other historians have tried to calculate the range of medieval ships in terms of how much water and food they could carry, and how much their crews would need.[36] These analyses can be extremely illuminating, but can also be misleading. They base the assumed needs of the medieval human and horse on the known requirements for calories and water of a healthy, well-built man from the modern Western world and a fully fit, modern horse. Yet calorific requirements and water requirements vary according to build, level of fitness and what the body is accustomed to receive. As will be explained in Chapter 4, horses can be trained to survive on less water if necessary, and the same applies to a man on campaign: with training, his metabolism will become more efficient in its use of food, and require fewer calories. Hence, while these detailed studies are useful in giving a general guide to the logistical problems of moving an army by land or on water, they cannot give us precise figures.

The question of how people fought is also difficult to establish. How far were warriors trained, and how far did they 'learn on the job'? Despite Vegetius's instructions that soldiers should train every day, there are very few references throughout the Middle Ages to warriors actually being taught how to fight. It has been suggested that the literature of the warrior classes, the epic and romance, provided some instruction to young warriors on how to conduct a campaign and about comradeship and responsibility; but most scholars believe that the martial feats described in such stories cannot have happened in reality. They argue that the 'heroic blow' by which Count Roland slices an enemy warrior in half, and his horse as well, would be impossible because, in raising his right arm for the blow, the knight would expose his right side to the enemy, who could easily slice his arm off. Certainly, the ninth-century writer Archbishop Hrabanus Maurus of Mainz advised warriors against using this blow for this very reason. Yet other scholars believe that these accounts, which also occur in the more (supposedly) 'factual' chronicles and histories, should be taken at face value. Another suggestion is that such a blow could be achieved by a warrior on foot, but not on horseback.[37]

Sometimes it is possible to suggest solutions to such debates, but as knowledge of medieval warfare is developing very rapidly at the time of writing, such solutions are likely to be only temporary. The aim of this study is therefore to clarify the issues over which scholars disagree rather than to impose answers. There is insufficient space here for a thorough analysis and criticism of the many excellent historians who have worked and are working on medieval warfare. Criticisms and analyses of the historiography can be found in many detailed studies of various aspects of medieval warfare and I refer my readers to these.[38] My purpose here is to give an overview and synthesis of recent research into warfare throughout the medieval period, in an attempt to establish trends and changes, and to indicate areas where work is needed, rather than attempting to give the last word on any subject.

1

The theory of warfare

Medieval warfare was such a supremely practical art that it may seem perverse to begin by considering theory. It is true that theory and practice were often far apart, yet the theory forms a basis from which the practice can be considered.

The theory of warfare during the Middle Ages can be considered under two broad categories: first, how to physically wage war and, second, considerations of honour and the moral foundations for war. The first was derived largely from Vegetius, and hence from classical, pagan, Roman writings on warfare, while the second developed from a mixture of classical, Germanic and Christian thinking. Nevertheless, both aspects came together in the body of military guidelines and standards of behaviour now labelled as 'chivalry'. As this body of military guidelines and standards is fundamental to what follows in later chapters, it is necessary to consider it at some length here.

* * *

Publius Flavius Vegetius Renatus wrote his *De re militari* under the late Roman Empire, possibly for the emperor Theodosius I, emperor of the East from AD 379 to 395.[1] He was not himself a soldier but a bureaucrat, although he does seem to have been an expert on horse breeding. He based his work not on his own experience in the field, but on his awareness of recent military developments and his reading of earlier authorities on the art of warfare such as Cato and Frontinus, whose work had come down to him in summarised form. His book dealt only with those aspects of imperial military practice which he considered to require reform, so he did not write at length on cavalry, for instance, as he thought that this was sufficiently up to date (although he did say a good deal about the role of cavalry in battle formations). His aim was to encourage the emperor to reform the infantry and restore it to the standards of the Roman Republic and the early Empire.

He divided his work into four books. The first dealt with recruitment and training: whom to recruit (the ideal size and shape of a soldier) and what they needed to learn. He also described the construction of army camps.

In his second book, Vegetius described the formation and structure of the army and the role of each part of it. He regarded the infantry as most important (as infantry could be used everywhere and is cheaper than cavalry and navy), but cavalry was also significant. He also noted that the army would contain engineers, carpenters, masons, smiths and so on to construct buildings, siege machines and weapons, as well as sappers to dig under enemy fortifications.

In his third book, he described field strategy and tactics, including the famous statement: '*Si vis pacem, para bellum*' – 'if you want peace, prepare for war'. He described the precautions that the general must take while the army was on the march and the best order of march; how to lay out a camp and how to cross a river. Battle should be the last resort; it might be better to embark on a long campaign of ravaging the enemy rather than risk all on the hazard of battle. The general should fight only if he had the advantage. Vegetius gave advice about the procedure of battle, how to retreat if the worst should occur, and also how to deal with camels, armoured cavalry, scythed chariots and elephants. The book closed with a handy list of rules of war, single sentences that could be easily memorised.

Book 4 covered how to besiege a city, how to defend a city under siege, and naval warfare. Vegetius referred to the use of 'incendiary oil' by the defenders, which sounds a little like medieval 'Greek fire'. The only role given to women in the siege was to supply their hair to power catapults, if sinews and horsehair ran short. Various siege machines were described. The book ends with a consideration of naval warfare, including instructions on when the timber for making ships should be felled.

Vegetius's book, based on secondhand material and often stating no more than the obvious (bravery is often more valuable than numbers, it is essential to ensure food supplies, hard work and training improve soldiers' morale), became the standard work on the art of war in western Europe for over a thousand years, until older works on warfare became readily available to European scholars in the sixteenth century.[2] But the extent of the impact of his work on the practice of warfare is difficult to gauge. Historians have attempted to assess Vegetius's influence by noting how many copies of his book were produced in the Middle Ages (over 130 in Latin: including translations and extracts, over 200).[3] Vegetius's work clearly exercised an enormous influence on writing about warfare: excerpts appear in other writing, and many writers adapted his work for their own use.[4] Yet this usage tells us little about Vegetius's impact on the actual practice of warfare.

The question here is how far medieval writers incorporated Vegetius's work into their texts in order to give their work historical authority and to emphasise their own scholarship, and how far copies and adaptations of Vegetius's work were made to be used in military affairs by military commanders. For example, in the ninth century a copy was produced by Archbishop Hrabanus Maurus of Mainz, and another by Bishop Frechulf of Lisieux for Charles the Bald (king of the West Franks 843–77, emperor of the West 875–7).[5] The production of copies of a late Roman manual of warfare may indicate that ninth-century political figures in western Europe were anxious to connect their authority and military activity to the authority and military might of the old Roman Empire; or it may indicate that Vegetius's manual was seen as a practical guide to warfare. The fact that Archbishop Hrabanus updated Vegetius's work to reflect current practice suggests that he expected the work to be a useful guide to the contemporary military practitioner; and on this basis the historian Bernard Bachrach has used it as a guide to the practicalities of Carolingian warfare.[6]

Yet it is difficult to identify Vegetius's work actually being used in practice, simply because he often stated the obvious, and described military practices which any competent and experienced commander would use. Bachrach has argued that Fulk Nerra, count of Anjou 987–1040, 'appears to have been very much influenced in both his tactical and his strategic thinking by the *De Re Militari* ... by the Roman military authority Vegetius'.[7] Yet Bachrach's arguments have not been generally accepted by historians. While Fulk's administration did use Roman imperial military terminology, this usage was standard in Latin documents of the period – at least those produced by reasonably well-educated clerks – and does not prove that Fulk was unusually influenced by classical precedent. Fulk's preference for avoiding battles and preferring to devastate the territory of his enemy is certainly the advice given by Vegetius, but was also sound military sense in the heavily fortified area of north-central France. Fulk need not have adopted this strategy simply because it was recommended by Vegetius; a good commander could have worked this strategy out for himself without assistance from a book.[8]

There is good evidence that Fulk's descendant Count Geoffrey V 'le Bel' of Anjou (d. 1151) possessed and read a version of Vegetius's work, as John of Marmoutier's *Historia Gaufredi* recounts an anecdote of a monk coming across the count reading Vegetius during the course of the siege of Montreuil-Bellay in 1151. Together they used advice from the book to win victory.[9] In the mid-twelfth century the count of Champagne owned a copy of Vegetius's work; but no anecdotes survive like those for Count Geoffrey of Anjou to show the count actually using it at a siege. John Gillingham has referred to the 'cautious mastery of Vegetian warfare' showed by King Richard I of England (d. 1199) in his campaigns;[10] yet, while this is true, there is no direct evidence that Richard had actually read, or listened to, Vegetius's book.

Vegetius's work was certainly well known to educated clergy by the twelfth and thirteenth centuries, on whose writing modern historians rely for much of their knowledge of that period. Preachers and scholarly churchmen quoted from Vegetius[11] and it is tempting to conclude from this that Vegetius's work was well known and used by the warrior nobility also, but this need not have been the case. Medieval stereotyping alerts us to the fundamental problem here: to use the words of M. T. Clanchy, 'the medieval axiom that laymen are illiterate and its converse that clergy are literate'.[12] While by the end of the twelfth century this stereotype was no longer completely accurate, in that 'some clergy were ignorant and some knights knew more of books than brave deeds',[13] the stereotype had its roots in late Roman views of the Germanic warriors who had taken over military power in the West from the fifth century onwards: not only could they not read, but they regarded learning as 'sissy'. Experience was what made a man a good warrior, not learning. If warriors could not read and despised learning, then they would not follow the advice of Vegetius, even if they possessed copies of his work. To take one example of the stereotype, in the sixth century the Byzantine historian Procopius (d. 560s) depicted the Ostrogoths of Italy as regarding learning as inimical to warriorhood. He described the leading German nobles of Ravenna in the 520s informing Queen Amalasunth of Italy that she must stop educating her son Athalaric in the classics:

> For letters, they said, are far removed from manliness and the teaching of old men results for the most part in a cowardly and submissive spirit. Therefore the man who is to show daring in any work and be great in renown ought to be freed from the timidity which teachers inspire and to take his training in arms. They added that even Theoderic [Amalasunth's father] would never allow any of the Goths to send their children to school; for he used to say to them all that, if the fear of the strap once came over them, they would never have the resolution to despise sword or spear.[14]

Procopius was ridiculing the Ostrogoths as barbarians, for the nobility of the Roman Empire had always been well educated in the classics and also successful in warfare. He supported the reforming and well-educated Queen Amalasunth, and set out to portray the Byzantine general Belisarius as her avenger. Yet his slurs against the Germanic warriors were not completely baseless. Despite the educational drives of Charlemagne in eighth-century Francia and Alfred in ninth-century Wessex, few warriors of western Europe below the highest nobility were noted for their learning before the twelfth century; they would listen to texts being read, but were unable to read them for themselves. Any benefit that they gained from the work of Vegetius or other writers was through the medium of a cleric who could read the Latin text.

Despite the revival of lay education in the twelfth century, even in the late twelfth century the composer of the first version of *Le Moniage*

Guillaume ('How William became a Monk' – a satirical epic poem aimed at a lay, warrior audience), depicted the hero, the great warrior William Shortnose, as unable to read.[15] Reading was depicted as something associated with the idle, worldly monks rather than the hardworking, austere warriors who would suffer and lay down their lives for God on the battlefield. The poem goes on to glorify the warriors and demonstrate that their vocation is more pleasing to God than the monks' vocation.

Even as the warrior classes learned to read from the twelfth century onwards, some warriors apparently preferred experience as a means of learning warrior skills rather than reading books. The noble knight Geoffrey de Charny (d. 1356) regarded knighthood as an order founded by God with an essential role in society, and, seeing that French knighthood was in crisis, he set out to reform it so that it could again play its proper role. He wrote three books on the practice of knighthood, which may have been commissioned by King John II of France alongside the king's foundation of a new secular knightly order, 'the Order of the Star'.[16] Given the prominence of Vegetius's work in other works on warfare written before and later, we might expect Charny to refer his readers to Vegetius. But in fact, in his *Livre de chevalerie* Charny did not envisage knights learning how to be warriors by reading. He argued that knights should learn by watching others and asking questions of those who are the best in the business of arms.[17] Charny said nothing about books; he did not even advise young warriors to study the deeds of knights of the past. For him, war was a practical art that could only be effectively learnt by taking part in it.

In short, it is not enough to conclude that warriors were using Vegetius's work because educated clergymen were using Vegetius's work in their writings, or because warriors are known to have owned copies of Vegetius's work in Latin. Simply because one anecdote survives of Count Geoffrey V of Anjou taking an idea from Vegetius's work, this does not mean that use of Vegetius was common; rather, that the event was thought worthy of record may indicate that it was very unusual. To suggest that warriors did actually use Vegetius's work in practice, we must look for instances where warriors either used Vegetius's work in their own writings (which Charny did not) or commissioned for themselves translations of Vegetius's work or works which referred to Vegetius's work. So, for example, as King Alfonso X of Castile (d. 1284) incorporated translated sections of Vegetius's work into his political manuals,[18] we might conclude that the king was using Vegetius as a guide in his own military activity. Alternatively, we might conclude simply that Vegetius's opinions lent the king's work classical authority and demonstrated his learning.

Eleanor of Castile (d. 1291) commissioned a translation of Vegetius's *De re militari* as a present for her husband, King Edward I of England (d. 1307), while they both were on crusade in the Holy Land in 1271–2.[19] It is possible that Edward read the book and put it into practice. Michael

Prestwich has noted that Edward's cautious strategy in the conquest of North Wales may have been based on Vegetius's advice, although there is no direct evidence of this.[20]

To take another example: in the 1270s Egidio Colonna ('Giles of Rome'), an Augustinian canon and doctor of the University of Paris, composed a work on the government of princes, *De regimine principum*, for the education of the future Philip IV of France, whose tutor he was. Book 3, Part 3 of this work deals with government in time of war, and was partly based on Vegetius's *De re militari*. Egidio cited Vegetius by name repeatedly: 'as Vegetius says in his work "The art of warfare"'. Clearly, he and his intended audience regarded Vegetius as the leading authority on warfare, whose name gave validity to Egidio's own study of the subject. The whole of Egidio's book was translated into French by order of King Philip IV in 1296, and was later translated into other European languages: Spanish, Portuguese, Catalan, Italian and Hebrew. It was very widely read, and was also excerpted in other works. As translations were being produced, this suggests that the work was being read by non-scholars, who hoped to put its guidelines into practice, although, again, this is only supposition.[21]

In 1284 Jean de Meun (best known for his completion of the *Roman de la Rose*) produced a prose translation of Vegetius's *De re militari* into French.[22] The fact that a translation into the vernacular was needed indicates that there was a contemporary demand for a translation from less educated people, those who could not read Latin. The obvious conclusion is that the laity who wanted the translation hoped to learn about warfare from it. Even more interesting is the fact that Jean de Meun's translation was soon rendered into verse in an edited form by one Jean Priorat de Besançon for a Jean de Chalon, probably in the late 1280s.[23] In the same way in England, in the fifteenth century Vegetius's work was translated into prose and into verse.[24] Verse was a medium intended for reading aloud to larger groups and could be more easily memorised than prose, and so these shortened versions of Vegetius's work could have been intended to educate lay people, particularly warriors, in the art of warfare. Christopher Allmand suggests that King Henry V of England read the first English prose translation and based his own military training on it, as his exercise regime was similar to that recommended by Vegetius.[25]

One of the most successful uses of Vegetius in a vernacular work was produced by the Italian-born author Christine de Pisan or Pizan, in 1408–9. Her *Livre des faits des armes et de la chevalerie* ('Book on Feats of Arms and Knighthood') survives in 15 sumptuous manuscripts, clearly commissioned by the highest nobility. In 1489 King Henry VII of England (who had won England in battle in 1485) asked the publisher/translator William Caxton to translate Christine's work into English, 'so every gentleman born to arms and all manner of men of war, captains, soldiers, vituallers and all others would know how they ought to behave in the feats of wars and battles'. Caxton added his own opinion of Christine's work: 'it is as necessary a book and as requisite as any may be for every estate, high and low, that attends to the feats of war, whether it be in battles, sieges, rescues and all other feats …'. In short, it was an all-round guide to warfare, essential reading for anyone who wanted to learn about war – and presumably King Henry VII had decided that it was the best means of teaching his newly acquired subjects how to fight effectively, to enable him to defend his realm against other potential usurpers. The translation had a wide circulation, as 20 copies survive.[26]

Christine's volume was not simply a translation of Vegetius, although he was her major source for the first book of the four that made up her work: how kings and princes should wage wars and battles. For her second book, on stratagems and how to attack and defend castles and cities and wage war at sea, she relied mainly on the classical writer Frontinus (who was also one of Vegetius's sources), but also used Vegetius; for her final two books, on the rights of arms and laws of war, she followed Honoré Bouvet's *Arbre des batailles*, 'Tree of Battles', produced in 1387. Bouvet, priest, academic and monk, had considered the customs of war, how war could be legitimate, how it should be legitimately waged, the proper treatment of prisoners and who should be exempt from violence during war (women, other non-combatants, those otherwise not involved).[27] Christine was frank about her reliance on Bouvet, and presented herself as his disciple, asking questions and sometimes disagreeing with him.[28] Yet she also used contemporary firsthand sources, military men whom she had asked about how sieges should be conducted and how war should be waged. Her work therefore contains much valuable information about the conduct of an early fifteenth-century siege, including the use of gunpowder artillery.

Christine explains at the beginning of her work that she has been asked by certain prominent and renowned warriors to write on this subject, following on the success of her earlier books. As those who are expert in the art of knighthood (i.e., warfare) are not usually well educated or skilled in the clever use of words, she will write in very plain language. Despite her self-deprecation, the surviving manuscripts indicate that her work was aimed at the high nobility rather than the 'ordinary soldier'. Christine may have done no more than persuade the French nobility of the early fifteenth century that their warfare continued the noble tradition of the renowned Roman army. Yet the fact that King Henry VII of England selected this book for translation into English in order to educate his warriors in warfare indicates that it did have some potential as a book for teaching the art of warfare. Hence, Christine's use of Vegetius's work is positive evidence that warriors were influenced by his work – at least, in France and England in the fifteenth century.

* * *

Vegetius and those writers who followed him did not cover every aspect of warfare. They set out instructions on the necessity of training warriors and how to conduct a campaign, but they gave very few instructions on the physical act of fighting. Until the fourteenth century, other medieval writers who considered the art of warfare gave little more information about how one should actually fight.[29] Fictional writing – epic and romance – described the activities of warriors using the sword and lance, but in an exaggerated fashion, intended to entertain rather than to instruct.[30] Writers instructing knights included some information about how one should learn warfare: Geoffrey de Charny urged young warriors to travel to see wars in progress; Alfonso XI of Castile, setting up his secular knightly 'order of the Band' in 1330, obliged the members of his order to attend tournaments on a regular basis, as these were valuable training for war.[31] Sydney Anglo has noted that those who composed treatises on how to fight stressed the importance of practical demonstration over books, stating that a book could never adequately show how a fighter should move.[32]

Descriptions of fighting in treatises cannot be taken at face value as representing actual practice on the battlefield. The earliest surviving treatise on combat dates from the turn of the thirteenth/fourteenth centuries, but Sydney Anglo judged that the method described does not appear very practical or effective, and suggested that possibly the treatise does not describe actual fighting but a series of exercises, or possibly the author was a poor swordsman.[33] In the fifteenth century a number of fencing manuals were composed, describing and illustrating various combat techniques with weapons such as swords, poleaxes, shields and daggers.[34] These detailed works presumably reflect actual moves used in one-to-one combat such as judicial duels, although the blows they describe could not necessarily be used in the confusion of massed battle.[35] The weapons are state-of-the-art fifteenth-century weapons; for early periods with different types and designs of weapons, different moves would be required. In around 1434 King Duarte of Portugal composed a book entitled 'The art of good horsemanship', which included instructions on how to learn to handle a lance and how to charge one's opponent. He stressed the importance of constant practice and added that a good deal depended on the quality and experience of the horse.[36] Presumably he was describing his own experience and usual practice, but as no similar sources have survived it is not possible to be certain. Nor can we know how far his treatise was used as a learning aid, nor how far what he describes was also true of, for example, the twelfth century. However, as his descriptions are borne out by manuscript illuminations from earlier centuries and the descriptions in epic and romance, it seems likely that he was describing the process by which mounted warriors did learn to use a lance in battle as well as on the tournament field.

Another type of martial treatise was the military plan, which set out a military strategy and the tactics necessary to bring it about; typically the recovery of the Holy Land from the Muslims after the destruction of the kingdom of Jerusalem in 1291. Scholars debate how far these recovery treatises were intended to be put into practice, and how far they were works of propaganda to emphasise their writer's or their patron's dedication to the defence of Christendom. Some were written by experienced military strategists, such as the masters of the military religious orders, or Charles II, king of Naples (died 1309); but none was ever fully put into effect.[37]

* * *

Moving on from the theoretical studies of how to wage war and how to fight, we should consider the moral foundations for war. The main problem here is that there were several threads of tradition and thought on this subject during the period 300–1500.

One extreme view of warfare was that war is never justifiable in any circumstances. This was the view of some Christians, based on Christ's teaching in the Gospels. From the twelfth and thirteenth centuries onwards it was the view of some western European heretical groups who based their beliefs on a careful reading of the New Testament, notably the Cathars and the Waldensians.[38] It was also the view expressed in the magical text *Picatrix*, translated in 1256–8 from an Arabic text (itself apparently based on late Hellenistic Greek writings, among other sources) into Castilian Spanish for King Alfonso X of Castile, and later into Latin. This view is the opinion of an educated man, but secular rather than religious. Describing the attributes of the planet Mars, patron of war, the writer states:

> Mars ... is misfortune, damaging, and the author of evil things. And it signifies loss, evil works, houses and cities depopulated, drought and preventing rain from falling, fire, burning, disagreements, blood, every impetuosity ... evil and warped judgements, oppressions, anguish, people's deaths and damage to everything, destruction, quarrels, wars, battles, terrors, discord among people, anxiety and misery, pains, wounds, prisons, misery, flight, contentions, stupidity, treachery and every cursed thing which comes about without sense or moderation ...[39]

The impact of war also includes illegal actions, false oaths, sexual depravity, killing infants in their mother's womb, 'and everything remote from truth and legality'. This was an unremittingly negative view of warfare, without even the glory and honour of fighting to relieve the dark picture, and with no suggestion that war could ever be just: far from imposing justice or right, this warfare creates injustice and every wrong.

The opposite extreme was that expressed by the landowner and warrior-poet of the Limousin (western France), Bertrand de Born, who died in around 1214:

> I am overjoyed when I see knights and horses, all in armour, drawn up on the field. I love it when the chargers throw everything and everybody into confusion, and I enjoy seeing strong castles besieged … Once he has started fighting, no noble knight thinks of anything but breaking heads and arms – better a dead man than a live one who is useless.[40]

This viewpoint implied that warfare was an end in itself, undertaken for the joy of fighting.

The 'official' view of warfare held by the institutional Catholic Christian Church during most of the Middle Ages fell between the two extremes, seeing warfare as sometimes necessary or permissible, but condemning excessive violence. This view was simply expressed by Honoré Bouvet:

> Now it is fitting that I should reply to the first question: 'What is war?' And I answer, following the master in law, that war is nothing other than discord or conflict that has arisen on account of certain things displeasing to the human will, to the end that such conflict should be turned into agreement and reason, and there is a law which proves this.[41]

War, then, has a legal purpose and function, to resolve conflicts and restore peace; but Bouvet went on to show that it should be kept within certain bounds.

These three viewpoints give us a broad, simplified impression of medieval thought on the subject of warfare. It is difficult, however, to judge how widely each viewpoint was held. The belief that 'all war is evil' was rarely expressed in the medieval period; and as this attitude became associated with heretical groups from the second half of the twelfth century, it would be dangerous for writers to express such views. *Picatrix* itself was a well-known text among the educated elite, surviving in at least 20 manuscripts, plus fragments, and translated into Italian, French and English.[42] However, those who read it would have been interested in its magical content rather than its moral views, and so it is not possible to say how far its negative view of warfare reflected contemporary opinion. What can be said is that actual events indicate that total rejection of all violence was not common during the Middle Ages. The 'war is good' viewpoint broadly derived from the warriors themselves and before the twelfth century is represented mainly by the few surviving examples of vernacular poetry. From the twelfth century onwards some writings survive which either represent the views of warriors or were written by warriors themselves. The moderate viewpoint expressed by Bouvet is represented in numerous writings, largely but not invariably by ecclesiastics, which have survived from the whole medieval period.

The number of surviving manuscripts would imply that the moderate view of warfare was the most widely held; but in fact this was not necessarily the case. For most of the period 300–1500, the majority of warriors were illiterate and could not express their own views in writing. The majority of writings promoting the view that violence should be limited were written in Latin, and were inaccessible to the bulk of the population. Therefore the number of surviving manuscripts is not an accurate representation of influence. In order to assess the influence of these different ideologies, it is necessary to consider writings on warfare throughout the Middle Ages and trace how these ideologies developed.

* * *

The debate over when warfare was right and when it was not went back to classical times, but for medieval Christians the most important opinions were those expressed in the Bible and by the Church Fathers. In the Old Testament, the sixth Commandment seems to condemn war in the statement: 'You shall not kill' (Deut. 5 v. 17). However, elsewhere in the Old Testament God's people are commanded to fight, for example, to win the land of Israel from idolaters (e.g., Josh. 8), and God is portrayed as a warrior god, a god of battles, who fights for His people. Therefore when God's people fought to punish idolaters or to defend God's holy places, they were fighting God's wars, holy wars.

In the New Testament, Jesus is recorded making various statements against violence, indicating that Christians should not fight.[43] Yet elsewhere it seems that it may be acceptable for God's people to fight; for example, in Luke 22, v. 36, Jesus told the apostles to buy swords to protect themselves as they went about preaching, while Acts 10 vv. 1–2 describe Cornelius, centurion of the Italian Cohort, a devout man who was the first non-Jewish convert to Christianity. These instances indicate that it is possible for a warrior to follow a pious lifestyle and win salvation.

Early Christian writers differed in their views on the subject of violence. St Paul had written (Rom. 13) that everyone must obey the governing authorities, since God had appointed them. However, the Church Fathers believed that God's command not to fight overrode the command to obey the authorities God had appointed. At the beginning of the third century, the North African Christian writer Tertullian recorded that although some Christians did fight, he did not approve. He observed that one of the last remarks Christ had made before He was led away to be crucified was when He told Simon Peter to put away his sword, indicating that this was His last word on the subject.[44] There were a number of famous cases of soldiers in the Roman army who threw away their weapons when they converted to Christianity and refused to fight any more; they were then executed for breaking their oaths to the emperor.[45] Some other Christian writings of the early Christian period assume that it is not possible to be a soldier and a Christian.[46] However, the great writer Augustine (354–430), bishop of Hippo Regius in North Africa (now Annaba or Bône in Tunisia), believed that it was possible for a soldier to please God. He condemned war, but acknowledged that it is necessary to use violence to protect the vulnerable against violence. Therefore, war is justifiable provided that war is waged with the right intention – that is, in order to gain peace.[47]

Under the Roman Empire, warfare was the responsibility of the emperor. When the Emperor Constantine adopted Christianity and made it the official religion of the empire (312) he maintained that it was one of his duties as God's vicar on Earth to defend the people whom God had entrusted to his care. This remained the view of educated Christian writers until the late eleventh century. In 747 Pope Zacharias (741–52) wrote to Pepin or Pippin III, the Short (mayor of the palace, 741–51, king of the Franks 751–68), father of Charlemagne, asking for military aid. The pope observed that society is divided into two groups, those that pray and those that fight; so Pepin, as leading representative of the fighters, had a duty to come to his assistance.[48]

Hincmar, archbishop of Reims (d. 882), writing to King Louis the German (ruler of the eastern part of the Carolingian empire, 843–76) in 858, set out these military duties of rulers very clearly. In Hincmar's view, the ruler's power comes to him from God for a specific purpose: to lead the people to salvation. So he must be a just judge, protect them, keep the peace and wage war against those who try to attack them. This is a sacred duty. As for other soldiers, Hincmar wrote that a soldier who killed was not guilty of homicide when he was acting under the king's orders, and cited the various New Testament examples of soldiers who were praised by God's servants or at any rate not instructed to stop fighting.[49]

It was only a step from Hincmar's views on the soldiers' duty to fight for the king to the concept of three 'orders' or sections in society: those who fight, those who pray and those who work. Near the end of the ninth century, the monk Aymon of Auxerre referred in passing in his 'commentary on the Apocalypse' to the three orders of the priests (*sacerdotes*), the fighters (*milites*) and the farmers (*agricultores*). At around the same time, King Alfred the Great of Wessex (871–99) referred in his translation of Boethius's *De consolatione philosophiae* to the instruments through whom the king must govern: those who pray (*gebedmen*), those who fight (*fyrdmen*) and those who work (*weorcmen*).[50] There was, then, a section of society who had a duty to fight for the protection of society.

In the tenth century, as central authority in France became less able to ensure the peace throughout the kingdom, Church leaders began to look to local secular lords to fulfil the function of defending the people. Sometime before 942, Odo, abbot of the monastery of Cluny in central eastern France, wrote 'The Life of Gerald of Aurillac', an account of a pious nobleman who held his lands in the vicinity of Cluny and who had renounced pillage and given his lance to the service of Christ, protecting the poor and needy and the churches against the bandit knights. Yet although he approved of what Gerald was doing, Odo was clearly ambivalent about the necessity of bloodshed, even when it was in the cause of protecting the weak. He claimed that Gerald of Aurillac never shed blood, and depicted him winning battles miraculously through God's aid without even drawing his sword, because he was fighting in a good cause. The warriors in Gerald's service, who had given him an oath of loyalty, also had God's approval and protection.[51]

Church leaders also took their own steps to curb violence and banditry. Through a series of Church councils from 975 onwards, leading churchmen assembled warriors and peasants together and exacted oaths from the warriors not to attack Church property or the peasantry.[52] These oaths were backed up with the threat of armed force against anyone who broke them: at the 975 council of Le Puy the bishop called on his relatives, the counts of Brioude and Gévadan, to supply troops to enforce the peace. In a previous era he would have called upon the king, but by 975 the king of France was unable to enforce the peace so far south.

In the eyes of the Church, Gerald and his warriors and the counts who enforced the peace of God at Le Puy in 975 were waging legitimate war. But the Church preferred to have no warfare at all between Christians, and in the 'truce of God' movement in France, beginning at the council of Toulouges (in Roussillon) in 1027, all violence was forbidden on certain days of the week, on pain of excommunication. We may assume that the men who committed violence against Church property and who pillaged the peasantry would not care very much about excommunication – being cut off from the community of Christendom and damned to Hell on their death – and so the 'truce of God', like the 'peace of God', relied on the support of leading secular lords, and their armies, to enforce it.

So, according to these ecclesiastics and leading lay authorities, legitimate war was possible in certain circumstances. From the twelfth century onwards canon lawyers developed the theory of the 'just war' whereby certain wars were legitimate and others illegal banditry. Although they generally agreed that all persons have a right to meet force with force, normally private individuals should not resort to war to enforce their rights, but seek justice through the courts. Legitimate war could normally only be waged by a proper authority, such as a king.[53] Maurice Keen has traced how the concept of a 'law of arms' developed in the later Middle Ages from a combination of canon law and civil law; this 'law of arms' applied to warriors and could be enforced in military courts. By use of this law, kings could take legal action against any subject conducting private wars.

Throughout the kingdoms of Europe, the constable or marshal of the kingdom judged such cases: in England from the reign of Edward III, the 'law of arms' was enforced by the Court of Chivalry, presided over by the constable of England.[54]

Yet even those involved in legitimate warfare were normally regarded as committing a sin (although not a crime) when they killed others. In contrast, it was not necessarily a sin to kill people in the course of holy war. 'Holy war', in Christian terms, was war against the enemies of Christendom: it could simply involve the defence of leading Church officials, such as the local archbishop or the papacy.[55] By the late eleventh century holy war was being depicted by ecclesiastical writers as bringing a reward from God, such as forgiveness of past sins. The theological thinking behind this was complex, and the finer details were probably beyond the understanding of most warriors: so what follows is a very simple outline.

In the early Christian Church, Christians who committed a sin had to confess it, put right the wrong in some way ('penance'), and could then be reconciled to God and admitted to worship with other Christians (the Church) again. Until the wrong was put right by penance, they were excluded from worshipping with other Christians. By the eleventh century this system of dealing with wrongdoings had been amended so that as soon as a sinner had confessed and begun penance, he or she was absolved and reconciled to God and the Church, on the understanding that the penance would eventually be completed. Taking part in holy war became an acceptable form of penance. In the second half of the eleventh century, Pope Gregory VII (1073–85) and his supporters urged all warriors to fight in his defence against his enemy, King Henry IV of Germany (1056–1106). Pope Gregory argued that in serving the pope, warriors would be serving God, for the pope was the heir of St Peter and he had jurisdiction over all things, spiritual and secular. According to his enemies, Gregory VII claimed that fighting for the pope wiped out all sins, and that anyone who killed a Christian in this cause would be forgiven, apparently without any necessity to do penance.[56] A generation later, Guibert, abbot of Nogent (died c.1125), wrote: 'in our time God has ordained holy wars, so that the knightly order and the wandering crowd – who had been engaged in mutual slaughter, like their ancient pagan forebears – could find a new way of earning salvation.'[57] He was describing the crusades: those who took part believed that the campaign was a substitute for all their penance.[58]

During the First Crusade of 1095–9 the western Christians encountered the popular Byzantine Christian cults of military saints such as George, Demetrius, Maurice and Mercurius, who – although they were known in the West – had not been as well known as they were in the Byzantine Church.[59] The warriors of the West adopted these cults with enthusiasm, for they seemed to endorse their own brand of religiously justified warfare. In the 1120s new military religious orders developed in the newly established kingdom of Jerusalem. These followed religious rules as monks and religious people did in the West, but with the particular duty of using arms to defend Christian pilgrims visiting the holy places in the East, and also helping to defend Christian territory by force. The best known of these orders would be the Templars and the Hospitallers. The cleric John of Salisbury, writing his *Policraticus* in 1159, remarked that the military religious order of the Templars was almost alone in waging legitimate war: following the example of the Maccabees (Jewish warriors who fought pagans in defence of the Temple before the time of Christ), they laid down their lives on the battlefield on behalf of other Christians, in defence of Christendom.[60]

The crusades and the military religious orders required warriors to leave their homes and families and travel to strange lands to serve God. Yet even warriors who did not fight in defence of Christendom could be regarded as serving God. John of Salisbury wrote that an ordinary warrior could act as a good Christian in the course of his normal duties: a faithful warrior who served his lord loyally, even if his lord was fighting illegitimately, was nevertheless a good warrior, not a criminal.[61] John described the function of warriors: they should guard the Church, fight unbelievers, venerate the priesthood, protect the poor, keep the peace and die to protect other Christians. 'Knights who do these things are sanctified.'[62] Likewise, Bonizo of Sutri (d. 1090), one of the scholars who had supported Pope Gregory VII, had written that ordinary warriors, the 'knights' of his day, should serve the Church, serve their lord and keep the oath of loyalty which they had sworn to him, serve the state and lay down their lives for it, protect the poor, widows and orphans, and avoid pillage.[63] These are the standards of warrior behaviour that are now regarded as 'chivalry': protecting the Church and the poor and keeping the peace.[64]

Yet, even though churchmen agreed that warfare could be legitimate in certain circumstances and that the warrior had a positive role to play in society, they were still anxious to limit the activities of warriors. The priest and writer Honoré Bouvet, for example, did not regard war as evil in itself, but wished to restrict war to those who were properly involved in it, and mitigate its evil effects on society as a whole. Jean de Venette (died *c.*1368), a Carmelite friar writing a chronicle of the same Anglo-French war which prompted Bouvet's writing, regarded the war as a chaotic breakdown of law and order in which the non-combatants were victims and the warriors had brought about the destruction of the French kingdom.[65]

How far did active warriors agree with this assessment of their lifestyle? As explained in the introduction, to discover the views of active warriors we must go to the vernacular literature written for them. We then find that the same war which Bouvet and Venette regarded as destructive and undesirable was depicted by Jean Froissart as a glorious performance of knighthood. While educated ecclesiastics of the late eleventh and early twelfth centuries debated whether fighting could ever win warriors favour in God's eyes, one Turold, redactor of the enormously popular Old French epic poem *La Chanson de Roland* ('The Song of Roland'), wrote that a man who did not fight bravely was not worth fourpence and was fit only to be a monk.[66] Comments such as these do not indicate that the warrior class took ecclesiastical admonitions to limit warfare very seriously.

Warriors agreed with ecclesiastics that war should be just – but what was 'just'? The Old French 'epics of revolt' in which the hero wars against his lawful king, typically Charlemagne or Louis the Pious, indicate that even a warrior fighting against his lord could be fighting in a just cause if he had been treated unjustly – and of course this was a matter of interpretation.[67] The romance literature of the warrior classes also contained its rebel characters who did not fight according to the rules and disrupted the idealised world of romance knighthood. Sometimes the story told how the hero destroyed these rebels and restored the balance of society, but it is clear that some 'rebels' attracted an audience following, notably Brun sans pitié, 'pitiless Brown', of the vulgate and post-vulgate French Arthurian romances of the thirteenth century. Initially an outlaw robber knight pursued fruitlessly by Arthur's knights in the vulgate *Lancelot* (composed perhaps between 1210 and 1225),[68] in subsequent works Brun was transformed into an anti-hero of considerable military skill and of long and illustrious knightly lineage whose actions were understandable if not strictly legal in a good Christian society.[69] The fact that this lawless warrior appeared repeatedly in different works and was developed into a well-defined personality indicates that he was a popular character with noble audiences, a person to whom they could relate. It appears that to those who regarded warfare as their role in society, war could be a justified activity in itself. Contrary to the urgings of the canon lawyers, they believed that they had a right to wage war on their enemies.[70] This view is obviously reminiscent of the views of Bertrand de Born quoted at the beginning of this section; but how does it relate to the ecclesiastical ideals of 'chivalry' just described? To answer this, it is best to trace the development of warrior ideals from the early Middle Ages.

The Ostrogothic culture which Procopius depicted in his 'Secret History' in the first half of the sixth century was one in which warrior skills were everything: a man who did not fight was worthless in society. Glory and honour were won by exercising warrior skills. A commander won additional prestige in society by gathering together the best warriors, and retaining their loyalty by giving them their bodily needs – food, drink and shelter – and bestowing gifts on them (of armour, horses, weapons and also of land; and ensuring that they made a good marriage). One of the most famous descriptions of early medieval warriors appears in the Old English poem *Beowulf*, whose date is much debated among scholars

– it may date from around 800, or earlier, or later. Its description of the successful warrior king, however, applied to most of the Middle Ages:

> Then to Hrothgar was granted glory in battle
> Mastery of the field; so friends and kinsmen
> Gladly obeyed him, and his band increased
> To a great company. It came into his mind
> That he would give commands for the construction
> Of a huge mead-hall, a house greater than men on earth
>   ever had heard of,
> And share the gifts God had bestowed on him
> Upon its floor with folk young and old.[71]

So Hrothgar's success in the field led more good warriors to join him; but in return he had to reward them. A good leader fed and armed his men well, to increase his own renown as well as theirs. *Beowulf* also underlines the importance of family relations: introducing himself to Hrothgar, Beowulf defines himself by his relatives. The noble warrior should have confidence in himself: Beowulf describes his past heroic deeds to Hrothgar in order to persuade him to allow him to fight the monster Grendal.[72] He makes a vow before the battle to overcome or to die; and he makes the deliberate decision to fight Grendal without weapons, because killing the monster with a sword would be too easy. A modern reader might regard Beowulf as boastful and rash, but his actions were those of a warrior who had confidence in his own abilities. Such confidence was praiseworthy, in contrast to pride, which was likely to lead a warrior into difficulties. Yet a good warrior should not be worried about staying alive; the essential thing was to fight bravely and honourably and die well.[73] The deeds of the warrior who was victorious, or who died valiantly, would be preserved forever in epic verse, while he or his family should be rewarded generously by his grateful lord.[74]

The women of the warrior classes also had a role to play: as mothers who should ensure the proper upbringing of their children and urge their sons to great deeds in battle, and as wives who should act in the place of absent husbands, honour and reward noble warriors appropriately, mourn the dead and avenge their menfolk's death if necessary; but they were not expected to fight as a matter of course.[75]

Loyalty was very important, but it was a two-way relationship. Warriors should be loyal to their commander and to subordinates, as well as to comrades and relatives. The commander who did not care for his warriors' needs and reward their courage would very quickly lose them to another commander who did. Those warriors who failed their commander in his hour of need were not only dishonoured, losing all standing among warriors, but would also forfeit all rights to gifts and support from their commander or his family.[76]

These were pious warriors, aware that God alone gives victories, although their own prowess also had an essential role to play.[77] We might argue that their warrior piety had little in common with the Christianity of the gospels, but it was none the less deeply felt. Those who worshipped a different god were regarded as enemies.

La Chanson de Roland, written in the late eleventh or twelfth century, also gives a clear view of 'heroic' warrior ideals. This poem commemorates a defeat of Charlemagne's army at Roncesvalles in the Pyrenees in 778, although altering certain details, and describes the deaths of Charlemagne's nephew and general Roland, his comrade Oliver, and many of his leading warriors in the battle.

The poet depicts Roland describing the duties of a warrior to his lord. When Oliver realises that they are under attack, Roland responds:

> May God grant it!
> We should certainly be here to fight for our king;
> On behalf of his lord, a man must suffer distress
> And endure great heat and great cold
> And lose both hair and hide.
> Now let everyone concentrate on dealing great blows,
> So that no one may ever sing an insulting song about us!
> The pagans [the Muslims] are in the wrong and the Christians
> have the right;
> I will never give a bad example of how a warrior should act.[78]

Meanwhile, his warriors declare: 'God's curse on anyone who flees; not one of us will fail you, even if we die.'[79] Roland even refuses to blow his great horn, the Oliphant, to summon Charlemagne for help, on the basis that he and his warriors would be blamed for cowardice if he did so.

Roland and his men go on to inflict terrible carnage on the Muslims, who at last retreat – but by this time all of Roland's men are dead, and he himself is dying. He takes his horn and his sword and goes to sit on a hill under a tree, his face towards the enemy, so that no one will be able to say that he died defeated. Even in his dying speech, he seems more concerned about the effect of his death on Charlemagne's military strength – listing his own great victories – and about the fate of his sword Durendal than about God ('Oh, Durendal! How beautiful and holy you are!'). Durendal is the female object that Roland apparently cares for most in the world, for in French the noun 'sword' is feminine. Alde, Oliver's sister and Roland's betrothed, is of secondary importance: while Oliver is angry and hurt that Roland's rashness in engaging the Muslims against overwhelming odds will mean that the marriage will never take place, and Alde herself drops dead at the news of Roland's death (and rather than marry Charlemagne's far less doughty son Louis), Roland himself never mentions Alde. As for his male comrades, although he is a popular commander because of his past generosity to them, only late in the battle does he realise that they are all going to die, by which time it is too late to call on Charlemagne for reinforcements. He grieves over Oliver's death, but in the face of his earlier indifference to Oliver's good advice this grief seems rather futile. What is more, only when he is at the very point of death does he pray to God to have mercy on his sins. His Christian faith is very simple; he recalls the miracles of Daniel in the lion's den and the raising of Lazarus from the dead. Yet this is enough to win him immediate access to paradise as a martyr.[80]

Roland is a warrior in the heroic tradition, for whom honour is everything, and a glorious death his greatest achievement. But even as Turold wrote his version of the epic, over 200 years after the battle actually took place, he was questioning the validity of Roland's actions. The modern military historian reading the text may observe how Oliver, Roland's faithful comrade, acts like the ideal wise and prudent commander described in the clerically composed chronicles of the late eleventh and early twelfth centuries. Edward Steidle has pointed out how contemporary commentators writing about the First Crusade criticised commanders who did not take adequate precautions before battle by sending out scouts to reconnoitre the enemy's forces and drawing up their army carefully before battle, and who sought honour and glory rather than victory. These commentators were contrasting the wise commander described by Vegetius with the honour-seeking commander of traditional epic poetry, and finding the traditional 'epic' commander wanting. Oliver, who goes to look at the approaching Muslim army and gives Roland advice about strategy, was acting more like the wise Vegetian commander than the traditional commander, represented by Roland. Certainly, Roland won undying fame for himself and his men, but his failure to call on Charlemagne for reinforcements led to the loss of Charlemagne's rearguard and of his best general. If only Roland had followed Oliver's advice and called for reinforcements, he could have won a glorious victory and stayed alive, going on to win more glorious victories for Charlemagne and for Christendom. Arguably, then, Turold's version of the death of Roland was intended to teach the warriors who listened to it about battle strategy. Such warriors would not read Vegetius, but they would accept Vegetian teaching about strategy and planning in battle if it were presented to them in a form that interested them: the traditional epic.[81]

Epic literature, then, not only expressed but also criticised warrior ideals, and in so doing indicated that these ideals could adapt and develop. To take another example, in Jean Bodel's *Chanson des Saisnes*, 'the Song of the Saxons', written between 1180 and 1202, the hero Baudouin, Roland's half-brother, dies on the battlefield because of his lack of experience as a commander. When the Saxons attack him, Baudouin rejects the advice of his wife Sebille and his barons to send to Charlemagne for help: it is too soon to ask for help, he says, and as young bachelors (young warriors still seeking their place in society), it is their duty to win renown and to conquer new lands. Only reluctantly does he give way to Sebille's urging and send a request for aid. When he leads his army out to fight the Saxons he is slow to retreat even when he gets into difficulties, because he fears that Sebille will call him a coward.[82] Finally, when Charlemagne comes with reinforcements, the Franks are overwhelmed by the Saxons and Baudouin and other leading warriors are killed, although Charlemagne goes on to defeat the Saxons. In contrast to Alde on the news of Roland's death, Sebille's reaction when told of Baudouin's death is first denial and then floods of tears. Regretting that she cannot drop dead as Alde did, she finally becomes a nun to pray for her husband's soul. Unlike Alde, Sebille represents the active wife of the warrior, who supports her husband's actions and gives him sound advice. Baudouin's failing was that he did not listen to her and his other advisors early enough; and his beliefs about the duties of young warriors and concern about his honour prevented him from taking the right action until it was too late. Certainly, Baudouin had a glorious death, but the vivid description of the impact of his death on those he loved, especially Sebille, might encourage warriors who heard the story recited to act a little more responsibly.

Baudouin and Roland were noble warriors, and their warrior ideals need not also have been the ideals of their followers. But during the course of the twelfth and thirteenth century, both noble and lesser warriors who fought on horseback with sword and lance came to use the same term for themselves: in French *chevalier*, in German *Ritter*, in English *knight*. They viewed themselves as belonging to the same 'order' in society, with the same social functions, and, to judge by the literature produced for them, they shared the same ideals of knighthood: called *chevalerie* in French (i.e., chivalry).[83] This social development will be considered in more detail in the next chapter. What should be noted here is that even as the status of 'the knight' rose in the course of the thirteenth century, so that many more warriors were no longer achieving the status of 'knighthood', they continued to share the same warrior ideals; for, while the ideals set out in 'knightly' literature specifically applied only to knights, any warrior who wished to win renown should aspire to these ideals.

Clearly, there was debate among warriors over these ideals, for example, whether discretion was the greater part of valour or whether the strategic withdrawal was cowardly. As social expectations of knights rose, the debates in knightly literature deepened. The Anglo-Norman poet Wace, writing his Old French version of Geoffrey of Monmouth's *Historia regum Britanniae* ('The History of the Kings of Britain') in the second half of the twelfth century, elaborated on the knightly behaviour of the warriors of King Arthur's court, and in so doing described the debate between the traditional warriors and the new ideals of chivalry.[84]

King Arthur receives an ultimatum from the Emperor Lucius of Rome, ordering Arthur to come to Rome to give satisfaction for the damage he has inflicted on the emperor. The king calls his council. As they assemble, the old warrior Cador gives his opinion that this challenge from the Romans is a good thing. The British, he says, are becoming idle and lazy, and given over to lechery. The young warriors have lost their prowess; they are only interested in love affairs, joking and playing games. Because the country has been at peace so long, the British have lost all their great reputation as warriors, but now they will have the opportunity to recover their boldness and energy. 'I have never loved a long peace, nor will I ever do so' (lines 10737–64).

Cador could have been speaking of England under Wace's patron, King Henry II: a country which had recently been affected by constant warfare, but where warfare was now a thing of the past so that knights had to go overseas to perform deeds of prowess. Presumably Cador was expressing views similar to those expressed by many people in Wace's expected audience, views like those expressed by the poet Bertrand de Born in the next generation. But Wace immediately gives the counter-argument, expressed by King Arthur's handsome young nephew Walwain (Gawain).

> 'Faith! My lord earl,' said Gawain,
> 'You are getting alarmed over nothing.
> Peace is better than war,
> The land is more beautiful and improved by it;
> Jokes are excellent,
> And love affairs are good.
> Knights do knightly deeds
> For the sake of love and to please their girlfriends' (lines 10765–72).

In short, peace need not damage warriors or make them unwarlike, for the young men will still wish to do doughty deeds in war in order to win the favour of the young women. Peace is also good for the country at large. Gawain was a suitable mouthpiece for this new knightly ethic: he went on to be famed in Arthurian romance as the wisest of Arthur's knights, one of the most doughty, and outstanding as a lover of women. Here he seems to represent the up-and-coming generation of young warriors who had a rather different view of warfare to their forefathers. No longer was war itself the only honourable activity for a young warrior: one could make a name for oneself in peacetime also, impressing the ladies with knightly deeds of a different sort. Gawain does not state what sort of 'knightly deeds' (*chevaleries*) he has in mind, but one can assume that the young warrior should attend tournaments, assist young ladies in distress, for instance by fighting on their behalf in legal cases – as Gawain himself was famed for doing – help other persons in need of aid, and learn the courtly arts of dancing, singing and playing chess and backgammon. For an example of such a warrior one need only think of William Marshal (d. 1219), contemporary of Bertrand de Born, who attended tournaments across France as a young man and won a great name for his knightly skill, was generous to others, imposed justice as he saw fit on miscreants whom he encountered, respected women and stopped to help a woman in Le Mans whose house was on fire, and was able to sing to accompany dancers; while also taking part in warfare for the king when necessary.[85]

This more measured, rounded model of knighthood obviously owed something to the ecclesiastical model of knighthood discussed by writers such as Bonizo of Sutri and John of Salisbury, but the fact that it appeared in knightly literature indicates that it was becoming accepted by knights themselves. So at the end of the twelfth century or early in the thirteenth, one of the composers of the first continuation of Chrétien de Troyes's famous romance poem *Le conte du Graal* depicted Gawain stating that the wise knight should not fight unless he must – in contrast to the traditional warrior, who had believed that he would be shamed if he did not fight on any pretext. In the 1230s the author of the prose romance *Tristan* depicted two of his characters attacking the tradition that a knight must fight when challenged: what use is honour to a dead man? This point of view was presented as a satirical attack on knighthood, and may not have been taken very seriously by listeners, but in *Guiron le Courtois*, composed in the late 1230s and incorporated into Rusticien de Pise's compilation of the 1270s, the same need for moderation is implied in the statement that a good knight should not kill another good knight except in self-defence. This was less a warning against imprudent violence and more a plea to defend the new 'class' of knights against needless damage: knights should protect each other, not kill each other. Yet, nevertheless, it suggests that warriors, at least the more noble warriors who would hear romances such as *Tristan* and *Guiron* read aloud, were realising by the 1230s that violence should be limited if it were not to damage knights rather than honour them. No one should attack another without warning. Knights should not attack two or more against one; if several knights attacked one, they should attack one at a time. Knights should not attack those from a different class: it was dishonourable to attack merchants, clergy or peasants, whose role in society did not require them to fight, or women – even noble women whose place in society did involve them in warfare, for women themselves should not have to fight except in cases of emergency. On the other side of the coin, knights should treat each other fairly. Treachery by knights against knights is severely criticised in *Guiron*; knights who imprison other knights and refuse to release them are regarded as evil, although apparently also an inevitable part of an evil world.[86]

So by the 1230s at least a more moderate, rounded view of the role of warriors in society had been adopted into the literature of the military classes. This combined elements of Christian tradition with warrior ideals of heroism and loyalty. The popularity of this literature throughout lay society indicates that its view of warfare was the most widely held: a positive view of warfare as a means of gaining status, but with the qualification that it should be limited and controlled. The question remains whether real warriors actually strove to live up to this moderated literary ideal, or whether they continued to act more like Procopius's sixth-century image of the uncultured Ostrogoths. Maurice Keen, in his great work *Chivalry*, believed that 'the secular code of honour of a martially oriented aristocracy' was a major influence on the behaviour of 'a martial estate that regarded war as its hereditary profession'.[87] But historians do not agree over what this secular code of honour actually was. Nicholas Wright, for example, has distinguished between 'the general code of chivalry' promoted by the Church, to which the highest nobility paid lip service, and 'the law of arms' which was the martial code actually followed by warriors.[88] Yet late medieval commentators did not distinguish between the two sets of ideals, although they might stress certain ideals at the expense of others. The accounts of Jean Froissart and others writing for, or from, the 'martial estate which regarded war as its hereditary profession' indicate that the warriors of the later Middle Ages took their secular code of ideal behaviour very seriously. This problem will be investigated here by examining one small aspect of the question: how warriors actually behaved on the battlefield.

* * *

The French nobility of the twelfth century onwards believed that knighthood had originated in France, and that they therefore had a responsibility to uphold its values.[89] The particular characteristic of knightly combat which set them apart from other warriors on the battlefield was the mounted charge with couched lance, and it is striking that the French nobility persisted in using this tactic even when it had been shown to be ineffective against suitably armed infantry. For instance, the cavalry charge was used by the French nobility at Courtrai on 11 July 1302 against the Flemings. The cavalry knocked their own foot-archers to the side or trampled them if they failed to get clear of the knights, but were unable to break the lines of Flemish infantry armed with pikes and wooden maces, and the French knights suffered heavy losses. French cavalry was again unable to drive the Flemish infantry from the battlefield at Arques on 4 April 1303; at Mons-en-Pévèle on 18 August 1304 the French remained in control of the battlefield, but were unable to defeat the Flemings decisively.[90] While the French cavalry had the advantage of mobility, the infantry were a more powerful defensive force and could withstand and break up a cavalry charge and pick off the more vulnerable mounted knights individually.

The next generation of French nobility do not seem to have learned from their fathers' experiences, for on 26 August 1346 at the battle of Crécy they again used the cavalry charge against well-armed infantry, this time against the foot-archers of the army of King Edward III of England.

Again the French mounted knights drove their own archers apart, trampling many in the process. In this battle the blind king of Bohemia insisted on being led into the fray by his own knights so that he could deal a blow with his sword against the enemy, and he was killed. Jean Froissart and the English nobles who gave him his information about the battle regarded the French action as foolhardy rather than an example of good knighthood. In contrast to the French, realising the problems of the battlefield, Edward III had ordered his men-at-arms to dismount and fight on foot.[91]

The French nobility were not blindly tied to their ideals, however. As Matthew Bennett has pointed out, in the battles that followed between the French and the English, the French commanders changed their tactics, including dismounting some or all of their knights.[92] This brought some success, but not consistently. Froissart described how at Poitiers in 1356 the French nobility again began the attack on horseback:

> Then the marshals and their battalion approached [the English lines] on horseback, and entered the path with the thick hedge on either side. As soon as they had entered, the archers began to fire rapidly from both sides, shooting the horses and firing long barbed arrows. The horses that were shot, feeling the iron tips of the arrows, were frightened and did not wish to go on. One turned across the path, another fell on its side, where they lay shaking beneath their masters, who could not get up. And the English men-at-arms fell on them and killed them, or took them prisoner at will.[93]

Those behind, seeing what had happened, fell back. When the next battalion saw what had happened, many mounted their horses and fled. The English then attacked on horseback. King John of France, however, refused to retreat, and ordered his men to dismount and fight on foot. Yet the English now had the advantage, and the French army was heavily defeated and the king captured.[94] After this defeat, the French improved the quality of their horse armour, and, as a result, at the battles of Cocherel in 1364 and Pontvallain in 1370 the English archers could not make any impact on the French cavalry.[95]

The French nobility again attempted to use cavalry against infantry with disastrous results at Agincourt in 1415. On this occasion, however, it was not the arrows that destroyed the cavalry charge so much as the muddy ground and the line of stakes which the English had erected in front of their lines. The eyewitness accounts of Jean Le Fèvre and Jean de Waurin describe the initial French charge under Lord Guillaume de Saveuses being turned back when the horses reached the English barricade of sharpened stakes: the ground was so soft that horses slipped and fell in the mud. The other horses were so troubled by the arrow shot of the English that they turned round and ran back into the French vanguard.

The battle lines of the vanguard were broken up, and many of the French panicked and rode away. The English then attacked and destroyed the French vanguard. The cavalry of the rearguard, meanwhile, which was still waiting undisturbed on horseback, on seeing the disaster, fled.[96]

In the early fourteenth century the English mounted nobility had initially encountered problems facing an army largely made up of infantry, most famously against the Scots at Bannockburn in 1314. However, the English nobility learned from this experience that alternative tactics were required against the Scots, and dismounted to meet them at Dupplin Moor and Halidon Hill in 1332 and 1333, using archers to break up the Scots' ranks. In this way they showed themselves prepared to adapt the knightly ideal of combat on horseback to meet military needs.[97] The French knights did attempt to adapt, but their lack of consistent success suggests that they, in particular, were especially devoted to the idealised concept of the noble knight fighting on horseback.[98]

The crusades against the Hussites suggest another instance of adherence to knightly ideals where a more pragmatic approach could have been more effective. The Hussites were Czechs who adopted a rigorous version of Catholic Christianity; the movement began in Prague in the first decade of the fifteenth century, and incorporated Czechs from every social level in Bohemia. It was condemned by the institutional Catholic Church, and crusades were launched against the Hussites to stamp out their beliefs. The leading Hussite military leader was one John Žižka (d. 1424), who was a member of the gentry, a squire and not a knight; and most of his troops were from the peasant farming class. Žižka was not knighted until 1421 or 1422. It appears that his relatively low social status led to his enemies underestimating him and his army. In addition, while his enemies were inclined to follow established military practice, Žižka, unencumbered by the obligation to follow a knightly code of warfare, showed initiative and resourcefulness unmatched by his knightly foes.

For instance, on 21 December 1421, Žižka and his army were surrounded in the city of Kutná Hora by the forces of King Sigismund of Hungary, heir to the throne of Bohemia, who was determined to crush Hussitism. Žižka had apparently lost the battle, but during the night of 21–22 December his forces broke out of the encirclement and retreated to Kolín. Sigismund did not pursue his defeated foe, but took control of Kutná Hora. His army was much larger than Žižka's, and apparently he saw him as no threat at this juncture: Žižka had, after all, been defeated. Žižka, however, did not remain defeated. Having gathered reinforcements, but still with inferior numbers, Žižka launched an attack on Sigismund's forces. Sigismund decided to retreat; Žižka pursued him. Sigismund attempted to stand and give battle, but his troops fled before the Hussites. Žižka and his army continued to pursue Sigismund and his army until they were driven out of Bohemia.[99] This was not accepted knightly practice; a defeated foe should be allowed to withdraw in peace. But Žižka did not follow knightly practice, and caught his foe unawares.[100] Perhaps if Žižka had been of knightly stock, Sigismund might not have underestimated him so disastrously.

These instances suggest that knightly ideals did have some influence over how warriors fought, although some warriors saw themselves as more bound by knightly ideals of warfare than others. Whether warriors also respected the moderating influence of ecclesiastical writers is less clear. As knightly literature set up moderation and courtesy as ideals alongside the ideal of fighting on horseback and allowing a defeated enemy to retreat, warriors obviously liked to hear about moderate, courteous warriors, but would not necessarily be so enthusiastic about emulating them.

* * *

To sum up: while many theoretical treatises on how to wage war were produced in the medieval period, it is rare to find evidence of such works actually in use in the field. Nevertheless, the great interest of many noble patrons, who themselves were active warriors, in commissioning such works suggests that they held some relation to actual practice. On the question of the moral justification for war there was considerable debate: canon lawyers and the ecclesiastical writers who followed them believed war could only be justifiable in certain limited circumstances, a viewpoint that rulers supported as a means of limiting warfare among their nobles, but for those who saw war as their hereditary profession the justification for war was much wider. For a social group defined by ability to fight, obviously, war would always hold a central place and tend to be regarded as an end in itself. Yet this centrality of war to the self-image of the nobility of Catholic Christendom boded ill for the peace and stability of society as a whole. Again, although the idealised model of western Christian society as consisting of three 'orders' and assigned the duty of fighting to one section of society only, the status which derived from military ability meant that in fact all parts of society would tend to become involved in warfare. This will become clear in the next chapter.

2

Military personnel

Gregory, bishop of Tours 573–94, describes in his 'History of the Franks' how, in AD 585, the army of the Merovingian King Guntram of the Franks set out to attack the city of Poitiers, whose inhabitants had rebelled against him. Having captured Poitiers, the army marched south to crush the army of Gundovald, who claimed to be a son of King Lothar I (d. 561) and therefore Guntram's brother and a contender for the throne. This army contained men on horseback and on foot. Gregory mentions that they were armed with javelins, or spears. The army had a large baggage train of wagons, which was left in the care of the less able-bodied when the army went to attack the church of St Vincent at Agen.

The army was made up of those in the realm who were liable for military service, including men identified by their towns of origin, Orléans and Bourges. Some of those who were liable for service failed to join the army, and were fined: the monks of one of the religious houses belonging to the church of St Martin of Tours were due to pay a fine for failing to appear to perform the due service, but were saved from the fine when the assessor fell suddenly ill. The army was led by leading officials of the realm, such as Ullo, count of Bourges, and Boso, one of the king's military commanders. When Ullo and Boso went to escort Gundovald, Ullo was carrying a lance with which he tried to stab Gundovald, but Boso apparently carried no weapon, as he picked up a stone and threw it at Gundovald. The impression that is given is of a large army, largely made up of town levies of men who only fought when summoned to do so – although they provided their own weapons – and led by professional commanders, either holding a high official military/administrative office, such as count, or having no named office but nevertheless exercising military command.[1]

Six and a half centuries later, when King James I of Aragon (d. 1276) set out to attack the kingdom of Valencia in 1233, he had an army of barons, the military religious orders of the Hospital, Temple, Uclés and Calatrava, the bishop of Saragosa, men of his own household under one of his own household knights, and the men of the town of Teruel. He had mounted warriors, *caballeros*, armed with lances, squires carrying the knights' replacement weapons, crossbowmen and other infantry. The army had assembled at the king's summons, although the military orders of the Temple and Hospital and the men of their towns did not assemble in the place directed, but undertook a raid of their own.[2]

Although more detailed information is available on James's forces, superficially these armies appear to have been similar. Both contained town levies; both contained men on horseback and men on foot. The lance, or a variation on it, was a weapon used by both armies. The basis of the army was the king's own military forces, to which the town levies and other officials were added. There were also leading religious men: King James had a bishop in his army, while Gundovald was actively assisted by Bishop Sagittarius of Gap, who threw missiles at King Guntram's army as they besieged Saint-Bertrand-de-Comminges. James had crossbowmen in his army; but this weapon was not apparently used by the Franks, although it had been known in France during the Roman period and was used by the Roman army. Gregory does not mention bows during the campaign against Gundovald. Although arrows are mentioned as a weapon on a few other occasions during this period, the bow appears to have been less important in Merovingian armies than types of lance or spear.[3]

If we consider the Carolingian armies of the eighth and early ninth centuries, we again find a similar picture: local levies from the towns, now armed with bows and arrows, commanded by their own counts (here the officials with authority over the towns), plus the nobles with their own personal armed followings. The levies from the towns were made up of free men who were liable to perform military service for the king by virtue of owning a certain amount of land. The nobles were military officials appointed by the king or emperor who owed military service as part of their office and were warriors by profession.[4]

These armies, therefore, were made up partly of part-time warriors who only fought when summoned by the king or ruler, and partly by professional warriors who fought because of a personal contract with the king: because they were part of his household, or because he had appointed them to an office which involved military service. James I of Aragon also made use of a small body of professional warriors who fought from religious vocation, the military religious orders. There was no full-time professional standing army employed by the king. These armies were considerably changed from those of the Roman Empire which the Merovingians had succeeded and which the Carolingians sought to revive. By the end of our period, however, full-time professional standing armies were again being employed by the leading rulers of western Christendom. This chapter will trace changes in recruitment of armies throughout our period, and then go on to consider what types of warrior and what categories of persons made up these armies.

* * *

The army of the later Roman Empire was described in detail by
A. H. M. Jones in his *The Later Roman Empire, 284–602* (1964) and his
description is still largely accepted by scholars. Jones described an army
that was largely permanent and professional, recruited, trained and paid
by the state.[5] The army created by Diocletian (d. 305) and Constantine I
(d. 337) consisted of cavalry and infantry. The bulk of the army was
stationed on the frontier of the empire, but there were also mobile field
armies, called *comitatus*, literally 'companies' or 'entourages' – the same
word applies to the warband surrounding a chieftain. The army consisted
of the traditional legions of infantry, made up of free Roman citizens
armed with the short sword and spear, complemented by *vexillationes*, or
detachments, of cavalry and cohorts of auxiliaries, who used a variety of
weapons. The actual organisation of the army was constantly under
review. The main question which concerns us here is who formed part of
the late Roman army and how they were recruited.

The core of Diocletian's army consisted of Roman citizens of free birth;
generally not volunteers, but conscripts. Slaves and freedmen, and even
men from certain 'dishonourable' professions such as cooks and bakers,
were not normally enlisted. By AD 313 sons of soldiers and of ex-soldiers
were expected to enlist if they were physically fit, in line with the government policy that every man should follow his father's profession. Their
sons, then, were expected to follow their fathers into a military profession.
But this was hardly the 'martial estate which regarded war as its hereditary profession' of the late medieval period. The late medieval martial
class was noble, or at least of relatively high social status; the hereditary
soldiers of the late Roman Empire were certainly not.

Most of the recruits for the late Roman army were raised as levies from
the provinces of the empire. An annual tax was levied, either in money or
in men. It was made on the same basis as the land tax, and landowners
were grouped together under the assessment, a certain number of
landowners being responsible for supplying one man and his equipment
for military service. As with other heavy burdens under the empire, privi-
leged persons were exempt from the assessment, as were those responsible
for administration in cities and towns, and the tenant workers tied to the
great estates. The recruit supplied to the army should be one of the free
tenants or one of their sons. Vegetius complained that too often landowners sent the men whom they did not want on their land – presumably
because they were lazy, troublemakers or physically unfit.

It is tempting to see a connection between these agricultural workers
who were recruited for the late Roman army, and the later medieval peasantry who owed military service to their lord. However, in the medieval
period those liable to provide military service were expected to serve in
person or to pay money to provide a replacement for themselves. In the

late Roman period, those liable to military assessment had to find a recruit to serve; it was not a personal military liability, but more resembled a modern tax assessment.

Once obtained, the new recruits to the late Roman army were examined to ensure that they were the correct age and height, and tattooed so that if they deserted they could be identified and brought back to the army. Recruits were locked up like prisoners to stop them running away. Once with their units, they would be trained as soldiers. None of these procedures applied to medieval armies. Anyone militarily fit was expected to serve, but there were no consistent procedures for dealing with those who ran away. They might be fined, or simply regarded as dishonoured by the rest of their society. But by the late Middle Ages the concept that a warrior was protecting public welfare on behalf of the king led to deserters being dealt with more severely.[6]

Non-citizens (either from within or without the Empire) were also recruited into the auxiliaries of the late Roman army. The fact that many of the units in Constantine I's army had the names of Germanic tribes suggests that they consisted mainly or entirely of men from these tribes, but A. H. M. Jones judged that the non-Romans were generally recruited as individuals rather than as groups from one area, and served under Roman officers rather than under their own chieftains. For such men the high standard of life in the army would have been an attractive inducement: they would eat well, be well housed and have fine equipment, a beautiful uniform and weapons, and be paid in kind and sometimes even in gold and silver. They might be promoted to high office and exercise power undreamed of in their homelands. Although these recruits were sometimes unwilling to serve far from home, and there are a few stories of intelligence leaks via a German recruit, in the main these recruits were reliable, loyal soldiers.[7]

In addition to the regular army, federates were employed. These were contingents of fighting men supplied by tribes outside the Roman Empire who had made a treaty of alliance with it, and they served under their own leaders rather than Roman officers. From the late fourth century, federates were employed more and more extensively, presumably because of the problems of persuading the free citizens to serve in the army.[8] The warriors employed as federates were sometimes drawn from tribes who had been given territory within the empire in return for helping to defend it against other tribes from outside: they could be wandering bands of warriors under a leader. They were not subject to Roman military discipline; their leader answered for their deeds, and he alone acted on behalf of the whole group in relations with the Roman military authority. He was responsible for collecting their pay, arranging their quarters and so on.[9]

There is an obvious similarity between these late Roman federates and the great mercenary companies of the fourteenth century; or one might compare the wandering bands of warriors that made up the federates to the wandering bands of knights in search of employment, tournaments and adventure in twelfth-century western Europe, described in the biography of William the Marshal and many works of romance. But, unlike the late Roman federates, these medieval wanderers came from within western European Roman Catholicism, not from outside it; the Germanic tribesmen employed as federates were either pagans or Arian Christians.

During the medieval period persons from outside western European Christian society were sometimes recruited into armies within western Europe (and western Christians were sometimes recruited into armies outside Christian Europe). In the ninth century various Frankish nobles, and the emperor Charles the Bald, used the military services of the pagan Vikings.[10] In the 950s when Liudolf (d. 957), son of Otto I, revolted against his father, he allied with the pagan Hungarians.[11] In the eleventh century the Spanish nobleman Rodrigo Díaz de Vivar, otherwise known as 'El Cid' (d. 1099), gave military service to various Muslim rulers within the Iberian peninsula.[12] In 1193 or 1194 King Richard I of England was employing Saracens at Domfront in Maine in northern France; in the thirteenth century the kings of Hungary employed pagan Cuman troops.[13] In 1237 the emperor Frederick II (d. 1250) employed Saracen archers from Lucera in his wars in northern Italy and in 1266 his son Manfred had Saracens in his army at Benevento.[14] In the early fourteenth century a Muslim Turkish force of horse and foot joined the Catholic Catalan Company in Gallipoli.[15] After their defeat at Tannenburg/ Grunwald on 15 July 1410 the Teutonic Knights accused their victorious Polish-Lithuanian enemies of employing heathen Wallachians, Samogitians and Lithuanians and (Christian) Russians in their army, whom they referred to (from crusading custom) as 'Saracens' and 'Turks', terms denoting enemies of the Christian faith.[16] The employment of non-Catholic Christians by Catholic Christian rulers during the medieval period usually caused alarm among their own people, much as the employment of federates in the late Roman army caused unease among informed contemporaries such as the fourth-century military officer and historian Ammianus Marcellinus and Vegetius.[17] But whereas Ammianus Marcellinus and Vegetius saw the employment of non-Romans as a security risk, in the medieval period the employment of non-Catholic Christians was also regarded as a sin which would anger God and lead to defeat.

It has been suggested that the medieval town levies were derived from the urban and rural militias set up by Valentinian III, emperor of the West 425–55, in the fifth century: every able-bodied male was expected to play a role in these militias in order to defend their own locality.[18] The Merovingian army raised its levies from the towns using the same sort of method of assessment, as did Charlemagne later in Aquitaine. James I of Aragon was still using town levies in the 1230s. Yet these medieval levies were crucially

different from the late Roman system, for the medieval town levies were
expected to join the royal army and serve outside their locality.

The changes to military recruitment and organisation in the former
provinces of the Western Empire obviously came about because of the
reduced resources and changed needs of government after the Western
Empire's disintegration from the fifth century onwards. Germanic kings
took over the government of individual regions as imperial appointees or
by usurpation, assisted by a noble class made up of Germanic warriors. In
northern Gaul in the late fifth century, for example, the Frankish leader
Clovis took over the civil adminstration, inaugurating the line of
Merovingian kings. When large professional armies returned to western
Europe in the late medieval period, they would be recruited on a more
voluntary basis than the late Roman armies.

It was stated above that, while the core of the late Roman army
was raised by a system of taxation based on land holding, in the medieval
period the obligation to serve was based less on land holding and more
on the individual's duty. Yet historians now disagree over how far this
was the case, and how to classify the new method of raising armies.

For many years historians called this method 'the feudal system', a term
derived from historians of the early modern period. In sixteenth-century
France, legal historians tried to work out a history of land law, and developed a historical 'model' which showed that in the Middle Ages men with
an obligation to serve their lord in war had been granted land called a
beneficium (benefice) or *feodum* (a fief). In exchange, they owed a vow of
loyalty to their lord, and various military services. They became the lord's
'man' (*homme*), hence the term 'homage' for the ceremony of loyalty.
These men (according to this model) were called 'vassals'. The historians
concluded that this system of military service in exchange for land began
during the Carolingian period. This theory has been amended by historians over the centuries, to allow for the fact that there was also freehold
land (called allodial land) which did not carry the obligation for military
service, and historians have decided that the original system of fiefs held
by vassals in exchange for military service was introduced by
Charlemagne as a method of governing his enormous empire. Historians
have also deduced that Charlemagne's system broke down during the
Viking invasions of the ninth and tenth centuries, and was redeveloped
with certain refinements in the eleventh century. This model of land holding in return for service has been given the name 'feudalism' from the
word *feudum*, or fief, as the fief was the basis for military service; although
this term was not used in this way during the Middle Ages.[19]

Recently, this theory of feudalism has come under fire from revisionist
historians, who have looked at the evidence afresh and concluded that the
prevalence of feudalism has been vastly exaggerated. The leading scholar
in the field is Susan Reynolds, and what follows is drawn largely from her
study *Fiefs and Vassals*.[20] Certainly, men did commend themselves to

lords, and did so from the early Middle Ages, but not necessarily in return for land. An oath of loyalty and/or good faith was also given by one person to another, called *fides* or *fidelitas* in Latin, *Treue* in German, or *fealté* in French. The people who made such oaths were not all warriors, and did not necessarily make these oaths in return for land, nor with an obligation to give military service. Oaths of fealty could be given between equals when a peace treaty was made without implying any obligation of military service. A subject was expected to swear loyalty to the king, without receiving any reciprocal obligations. Reynolds has concluded that although interpersonal relations between a lord and the subjects of that lord clearly mattered a great deal in medieval society, and that ceremonies surrounding the giving of oaths of loyalty were obviously important symbols of the obligations of lord and subject, these relations and ceremonies were not the basis of military service.[21]

The word 'fief', Reynolds deduced, as a term applied to the land holdings of nobles and other free subjects, was not used until well after 1100, and it was not used consistently to mean the same thing. Before 1100, free landholders did not hold their land in return for service. They expected to hold their land with full property rights, including the right to dispose of it and to pass it on to their children, although in fact their tenants and their relations would also have a say in anything they wanted to do with their land. Their use of the land was governed by custom. Officials such as counts and dukes owed military service to the king, but this service was due by virtue of their office, not by virtue of their landholdings. After 1100, with the rise of the study of Roman law and canon law, rulers claimed that all land actually belonged to them and was granted to their subjects only for life and in return for certain services, including an oath of homage. Reynolds argued that the concept of the 'fief', the land holding for which military service was due, spread from Italy from the early twelfth century, as a result of the study of Roman law in Italian schools. From there it influenced France, England and eventually Germany – her study does not consider the Iberian Peninsula. Freeholdings or alods were redefined as 'fiefs', which carried obligations of service. If the holder was a noble or from the warrior class, this would be military service.[22]

But not all land in western Europe was redefined as 'fiefs'; and landholders could owe oaths of loyalty to several different people. Women as well as men held land and gave oaths of loyalty to lords, and owed military service, as did Church leaders. In 1181 King Henry II of England (d. 1189) issued his Assize of Arms, which stated that each free man should bear arms in the king's service as the king might command, and laid down which arms and armour he should carry, according to his status. There is no mention of land holding as a basis for military service; the obligation is a result of status, not of land held.[23]

Not all historians agree with Reynolds in her reappraisal. We may agree that 'feudalism' has been greatly exaggerated. Yet if we allow that the essence of 'feudalism' was that military service was based on, first, the personal bond between lord and subject and, second, land holding, then we can see instances of these two factors acting as the basis for military service throughout the period from the eighth century to the fifteenth century, even if their importance has been exaggerated for the period before 1100 and vastly over-simplified for the period after 1100. For instance, Charlemagne took oaths of loyalty from all free men, and laid on all free men with sufficient means an obligation for military service: they needed sufficient means because they had to supply their own equipment. In 792 Charlemagne also ordered that the slaves (*servi*) who formed the armed bands of his magnates should swear an oath of loyalty directly to him.[24] Military service under Charlemagne was sometimes based on land holding, although the counts and dukes served by virtue of their office. Landholders holding at least 12 'manses' (an area of land) had to come to the army with their own coats of mail armour and if they failed to appear, they would lose their land. Those whose landholding was less than four manses could not afford to equip themselves to serve in the local levies, so Charlemagne ordered that those holding one or more manses, but less than four, should form groups to equal four or more manses and between them should send one of them to the army.[25] So far, this resembles the classical theory of feudalism. Yet, while this regulation linked land holding to military service, as under the 'feudal system', it is also reminiscent of the assessment of conscripts in the fourth-century Roman Empire.

In short, what Reynolds has done is to demonstrate that the 'feudal' model is too simplified to explain in every respect the obligation for military service in medieval western Europe. The model is more useful after 1100 than before 1100, but even after 1100 it may be misleading and should be used with care. Nevertheless, it does provide a framework within which historians may work, provided they remember that 'feudalism' is a model not necessarily reflecting actuality.

* * *

The core of the medieval army was always the leader's personal troops: the personal warband or *comitatus*. These were typically younger men without family ties wishing to win a name for themselves, to earn their lord's approval and so win wealth and, in time, land and a wife and to continue their family name. They were bound to their lord by ties of honour and friendship, of gift giving and reward, as described in Chapter 1.[26] The military leader's household warriors could also include older warriors attracted to the lord's court by tales of his success in battle and his generosity. The lord's personal entourage continued to form the core of his army throughout the Middle Ages. These were the troops who were taken out on lightning raids when there was not time or need to call up a larger army. But the number of these elite troops was necessarily few.

Beyond this, a ruler could call on those who were bound to provide military service. This summons could recruit warriors who belonged to families who regarded it as their hereditary duty to win fame on the battlefield. Under King Edward I of England, such people were expected to serve at their own expense, supplying their own weapons and other equipment. But if they had to serve far from home – for instance, in Scotland – they would not be able to afford to serve for a long period; and some of those summoned for service would perform the due minimum and then return home. Peter Coss cites the case of Hugh fitz Heyr, who came to serve in Edward I's army in 1300 with one bow and one arrow, as he was bound to do; when the Scots were sighted, he fired his arrow and then went home.[27] One of the reasons that the kings in the Iberian Peninsula were so anxious to found and support the new military religious orders from the 1120s onwards was that they would stay in the field after the local levies had gone home to get the harvest in.[28] Town levies produced troops of unreliable quality: they were reluctant to assemble, anxious to get home, and were likely to desert during their period of service, or to run away when battle was joined; as, for instance, Duke Charles the Bold of Burgundy (d. 1477) discovered when his levies of Flemish pikemen ran away from the French at Amiens in 1471.[29]

In the city communes of Italy from the twelfth century, all adult males were bound to provide military service, for which they were paid. The nobles and wealthy citizens had to supply a horse for cavalry service in the city's army, while others served in the infantry. The obligation to supply a horse fell on the family rather than the individual, so that it might be the responsibility of a number of citizens to supply one of their number to serve in the cavalry. Those who served were paid, and given an allowance for their horse, and were compensated if it was injured or killed; officials were appointed by the city to inspect the horses, arrange for compensation and so on. The cities also employed mercenaries as required, despite the high costs involved; on which more below.[30]

On the Christian/Muslim frontier in Spain from the late eleventh century, those Christians who settled on the land 'reconquered' from the Muslims were given favourable terms of tenure, but had to provide military service. In Castile, all colonists were obliged to serve, whatever their status, either as cavalry or as infantry. Anyone could serve in the cavalry as *caballeros* (knights) if they could afford a horse and the necessary equipment and arms. As in Italy, a cavalryman was compensated if his horse were injured or killed on military service. The effect of opening the cavalry to men of all classes, provided that they had the means to equip themselves, was to produce a class of 'peasant knights', *caballeros villanos*, who dominated the government of the frontier towns despite their lowly birth.[31]

For most of the Middle Ages, a large army typically consisted of many smaller units, whose members were not directly under the authority of the supreme commander. For example, when King Louis IX of France was raising an army to go to the Holy Land on crusade, from December 1244 when he took his vow of crusade, he provided only around half of the troops himself. The rest were provided by the nobles who accompanied him, notably his younger brother, Count Alphonse of Poitiers. Alphonse recruited his barons and knights, and paid their wages; he also recruited mounted crossbowmen and footsoldiers, and provided bows, arrows and crossbow bolts for their use. A baron would bring so many knights with him; a knight banneret (carrying his own banner) would lead a small group of ordinary knights, and each knight was accompanied by 'sergeants' (on which see below) and footsoldiers. William Jordan has calculated that the 35 knights banneret from Champagne who were reported to have died during the crusade would have been accompanied by over a thousand support troops.[32] In this way, Louis recruited an army of over 15,000 men – although most of them were not recruited directly by him, and were beholden to him only indirectly.

By the late thirteenth century, nobles who were bound to provide military service to the king or who regarded it as their duty to do so were making formal arrangements through written contracts to ensure that they would have sufficient warriors to accompany them to war. These contracts between lords and their warriors were called *alliances* in France, *accomanigia* in Italy and indentures in England, and were not necessarily linked to a specific campaign. Warriors would be granted payment and privileges by a lord in return for providing military service when required. The agreement was recorded in writing, and would specify, for instance, whether a warrior was bound to follow his lord if his lord went to fight in another country, or if his lord went on crusade. The English nobles were making use of indentures to raise troops by the late thirteenth century, taking their indentured retinues with them when they were summoned to serve in the English king's army. By the fourteenth century the English king was also drawing up indentures with his nobles, whereby the noble agreed to provide a set number of men-at-arms and footsoldiers, and a rate of payment was settled. Not all nobles served under these terms – the change in organisation was gradual, and in the first three decades of the fourteenth century many nobles served according to the old custom of military duty.[33] By the mid-fourteenth century, the English government was paying its troops, and the contracts made included arrangements for compensation for damage to war-horses and correspondingly lower shares in booty for those who were employed. But the government did not deal directly with the individuals involved. Those who made the contracts were responsible for paying the men they had contracted.[34] The result was a fragmented force rather than a united force unified by loyalty to the king or a cause.

In the fifteenth century, the English government continued to use indentures or contracts as a means of recruiting military captains for service in the army, stating the number of men of different types (men-at-arms, archers) to be provided and the length of service, rates of pay and due dates of pay. The captains collected the pay for distribution to their men, but had to show that it was properly accounted for. Within conquered territory in France, the government could also call upon the services of ex-servicemen for military garrisons of fortresses and towns. Field armies were also raised in France, from ex-servicemen and from the garrisons, by calling on feudal obligation, and by calling on the local French nobles to serve from duty, as they would serve the French king.[35]

While these armies were recruited afresh for each campaign, they were increasingly made up of paid professional warriors who made their living from fighting. The concept of the paid, professional warrior was already very familiar to medieval rulers, but on a smaller scale. The members of a lord's warband had traditionally received payment in gifts of booty and property in return for their military service, and warriors had always travelled in search of the lord who would best reward them. By the late tenth century, European rulers had been routinely hiring warriors for pay to supplement the traditional levies, as the latter were often reluctant and not always suitably equipped. The French word for pay, *solde*, gives us the modern word for the professional warrior: 'soldier'. In this respect these mercenaries (literally 'men who are paid') were professional warriors, but unlike the professionals of the late Roman army, they fought not for the state but for an individual. These mercenaries made up an increasingly significant portion of the medieval army.

As those who fought for money rather than for honour or duty or because it was their role in society to do so, and because they were typically of non-noble birth, mercenaries were despised by the Church and by noble warriors who fought primarily for honour and duty. They were accused of having no loyalty except in so far as they were paid, and of deserting their employers for one who would pay better. In fact, it appears that those who fought for pay followed the same code of loyalty to their employer as would be expected from a warrior fighting for his ruler or his landlord.[36]

The resentment against paid warriors arose partly because such warriors knew their own worth to their employer and could dictate their own terms. In the late fourteenth century Jean Froissart referred slightingly to the German warriors who would do nothing without money and who wanted to be paid every fortnight.[37] In 1261, Brother Thomas Bérard, master of the military religious order of the Temple, wrote to the grand commander of the order in England, Brother Amadeus, that the order in the Holy Land was having great difficulties in employing mercenaries, because they wanted to be paid not only their living expenses but also danger money.[38] To the modern reader, this demand may seem entirely reasonable given the danger to Catholic Christendom in the Holy Land from the Mongols and from the Mamluk regime in Egypt, but as an employer Thomas Bérard found the costs intolerable.

There was also the problem that such paid warriors were often foreign-
ers who knew nothing of local customs and had no respect for local
people: hence the hatred of the English barons for King John of England's
mercenary bands, expressed in the clause of Magna Carta in 1215 which
required that all foreign warriors should be expelled from the realm.[39] A
large professional army in search of employment or its fortune was virtually a small nation in its own right, acting in its own interests, and intent
on making its own living. It would include women and children and support forces, as well as fighting men, both cavalry and infantry. While the
names of individual mercenary captains are known from earlier centuries,
it is generally agreed that the first large professional army of this sort was
the Catalan Company, founded by Roger de Flor at the beginning of the
fourteenth century. Employed briefly by the Byzantine emperor, it went on
to carve out a state for itself in Achaea in what is now Greece, and until
1388 was a major political player in the north-eastern Mediterranean. Its
career is well known through the chronicle of Ramón Muntaner, who was
a member of the company in its early years.[40]

The great mercenary companies that were employed in the Hundred
Years War had shorter lives. When peace was made in France in 1360 and
they were unable to find employment from kings or lords these companies
harassed the countryside, preying off French and English supporters alike,
and fighting each other. In 1361 at Avignon, Pope Innocent VI called a crusade against them. In 1365, under the leadership of Bertrand du Guesclin,
the Great Companies went to fight in Spain against King Pedro of Castile,
with the promise of going on crusade to the East afterwards. In the event,
they returned to France instead and became involved in the renewal of
hostilities. Kenneth Fowler dates the end of the Great Companies to the year
1370, with the defeat of the English army by the French under du Guesclin
at the battle of Pontvallain. By this time many of the original captains had
died, while many of the soldiers had effectively become part of the English
or French armies. Mercenary armies continued to operate, but they were no
longer on the scale of the Great Companies.[41]

It was a logical step from employing a semi-permanent company to setting up a standing army. King Charles VII of France (1422–61) effectively introduced a permanent army to his kingdom in 1445 when, instead of
simply disbanding his whole army during a truce with the English, he
appointed royal captains to retain the best troops from the mercenary
companies then in his employment and to disband the rest. In a series of
ordonnances over the years following 1445 he set up a series of companies of mounted men, with infantry made up of archers and pikemen. The
army was paid for by a system of taxation, the *taille*, originally devised to
finance the army on a temporary basis but now made permanent.[42]

Charles the Bold, duke of Burgundy, used various means of raising
armies. The army he led against Liège in 1467 was made up of his
courtiers and nobles and their military followings, military captains and

their forces, English archers and levies of pikemen from some, but not all, of the Flemish towns.[43] However, in 1469 the duke decided to reform his army to make it far more efficient. Although this took several years and did not actually materialise until 1471, what resulted was, in the words of Richard Vaughan, 'virtually a new army of permanent mercenary companies of volunteers'. The duke recruited volunteers into 'companies of ordinance', each made up of mounted archers, archers on foot, culverineers (the culverin was a handgun), pikemen and men-at-arms. Each company was commanded by a captain, and their organisation and administration was closely regulated. By the end of Charles's career the 'ordinance' companies made up almost the whole of his army.[44]

> Charles the Bold's field army, then, had been transformed from one composed of paid but conscripted feudal levies and civic militia, raised separately for each campaign among those obliged to perform military service, to ... a standing army of mercenaries.[45]

Despite having professional troops that were routinely drilled and well organised on the battlefield, Charles the Bold's expansionist strategy failed, and he himself was killed at the battle of Nancy in January 1477. Nevertheless, it was clear to contemporary rulers that paid, professional troops were the best means of obtaining an effective field army, and the development of such armies has been identified by military historians such as Geoffrey Parker as part of a 'military revolution' which took place in the late medieval and early modern period.[46]

The employment of large paid armies was only possible if an employer could command an efficient system of administration and taxation. Early medieval rulers, unable to rely on systems of direct taxation and ruling by custom, were restricted in what funds they could take from their subjects to finance their wars. By the second half of the twelfth century in England it was acceptable for a landowner to pay a shield-tax, 'scutage', in place of the military service due; the king could then use this money to hire warriors. Employers without the right to levy taxes must find some other way to raise money to pay their troops, but not every warlord was as blatant in raising funds for war as Roger de Flor, who in the mid-1290s simply sailed along the western Mediterranean coast taking everything of value he could find so that he could recruit a military company.[47] Booty, ransoms and tribute helped to pay for war, but simple financial and logistic constraints restricted the size of armies.

This said, historians disagree over how large medieval armies could be. Obviously, the size of the army raised would vary with its purpose: a raiding party would be smaller than an army to conquer a kingdom. Bachrach estimates that Carolingian armies could be as large as 100,000 fighting men,[48] but historians of earlier and later periods see armies as much smaller. Stephen Evans concludes that the British and Anglo-Saxon warbands of the late fifth to eighth centuries were small, of hundreds rather than thousands, with some bands well under a hundred men. John France calculates that from the eleventh to the thirteenth century armies were in the low thousands; Frederick II led an army of around 20,000 warriors in northern Italy in the autumn of 1237, while Philip III of France led 8000 warriors against Aragon in 1285.[49] Richard Vaughan calculated that at the battle of Murten (Morat) in 1476, Duke Charles the Bold of Burgundy had an army of no more than 15,000 in total, while his opponents had 25,000 warriors. At the final battle at Nancy just over six months later he had 5000 warriors while his opponents had 20,000.[50] In general, military historians agree that the armies of the fifteenth century were much larger than they had been in earlier centuries, and that because they were expensive to maintain only wealthy rulers with an effective system of taxation could maintain an army by this period.[51]

* * *

The actual mustering of the army proceeded in a similar way throughout the Middle Ages. The commander in chief (king, lord or simple warleader) could always call on the immediate services of the military entourage in the commander's own household. The decision to wage war using only these forces could be taken by the commander alone (for example, in the case of a lightning raid), but larger campaigns would normally require discussion with the leading members of the military class in the realm, and/or those who would be responsible for financing the war. So a king of the early Middle Ages might take advice from his council of leading lords of the realm, including Church leaders; a king of the later Middle Ages would probably also consult the representatives of the towns, which would have to send levies to the army, in a larger council which in England was called 'parliament'. Once the decision was taken to go to war, written or oral summonses were sent to those who were due to furnish armed warriors for the war: so that a king would send summonses to the secular and ecclesiastical lords of the realm, the chief officials of towns which furnished levies, and various individuals who were required to provide military service. They would be told to lead or send their forces to a certain point with certain equipment and supplies, to arrive by a certain date. In England in the twelfth century it was the task of the sheriffs to recruit infantry for wars, but from the late thirteenth century 'commissioners of array' were specially appointed to recruit infantry, and later to bring together all those due to supply military service.[52] The commander of the army would also have to draw on available funds to hire the necessary numbers of warriors, engineers and craftsmen for the army which were not already due to be supplied by those who owed military service. In England, again, the commissioners of array became responsible for hiring these people for service. Those lords and vassals responsible for supplying troops to the army would either serve in person or hire troops to serve in their place.

* * *

The best known member of the typical medieval army nowadays is the knight (*miles* in Latin, *chevalier* in French, *caballero* in Spanish, *Ritter* in German). In the modern world these terms are synonymous with nobility, but that was not the case when the term first appeared: the French, Spanish and German terms all refer to a 'horse rider', and indicate that the knight was mounted, which was not necessarily the case, while the English term, 'knight', originally meant a servant. The Latin term, *miles*, meant in classical Latin 'a soldier', and in the tenth century meant 'a servant'. Before the mid-eleventh century, the term 'knight' was not prominent in warfare, and so when historians are writing about warfare before 1050 they must write of warriors or arms-bearers rather than knights. Historians have wondered how the term that was used to refer to a soldier-servant, who was more prestigious than the peasant footsoldier but definitely not noble, came to refer to the most noble warriors.

One of the most important studies of this development is by Georges Duby, in his study of nobility in the tenth- and eleventh-century Mâconnais (in what is now eastern-central France). He traced the breakdown in public authority in this area between 971 and 1032, and deduced that during that period there was a fundamental change in the meaning of *nobilitas*, 'nobility'. In the tenth century it indicated that a person was virtuous and therefore had a moral right to rule. By 1032 authority in the area rested on military capacity, not on hereditary right, so that anyone who had armour, weapons and a horse could exert authority. In fact, it was necessary to be wealthy in order to have the armour, weapons and a horse, so in practice there was little change in who held authority; but the basis of this authority had changed. By 1032 warriors were proud to call themselves *milites* or 'knights', because knights had military skill; in effect, if a man had military skill, he could hold authority in the area. Duby concluded that by 1075 in the Mâconnais the words 'noble' and '*miles*' were interchangeable terms.[53]

Yet when Duby and other scholars looked at other areas, they found that this change in *milites* or 'knights' from being servants to nobles did not occur, or occurred much later. In Germany, in general the change took longer than in France: in Brabant, in the Rhineland, the nobles were calling themselves knights by 1175. In the Iberian Peninsula not all knights were nobles, for alongside the *caballeros* of noble extraction were the peasant knights, the *caballeros villanos*. In Italy a knight was a knight not by birth or deed but: 'a knight is a man who is ... a knight by public repute.' In Namur it was not until 1280 that the distinction between nobles and knights vanished, and it was not until the late fourteenth century that the noble families and knightly families intermarried. Historians also discovered that in other areas where 'knights' had changed from being servants to nobles there had been no breakdown in central authority to stimulate the change; in Normandy or England, for example. In these areas the term *miles*, 'knight', could not have become a noble term simply because power and authority rested on the sword.[54]

Historians have put forward various suggestions as to why the word *miles* came to designate a noble. First, they suggest that the *milites* rose in status in society as warfare became more specialised, with the use of the cavalry charge with couched lance from the late eleventh century (although this date is also disputed). New fighting techniques required daily training, and could be learned only by those with the leisure time to train on a daily basis. It is true that knights continued to dismount in battle and fight on foot, as at Tinchebrai in 1106, when Henry I of England (d. 1135) fought his elder brother Robert of Normandy (d. 1134), and at Lincoln in 1141 when King Stephen of England (d. 1154) fought the forces of his cousin the Empress Matilda (d. 1167). Nevertheless, at the same period the tournament was developing, which was primarily a means of practising mounted combat; and mounted combat with the couched lance became the distinguishing mark of the knight in the fictional literature of the warrior classes, the epic and the romance. Hence this theory has some merit as a basis for the rise in status of the mounted warrior in the late eleventh and twelfth centuries.[55]

Second, it has been suggested that as Church attitudes to violence changed and certain sorts of warfare became theologically acceptable, as considered in Chapter 1, the warrior rose in status.[56]

Third, it is undeniable that, at least in some regions, knights were becoming more respectable. In twelfth-century England, knights were given land by their lord, they married and settled down and became parents and respectable pillars of their community. As noted in Chapter 1, ecclesiastical writers such as John of Salisbury deduced that knights could be useful in society if they acted correctly; and kings and other rulers made much use of them. Henry II of England used the 'knights of the shire' on juries and gave them various administrative duties to perform. William Marshal regarded it to be his duty as a knight to dispense justice as he rode about northern France; if necessary against other knights who damaged society.[57]

Finally, the growth of the knightly ethic increased the status of warriors. The epic and romantic fictional literature which appeared in the twelfth century set out various standards of behaviour which were recognised by all who called themselves 'knights', even though they disagreed over some of them. Their status became a sort of institution, *chevalerie*, knighthood, a separate order in society.[58]

However, in the thirteenth century in England and northern France, as knights became more noble, warriors of lesser means stopped calling themselves 'knights' – *chevaliers*, *Rittern*, and so on. They could no longer afford to 'take on knighthood', to undergo the public ritual which would make them a knight. The social expectations of knights and the public responsibilities which they were expected to take on exceeded their means. So knighthood, *chevalerie*, became an exclusive caste. In other areas the change took more time or less, but it occurred all over western Europe.[59] Within knighthood there remained a distinct divide between the knight of the high nobility and those who claimed the title of knighthood, but who were not from the high nobility.

Yet those who failed to take up knighthood, whose ancestors would have called themselves 'knights' but who could no longer aspire to the title now that it was worth aspiring to, were still warriors, albeit of lower status. Such warriors are called in the sources 'squires', *escuiers* in Old French, the shield-bearers who assisted knights, or 'sergeants', *sergents* in Old French or *servientes* in Latin, again those who assisted the knights. Together with the knights they were termed 'men-at-arms', *gens d'armes* in French or *armigeri* in Latin. While for the late eleventh, twelfth and thirteenth century the term 'knight' is quite acceptable as a catch-all phrase for mounted warriors with a certain level of skill and equipment, outside these periods the term was far more exclusive. Before around 1050 it meant a lower status warrior, or a servant; after 1300 it meant a noble warrior.

The squires and sergeants remain elusive figures in the army and on the battlefield. As they lacked the status of the knights, and lacked the wealth to patronise chroniclers, they were very seldom mentioned by contemporary commentators. Their original function was as 'support troops', either mounted or on foot, less well equipped than knights and possibly lacking knightly skill. Yet epics and romances of the twelfth and thirteenth centuries indicate that squires, such as Governal in *Tristan*, could be older warriors who were given the responsibility of taking care of a young noble warrior and looking after his training. Such squires were arguably of much greater skill than their young charges.[60] On the other hand, the hierarchical statutes of the rule of the military religious order of the Temple, written in the second half of the twelfth century, regard the squires purely as assistants. The sergeants in the order could be either armed or unarmed: those who were armed were to fight following the same regulations as the knights, while those who were unarmed could fight or not as seemed best to them. Those who were armed did not charge alongside the knights, but acted as a support unit, advancing behind the knights and coming to their assistance if necessary.[61]

While the other military religious orders also had brother-sergeants, their regulations tell us little more about them than the Rule of the Templars. It seems that sergeants were of two ranks, those who were the equivalent of squires, and those who were the equivalent of servants. The former could fight on horseback or on foot; the latter might not fight at all. For instance, knights who entered the order of Santiago could bring their 'men' with them, who were admitted as brother-sergeants. This indicates that the sergeants could be the warriors of non-knightly rank who formed the personal entourage of a knight. But it should also be noted that nobles who were not knights entered the order of Santiago as 'sergeants'; so that the term included those who were eligible for knighthood but who had not taken it up, for whatever reason.[62]

Some medieval squires were certainly trainee knights, the sons of knightly families who expected to receive the rank of knighthood one day. In the romance literature of the thirteenth century and later, these young men are also called *vassaux*, a term which in the early twelfth century in the *Chanson de Roland* had been synonymous with 'doughty warrior', but which a hundred years later meant something nearer the English term 'page' – a noble youth still training as a warrior and as a nobleman. The equivalent term in medieval Latin was *valettus*. Such young men were *gentils*, 'gentle' in the sense of being noble or with the potential of becoming noble.[63] But the word could also be derogatory: in the late fourteenth century, Jean Froissart referred to the 'varlets' on the battlefield as the non-noble footsoldiers who killed without mercy.[64]

Other squires would never become knights because their families could not afford the honour, or did not wish to carry the social burdens that went with the distinction. Squires who were descended from squires rather than knights were less associated with nobility than the sons of knights, but were nevertheless regarded by society as having some gentility – in English they were not 'common folk', but 'gentry'. They might receive knighthood in the course of their career in recognition of their courage and skill. With the institutionalisation of knighthood, battlefield knightings and their like became far less common by the late thirteenth century,[65] although it was still possible for a squire of non-knightly descent to be promoted to knighthood: in 1421 or 1422 John Žižka, the Hussite leader of squirearchical descent, was knighted in recognition of his victories over King Sigismund.[66]

Those warriors who fought on horseback might also include mounted archers, who were of lower social status to those who fought with lance and sword. Mounted archers were much used by the Cymro-Norman commanders who invaded Ireland in 1169, for as Gerald of Wales, archdeacon of Brecon (d. 1223), explained, mounted archers were able to keep the Irish stone-slingers at bay.[67] The Catholic Christians who settled in the Holy Land after the First Crusade (known as 'the Franks' as many of them came from areas of Europe colonised by the Franks) employed light cavalry to counter the Muslim light cavalry; some of these were mounted archers.[68] The English army made use of mounted archers during the Hundred Years War.[69]

The cavalry, then, was made up of warriors of various status and arms, who might also dismount in battle and fight as footsoldiers. In the same way, those who generally fought on foot could be of many types. In certain circumstances noble warriors preferred to fight on foot: historians have generally agreed that even though they rode to the battlefield, until at least the eleventh century the noble Irish, Welsh and Anglo-Saxons usually fought on foot – although recently this view has been challenged, and certainly by the early twelfth century the kings of Ireland were using cavalry.[70] Like the mounted squires and sergeants, the common footsoldiers were generally overlooked by medieval chroniclers except as support forces for the knights. In a battlefield situation where cavalry was used, archers on foot typically had the task of opening up the enemy ranks with a hail of arrows before the cavalry charged; after the cavalry had charged, the footsoldiers, armed with pikes and spears, could follow and kill those whom the cavalry had unhorsed. In a march across country, archers could keep an attacker at bay, but footsoldiers might have trouble keeping up with the mounted troops, particularly if they had to carry their own baggage. They were less mobile than the mounted troops, and if they broke rank they were very vulnerable to enemy attack.

In order to be effective the infantry had to be trained, with frequent drill; but training, as will be discussed in Chapter 5, was very unusual in medieval armies. Town militias might drill together if there was money to pay an official to drill the men. The English government in 1337 ordered archers to practise their skills; but only a strong and respected government could expect such an order to be carried out.[71] Drilling could only take place if there was a strong central authority to organise it, or if drill was incorporated into everyday life. Hence, as Stephen Morillo has argued, in a period where central government was weak – as in France in the tenth to twelfth centuries – infantry was less effective than cavalry in battle. As governments grew stronger, so infantry became more effective again; as in the Flemish towns in the early fourteenth century, and in Burgundy in the late fifteenth century.[72]

The ineffectiveness of undrilled non-noble infantry was one reason why the nobility traditionally held them in scorn. The *Annals of St Bertin* recorded how in 859 some peasants banded together and defeated the Vikings, but were then in turn defeated by the local nobility.[73] In the early 1180s in the Languedoc, a band of peasants led by a carpenter formed a confraternity (or brotherhood) to fight ravaging unemployed mercenary bands. Their uniform was a white hood. In 1183 they defeated two troops of mercenaries in battle. But when they tried to use their success to demand better legal rights from the local lords, Bishop Hugh of Auxerre led an army against them and crushed them.[74]

Yet from ancient times onwards, footsoldiers usually formed at least the bulk of the army, although in certain circumstances, such as a fast-moving raid, the presence of footsoldiers might not be appropriate. Although an army consisting largely of footsoldiers rather than cavalry is more effective at defence than attack, footsoldiers were well able to defeat cavalry if they could stand firm against the cavalry charge. A large army of footsoldiers could be usefully combined with a small cavalry force. At Jaffa in August 1192, under attack from Saladin's light cavalry, King Richard I of

England drew up a line of spearsmen, half-kneeling on the ground with a spear planted in front of them to form a spear wall pointing towards the charging enemy, and behind them crossbowmen, each with an assistant who would reload the bow between shots. He also had around ten cavalrymen, all notable warriors although not, apparently, all knights, and himself. The Muslim army attacked, but the spear wall held. When the Muslims drew back, Richard's small cavalry force attacked them, and Saladin's army withdrew.[75] The battle of Courtrai in 1302 has already been considered in Chapter 1. Here the well-trained and determined Flemish infantry took up a good strategic position and maintained their lines, armed with pikes and *goedendags* (wooden maces or staves called 'good-days' in a twist of black military humour) against the cavalry charge of the French nobility.

Modern historians of warfare have written of the 'infantry revolution' of the fourteenth century, when the common-born but well-drilled infantryman with wooden pike or bow overcame the mounted nobility of western Europe, leading to a change in the organisation of war, its costs (as infantry are cheaper to employ than cavalry), social prestige of the classes involved and the nature of battle.[76] This 'infantry revolution' formed part of the wider 'military revolution', which also saw the development of professional standing armies.[77]

Yet the demonstration of the value of infantry on the battlefield did not make King Sigismund of Hungary, for example, respect his Hussite enemy. On the whole, infantry continued to be used alongside cavalry on the battlefield, rather than replacing it. Even when infantry had shown its value in battle tactics, the prestige of cavalry action meant that the nobility were reluctant to give up fighting on horseback; and there would always be a role for fast moving, shock troops in warfare.

Other specialised persons could also be included in an army. Surgeons are occasionally mentioned in medieval armies.[78] An army should also include skilled engineers. Vegetius had envisaged that an army would contain engineers, carpenters, masons, wagon-makers, blacksmiths and painters to construct buildings for a winter camp, to make siege engines and to forge weapons.[79] Ramón Llull (died c.1316), in his *Liber de fine*, written in the late thirteenth century, indicated that his proposed crusading army should include sappers and engineers, as well as other non-military administrative staff such as a treasurer to pay the troops.[80] Christine de Pisan set out at length in her *Livre des faits des armes* the workmen who would be needed in her proposed army for besieging a fortress: each siege engine would require two men (Caxton's translation states four), plus a master and two masons to make the stone shot; there would be 600 carpenters, each with an assistant, to construct the siege equipment such as mantles, cats and siege towers; and 2000 labourers to make trenches and ditches. There would also be 50 carpenters and 20 labourers to construct mantles and mountings for the guns, and other labourers to set up the siege engines. A hundred knights and squires would be responsible for overseeing the construction of the panels of stakes and the ditch to defend the besiegers' camp: each would employ ten carpenters, ten assistants and 30 labourers. These workers were organised in gangs of ten: their employer would write down the name of the leader of each gang, who would be responsible for organising and paying his fellows. Christine also listed the carts that would be needed for carrying the machines and equipment for the siege, with their drivers and draught animals.[81]

Despite the fact that any effective army would need large skilled support forces of these sorts, the engineers are seldom mentioned in medieval accounts of war. King John of England's sappers receive a brief mention for their successful mining of Rochester Castle in 1215.[82] There are occasional hints that sappers and engineers could have their own policies, and might clash with the military commander. At the siege of Acre in 1191 the French sappers, meeting the Turkish sappers under the walls of Acre, came to a mutual agreement whereby there was an exchange of prisoners and both sides withdrew – not necessarily what their officers would have wished for.[83] The final reworking of the first version of the Old French Crusade Cycle, the so-called 'London-Turin continuation' composed at the beginning of the fourteenth century, includes an episode in which the crusaders plan to fire bees' nests from stonethrowers, over the walls of Acre against the Muslims; the barons shout at the engineers to get on and fire the bees because they have delayed too long.[84] This is fiction, but the friction between the two groups has a ring of truth about it.

From the 1320s onwards, gunners were also skilled professionals. As the anonymous early fifteenth-century German work the *Feuerwerkbuch* (literally, the 'Firework book') explains, every prince, earl, lord, knight and squire wanted good craftsmen, and especially good marksmen and master gunners. The master gunner, the author explains, must have extensive knowledge of powder, oil and various forms of missile, as well as how to operate the gun. He must be a pious man, moderate in his habits and self-controlled, brave and very careful. He must be able to read and write because his work is so complex he could not possibly commit to memory everything he needs to know. Such an expert would be in great demand among commanders of armies.[85]

* * *

Many other people would be present in the army, some against their will, as prisoners or slaves, others as servants or accompanying the troops as family or to provide services. These 'support forces' in the medieval army were usually made up of those whom medieval Christian society regarded as non-combatants. For instance, peasants might accompany the army as servants, craftspersons,[86] herding animals, or to fight. According to the socio-political model of 'the three orders', the peasants' task in society was to labour on the land, not to fight; yet very often they were forced to fight, either because they were summoned by their lord or in self-defence. The infantry of medieval armies might be, although need not be, of peasant stock. Nicholas Wright has demonstrated that the French peasants during the Hundred Years war were well able to resort to violence if necessary to defend their own property and people; many fought in the armies which ravaged France during the period, some turned to brigandage, while others were involved in local defence against such armies.[87]

Ecclesiastical writers also regarded women as being outside warfare, a view that derived from classical precedent. Honoré Bouvet expressed the ecclesiastical view: 'Women should not be compelled to go to war, even though they were wise, rich and strong.'[88] There has been considerable debate over the last two decades as to whether women did actually take part in warfare during the medieval period. The question remains undecided, but at present the best summary of the debate seems to be that of Carolyne Larrington: 'there is some historical evidence for women actually taking to the field themselves ... women may never have fought as a matter of course, but writers throughout the period relished the depiction of fighting women.'[89]

The fact that 'fighting women' made a good story, and the fact that medieval writers were influenced by various traditions and social expectations of women's involvement in warfare, means that the narrative sources on the subject are very difficult to interpret. Women warriors in classical literature were invariably regarded as operating outside the proper scheme of things and were firmly returned to their place in society – usually by being killed by the hero.[90] Thus in Virgil's *Aeneid*, Book IX, the warrior Camilla is killed through the intervention of the god Apollo because she is a serious military threat to her male foes. However, among the 'Germanic' peoples whose government superseded the Roman Empire in the West, the women of the warrior class were expected to take an active role in warfare. They should support their menfolk in battle, lend them their resources, encourage them to fight and advise them wisely, and if necessary fight in place of their husbands/ father/ brothers/ sons if the menfolk were absent, killed or defeated. In the twelfth-century Old French translation and adaptation of the *Aeneid*, Camilla dies not because she is acting beyond her proper role in society but because she commits the error of pausing to take booty, thus laying herself open to surprise attack.[91] Women fighting in medieval vernacular fictional literature were usually portrayed favourably, and were often used by the author to show the failings of the male characters.[92]

These two traditions may have influenced the way that medieval writers recorded women's involvement in warfare. In Latin, clerically authored literature, written by men trained in classical literature and therefore informed by classical tradition, the role of women in warfare would seldom be mentioned or it would be minimised. In vernacular literature, written by authors influenced by Germanic epic tradition, women's involvement in warfare would be given more attention or even exaggerated. To give one example in support of this theory, the Latin *Libellus de expugnatione Terrae Sanctae* minimises the role of Eschiva, lady of Tiberias, in defending her castle of Tiberias against Saladin (d. 1193, ruler of Egypt and Syria) in July 1187, while the French continuations of the history by Archbishop William of Tyre give Eschiva a more prominent role.[93] Yet, in fact, if we examine the context of these works, we see that literary precedent would not have been the most important influence on these writers. The French writers had a political agenda, supporting Eschiva's husband Count Raymond III of Tripoli and his allies against their critics, and so would have tended to emphasise Eschiva's role. Literary tradition did influence how authors wrote of women warriors, but it was just one influence among many.

The most famous medieval woman in warfare is Joan of Arc (d. 1431), who was central to the French military successes against the English in 1429–30. Yet historians differ in their interpretation of her role. Some regard her as a good military strategist, taking an active role in command of the French forces against the English; others have seen her role as more passive, inspiring the French forces to fight effectively but not actually taking part in military action. It has been pointed out by Deborah Fraioli that her role was seen by French contemporaries in the context of Old Testament models of female prophets and women inspired by God to save God's people by personal action, women such as Deborah, Esther and Judith, none of whom took part in warfare. Joan was not depicted as a successor to the Amazons, although these classical female warriors were well known to educated writers of the period. The only contemporary illustration of Joan shows her wearing a dress, not in armour, although she is holding a sword; and she herself claimed never to have killed anyone – a claim difficult to substantiate in battle, unless Joan had never aimed a blow at anyone.[94]

Looking away from the controversial and exceptional figure of Joan to more 'everyday' women, it is clear that, as landowners, women could owe military service to their lord. They were not expected to serve in person, but should provide a substitute.[95] A noble woman was responsible for the defence of her own estates if they were threatened. Thus Countess Matilda of Tuscany (d. 1115) commanded her army against King Henry IV of Germany,[96] and Christine de Pisan instructed noblewomen that they must learn military skills in order to defend their own property.[97] The noblewoman was also deemed to be responsible for defending her husband's lands if he were unable to do so; and as the mother of an underage son, she was responsible for the defence of his inheritance. So Æthelflæd of Wessex (d. 918), wife of Æthelred, lord of Mercia, became ruler of the Mercians after her husband's death (and possibly before he died), and initiated and led military activity.[98] In 1341 Jeanne of Flanders, countess of

Montfort, rallied support for her infant son Jean, who was heir to
Montfort and claimant to the county of Brittany. Jeanne's husband Count
Jean of Montfort had claimed Brittany on the death of the previous count,
but his claim was disputed by Charles of Blois, who had married the rival
heir Jeanne of Brittany. Count Jean had been captured by Charles and died
in prison. Jeanne of Flanders not only gathered an army to fight Charles's
forces, but also armed herself and led a daring raid on the enemy. Yet
despite this, her men would have surrendered Hennebont to the enemy
behind her back if English help had not arrived.[99] Following the death of
Charles, his widow continued to promote her cause in Brittany. Froissart
described the knights of the two commanders – Jeanne of Flanders and
Jeanne of Brittany – as claiming to fight 'for love of their ladies', in chivalric fashion; but perhaps this was a joke, simply an excuse for a fight.[100]

For women who were not landowners, warfare was not a duty, except
in so far as a mother must protect her children, and a wife support her
husband. Women were inevitably present in armies as the partners of warriors, but they were seldom noticed by chroniclers, except to be dismissed
as 'loose women'. Some no doubt were women without permanent
attachments, associated with any suitable warrior who would support
them, but others were in more-or-less permanent relationships.[101] Very
little evidence survives for these women, but one was referred to inciden-
tally by Jean Froissart when he was revising his history at the end of the
fourteenth century. He told a tale of one Aimery of Pavia, a Lombard
knight who had been involved in the Anglo-French war and had incurred
the wrath of Geoffrey de Charny and his friends, who decided to pay him
'an early morning visit'. When they burst in, Aimery was in bed with his
girlfriend (*amie*), an Englishwoman named Margaret; on hearing of his
enemies' arrival, he remarked to her that 'our companionship is about to
be ended', at which Margaret burst into tears. Charny and his friends took
Aimery, Margaret and Aimery's servants to Saint Omer, where they
beheaded and quartered Aimery and killed some of his servants, but
spared Margaret because they were sorry for her and because she was not
involved in Aimery's misdeeds. Froissart then states that a squire of the
region, Robert de Frolant, asked for Margaret. She was given to him, and
stayed with him as long as she lived.[102]

Who was Margaret? Where did she come from, and how did she come
to be with an Italian knight in Artois? Her relationship with him was
clearly regarded as long term by both of them, given their reaction to their
sudden parting. Nor does Froissart tell us why Robert de Frolant wanted
Margaret. Presumably, as there is no mention of his marrying her, he lived
with her on the same basis as she had lived with Aimery.

The courtier and writer Antoine de la Salle, born in Provence in 1385
or 1386, was the child of possibly a similar arrangement. Antoine's father
was a mercenary captain and was not married to Antoine's mother, but
when he died he bequeathed his assets to her.[103]

In action, such women could perform useful support roles in the army, bringing water to the soldiers on the battlefield,[104] and might also care for the wounded. There are occasional references to women providing other support services: urging on the men to fight;[105] women as laundresses (a role invariably performed by women during this period);[106] women boiling water to pour on the enemy during a siege (Christine de Pisan implies that only women were capable of boiling water);[107] and women picking lice and fleas from the men's bodies.[108] Women could also operate a stonethrower, use bows and were trusted to defend a fortress when their menfolk were elsewhere.[109]

Yet male pride and social norms demanded that when men were present they should perform the active martial roles. There were sound reasons for this: as women's prime social function was the production and care of children, their bodies should not be risked in the heavy physical exertion of warfare. There was also the fact that the men were likely to be distracted by having women in the front line, and spend more time trying to protect the women than fighting the enemy. In addition, the presence of women in the military camp could lead to rivalry and arguments among the men. As a result, a military commander would prefer to limit women's presence in an army to a minimum. In his ordinance of 1473, Charles the Bold of Burgundy forbade his troops to bring their own women to his army; instead, there were to be no more than 30 'common women' in each company, to be shared equally among the men.[110]

Like women, children were conventionally excluded from warfare – despite the popularity of tales about the 'heroic childhood' of men who later went on to become great warriors, such as Cuchulainn or Roland. Although the sons of the warrior classes would be trained in warrior skills from childhood, their parents would not expect to risk them on the battlefield until they were old enough and skilled enough to stand a good chance of survival; that is, not before their mid-teens. King Richard I of England, for example, was made duke of Aquitaine when he was 14, was knighted when he was 15, and his first involvement in military action (in rebellion against his father Henry II) was at the age of 16.[111] But in law a noble boy did not become an adult able to inherit land until he was 21, and he was not expected to play a leading part in war until that age.[112] Honoré Bouvet grouped children with women and old men as a group in society that should not be imprisoned during war, as they took no part in it.[113] In real life children were more often victims than active in war, but Nicholas Wright has drawn attention to the involvement, willing or unwilling, of some children during the Hundred Years War in France. In particular, Thenein Flamendeau at the age of nine or ten was captured by an English squire, Jack Spore, in a raid on his home village of Saint-Julian-du-Sault in around 1358. Instead of killing or ransoming his prisoner, Jack Spore made use of him, mounting him on a horse and giving him his lance and bascinet to carry. Thenein travelled with the military companies in

Burgundy, Brittany, Spain and France for ten years before returning to his home village, which he no longer recognised.[114] We may assume that on the occasions when the women of the army were enlisted to throw stones at the enemy, operate siege engines or boil water, the children in the army would be pressed into the same sort of essential support tasks.

Religious men and women should not be involved in warfare, for the shedding of blood would defile them. Yet the bishop with spiritual care of a city (for example) must also take care of its physical defence in time of war, and so those holding spiritual authority also came to hold military authority. Gregory of Tours describes Bishop Sagittarius's involvement in the defence of Comminges against King Guntram's army, although he also goes on to describe how a local religious house refused to give military service, as the monks claimed not to be involved in military affairs.[115] Charles Martel expected his ecclesiastical magnates to provide military service just as his lay magnates did. Bachrach argues that the downfall and exiling of Bishop Eucherius of Orléans in 732 came about because the bishop had failed to provide military levies from Orléans to fight at the battle of Poitiers against the Muslims of Spain under Abd ar-Rachman.[116] Charles Martel also drew on the resources of the Church to support his wars.[117] Clerics should also provide spiritual support for warriors, leading prayer, preaching to the troops and blessing them as they went into battle.[118] In legend, Archbishop Turpin accompanied Charlemagne's army and died fighting the Muslims at the battle of Roncesvalles, as told in the *Chanson de Roland*; in actual fact, Bishop Odo of Bayeux did fight at the Battle of Hastings in 1066. Such high-ranking ecclesiastics would normally fight as commanders. Ordinary priests also took part in warfare, and given the religious nature of the campaigns it is not surprising to find military priests on crusade. The Byzantine historian Anna Comnena, writing in the 1140s, described in detail and in shocked tones the military activities of a priest among the crusaders who reached Constantinople in 1097.[119] Another fighting priest is mentioned by contemporary chroniclers of the Third Crusade in 1191, irritating King Richard I by giving him unasked-for military advice.[120] The prohibition in canon law against priests shedding blood was increasingly enforced from the eleventh century onwards, but never entirely succeeded in preventing the clergy from getting involved in fighting; in fact, a few of the prominent masters of arms who took students and wrote treatises on fighting from around 1300 onwards were priests.[121] According to twelfth-century churchmen's views on warfare, the only religious who could legitimately fight were the military religious orders, founded from the early twelfth century onwards to defend Christians and Christian territory. These orders' military role had been specifically approved by the Church, and as most of the members were not ordained they were not affected by the prohibition on shedding blood.

Merchants, again, were not regarded by society as suitable warriors. The warrior nobility believed that merchants' concern for prudence and protecting their property made them neither willing to risk all in battle nor generous in giving as a noble should be.[122] In some respects the distinction between 'merchants' and 'knights' is a false one, as many merchants in Europe came from rich families, linked to the nobility; in the Italian city states the nobility were also the merchants. Yet contemporaries saw a distinction. In the 1240s the composer of a version of the continuation of the chronicle of Archbishop William of Tyre noted that the French despise the Italians because the Italians are mostly usurers – moneylenders – or corsairs, merchants or mariners rather than knights like the French. Such persons were regarded by the French as non-noble, *vilains*.[123] Even the Italian nobility who drew much of their wealth from commerce and finance regarded such business as ignoble and socially degrading, preferring to emphasise their chivalric credentials.[124] Sylvia Thrupp and Peter Coss have noted that few of the London aldermen were knighted during the fourteenth century, apparently because they were not interested in receiving knighthood; perhaps they did not regard it as something in which they should have an interest, or perhaps they did not see it as a rank to which they should aspire. Nevertheless, London merchants could be involved in military activities; if the rank of knighthood seemed outside their interests, military activities – for instance, against pirates, who threatened their trade directly – certainly were not. In 1378 John Philipot, a leading London merchant, raised and equipped a fleet to seek out and capture pirates, which he did successfully. As a reward, King Richard II knighted him in 1381.[125]

In short, while those who wrote on the theory of warfare might claim that warfare should only involve a small section of society – the fit adult male of the hereditary warrior classes – in fact, warfare could involve anyone and everyone.

3
Military buildings

A military building is any building that plays a role in military activity, from the army camp to the fortress. It can be temporary or relatively permanent. Yet not all buildings which are generally regarded as military had a solely military purpose. Walls of stone or earth, such as the late Roman *limes* on the German frontier, or King Offa of Mercia's dyke on his western frontier, could simply mark a boundary, the 'cut-off point' between one ruler's region of authority and the next. A castle, while being built to offer secure housing against marauders and to house warriors who could conduct hostilities against other warriors, was also a centre of administration and a home and could display the wealth and artistic taste of its owner; it could be a palace as well as playing a role in war.

Military buildings vary in size and purpose. Famously, the Teutonic Order in its early years in Prussia constructed fortresses in trees in order to provide places of defence for its warriors against the fierce Prussians.[1] A stone-built church tower could become a fort if necessary: examples include the sturdy church towers of south Wales and of France – the latter being used during the Hundred Years War. Such church fortresses could be used for aggressive purposes, to house a band of warriors on their way through the countryside, or for active defence against marauders – for instance, by hurling missiles from the parapet of the tower – but were more usually used for passive defence, with the villagers hiding inside the church with their property until the enemy had passed through.[2] The danger of such small fortresses was that a determined band of attackers could easily surround them and destroy them with fire or mining.

The amount of construction work that went into a military building varied. Caves could be used as refuges, as they were by the French peasantry during the Hundred Years War, or by the Italian peasants during the wars of the early sixteenth century. Any enemy venturing into such a refuge could easily be killed by the defenders, so the attackers usually remained outside and tried to smoke the peasants out. As there was generally no second exit or even alternative air holes, such cave refuges quickly became death traps.[3] But caves could also be used as fortresses: Archbishop William of Tyre (died *c.*1184) described such a cave fortress in Transjordan in the kingdom of Jerusalem, whose defence King Amaury of Jerusalem (1163–74) entrusted to the military religious order of the Templars.[4]

The classic defensive fortification is the hill fort, which in its most basic form is a steep hill with an earthen rampart surrounded by a ditch encircling the top. The rampart can be reinforced with a wall of wooden stakes, but on a good site this is hardly necessary. In early medieval Europe such forts were not necessarily intended for permanent occupation, but could be refuges into which the local population could withdraw in time of enemy raids, to emerge when the enemy had retired. If the fort was intended to be occupied for no more than two or three days at a time, it would probably have no well, relying on rainwater collected in cisterns or on what the local people could bring with them when they retreated inside the ramparts. Such a fort would also be difficult to keep supplied, as it was inaccessible by road. The expectation was that the enemy would be simply raiders from the neighbouring region who would rush through the locality taking anything moveable and then retreat to their own land. They would not have the expertise or means to conduct a siege, their intention being to keep on the move and then to retire before any large army could be gathered to oppose them. Therefore the fort would not have to withstand a long siege. Ideally, the hillsides would be so steep and so high that these forts could not be taken by storm or by bombardment.

The fortresses constructed by the Germanic peoples who settled in the Western Roman Empire in the fifth and sixth centuries were of this type, built in places with good natural defences, sometimes assisted by earth ramparts, perhaps assisted with barriers of stones and wood.[5] Arguably, most of the Welsh castles built by Welsh princes between the late eleventh and late thirteenth centuries were based on the concept of the traditional hill fort, on a high and inaccessible site – but constructed in stone rather than earth and wood. Some of the castles built by the Anglo-Normans in Wales were of the same basic concept.[6]

In complete contrast to these largely natural features, but with the same basic function as a place of retreat in time of war, were the defensive/aggressive towers built within their city walls from the eleventh century onwards by the city-based nobility of the Italian city states. A tower would be built by a family or group of families who were allied together, and when war broke out between the rival noble families within the city, they could retreat into their towers. The towers reflected both the state of constant political unrest within the city and the need for display, to impress other nobles and the rest of the population of the town. A Jewish traveller from Spain, Benjamin of Tudela, described in the 1160s the Genoese fighting each other from the tops of their towers within the city. The towers could also be attacked from the ground with siege machinery such as stonethrowers. A thirteenth-century observer described the towers at Lucca, clustered like densely growing trees, as looking like 'a little wood'.[7] The burghers of the wealthy trading towns of Ghent and Regensburg also built tower houses within their towns, for prestige and for self-defence.[8]

Technically these towers were also houses; conversely, any stone house could be used as a fortress. Jean de Venette described how in the 1350s, during the Hundred Years War, a group of French peasants fortified, with the permission of the local lord, a farmhouse at Longueil-Ste-Marie near Compiègne (Oise). In 1359 it was attacked by the 'English' garrison of the nearby castle at Creil, but the peasants beat off these professional warriors.[9] In 1369 a party of English noblemen took refuge in a house of the Hospital of St John in Purnon in Anjou and fought off a French attack until they were relieved. Although the Hospital of St John was a military religious order, this house was not fortified and was the equivalent of a manor house.[10]

Being built of stone and designed to keep outsiders out and the inmates secure from the influences of the outside world, monasteries were also obvious fortresses for refuge in times of need.[11] Ewenny Priory in West Glamorgan, south Wales, is unusual in the British Isles for its castle-like fortifications; but Ewenny, founded by the local Anglo-Norman landowner Maurice of London, was not only threatened by rival Anglo-Norman and Welsh lords, but also by Irish pirates who sailed up the Bristol Channel and ravaged the coastline. In the Iberian Peninsula, where there was a frontier with the Muslims, in areas troubled by war (such as central France in the fourteenth and fifteenth centuries) and areas without a strong central authority keeping the peace (such as Ireland), religious orders, who had sufficient liquid capital to build permanent defences, constructed their buildings to protect themselves. The monasteries in the Iberian Peninsula have been described as 'fortified ranch houses'.[12] In the Larzac region of central southern France (Aveyron), many small villages were given high fortified walls during the fourteenth century, paid for by the religious orders who owned the land: those at La Cavalerie, La Couvertoirade and Sainte-Eulalie de Cernon were paid for by the Hospital of St John, while those at Saint-Jean d'Alcas were paid for by the abbess of the Cistercian abbey of Nonenque.[13] In Ireland the Augustinian canons, for example, had an abbey at Athassel in Co. Tipperary surrounded by an embattled wall, while the Benedictines had a 'fortress-like' priory at Fore Abbey in Co. Westmeath.[14] Bishops also built fortresses, for security or to display their power and wealth, most famously the castles built by the archbishops of Mainz, Cologne and Trier in the Rhineland.[15] In Britain one might think of the castle of the bishop of Durham (uncomfortably close to the Anglo-Scottish border) or of the bishop of St David's at Llawhaden (on the Welsh/English frontier in south-west Wales), in contrast to the castle of the bishop of

Salisbury at Sherborne in Somerset, England, which was built in a peaceful locality.

At the other end of the scale were the temporary constructions built by armies to house themselves during a siege. Guntram's army that besieged Comminges in 585 camped in tents in the countryside around the hill on which the city stands. The late twelfth-century continuations of Chrétien de Troyes's *Conte du Graal* or *Perceval* describe how the soldiers who had arrived to besiege a castle either pitched silken tents and pavilions or, if they had none, went into the forest and cut themselves leafy branches to make themselves huts. This is a fictional description, but based on contemporary practice. Descriptions of the crusader camp during the siege of the city of Acre in 1189–91 describe more permanent dwellings, containing various rooms, even a baker's oven, and with gardens attached where vegetables were grown.[16]

Arguably the forms of military building constructed in Europe remained fairly constant throughout our period, although some historians have regarded the castle as something new: this will be considered in more detail below.

* * *

The Roman Empire had seen a variety of forms of military building. Vegetius's work considers the construction of military camps, giving advice on where they should be sited and how they can be fortified. He regarded a fortified camp as essential as a point to which a beleaguered army could fall back, and as a place where the army could rest safely without being harmed by the enemy. He envisaged such camps as being able to repel sieges of several days, being effectively a portable city. He described them as being fortified by an earthen rampart and ditch; the earthen rampart could be further strengthened with wooden stakes. A permanent garrison camp or fortress, such as those at Inchtutil in Scotland or at Caerleon on Usk in Gwent, would be built and fortified in stone.[17]

Vegetius also described how cities should be fortified and the preparations for a siege, both by besiegers and by defenders.[18] His instructions were repeated by his translators and adapters throughout the Middle Ages, indicating that the basic principles involved did not change in over a thousand years. He noted that natural defences should be utilised where possible, such as mountains, the sea, marshes or rivers; but where these were not available, the builder would have to employ labour to dig a ditch and build a wall for defence. Walls should be winding or have many angles, to make them more difficult to destroy with rams or bombardment. This principle would remain true even after the introduction of gunpowder artillery. He suggested using outworks to strengthen the walls, such as constructing an additional lower wall outside the main one and filling it with earth. Ditches should be wide and deep, and if they were filled with water, the wall of the city would be more difficult to mine. It is necessary to ensure a reliable water supply; perhaps there would be natural springs, but, if not, wells must be dug. If there was a spring outside the city, it might be necessary to fortify it so that the citizens could still retain access to it even when under siege. If the fortress was built on a dry site (such as limestone, which is porous and allows water to escape underground) then cisterns should be constructed to catch rainwater.

It was usual for cities and towns in the late Roman period to be fortified: from the reign of Diocletian, it was imperial policy that cities and towns should be walled in stone, and where no walls existed they were built.[19] The most famous of these are the land walls of Byzantium. The city was refounded in 330 by the emperor Constantine I as Constantinople, but the land walls were constructed in their present form from AD 413. Byzantium/Constantinople stands on a triangular promontory between the stretch of water named 'the Golden Horn' and the Sea of Mamora; the wall runs along the third side, from the sea to the horn. The great wall is 15 feet (4.6 metres) thick at the base, built of stone layered with courses of brick, with a concrete core. A rectangular tower juts out from the wall every 60 yards (55 metres). A lower wall was built in front of the great wall, six and a half feet (two metres) thick, with towers jutting out from the wall. There was a moat in front of this. The arrangement of the fortifications meant that it was possible to have archers stationed on both walls, firing at the enemy outside, so doubling the level of fire.[20]

Ammianus Marcellinus explains that Constantius Caesar (d. 361) deliberately fortified the city of Amida in Mesopotamia with strong walls so that it could act as a place of refuge for the people of the region against Persian attack. The fortifications consisted of walls punctuated by towers, and there was a central citadel. At the base of the citadel there was a spring of drinkable water.[21] Amida was finally captured by the Persians in AD 359 after a fiercely fought siege. In the West, the city and imperial residence of Trier (then in Gaul) also received impressive fortifications, designed to cow onlookers and impress upon all the power and authority of the emperor as much as to defend the city from attack.

The city walls built during this period continued to act as fortifications throughout the medieval period, although they needed to be regularly repaired and might be allowed to crumble with neglect during periods of peace.[22] In Spain, the walls of the city of Avila, rebuilt between 1090 and 1099 and including 88 towers within the perimeter, were probably constructed reusing the Roman walls of the city.[23] Gregory of Tours's *History of the Franks* indicates that when he was writing, in the late sixth century, the cities and towns of Gaul still had their Roman walls and that they were in regular use; although he also records that the walls of Angoulême collapsed under their own weight when King Clovis went to besiege the city in 508, suggesting that they had not been kept in good repair, or that they had originally been built in a hurry.[24] Other city fortifications survived in good order: Gregory of Tours describes the walls of Dijon as being constructed of large squared stones to a height of 20 feet, then with smaller stones to a total height of 30 feet, and being 15 feet thick. These were clearly late Roman in construction. New fortifications were also constructed after the dissolution of the Western Empire on suitably defensible sites, such as Chastel-Marlhac in Gaul which was surrounded by sheer cliffs and had a pool of drinking water and many springs inside the natural fortifications. This had obvious parallels with the traditional hill fort. Fortifications were constructed for 'new' towns throughout the Middle Ages as required, but by no means all medieval towns were walled.[25]

Gregory's descriptions indicate that the walls around the Gallic cities in his day were wide enough to walk about on with ease in time of peace or for defenders to use as a platform for hurling down stones on attackers in time of siege. (At Amida the battlements had been wide enough for stonethrowers to be mounted on them.) City walls were pierced with a strong gate or gates through which the main roads entered the city; Dijon had four gates, on the north, east, south and west. The city gates should be guarded by gatekeepers at all times, to arrest any undesirables who tried to enter the city or prisoners who tried to escape. Towns built on flat land might have a deep ditch to add height to the walls, but others made best use of natural defences. At Comminges in south-western Gaul there was a deep ravine all round which the attackers tried to fill in with bundles of sticks. The spring was outside the town walls, at the bottom of the hill on which the town stood: a fortified tower had been built over the spring and the townspeople went down a covered way from the town to draw water, as in Vegetius's description of such a situation.[26]

The purpose of these fortifications was to protect both the people who lived within the city and those of the surrounding countryside who fled there in time of upheaval. They were able to withstand a determined siege, although Gregory's accounts indicate that they did not normally attempt to hold out for long against a determined enemy. Their main usefulness was to protect the citizens for short periods against bands of bandits and passing raiders (including kings and their officials). At Chastel-Marlhac in 532, despite their strong fortifications, the citizens paid King Theuderic to go away; at Comminges, Count Mummolus, realising that the town could not hold out for much longer against King Guntram's army, agreed to hand over the pretender Gundovald to the generals of the army.

Another form of military building that continued from the late Roman period was the long boundary line, the *limes* (plur.: *limites*). Such boundary lines included Hadrian's Wall across Britain, between Carlisle and the mouth of the River Tyne, and further north the Antonine Wall, between the Firth of Clyde and the Firth of Forth. Hadrian's wall, built in AD 122–3, was constructed of stone, punctuated with towers, with a rampart along the top wide enough for a chariot to be driven along it and a deep ditch on the northern side. It replaced an earth and wood rampart and trench built in AD 81 by Governor Agricola. The Antonine Wall, built AD 139–43, was again an earth and wood structure with a ditch. It is difficult to see how such a structure could ever have been regarded as defensive, although it might reduce lightning raids and sheep stealing. Its main function was probably to mark a boundary line, and it was abandoned when the boundary was moved back to Hadrian's Wall in the 150s.[27]

Such boundary lines were also constructed in northern Africa: the *fossatum Africae*, an earth wall 2–2.5 metres high with a ditch 4–6 metres wide and 2.3 to 3.4 metres deep (6.5–8 feet high, 13–20 feet wide and 7.5–11 feet deep).[28] Along the northern frontier of the empire with Germania a line of forts was constructed, with trenches and wooden palisades; a stone wall was built further east beyond the Danube, and ditches were dug in Mesopotamia.[29] Such lines marked the edge of imperial jurisdiction, but they were not final frontiers; they could be advanced or retreated from. While some historians have criticised Roman military strategy in laying out such lines, arguing that their construction in the second century marks the end of a dynamic, expansionist policy and the beginning of a defensive, stagnant military policy, others would argue that this is to misunderstand their purpose. Such walls could not be fully defensive; a determined enemy could easily jump a ditch or scale a wooden palisade. Differing interpretations of the functions of these lines have been proposed, for example by Benjamin Isaac[30] and Everett Wheeler.[31]

It could be suggested that, like the later medieval castle, the *limites* were intended, at least to some degree, to overawe outsiders and impress those living within the empire, as the scale of the work involved demonstrated the power of the empire. They also enabled administration to proceed more efficiently: at its simplest, if you lived on the inner side of the *limes*, you were subject to Roman jurisdiction and you paid Roman taxes. If you lived on the outside, you did not. If you lived on the outside and you were found on the inside without good reason, you would have some explaining to do.

Whatever the function of *limites*, the concept of the boundary line did not die with the Roman Empire. In the second half of the eighth century King Offa of Mercia (757–96) ordered the construction of a ditch and rampart along the western boundary of his kingdom of Mercia in central Britain, now known as 'Offa's Dyke'. Although the historian Asser, writing a hundred years later, recorded that it was built from 'sea to sea' – that is, from the Severn Estuary in the south to the Dee Estuary in the north – in fact, an earlier ditch and rampart existed along the north part of the line, 'Wat's Dyke', and Offa's Dyke ran alongside and south from this to the mouth of the River Wye, where it meets the Severn. There are gaps in Offa's Dyke, and it has been ploughed in by farmers along part of its length, particularly in the Wye Valley; but archaeological excavation now suggests that the Dyke was originally continuous. For at least part of its length a stone wall ran along the top of the earth bank. The Dyke was partly defensive: built at a time when the Welsh and the Mercians were continually raiding into each other's territory, it offered some obstruction to Welsh raiders. It also attempted to overawe the irrepressible Welsh, offering visible evidence of the unity and organisation of the Mercians and the power and authority of their king.[32] In addition it formed a boundary line: in later years, local law decreed severe penalties to any Welsh person found on the English side of the Dyke after sunset. Historians are not in agreement over which was its primary function.

Offa's Dyke is certainly reminiscent of the Roman *limites*, but it was not constructed by the army as were the Roman boundary lines. Archaeological work has indicated that it was dug by gangs of workers, as it is possible to trace where one gang's work ended and the next began; and a marker ditch was dug first to show workers the intended line of the Dyke. It has been suggested that it was dug by workers raised in local levies, so many from each town or region, in the same way as the army was raised, and presumably as large monuments had been raised in the past in Britain. Patrick Wormald noted: 'Major public works of this order were being erected in Britain as far back as the early Bronze Age. ... The proper conceptual counterpart of Offa's Dyke is not Hadrian's Wall but Stonehenge.'[33]

In constructing such a line, Offa was certainly following Roman precedent, and as a king who claimed authority over the whole of Britain, who conducted diplomatic contacts with Charlemagne and who issued coins obviously based on Roman models, it was entirely natural for him to imitate his Roman predecessors. But the earthwork and ditch was not peculiar to former Roman territories. The Danevirke was built across the base of the Jutland peninsula possibly in around 757 – before Offa's Dyke. Historians agree that this was primarily a defensive military structure.[34]

The late Roman Empire in the West also saw the construction of many permanent coastal forts along the east and south coast of Britain, such as at Brancester in what is now Norfolk, Walton Castle in Suffolk, Bradwell in Essex, Reculver, Richborough, Dover and Lympne in Kent, Pevensey in Sussex and Portchester, near Portsmouth. These housed troops and enabled a quick reaction against sea-borne raiders attacking the coast. A system of signal stations were built along what is now the Yorkshire coast, to enable warning of raiders to be quickly passed on. Such fortifications were active rather than passive; the troops in the forts did not expect to wait to be attacked, but would go out to meet an approaching enemy.

Not only the Romans built fortifications. The traditional hill fort has already been mentioned. Stone brochs were built in north and west Scotland and in the Isles: these consisted of a double stone wall, rising to a height of ten metres or more, enclosing a circular area. Animals and people could take refuge within the enclosure; in extreme circumstances it was possible to retreat into the area between the walls. These were essentially refuges from pirates, and were not necessarily built on high ground, as much of the Isles landscape is quite low-lying and flat. Likewise, ring-work forts or refuges were constructed in the Baltic region, Scandinavia, Poland and Germany.[35] Henry of Livonia, a Catholic priest involved in the German mission in Livonia (now Latvia) in the first half of the thirteenth century, calls the forts of the Livonians *castra* (singular *castrum*), that is, 'castles'. They had a defensive ditch and high fortifications, and were able to withstand a siege of several days by western Europeans.[36] In Norway, to take another example, between AD 600 and 1000 many hill forts were constructed with dry stone walls and timber fortifications added at vulnerable points.[37] These refuges were not places of regular habitation, only being used at times of danger. In normal times, the nobility and rulers of the land lived in halls built of wood or stone, which were impressive dwellings but had limited defences, such as an outer palisade and ditch. Like Hrothgar's hall in *Beowulf*, they were built primarily to impress, to entertain and to bring people in to look on their lord, not to keep people (or monsters) out.[38]

The military problem with defensive fortifications, to put it simply, is that it is possible for an army to get stuck behind them, unable to defend itself effectively and unable to escape an enemy's attack. Some historians have argued that the Germanic peoples who inherited the government of the Western Roman Empire preferred not to tie themselves down with fortifications. While the Merovingians, the Visigoths and the Lombards used the fortifications of the cities which the Roman government had had built and fortified hilltops, they did not build to the same degree as the Romans. Monasteries were defensive structures because they were usually built in stone and had a tall outer wall enclosing their buildings, and churches built in stone could also be used as military structures in time of need, but neither of these were specifically built as fortifications. The emphasis of military strategy (this theory goes) had shifted away from static fortifications to more dynamic strategies. Armies did not sit in military camps or in fortresses, but went out every summer on campaign, raiding into enemy territory and returning with booty and honour, or capturing territory and subjugating it. Of course those being raided would still require defensive fortifications as refuges against the raiders.

While the Carolingians, who succeeded to the government of Gaul in the eighth century, did build some fortifications, historians disagree over how significant fortifications were in their military strategy.[39] In particular, one of the most famous deeds of Charlemagne in connection with fortresses was not constructing, but demolishing the walls of Pamplona in order to cow the unruly Basques. The Basques repaid him by ambushing and destroying his rearguard at Roncesvalles in 778, a battle immortalised in the *Chanson de Roland*.[40] It is possible to argue from this episode that Charlemagne certainly saw the value of fortifications, in that they enabled rebels to defy his authority. He therefore destroyed them where they were a threat to him. He himself used or constructed fortresses where he saw that they could play a useful role in maintaining his authority over an area, but he often preferred to use other methods such as taking hostages, imposing Christianity and establishing churches, controlling the election of bishops, imposing oaths of loyalty on his subjects and giving territory to men whom he could trust to remain loyal, establishing sub-kings within his realm and governors in the frontier zones.[41] As Viking attacks on his coastlines became a menace to his subjects and their property, he followed Roman precedent in setting up watches along the estuaries of the Low Countries, with fortified guard posts whose garrisons could sally forth to drive off Viking raiders.[42]

The usefulness of fortifications became more apparent during the Viking raids of the second part of the ninth century. The word 'Viking' itself is difficult to define precisely. Originally, it meant a person from the area of Víken in southern Norway, but from the late eighth century the term came to mean a 'sea pirate', typically originating from the Scandinavian region, and that is the sense in which it is used here.[43] Vikings would sail or row their ships up the Seine and attack the towns along the river, sacking the great monastery of St Denys in October 865. The nobles and officers of the kingdom were unable to prevent these raids; the best they could manage was to attempt to ally with some of the Vikings against the others. Charles the Bald first raised a tax to pay the Vikings to go away, and then had a fortified bridge constructed at Pont-de-l'Arche, near Pîtres (Eure) and another at Treix on the River Marne.[44] It is not possible now to reconstruct these bridges completely, but it appears that they had large stone bridgeheads on either side of the river and wood spanning the river. Troops could be stationed in the bridge-heads.[45] There were also fortresses with earthen ramparts around the bridgeheads, which may have acted as refuges. These bridges were apparently very successful in barring the Vikings' route upriver, and Charles went on to plan further fortified bridges. Again, it is possible to draw parallels with Roman river defences in this case, although the Romans had had river patrols as well as fortresses on the rivers. Charles would have appreciated such parallels, for he was a ruler who claimed that his authority was a continuation from the authority of the Western Roman Empire.

Between 875 and 900 possibly as many as six fortresses were constructed in Zeeland as refuges for the local people and their property against Viking attack. These consisted of a circular rampart constructed from clay sods stacked up on the outer and inner sides and infilled with sandy clay or sand. The diameter of the fortress varied, from 144 metres (472 feet) at Oost-Souburgh to 265 metres (870 feet) at Domburg. There may have been a wooden palisade on the top of the rampart or on the inner side. There was a water-filled moat around the outside, from 30 to 50 metres (100–160 feet) wide. Two paths passed through the fortress, crossing at right angles in the middle and passing through a passage through the rampart and then by a narrow bridge over the moat. Around the same period, defences were built around the church of St Omaars, constructed from wood, earth and clay sods.[46]

The Viking threat also prompted rulers to build warships – which will be considered in Chapter 6 – and to refortify towns. It was probably King Alfred of Wessex who began the systematic construction of fortified sites or *burhs* in that kingdom: at least, this is what we are told by his biographer Asser, Alfred's *Anglo-Saxon Chronicle*, and the twelfth-century historian William of Malmesbury. These *burhs* were scattered across the kingdom so that none was more than 20 miles (a day's march: 32 kilometres) from the next. Some were new towns such as Wallingford on a crossing point on the River Thames, some were old hill forts such as Chisbury, Roman towns such as Portchester, or naturally fortified sites such as promontories, for instance Malmesbury. They had an earth wall and a ditch all around. Some *burhs* were probably used as temporary refuges, but the towns, which had a network of streets laid out to a common plan, were intended as centres of trade and commerce. A document called 'The Burghal Hideage' probably dates from the reign of Alfred's son Edward the Elder (899–924), and explains that a certain number of 'hides' of land were associated with each *burh*. Each hide represented one man, and from the number of hides assigned to each *burh* was calculated how many men were assigned to defend and maintain the *burh*'s walls.[47] This document is invaluable evidence to military historians in that it indicates how many men were reckoned to be needed to defend a certain length of town wall in early tenth-century Wessex: four men for each pole or five and a half yards (five metres). It would be unwise, however, to assume that this concentration of defenders applied to any other time or place.

In 924–5 King Henry 'the Fowler', king of East Francia, set up a system of defence which was apparently similar to the Wessex *burh* system, with warriors assigned to towns to defend and maintain them and their region. It is not clear which towns were involved.[48] Henry was concerned about attacks by the Magyars rather than by the Vikings.

The Vikings themselves, mobile pirates or horsemen as they were, also built fortifications. They constructed *longphuirt*, fortified naval bases, for their ships to overwinter; these would often be on an island for additional security, or could be at the mouth of a river. They contained huts where the Vikings lived and kept their prisoners and plunder. The Vikings also established winter camps inland, without their ships. Archaeological remains indicate that these fortifications, on islands or inland, were surrounded by an earth embankment with an exterior ditch. They might incorporate an existing building into the fortifications: at Nijmegen in the Netherlands in 880–1 Vikings used the royal palace as a winter base and built fortifications around it; a few years later a band of Vikings used a farmhouse as a base. At Repton in Derbyshire, England, in 873, they built the church into their outer rampart. Although these fortifications do not sound very impressive, at Nijmegen the royal army was unable to dislodge them. Where the Vikings founded towns, these were also fortified against raids by other Vikings. At the Viking town of Dublin (itself sacked by Danes in 851) earth ramparts strengthened with wood were built in around the mid-tenth century and the end of the tenth century, and rebuilt in stone at the beginning of the twelfth century.[49]

It is clear that earth and timber were regarded as being good material for a military building during the early medieval period. Earth and timber had in their favour that they were relatively cheap – timber was readily available in most parts of Europe – and could be put together quickly, with relatively unskilled labour. Apart from the classic military campsite – as used by the Romans and the Vikings – and the hill fort, the other typical earth and timber military construction familiar to medieval historians is the motte and bailey castle. The motte and bailey castle has a simple basic plan: a mound of earth (the motte), on which is built a wooden tower, and which is surrounded by a ditch; and adjacent to it an area (the bailey) enclosed by an earth rampart topped with a wooden palisade, the whole surrounded by a ditch. This design did not have obvious origins in ancient times, but apparently developed in western Europe (including Italy and Denmark) in the tenth and eleventh centuries.[50] It has been suggested that it originated in defences against the Vikings and Magyars. As it was small, cheap and quickly constructed, it was within the means of most lords, unlike fortified bridges, which required the resources of the western emperor to design and build. The Bayeux Tapestry, originally embroidered in the late eleventh century, shows a number of motte-type wooden castles of this kind. In France, the earliest motte and bailey castles were apparently built by Fulk Nerra, count of Anjou (lived 987–1040), and his son Geoffrey Martel, 'the Hammer' (d. 1060). They were then built in the neighbouring county of Normandy; and in England, under the pro-Norman rule of King Edward the Confessor (d. 1066). After William the Bastard's conquest of England in 1066 they were built extensively throughout England,[51] and also – as the Normans moved west – in Wales. But motte and bailey castles were also built in Denmark, Norway, the Low Countries, and the Rhineland and Southern Italy,[52] all regions which came under Norman or Viking influence, and we might surmise that the motte and bailey castle was a Viking invention, or, if not, one which the Vikings took up and exported.

Such a fortress could house warriors who could launch raids on the surrounding region, or keep a look out for raiders coming into the region and attack them. The bailey could form a refuge for local people, and it is interesting to note that the motte and bailey castles built in Zeeland in the Netherlands in the eleventh century are in fact called 'refuge mounds' (*vliedberg*).[53] Again, like the traditional hill fort, the motte and bailey castle could not withstand a long siege – it was too small to hold large volumes of supplies and the wooden defences could be fired or chopped up relatively easily. But it formed a strong point, and was an indication of prestige.

We might ask why, after a period between the sixth and the tenth centuries when fortifications received less emphasis, European rulers and their nobles once again started building fortifications. The answer lay partly in the nature of warfare and weaponry: a highly mobile enemy such as the Vikings could not be met simply with a field army, because whenever the army got there the Vikings had gone; it was necessary to build fortified dwellings for protection, and fortresses as local bases from which warriors could look out for the Vikings and sally out to meet them in the field when they appeared. Fortifications were also built partly to meet the need for administrative centres and social display. Also, the economic recovery of Europe from the eleventh century onwards meant that more lords could afford to build fortresses; they could afford to develop systems of administration, so that they needed formal administrative centres; the population was rising, so that there were more people to administer; and so on. Having said that, strong rulers generally imposed limitations over who could build fortifications.

Motte and bailey castles were initially constructed simply from earth and wood, but in the late tenth century stone castles were being constructed in Catalonia, not only along the frontier with Muslim-held Iberia but also in the middle of the country. These were tall, circular towers, and have been defined as having economic and administrative roles as well as strategic functions such as defending a dependent village.[54] In northern France, Fulk Nerra of Anjou may have constructed a stone tower at Langeais on the Loire River, and at Montbazon on the Indre River, in the late tenth century. If he did, then it is also possible that his neighbours in Blois, Angoulême and La Marche, and the Île de la France were building stone castles in the late tenth century. However, historians do not agree over the date of these stone fortresses; it is possible that the stone ruins that now exist at Langeais and Montbazon date from the late eleventh century, and replaced an earlier wooden fortress built by Fulk.[55]

These designs of castles were built in stone rather than wood because stone withstands fire better, and does not rot, but, as most of the surviving medieval stonework shows, it required a skilled stone mason to cut and put it together to form a wall which would not fall down, building stone fortresses was more expensive than building in wood. A suitable supply of stone was needed, and this might have to be carried many miles, at great cost. In some parts of Europe building stone is not available; so that in the Baltic lands of Prussia, Livonia and Estonia, and in parts of the Low Countries, the fortresses which were constructed were built of brick. Building in stone, while slower than building in wood, could still be relatively quick – the castle at Jacob's Ford in the kingdom of Jerusalem was constructed in six months between October 1178 and April 1179.[56] Some stone castles were built as motte and bailey castles, such as Batenburg Castle in Guelders province in the Netherlands, where earth was piled up around the base of the stone tower to a height of seven metres.[57] This earth mound around the base made it far more difficult for a would-be attacker to undermine the base of the castle walls.

Stone castles, being permanent and more expensive to construct than earth and timber motte and bailey castles, fulfilled somewhat different purposes. The stone castle was a military centre; it could withstand a long siege and would normally be larger than a motte and bailey castle. Because of its cost, a stone castle necessarily conferred more status on its builder and reflected more authority than an earth and timber motte and bailey castle. The development of this type of fortress has been regarded by some historians as critical in the development of medieval warfare, for (they argue) as a result of the new fortifications warfare became based around sieges rather than on raiding or battles.[58]

But where did the stone castle originate? In some respects the stone fortress had never disappeared from Europe. In so far as it was a centre of population and a seat of government, the stone castle succeeded the stone-fortified imperial cities of the Roman Empire, such as Trier, Sirmium and Milan. In the Middle East the Byzantines and Arabs built stone fortresses, so that when the crusaders arrived at the end of the eleventh century they found castles already *in situ*.[59] Whether earlier pilgrims to Jerusalem in the tenth and eleventh centuries, such as Fulk Nerra, were influenced by seeing these fortifications is not known. Again, how did the fortresses captured by Charlemagne in his expedition to Spain in 777–8 differ from the castles of Spain and France of the tenth and eleventh century?[60] We may assume that these eighth-century fortresses were fortified towns and refuges rather than stone towers, but the writers of the period do not tell us. But although in some cases stone castles were simply reconstructed hill fortresses, the Catalonian and French castles of the late tenth century seem to have been a new development: more permanent and more politically significant.

This brings us to the problem of definition. What was a castle? Our problem is that medieval writers used various terms to describe a castle, such as 'municipium', 'oppidum', or 'castrum', although the name 'castrum' became dominant. *Castrum* in classical Latin referred to a fort or fortress; in the plural it meant a fortified camp. As *castrum* or *castellum* (a walled enclosure) it became a *chastel* in Old French, and 'castle' in English. It is worthy noting that the words 'municipium' and 'oppidum' could also mean 'town' or 'village'. These hint at the fact that the castle was not simply a place where warriors lived: it was a fortified dwelling or collection of dwellings. When in the Old French romances of the late twelfth and thirteenth centuries the hero comes to a *chastel*, what he is approaching is usually not simply a castle in the modern sense but a fortified town; within the *chastel* he will ride to the *maistres chastel* or the *petis chastel*, the citadel or castle within the fortified town.[61] The author could have been thinking of many fortified towns and cities in western Europe with a 'castle' within the fortified town: from towns such as Ghent in the Low Countries to Le Mans in northern France, Blois and Tours in the Loire Valley, Carcassonne in the south, Burgos in Castile (both 'burgos' and 'castile' mean 'castle'), and in Britain new towns such as Caernarfon and Conwy in North Wales. In fact, if we recall that late Roman Amida had a citadel within the ambit of its massive walls, and that Antioch in Syria has a citadel likewise on the highest point within the city, we may see that this use of the term 'castle' was the classical one, where the 'fortress' is the whole fortified settlement, not simply the central strongpoint; and the primary purpose of the walls is to be defensive.

Modern students of castles must therefore take care, for when medieval writers referred to a *castrum* they did not necessarily mean what the modern student expects. Nowadays the term 'castle' is popularly used to mean not a fortified town or city or a defensive refuge such as a hill fort, but the fortified residence of an individual that was designed to dominate the region around it: offensive rather than defensive, and acting as an administrative centre.[62] By regarding a castle as primarily offensive, a castle is defined as a point from which its owner could control the countryside around, and from which warriors could set out to raid enemy territory. When the castle became no more than a refuge, this meant that its lord had lost control of the surrounding territory and was probably about to become an ex-lord. Conversely, as lord's residence the castle invited people in to be entertained, attend the lord's court, and to pay their taxes.[63] The classic 'fairy-tale castle' perched on an inaccessible crag would make a poor administrative centre, for no one could easily enter to pay taxes or go out to war! So a successful castle must have two-way relations with its region; the lord and his warriors ride out to dominate the region, while people outside come in to be entertained, pay taxes and so on.

Yet, in fact, many of the buildings now called 'castle' do not fit this definition. Where we find a castle that was so difficult of access that its inhabitants could not have two-way relations with the locality around, we may surmise that it was defensive rather than playing a role in administration. For example, Carreg Cennen, perched on a rocky cliff in Dyfed (west Wales) and far from any centre of population, never played any decisive role in the government of the region. Such a castle was effectively a hill fort rebuilt in the latest style, a refuge from which bandits could sally out to trouble the local farmers or to prey on travellers, but unsuited to become a permanent centre of administration.[64]

Many castles had a wholly or primarily military purpose rather than a residential function. Some were built to dominate rivers, to collect tolls or to prevent enemies from travelling up the river: such as the castle of Amposta (or Montsià) at the mouth of the River Ebro in the kingdom of Aragon, then on the frontier with the Muslims, which was given to the

Hospital of St John in 1149 'for the propagation of the Christian religion and to crush and confound the Moorish people'.[65] In 1095 Bishop Otbert of Liège led a force to besiege the castle of Clermont on the River Meuse, which had become a serious obstruction to trade. Giselbert, lord of the castle, opted to abandon his castle and join the First Crusade. In the thirteenth century the cities of the Rhine valley, where the Rhine merchants lived and traded, formed leagues to oppose the lords who built and operated the castles.[66] Conversely, some buildings were built like castles simply from defensive necessity and with no intention to dominate the locality, such as the Irish monasteries mentioned above.

In general, we may apply the term 'castle' to fortresses with a primarily military purpose and to fortified dwellings intended primarily to house one lord's household (that is, including all the owner's employees and direct dependants), whether they were primarily residences, intended to dominate the region, or refuges. They were a new military development in that they were compact offensive/defensive structures that could withstand prolonged sieges; and they were a new architectural development, in that they combined military, residential and administrative functions to a far greater extent than did the traditional halls or the fortified towns.

* * *

Castle design was dynamic and changed rapidly from the tenth to the fifteenth centuries, to meet military, administrative and cultural requirements. The single tower with surrounding protective walls continued as a basic design throughout the medieval period. Castles of this type were built in Norway from the late twelfth century (where King Sverre built stone keeps with ring walls on the high cliffs outside the towns of Bergen and Trondheim),[67] and in Scotland, such as the Macdonalds's fortress on the island of Kerrara, as well as in areas of Norman or French dominance: France, England, Wales and Ireland and Sicily, and also the Iberian Peninsula. But the basic design was adapted. It is unclear where the initiative for new castle designs lay: while skilled architect/masons would presumably bring their own experience to bear on the best way to design a defensive building,[68] the commissioning lords were also active warriors who had besieged fortresses and had themselves been besieged, and must have had their own views on how to design a fortress for best effect. In addition, while architect/masons travelled around Europe, so did the castle-building lords: on pilgrimage or crusade, or following their ruler on campaign or as he perambulated his domains. Presumably they would take note of any fortresses which they saw and remember impressive features. So, for instance, when Llywelyn ap Iorwerth, prince of Gwynedd (North Wales), was building Criccieth in the 1230s, the gatehouse was built to the latest design with twin D-shaped towers, which presumably Llywelyn had seen in the territories of his English allies and rivals: at

Beeston Castle, built by Ranulf de Blundeville, earl of Chester (d. 1232), and at Montgomery, built by Hubert de Burgh (d. 1243) for King Henry III (1216–72). He may have brought in outside masons to do the work, as his local workers would never have seen anything similar before.[69]

Both rectangular and circular designs were used for the main central tower of castles. Count Henry of Troyes's (d. 1187) many-sided great tower at Provins included in the thickness of the walls small rooms that allowed members of the household to retire from the public life of the communal central hall and enjoy a little privacy. At around the same period, at Conisbrough near Doncaster in South Yorkshire the central tower was built with a circular ground plan with six solid buttresses built up the sides, giving better visibility around the keep. Although, again, a few small rooms were built into the thickness of the walls, the general result was not a striking improvement on the old rectangular keep in terms of comfort, size or defensibility: except for the chapel, the buttresses at Conisbrough have no windows or arrow slits to allow visibility around the wall, although they would act as protection for the main body of the tower. Here the keep was not the main living area, but a military stronghold and final refuge; the main accommodation was built against the walls of the inner bailey, where there was more space. At Orford in Suffolk the new keep, built 1165–73, was much smaller than at Conisbrough and was many-sided, but here it formed the main living area, with fine halls and small private rooms built into the thickness of the walls. It is possible that King Henry II of England (1154–89) used it as a residence.[70] While the central towers of the first castles in the Welsh March were rectangular, by the late twelfth century circular towers were being built at (for instance) Pembroke, by William Marshal, earl of Pembroke, and at Ewyas Lacy in the Welsh March, now Longtown. Built by the powerful Lacy family, the latter had a circular tower as the strongpoint of its castle at one end of its new, fortified town in the shadow of the Black Mountains. Such towers varied considerably in scale. The round tower at Pembroke is 16 metres in diameter and around 24 metres high; the tower at Ewyas Lacy is less than half as tall.[71] At Coucy in what is now north-eastern France, a massive circular tower was built between 1225–42, covering an area 31 metres in diameter and more than 55 metres high. The whole castle was not only a fine military fortress, but included beautiful vaulting, delicately carved stonework and many fine residential rooms.[72]

Above all, castle design was adaptable in line with the owner's requirements. Where a motte existed, it was possible to replace the wooden fort with a stone keep; but this would be a hollow 'shell keep' rather than a solid keep. This was the design at Pickering Castle in Yorkshire, England. The shell keep consists of a circular wall with buildings constructed of stone or wood within the wall. It is not as heavy as a solid rectangular keep, so suitable for building on ground which is liable to subsidence – such as an artificial earth mound like the motte. The shell keep had the advantages of the round tower: no corners to be undermined by besiegers, and offering better visibility to defenders than a rectangular tower.[73]

The emperor Frederick II followed the latest trends in castle architecture in his magnificent new castle, Castel del Monte, built near Foggia in southeastern Italy from 1240. This has an octagonal tower with eight small, circular towers attached, one to each of its corners. Situated on a high point with fine views all around, it was nevertheless apparently essentially a hunting lodge rather than an example of offensive military architecture; despite its defences, it was too small to stand a long siege. It was built to impress rather than to dominate.[74]

From the mid-twelfth century, a new form of castle design began to appear in the crusader states in the Middle East and in the Iberian Peninsula. This was the so-called concentric castle, which has no central tower as a final point of retreat, but has a series of enclosing walls, one inside the other, punctuated by towers. The inner enclosure has the highest walls, overlooking the lower walls around it. An enemy breaching the outer circle of walls is open to attack from above; the defenders of the inner enclosure may be able to fire right over the outer walls to the enemy outside. The design may include staggered gateways, open areas into which the enemy is 'lured' which are open to easy attack by the defenders, and outer works such as barbicans to defend the gates. The general effect from outside is not unlike a late Roman fortified city such as Constantinople.

Historians do not agree as to why this design developed. Some point to the fact that one of the earliest examples of the new design was the Hospitaller castle of Belvoir in the Jordan Valley, rebuilt in the new style in the late 1160s and 1170s. The order of the Hospital was a military religious order, whose members followed a religious rule and daily routine of prayer and services in chapel. In order to follow this lifestyle without being disturbed by the secular mercenaries whom they had to employ, they could have designed their castle to have an interior courtyard where the Brothers alone lived, then outer courtyards where the secular warriors employed by the order might live. This would produce a concentric castle. Alternatively, it has been argued that castle design in the crusader states of the Middle East began to adapt to meet new developments in Muslim siege techniques. The Catalan historian Joan Fuguet i Sans has pointed out that the castles of Gardeny and Miravet in Catalonia, rebuilt by the order of the Temple after they were given to the order in the 1140s, have aspects of concentricity and also reflect Muslim religious architecture. This again suggests that the concentric design was developed to meet the needs of military religious orders, with some influence from Muslim architecture. Other historians point out that the crusaders were taking on Byzantine defensive design – hence the similarity between the concentric castle and the fortifications of, say, Constantinople. Yet many military historians and archaeologists see no need to posit Muslim or religious influence. The concentric plan has obvious military advantages and could have been developed by skilled secular castle architects and designers as a logical progression from what had gone before, in response to new siege technology.[75]

If the concentric castle were invented in the Middle East, it must have been brought to the West by returning crusaders; but early concentric castles in the West are not clearly based on those in the Middle East. The early European 'concentric' castles, such as Dover in England, begun by King Henry II of England, retained the central tower strongpoint, which concentric castles in the East such as Belvoir had discarded. Castle Hedingham in Suffolk, built at the end of the twelfth century, had only one enclosure and no central tower, with the living accommodation built against the walls of the enclosure. It is hardly concentric, more like a giant hill fort – except that it is built on level ground. At Najac in Aveyron, begun by Count Alphonse of Poitiers in 1253, the main tower was built into the concentric wall, rather than being free-standing in the centre of the complex. One of the earliest true concentric castles in Britain is Caerphilly Castle, constructed in the 1270s. It has sometimes been assumed that this was influenced by crusader castles such as the Hospitallers' Crac des Chevaliers in the county of Tripoli (now in Syria), but as Caerphilly Castle was built by Gilbert the Red, earl of Gloucester (d. 1295), who had not been on crusade, this seems unlikely. It therefore seems most likely that the concept of the concentric castle developed as part of the ongoing development of defence, in response to new siege machines (which will be considered in Chapter 4), rather than as a direct result of developments in the Middle East, although input from architects and other travellers such as pilgrims may have played a role in some instances.

In the concentric design, the gatehouse came to be the central focus for defence. As the point of entrance, it was the weakest point of the castle. With the concentration of building on the gatehouse, the main living quarters of the castle came to be based here: as at Edward I's castle of Beaumaris on the island of Anglesey, built at the end of the thirteenth century, Caerlaverock Castle near Dumfries in Scotland, built from the end of the thirteenth century, and Båhus Castle in Norway, built in the first decades of the fourteenth century.[76] The inner courtyard then housed other domestic buildings such as the kitchen, perhaps a great hall (if the gatehouse was not big enough) and other 'service' buildings. The gatehouse of Fort St André at Villeneuve lès Avignon, on the French frontier with Provence (independent of France until 1480), was rebuilt, probably between 1362 and 1368, with a massive circular tower on each side of the gate, as was normal in this type of design. Extensive machicolation crowned the towers: battlements overhung the ground below, with many slits in the floor so that missiles could be dropped on an attacking enemy.[77]

The gatehouse was also the main focus of design in the typical German castle, which did not follow the keep and bailey model, but more resembled a fortified hilltop with a strong gatehouse and surrounding wall and a collection of living accommodation within the wall. In regions where all children inherited their parents' land jointly, the accommodation within the walls would be scattered and divided, so that each of the inheriting families had their own home within the walls: this can be seen at castles such as Burg Eltz (on a tributary of the Mosel) and Schönburg at Oberwesel, on the Rhine.[78] A variation on this design was the castle sited on an island or peninsula that was essentially a collection of living accommodation surrounded by formidable walls and towers. Such were the Finnish castles of Kuusisto and Turku, both apparently built in the second half of the thirteenth century (as they are first mentioned in the sources at the end of the thirteenth century).[79]

While a castle had to have military integrity, in the increasingly settled conditions of twelfth and thirteenth century Europe how a castle looked became increasingly important. The 'fictional' romances of the period stress that castles should be beautiful, which included a strong site (on a high point, in a marsh, on an island in a river and so on) and high, strong walls, but also included delicately carved windows, fine vaulting in the inner chambers, a magnificent stairway rising up to the main doorway into the great hall, beautiful painting on the interior walls, banners hung from the upper ramparts, tall, elegant and finely carved chimneys rising above the battlements, and so on. A number of castles in the West, such as Caernarfon in North Wales (built by Edward I of England) and Angers in Anjou in central northern France, imitated the construction of the land walls of Constantinople with alternating courses of stone and brick, producing a striped effect which enhanced the appearance of the fortress and implied a parallel between the power and authority of the builder and that of the emperor Constantine I and the emperors of the East.[80] Once inside the castle walls, Philip Dixon has drawn attention to how the internal layout of a castle could be designed to impress and subdue visitors and to emphasise the dominance of the lord. In the great hall at Castle Rising in Norfolk, for instance, the windows were placed to ensure 'that the occupant of the principal chair was the most prominent feature in the hall'.[81] The beauty of the castle in itself played a strategic purpose, for it would impress on others the power and authority of the owner of the castle. In this period of increasing economic prosperity, it was not only castles that looked impressive; churches, cathedrals and abbeys, and even rich merchants' houses could vie with the castle for visual dominance. But a beautiful castle was also a well-kept castle, a well-stocked and well-garrisoned castle that was well able to defend itself and well able to dominate the land about it.

* * *

The design of fortresses changed dramatically in response to gunpowder artillery, which first appeared in western Europe in the 1320s. Tall walls presented a fine target for cannon balls, and the traditional fortress wall, while thick, nevertheless was easily broken up by the more powerfully propelled shot. Castle and town walls were therefore built much lower and much thicker. Round towers deflected shot better than rectangular towers, but some 'dead ground' was left between the towers which defenders could not cover. Larger machiolations and sharply angled walls were the answer. Italian military architects were the first to adopt bastions and sharp angles pointing outwards from the defences to deflect fire and leave no 'dead ground' unprotected. The base of a stone fortress wall was usually 'battered', built sloping outward to the base, to deflect shots from stonethrowers and to make it more difficult to place a scaling ladder next to the walls and climb up; this battering now became more dominant with the need to deflect cannon shot. Towers placed along the wall were now built at a level with the wall and used as artillery platforms. Walls were pierced with round holes for guns rather than long narrow slits for arrow shot as in the previous centuries. The use of outworks increased, with (for example) barbicans protecting gates from direct fire, and long boulevards, built of stone and filled with earth, running outside the wall and parallel with it so that a besieger could not fire directly at the wall. The defences of the town of Rhodes constructed by the Hospital of St John at the end of the fifteenth century and the early sixteenth century reflect these new developments, as do many towns in Italy.[82]

This new form of architecture is one of the changes identified by historians of sixteenth-century warfare as part of the so-called military revolution of the late Middle Ages and early modern period.[83] The new developments did not come to their full growth until after 1500: one of the best examples being the defences of the city of Nicosia in Cyprus, built in the 1520s on a star plan.[84] In the northern Netherlands in the conflict between the duke of Gelre and the Habsburgs, castles were adapted in the late fifteenth and early sixteenth centuries (1492–1513) to meet the danger from the new smaller-bore, more controllable cannon. Written sources refer to earthen bulwarks being raised to protect castle walls, and low, circular, brick-built bastions being built to house cannons and defend vulnerable points. Parallel moats were dug around castles, with the bank between planted with thorn bushes, to keep the enemy away from the walls. Both sides also built 'blockhouses' to block roads and so cut off supplies to their enemies: these blockhouses were apparently built of earth and timber, and could house a large number of soldiers (130 men in one instance) but were only temporary structures. These were all *ad hoc*, temporary adaptations; it was not until after 1513 that permanent changes began to be made.[85] The fortress at Tarascon in southern France, on the frontier with Provence until the French king annexed Provence in 1480, was reconstructed in the first half of the fifteenth century with the enclosing walls and towers built to the same height so that defenders could move around more easily, and guns could also be conveniently moved and positioned.[86]

At the same time, most castle dwellers would not expect ever to withstand a siege by gunpowder weapons, and by the late fourteenth century many of the nobility, instead of building new castles, constructed comfortable residences that included some defences. The castle remained a prestigious dwelling place, but those castles of Europe that remained inhabited were gradually converted in time of peace to become comfortable homes rather than military buildings. This said, in the wars of early modern Europe castles and fortified towns remained significant strategic points.[87]

4

Military equipment

Christine de Pisan, writing in 1408–9, set out the military equipment required for a siege. She was apparently listing the materials actually used in a real siege described to her by the military men who were her informants on current military practice. The equipment required to besiege a *tresforte place*, a very strong place, included some impressive ordnance: 'Again, four great cannons, one of which is called garite, the next rose, the next seneca and the next maye.' These were presumably cannons that had recently fought for France; it was normal to give large artillery pieces names, be they stonethrowers or gunpowder weapons. They might, however, have been particular types of cannon. Garite, Christine tells us, hurls weights of 400–500 pounds (180–225 kilograms); Rose hurls weights of 300 pounds (135 kilograms) and the last two hurl weights of 200 pounds (90 kilograms) or more. Finally, there was a gun called Montfort hurling 300-pound weights. Interestingly, Caxton's translation of this section of her work gives 500 pounds for Garite and 400 for Rose; perhaps his manuscript gave different figures, or perhaps the larger cannon of his day were more powerful.[1]

Christine listed additional equipment she regarded as necessary to besiege a fortress.[2] She included a few of the traditional stone-throwing machines: the British Library Harleian manuscript lists 'two big engines and two others' which are less powerful, and four *coillards*, newly fitted out with cables and cords. Christine would also have a brass cannon called 'Artique' hurling 100 pounds weight (45 kilograms), 20 'common' cannon firing stone shot, and small guns firing small lead balls and 'common stones' weighing 100 or 120 pounds (54.4 kilograms); and so on and so on, 248 cannons in all, all with feet of strong timber and other equipment. The 'other equipment', we soon discover, included 30,000 pounds of gunpowder and enormous quantities of charcoal and the carts and horses to carry it all. Then every gun required its wooden 'mantle' to protect it from the elements and enemies while it was in operation; and Christine explained how these mantles were to be constructed.

Immense quantities of shot were to be brought: 150 stones ready dressed for the Montfort gun ('*le canon de Montfort*') and 120 stones rounded and ready dressed for the other great guns, with 300 other stones for the small guns and a further 600 stones which had not yet been finally shaped. She also mentions 400 stones all ready for the engines (the non-gunpowder artillery), and 500–600 which were only roughly shaped.[3] She also required 6000 leads to make lead shot.[4]

There would also be other siege equipment, which Christine sets out: timber for constructing wooden towers to attack the enemy and defences to defend the besiegers' camp; equipment for making siege machinery and for digging mines under enemy defences; and the means for setting fire to the wooden props so that the mines would collapse, bringing down whatever building was on the surface of the ground above.

When she went on to consider other weapons, Christine considered what the besieging general would require: 200 crossbows, 30 other crossbows which were primed by turning a crack or using a pulley, and 100 others primed by using a hook to draw back the string. Two thousand crossbow bolts would be needed. She reckoned that 300 hand bows would be needed, each with three strings (one in use and two spares) and 1,200,000 arrows. Then there were the bowstrings, and the machinery for winding back the crossbows.

This was the equipment to be provided by the commander. Christine did not list the armour to be worn by the individual warriors and their own personal weapons: swords, shields, axes, spears and lances. Presumably, in the army that her informants were speaking of, these were the concern of the individual and not of the commander.

The fact that Christine spent so much space considering the size and type of cannon to be used in a siege is a measure of the increasing importance of cannon in warfare by the early fifteenth century.[5] A decade after Christine was writing, John Žižka's Hussite army carried guns (called 'snakes') on their farm wagons that they used as battle fortresses: not only the heavy guns, but also hand-held weapons. While it may not have been possible to fire the guns accurately, they played an important role in frightening the enemy and the enemy's horses. At Kutná Hora in December 1421 the Hussite artillery kept King Sigismund's cavalry at bay until nightfall. During the darkness the Catholic army surrounded the Hussites. At daybreak the Hussites advanced, the battle wagons leading the way, shooting at the enemy from the guns on the wagons. The guns drove the Catholics back, enabling the Hussites to advance through the Catholic lines and escape. Frederick Heymann declared that this is the first clear use of field artillery in battle; although, in fact, the Roman army also used field artillery.[6]

A drawing of around 1450 shows a Hussite wagon camp with the Hussites in their wagon, armed with guns and crossbows, while another wagon with heavy guns mounted in it stands on another side of the encampment; a third wagon is filled with swords, while a battle flail stands to one side.[7] Old and new weaponry stood side by side and were used together.

Arguably, the development of cannon was the first major step forward in warfare in Catholic Europe since the old Roman Empire. With this exception, and setting aside improvements in materials and basic designs, most military equipment changed very little during our period.

* * *

In the late fourth century, Vegetius had envisaged the late Roman army using short stabbing swords and shields, throwing javelins, and using the bow, the sling, lead-weighted darts (thrown like javelins, with an impact like arrows), and the lance. The horse also formed part of military equipment.[8] Vegetius also described many different sorts of artillery and siege equipment. There were 'tortoises', wooden frameworks covered in hides, containing a beam slung from the framework, with an iron hook on the tip, which would be swung against a wall to tear away the stonework, or else tipped with an iron head and called a 'ram' because it butted the wall like a male sheep. There were wickerwork frameworks constructed to protect sappers while they were undermining walls. There were also *musculi*, which Vegetius says means 'mussels' but which may mean 'little mice'. These were wicker head and body coverings to protect those who were carrying earth about in front of the wall, filling up the defensive ditch so that siege machines could be brought up to the wall. There were ladders to scale the walls. There were mobile towers on wheels that contained other siege equipment – rams, ladders and a bridge to enable warriors to cross on to the enemy's battlements. There were also catapults of various sorts: mostly torsion machines, which took their firing power from twisted fibres, but also tension machines, which worked roughly on the same principle as the traditional bow and arrow, by stretching fibres. These included mobile field artillery that could be used in pitched battles. Catapults hurled various sorts of ammunition to damage fortifications and kill defenders. Attackers could also build earth mounds near the besieged site as a platform from which to fire missiles.[9] Most of this military equipment continued in use throughout the Middle Ages.

Historians do not agree over whether the torsion catapult was one of the machines which remained in continuous use. Many have concluded that torsion machines, which were powered by twisted fibres, were largely abandoned after the dissolution of the Western Empire, in favour of tension-driven machines such as the hand-held crossbow, and traction stone-throwing machines that gained their firepower from being pulled hard and suddenly. Bernard Bachrach, in contrast, argues that the torsion machine remained in use throughout the Middle Ages.[10] The obvious reason for the torsion machine to fall out of use was that it required expertise and considerable expense to build and maintain, whereas although tension machines were less powerful they were also cheaper, easier to build and to operate. On the other hand, the technology of the torsion machine is not particularly complex, and its superior firepower made it worth the extra investment of time and money.

The evidence is so sparse and inconclusive that some historians have concluded that stone-throwing siege machines were abandoned altogether in western Europe by the sixth century. It is notable that Gregory of Tours mentions Leudegisel, King Guntram's count of the Stables and therefore a high military official, preparing siege machines at the siege of Comminges in AD 585, but the only machines he describes are rams; he does not mention catapults or other stone-throwing machines. (Rams, ladders and siege towers were *machinae* as much as catapults and stonethrowers.) Bishop Sagittarius threw stones at the enemy, but he did this by hand, not with a machine.[11] In the Eastern Roman Empire, from the sixth century AD the tension catapult replaced the torsion catapult,[12] but the 'barbarians' did not adopt this technology. There is a reference in the work of John, archbishop of Thessaloniki, to the Avaro-Slavs using *petroboles* or 'rock throwers' at their siege of Thessaloniki in 597, but these were propelled by traction, not tension or torsion. A stone was placed in a sling that hung from a rotating beam, with a rope hanging down from the other side of the beam; the stone was hurled by the operators giving a sharp tug on the rope, jerking the sling and the stone up into the air. Apparently, a captured Byzantine soldier had shown the Avaro-Slavs how to construct these machines.[13] This was very simple technology, requiring only basic carpentry skills, good timber to form the frame and some lengths of strong rope and cloth for the sling – and a team of strong men to fire it, as it was propelled purely by human strength. The basic design of this traction stonethrower was invented in China between the fifth and third centuries BC, and was being used by the armies of Islam by the end of the seventh century AD.

Contemporary sources give a few more references to the use of siege machines in western Europe over the next three centuries. Bachrach draws attention to a late seventh-century reference to the Visigoths using a *ballista*.[14] In 737 Duke Childebrand of Aquitaine went to besiege Avignon *cum apparatu hostile* (literally, with hostile equipment), including *machinae*, and at Bourges in 762 Pepin III had *machinae* with which he breached the city walls;[15] but, as has been noted already, *machinae* could be simply rams, ladders and siege towers. Less ambiguously, in 806 Charlemagne required Abbot Fulrad of Saint Quentin to bring *fundibulae* to a campaign with men skilled in their use and the stones required as ammunition: a *fundibula* was a stone-throwing machine.[16] Bachrach has also noted that Paul the Deacon, who worked at the Frankish court in the 780s, mentions a *petraria* (literally a 'stoner', or stone-throwing machine like the *petroboles* used at Thessaloniki) which hurled a human head over

a wall. Bachrach has additionally set out further examples from the eighth
century referring to *palestrae*, *petrariae* and *ballistae*: the first two being
stone-throwing artillery and the last an arrow-firing machine.[17] He notes
that the *Annales regnum Francorum* – the 'official' Carolingian history –
mentions the Saxons using a *petraria* in 776.[18] In around 850 a biographer ('the Astronomer') of Louis the Pious wrote of *mangana* being used
alongside other siege equipment such as rams in the siege of Tortosa in the
Iberian Peninsula in 808–9.[19] The word *mangana* ('mangonels'), is apparently derived from a Byzantine Greek name for a type of hurling
war-machine.

The Franks also used stone-throwing machines during the Viking siege
of Paris, 885–6. The commentator who mentioned these machines, Abbo
of Saint-Germain des Prés, called them *mangana*. He did not explain how
these were fired, although his description suggests that they may have
been driven by traction (i.e., a hard tug on a rope). It is not known where
the Franks learnt how to make *mangana*, and it has been suggested that
Charlemagne brought back the concept from Muslim Spain in the late
eighth century.[20] According to Abbo, the Vikings besieging Paris were
using catapults (*catapultis*), presumably tension rather than torsion
machines, as torsion machines had not been definitely sighted in the West
since the fifth century. He also mentions the Franks having a *ballista*, a
tension-driven crossbow, which fired flaming arrows. But Abbo may have
borrowed his description of siege machines from classical sources.[21]

However, taking all the above evidence together, it appears that stone-
throwing siege machines were in use in the eighth and ninth centuries,
although not to the extent that they were in the thirteenth (for instance)
as they were not mentioned as often in contemporary accounts. For the
highly mobile armies of the West from the sixth to the eleventh centuries,
large stone-throwing siege machines which had to be carried in baggage
trains and set up were an inconvenience, especially as skill was required
to construct them and to fire them without doing more injury to the operators than to the enemy.[22] It has been suggested that Charlemagne and
Louis the Pious would carry dismantled siege machines in the baggage
train, to be set up on site as required.[23] But because of the logistical problems involved in transportation, it is possible that even though the technology was known throughout the early Middle Ages – after all, the
machines were described by Vegetius – stone-throwing machines were
only used at prolonged or particularly difficult sieges.

The first universally acknowledged appearance of the traction-driven
stonethrower in the West was at the siege of Lisbon in 1147, during the
Second Crusade. A German source on the crusade refers to these as mangonels.[24] An eyewitness account of the siege by an Anglo-Norman priest
refers in passing to five stonethrowers belonging to the crusaders from
Cologne and Flanders, which he calls *fundae Balearicae*. These machines
appear to have been large slingshots operated by tension or traction (the

terms used allow for either form of propellant). The priest was far more interested in the siege towers constructed by the various national groups at the siege, and the German mine that made a breach in the city walls.[25] This suggests that the stonethrowers were not decisive in the fall of the city.

If stone-throwing machines were present during the Second Crusade, we might ask whether they were also being used during the First Crusade of 1095–9. Anna Comnena refers to such machines, but Western historians have doubted her account.[26] The anonymous contemporary eyewitness account known as the *Gesta Francorum* ('the deeds of the Franks'), gives no definite indication that stone-throwing machines were used: there are references to *instrumenta* of wood and *machinamenta*, but these may have been rams, sows or cats, or siege towers.[27] However, the eyewitness account of the priest Ralph of Caen, the *Gesta Tancredi*, refers to *fundis balearibus*, which struck the wall of the besieged city, although he does not state whether they were firing darts or stones.[28] Later, non-eyewitness, accounts also mention such machines.[29]

This evidence indicates that there were a number of siege machines in use in the late eleventh and early twelfth century which were variants on the large mounted slingshot. The terms used to describe them may have varied depending on the exact nature of the machine – or the difference in nomenclature might be due to the ignorance of non-military writers. Although they relied only on combined human strength for their power, contemporary descriptions indicate that the firing power of these machines could be impressive. They were used to batter city walls and, combined with mining, were a factor in the breaching of the walls of the city of Acre in July 1191, which led to the surrender of the city to the forces of the Third Crusade. The machines used in the siege of Acre of 1189–91 were called *petrariae* and *perrières*;[30] simple traction machines, yet they seem to have been very powerful. The Muslims within the city had *petrariae* which could hurl enormous stones which crushed everything that they hit; on the other side, King Philip II of France (d. 1223) had a *petraria* he named 'Bad Neighbour', which eventually broke down the main wall of the city and shattered one of the towers in the wall, while King Richard I of England had a *petraria* which killed 12 Muslims with a single stone. It was said that Richard transported special hard stone from Sicily specifically to use for ammunition in his stonethrowers. Many of the stonethrowers were given names: apart from King Philip's 'Bad Neighbour', the Muslims had a machine named 'Bad Relation', and the crusader army had another which was maintained by charitable donations from the crusaders themselves, called 'God's Stonethrower'.[31] But the power of these machines was such that the question must arise whether these were actually simple traction stonethrowers or counterweight trebuchets.[32] Arguably, any stone-throwing machine was a *petraria* or *perrière* (as the word simply means 'stonethrower') and a writer who was not quite sure of the correct term, or needed a word to rhyme or scan well, could use *petraria* or *perrière* simply to mean 'a stone-throwing war machine'.

Another missile-hurling machine that is much featured in twelfth- and thirteenth-century writing is the crossbow or *ballista*, which was a tension-powered machine. While it is not always clear in twelfth-century chronicles whether references to *ballistae* mean the small, hand-held crossbow or a large siege crossbow, it appears that a large machine was used during the siege of Damietta during the Fifth Crusade (1217–21), where a contemporary Provençal commentator referred to it as *j alboresta de torn* – a turning crossbow, presumably a large machine mounted on a pivot, which could be swung around to be aimed at the enemy.[33]

Also at the siege of Damietta, on the western European side, were three powerful trebuchets, belonging to the Romans, the duke of Austria (who later gave it to the Templars), and the Hospital of St John respectively, and a *perrière* which belonged to the Hospital. The writer regarded the trebuchet as different from the *perrière*, much bigger, more powerful and more expensive.[34] He was evidently referring to a counterweight trebuchet, a machine that appeared in the Mediterranean area at least by the mid-twelfth century and then spread into northern Europe and the Middle East and Africa. Instead of being powered by humans pulling on ropes, it had a fixed counterweight such as a box filled with stones or sand. The box was wound up, and then dropped, supplying the energy to power the missile.[35] Such a machine could be operated by anyone who knew how to use it, old or young, male or female. With this in mind, it is interesting to note that the stonethrower which was being operated by women and girls and which killed Simon de Montfort the elder at the siege of Toulouse in 1218 was either a mangonel or a *perrière*, not a trebuchet; although there were also trebuchets and *machafundis* (slingshots) in use at the siege.[36] Given that women are usually physically weaker and lighter than men, one wonders how many women were needed to hurl a missile from a traction stonethrower with sufficient force to kill a man.

This famous mangonel or *perrière* had been constructed by a local carpenter; perhaps a trebuchet was beyond his abilities. The counterweight trebuchet at that time was a high-class, exclusive machine. During the Barons' War in England, 1214–17, the Lord Louis of France (d. 1226), eldest son of King Philip II of France, was invited by the rebel barons of England to become king of England in place of King John (d. 1216). Louis arrived in England in May 1216 and settled down to besiege Dover Castle, setting up his *perrières* and mangonels, a siege tower, and a 'cat', in this case apparently a cover beneath which his miners could dig a passage under the wall. The siege dragged on and on with little progress, and in February 1217 Louis himself went back to France to collect men and supplies. In April 1217 he returned. 'He brought a trebuchet with him,' wrote a contemporary, 'there was much talk about it, for at that time few had been seen in France.' (The writer, an eyewitness, was a professional military man.) However, when Louis finally arrived at Dover and had the trebuchet set up (*drechier*), our informant recorded that did it very little damage to the garrison at Dover. After the defeat of his allies at Lincoln in May, Louis had his trebuchet taken down (*abattre*) and prepared to leave Dover.[37] While the carpenter at Toulouse could knock a mangonel together at need, a trebuchet could not easily be constructed on the spot; it had to be carefully engineered by an expert. While a defeated force might simply abandon cheaply built catapults, a trebuchet was valuable and was taken down with care and transported with the rest of the army's equipment.

As the earliest undisputed recorded use of the machine, at the siege of Zevgminon in 1165, was by the Byzantines, the counterweight trebuchet was probably a Byzantine invention.[38] Paul Chevedden has argued that the machines used at the siege of Nicaea in 1097 were counterweight trebuchets. He attributes this usage to the Byzantines, as the Emperor Alexius I was assisting the crusaders.[39] As noted above, it may have been counterweight trebuchets that were in use on both sides during the siege of Acre of 1189–91. Whenever it was first used, the counterweight trebuchet was certainly much used in the second half of the thirteenth century in the Middle East by the great Muslim generals such as Sultan Baybars (d. 1277) and his successors, but it was also used throughout Europe. It has been calculated that it could hurl a stone weighing 33 pounds around 200 yards, or, alternatively, a stone weighing 100 kilograms more than 400 metres. With counterweight trebuchets at its disposal, a besieging force at last had the advantage in sieges, and it was probably the appearance of the trebuchet which prompted the changes in castle design from the mid-twelfth century onwards which were described in the previous chapter: the move from rectangular to round or multiform towers (reducing the flat target area offered to the besieger) and the change to the concentric design in preference to the single tower surrounded by a wall.[40]

Traction, tension and counterweight stonethrowers continued to be used in sieges until at least the fifteenth century. Froissart mentions their use at a siege in 1370.[41] Christine de Pisan refers to them in her work, and they were mentioned in French arms inventories until the middle of the fifteenth century. By that time, however, they seem to have been effectively obsolete.[42] Although Guillaume Caoursin mentions traditional and classical siege machines at the siege of Rhodes by the Ottoman Turks in 1480, other contemporary evidence indicates that in fact only gunpowder artillery was being used; Guillaume was simply following contemporary humanist style in preferring classical equivalent terms to the modern ones.[43]

Other siege equipment changed very little from the time of Vegetius. Many *machinae* were named after animals, although exactly what was meant by 'cat' or 'sow' seems to have varied. A 'cat', for example, could be a wickerwork frame to protect those mining the walls or guiding a siege tower, or it could 'cling to the wall like a cat'. A 'sow' might dig away at the base of the wall, or be the cover for a battering ram.[44] A siege tower might also be called a 'belfrey', as it was as tall as a bell tower.[45] A besieging force might also set up a small, fixed timber castle outside the besieged fortress, as King Richard I of England did at Messina in Sicily and at Acre.[46]

Ammunition changed little from the ancient period: usually specially shaped stones, but also the severed heads of prisoners or the whole prisoner (who would normally be killed by the impact of the fall), the carcasses of dead animals or other rubbish: anything which would demoralise the enemy or damage the enemy's defences. The exception was the use of Greek fire. Exactly what went into this substance is not known, but it appears to have been based on oil or pitch. It could be stored in jars and even fired in jars; it could be fired burning from a catapult and would set fire to whatever it landed on; it burned anywhere, even on water, and could only be extinguished by being smothered (for instance, with sand) or with vinegar – presumably, acid. While this incendiary device was known and used by both the Byzantines and the Muslims throughout the medieval period, it is difficult to find references to it being used by the Catholic Christians of western Europe. In the eighth century an incendiary paste was in use: it was smeared on arrows and lit before the arrows were loosed, or smeared on stones and lit, and the stones were then hurled from a machine into the enemy's fortifications.[47] Whether this was Greek fire or not, the purpose was the same. Greek fire was probably used at the siege of Montreuil-Bellay in 1151 by Count Geoffrey V of Anjou; it may have been used by Frederick II at Viterbo in 1249, and during a river siege of Cologne by Archbishop Konrad of Cologne in 1252. Jean Froissart describes the English and Germans discussing how to capture a castle in the 1350s by hurling burning material into it by cannon 'in the manner of Greek Fire', but this was not in fact Greek fire.[48] The recipe was a secret, guarded by the technical experts who manufactured it, but it would have been possible for a western ruler to employ one of these experts; it is not clear why they seldom did. Possibly it was not widely used because the essential ingredient, pitch, was not easily obtainable in the West.[49] It is also possible that it was regarded as such a destructive weapon that it should not be used, either because it was dishonourable, or because it was a sin, or because no one wanted it to be used against them and therefore they did not use it; as if they were observing an unwritten 'arms ban' treaty.[50]

Gunpowder was invented in China in the eighth or ninth century AD, where it was used in bombs, grenades, rockets and fireworks. It may have been used as a propellant in a type of gun in India as early as the early twelfth century; the Chinese themselves developed cannon in the late thirteenth or early fourteenth centuries. Gunpowder was known in Europe by the second half of the thirteenth century, as it is mentioned in the works of Albert the Great (d. 1280) and Roger Bacon (d. 1291). However, there is no definite evidence of its being used as a propellant in a weapon of war until the 1320s, when guns were used at the siege of Metz in 1324, and appear in a Florentine armoury inventory in 1326. The earliest known pictures of guns show dart-firing machines: the barrel resembles a vase, laid on its side, mounted on a table-like surface, and being ignited from a safe distance by a soldier holding a long taper to a hole in the base of the 'vase' (the 'breech').[51]

It is not known how effective these early guns were. Certainly, simply the terrible noise that they made in firing would be enough to throw the opposing army into panic, at least in the early days. Documentary records indicate that guns were being manufactured in France by 1340.[52] Froissart states that there were cannon at the siege of Calais in 1347,[53] and indicates that 'cannons' and 'bombards' were being used regularly in sieges by the 1350s, not only to fire stone shot or darts but also incendiary devices.[54] In 1377, Duke Philip the Bold of Burgundy set up his cannon to attack the castle of Odruik, and fired up to seven shots of 200 (pounds) weight to scare the people inside. Some of these shots went straight through the walls, holing them, to the great alarm of the besieged.[55] Similar stories had been told of the effects of a counterweight trebuchet at Castelnaudry during the Albigensian crusade in 1211. Froissart's stories may have been exaggerated, but they indicate that by the 1370s gunpowder artillery was equal to the best of the old stone-throwing artillery. Thirty years later, when Christine de Pisan was writing her treatise on warfare, she gave the old stone-throwing engines far less attention than the new technology; a commander preparing a siege needed cannon, and the bigger the better. As the big guns needed to be set up on legs under a mantle, they were not easily portable. Hence big guns were not much used on the battlefield until the Hussites mounted them on battle wagons in the 1420s.

The terms 'cannon' and 'bombard' were used to describe the great guns of the fourteenth century onwards. It has been suggested that the bombard was invented in the 1380s by a German alchemist friar named Berthold Schwarz, who was credited by fifteenth-century tradition with the invention of both the gun and gunpowder.[56] Christine de Pisan preferred the term *canon*, 'cannon', but by the late fifteenth century the term 'bombard' was usually used for the great guns, such as Mons Meg, which was given to King James II of Scotland by Duke Philip the Good of Burgundy in 1457 and still stands in Edinburgh Castle; Dulle Griet, made in the mid-fifteenth century for the dukes of Burgundy; and the Basel Bombard, captured by the Swiss from the defeated army of Charles the Bold of Burgundy in 1476. Dulle Griet is 5.01 metres long with a bore of 0.64 of a metre (16.5 feet long, bore just over 25 inches); Mons Meg is 4.04 metres long with a bore of 0.5 metres (13.25 feet long, bore nearly 20 inches); the Basel Bombard is smaller, 2.71 metres long with a bore of 0.34 of a metre (nearly nine feet long, bore just over 13 inches). They are all constructed from hammer-welded wrought iron. While historians have reported that some cannons had removable powder chambers to make transportation easier, these massive bombards were not designed to be taken to pieces.[57] It is particularly interesting that all three were built in the duchy of Burgundy during the central part of the fifteenth century. The wars of the dukes of Burgundy, their territorial ambitions, their military aspirations, their wealth, their support of learning and their innovative approach to their affairs all help to explain why this was so. It is notable, however, that – as Contamine pointed out – clear superiority in artillery in the field did not give Charles the Bold victory at Grandson or at Murten in 1476.[58]

Such huge guns would fire stone shot, as Christine de Pisan described in her treatise. She also mentions lead being used to make smaller shot. Cast iron was of such poor quality at this period that it might explode in the barrel.[59] There is also some evidence of incendiary materials being fired from cannon.[60]

As the cannon displaced the traditional stonethrower from the field, so the handgun would eventually replace the crossbow. It is not clear when hand-held guns first appeared; possibly in the 1330s, but probably not until the early fifteenth century.[61] For a long time the main use of handguns was to terrify the enemy, and any shots which actually killed a man were simply bad luck for him. When the famous warrior Bayart and the duke of Nemours charged the Venetian lines at Brescia in 1512, the Venetians were firing their cannon and *hacquebutts*, but were unable to halt the charge. Bayart was wounded in the thigh, but by a pike in hand-to-hand fighting, not by a gun. Again, at Ravenna in 1512, the French advanced despite the cannon, coulevrines (or culverins) and hacquebutts being fired by the enemy; and when Bayart was shot by a faulconneau (or 'falcon') at a battle at Pavia in the same year, his men stanched his wound and he recovered. He was finally killed by a shot from a Spanish hacquebutt during the retreat from Robecco in April 1524; the horror and sorrow of his men and the Spanish suggests that they had not expected such a death, and that such deaths were still unusual.[62]

The culverins and hacquebutts were smaller guns, which could be carried by hand and could be set up on a stand to be fired. The name 'culverin' (a mythical fire-breathing serpent), like the 'snakes' which the Hussites used, refers to the long, narrow shape of the weapon. The 'falcon' was a larger gun, too large to carry by hand, but small enough to be conveniently moved and used in a battlefield situation.[63] Mortars were short guns, with their barrel about the same length as the width of their bore, and intended to fire shells with a high trajectory.[64]

* * *

The crossbow, however, survived long after the coming of the handgun, as the early handgun was inaccurate and took even longer to load than the crossbow. The crossbow was also much quieter, which was an advantage in, for instance, a night attack. The technology of the crossbow is similar to that of the simple bow, but in the crossbow the string is held under greater tension than in the simple bow, and is held back with a trigger until the archer is ready to fire. Like so many instruments mentioned in these pages, the hand-held crossbow was invented by the Chinese, in the fifth century BC, and probably came into the Roman world in the first century AD, where it was used for hunting. Initially called simply a *machina*, the Latin term *ballista* seems to have been applied to it by the fourth century, although the large *ballista* that the Romans used as field artillery was powered by torsion rather than tension. The hand-held crossbow was probably used in the Byzantine Empire, but by the twelfth century the historian Anna Comnena regarded it – at least the version used by the crusaders – as a barbarian weapon. It was not mentioned in western European sources between the fifth and the tenth centuries, although archaeological evidence indicates its continued use. It is mentioned at the siege of Senlis in 947 and at Verdun in 985, and was used in Islamic countries from the late ninth century.[65]

The fact that more references to crossbows appear in European sources from the eleventh century onwards indicate that the crossbow had become a more popular, and therefore probably a more effective weapon, although historians differ over how it had improved.[66] It was not a quick weapon to use, because spanning the bow (drawing back the string, locking it back with the 'trigger' and placing the arrow or bolt in position, ready to fire) took much longer than for the simple bow. But it could be used effectively by a comparative novice and was much more powerful than the simple bow. In a siege situation, or where a large group of crossbow archers were operating together on a battlefield, it could be devastating, for it could pierce chain mail. Because it could kill at a distance, and did not need extensive training for effective use, it was regarded as a dishonourable weapon, although kings were well able to use it: King Philip II of France and King Richard I of England used crossbows during the siege of Acre in 1191.[67] From the twelfth century onwards crossbows improved in effectiveness, although even more time must be spent in spanning the weapon before a shot. In the fifteenth century steel crossbows were produced, spanned with the aid of a windlass – a system of pulleys and ropes to wind back the bowstring – or a winch called a *cranequin*, a rack and pinion device wound by a handle.[68] The crossbow was still used as a military weapon at the beginning of the sixteenth century in France, Spain and Germany, although it was passing out of general use; it remained an important military weapon until the 1570s in Scandinavia.[69]

Spanning a crossbow could require considerable physical strength. In contrast, anyone could use an ordinary bow, including women, children and the elderly; and so the 'simple bow', which was cheaper and simpler in construction than the crossbow, continued in use. Mounted archers had

been used by the Roman army, but were less used by the armies that succeeded them. The lack of use of bows in warfare in the Merovingian period has been considered briefly at the beginning of Chapter 2. In the
Carolingian period, however, the bow came back into favour: in 802–3
Charlemagne laid down that all infantry should carry a bow, with a spare
string and 12 arrows.[70] The Muslims of Spain and the Middle East made
much use of horse-archers, and to some degree their Latin Christian opponents imitated them.[71] Evidence from the Bayeux Tapestry indicates that
the Normans made effective use of foot-archers alongside their cavalry.

The length of bow staves varied: the Franks used long bows of around
six feet or up to two metres long, as well as shorter bows. Jim Bradbury
has suggested that the Normans' bows used at the Battle of Hastings in
1066 were around five feet long.[72] He has also argued convincingly that
the so-called 'long bow' of the later Middle Ages was simply the traditional wooden bow, produced slightly longer than in the eleventh century
as a consequence of improvements in manufacture and in response to user
requirements. He suggests an average length of around six feet, but adds
that the length of the stave must have varied with the height of the
archer.[73] The use of these bows by the English army at Crécy, Poitiers and
Agincourt has already been described. Even the Teutonic Order in Prussia,
which made extensive employment of Genoese crossbowmen, saw that the
English 'ordinary wooden bow', as Bradbury terms it, could be a better
weapon, for archers using these bows could keep up a continual stream of
arrows, whereas crossbowmen had to stop to 'reload'. The problem was
that skilled archers were in short supply; the English king employed most
of those available.[74]

By the twelfth century the bow, as a 'peasant's weapon' which could be
operated at a safe distance from the enemy, was looked down upon by
knights,[75] even though they all learnt how to use it. Other weapons suffered similarly: the sling was typically the weapon of the animal herder;[76]
the Taborites' battle flails, used during the Hussite wars of the 1420s, were
simply their agricultural flails adapted to a new use; while the mace, or
club, was obviously a weapon that even a peasant could afford to make,
although the knightly mace was a more impressive object, with either a
flanged or knobbed head. Although Duke William of Normandy is depicted on the Bayeux Tapestry carrying a mace at the Battle of Hastings,[77] the
weapon later lost status. In 'fictional' literature of the thirteenth century
onwards the mace was always the weapon of the giant, invariably a barbarian without knightly skill or courtesy; possibly this role also indicates
that the mace was regarded as somewhat old-fashioned and simplistic. On
the other hand, in the fourteenth and fifteenth centuries fine maces were
manufactured for noble clients; perhaps the weapon's ferocious reputation
could be a point in its favour.[78]

The axe was another traditional weapon, which was also available to
peasants and thus could be regarded, by the twelfth century, as a non-

knightly weapon. It was used by the Germanic tribes during the Roman Empire, not simply as a hand-held weapon but thrown as a missile.[79] The throwing axe became less important by the end of the sixth century, but the hand-held axe became a major weapon. Most famously used by the Vikings, it was wielded by the Anglo-Saxons at the Battle of Hastings (according to the Bayeux Tapestry), by King Stephen of England at the Battle of Lincoln in 1141, and by the famous noble knight Geoffrey of Lusignan during the Third Crusade.[80] Though it was still used by the nobility after the late twelfth century, the axe, like the mace, was 'not quite' a noble weapon; perhaps seen as barbarous, or old fashioned. It was, after all, the weapon used by the barbarous Irish, as emphasised by Gerald of Wales – Gerald noted that the Irish had taken it from the Vikings.[81] But the axe was also a vicious weapon in skilled hands, and therefore frowned on in some quarters and admired in others. So, for instance, Froissart commented on the doughty Sir John Chandos using an axe at the battle of Auray in October 1364.[82] In the fourteenth century the battle-axe was reborn as the poleaxe, the halberd and other 'staff' weapons – that is, weapons consisting basically of a blade on a long staff.

While these were, in theory, obvious developments from farming tools, they developed into high precision killing instruments. By the late fourteenth century the poleaxe had become the principal weapon of the knight when fighting on foot, requiring considerable practice to handle it with skill, and capable of killing an armed man in combat. It had a pointed spearhead on one end and a sharp axe head and hammer on the other; it could be spun around in combat to hit first with axe, then hammer, then stab with the spear. Its sharp points and blades could penetrate the new plate armour, which was capable of withstanding a couched lance in the cavalry charge or an arrow or crossbow bolt.[83] Yet, because it was not well balanced, it was predominantly a weapon of single combat, not of the battlefield.[84]

Other such infantry weapons which did not become weapons of the nobility included the *goedendag* or 'good day', already noted in Chapter 2, a long pole with spear head at one end and a mace head at the other that was wielded by the Flemish infantry. Another was the halberd, a spear with a spearhead combined with an axe head. It was also possible to include a billhook on its multiform head.[85] Frisian warriors from at least the twelfth century carried long pole-spears, over 13 feet long, with a spearhead at one end and a small thick disc at the other. These performed a double function; they acted as weapons, and were used as poles to leap over the ditches and watercourses which criss-crossed their land. The disc was to prevent the pole from sinking into the mud when it was used to vault over ditches.[86]

* * *

The primary weapons of the nobility during the period from the late eleventh century to 1500 were the lance and the sword. The lance, made from wood – ash wood was preferred [87] – varied in thickness and in length, but an average cavalry lance would be around four metres long (13 feet).[88] It could be shortened to make it more easily aimed or to enable it to be used for fighting on foot; Froissart describes lances being cut down to five feet long (1.5 metres) for this purpose.[89] Richard I and his knights fought with canes outside Messina in Sicily for their own amusement; but lances could also be very much thicker.[90] Presumably thickness and length could be varied for the strength of the person who would be wielding the lance.

The lance obviously developed from the spear, and the terms for the two weapons can be interchangeable in the sources. The spear could be an infantry weapon or a cavalry weapon, and had been used as both by the Roman army. The Roman infantry used a short, throwing spear, the *pilum*, as well as spears to be wielded by the cavalry. The early Franks used throwing spears;[91] but the Carolingians used their spears generally for thrusting rather than as javelins. In 802–3 Charlemagne decreed that his infantry should carry lances. In 792–3 and again in 804 and 811 he declared that his cavalry should be armed with spears.[92]

Charlemagne's insistence that his cavalry be armed with spears immediately calls to mind the later descriptions of the cavalry charge with the couched lance. Formed into a tightly grouped squadron, the cavalry would lower their lances so that they stretched out horizontally in front of them, far beyond their horse's nose ('couched' means 'stretched out'). They swung their shields (normally carried slung over their backs from a strap around their necks) on to their arms, and spurred their horse forward at a gallop. Just before the moment of impact on the enemy they let go of the reins and gripped lance in right hand, shield in left. With the impact of horse and rider together, if the lance hit its target, it could go straight through a shield, through chain-mail armour, and straight through the opponent, throwing him backwards off his horse or spitting him on the lance.

That is how the cavalry charge is described in the knightly literature of the twelfth century onwards. But when was it first used? The Bayeux Tapestry shows knights holding lances in various poses; as if to throw them, as if to stab with them or as if charging with them couched. This suggests that the charge with couched lance was not the invariable practice in 1066 – although admittedly the knights on the Tapestry were charging infantry, not other knights. Although it used to be believed that the cavalry charge was a revolutionary development of the late eleventh century, historians now suggest that the charge was a tactic that developed over a long period of time, or that had long been known but which became more significant from the twelfth century.[93]

Historians have debated why the cavalry charge developed. Lynn White in his *Medieval Technology and Social Change* (1962) argued that the cru-

cial factor was the introduction of the stirrup, which enabled the warrior
to sit firmly in the saddle and not to be thrown off by the shock of impact
with the opponent. However, the stirrup was first used in western Europe
long before evidence indicates the use of the couched lance, and it seems
much more likely that the crucial change was the development of the high
pommel saddle, which held the warrior tightly in position on the horse
whatever blows were struck or received.[94] While it was possible to conduct a cavalry charge without this type of saddle, it was far more likely to
be effective with such a saddle.

The cavalry charge was the military manoeuvre *par excellence* in later
medieval warfare. Properly executed, it could break the enemy's battle-
lines and enable the enemy ranks to be divided and cut down. The infantry
could follow the cavalry, cutting down those who had been struck aside
by the cavalry. However, a cavalry charge was not always effective against
archers (the horses had to be properly armoured) or on treacherous
ground, or against well-drilled infantry who held their ground and did not
give way – or who divided to allow the charge through, and then reformed
ranks to attack the infantry. Vegetius pointed out that caltrops could be
used against chariots; arguably they could also be used against horses
without the chariots. The cavalry had to be well disciplined; after the initial charge, they must reform and charge again. Yet the problems of using
cavalry could be overcome to some extent by a careful commander. Being
on horseback gave the cavalry speed and manoeuvrability, and as they
were invariably of higher social status than most of the infantry, the
cavalry received the most attention from commentators.

Once a warrior's lance had broken, he should draw his sword.[95] This
again was a weapon with a long history. The Gauls had used long slashing swords, which bent when they had been used and had to be straight-
ened again before the battle could continue.[96] The classic weapon of the
Roman army was the *gladius*, a short, stabbing sword; Bachrach argues
that the Frankish short sword of the seventh and eighth centuries developed from this. But the Franks also used long, double-edged swords for
slashing.[97] The sword was expensive to manufacture; a sword that would
not bend or smash in use had to be forged with care. So swords were very
valuable, to be passed down from one generation to the next. Famous
swords were named; and the most famous, in the French epics of the
twelfth and thirteenth century, were ascribed to the craftsmanship of
Galaan the smith, the divine Wayland of Norse epic. Descriptions of
swords in twelfth-century epic, such as the *Chanson de Roland*, state that
the hilts contained relics of saints, such as bones and teeth, as well as valuable jewels, and that words might be inscribed on the blade, particularly
the name of the manufacturer (Galaan in the epics).[98] Swords were a
means of displaying the wealth of the owner.

The manufacture of the sword followed a standard pattern from the
ninth century to the mid-fourteenth: swords were long and flat, with sharp

edges, designed to slash and penetrate leather or chain mail armour at a distance. Some historians have argued that, with the introduction of plate armour during the fourteenth century, the old design of sword was no longer effective; the sword had to thrust (as in Roman times) rather than slash. Hence swords again became shorter, with sharper points. Anglo's study shows that fourteenth- and fifteenth-century masters of arms recommended both cut and thrust in sword fighting. Nevertheless, the shorter swords produced at this period would seem to favour the thrust.[99] The fourteenth- or fifteenth-century prose work *Saladin* has the famous French knight Andrew de Chavigny declaring that a short sword brings a man closer to his enemy, implying that it was cowardly to stay too far away.[100]

The most crucial part of the noble warrior's equipment was the horse. The horse could be used for transport to battle, or for transport in battle; one would not use the same animal for both. It is true that in some parts of Europe horses were hardly used by warriors: in Frisia, horses were merely an inconvenience, for they could not easily cross the ditches; in the rough terrain of Ireland, Wales and Scotland, and the forests and marshes of Prussia, Lithuania and Livonia, warriors might well prefer to ride to battle and then dismount to fight. But possession of a horse was a sign of status everywhere. A riding horse could be a gelding or a mare; a warhorse, a *destrier*, should be a stallion. The fictional literature of the twelfth to fifteenth centuries suggests that medieval war-horses could be very tall, but the evidence of archaeology and medieval art indicates that actually this was wishful thinking. Knights might dream of Gringalet or Bayart (the horses of Lord Gawain and the Four Sons of Aymon respectively), wonderfully tall, strong horses which could gallop all day without getting tired and carry four adult men with ease, but they were stuck with an animal not over 15 hands high, so that the knight would have stood shoulder to shoulder with his horse.[101]

Some might wonder why the nobility persisted with the use of the horse in battle. They were troublesome to transport overseas, requiring special slings to carry them by ship; when they arrived they took several days to recover from the ordeal.[102] When they went on crusade to the Middle East they had to be trained to become accustomed to the shortage of water, just as the Australian cavalry were trained when they campaigned in the Middle East during the First World War. During the Palestinian Campaign of 1914–18 the horses sometimes had to go without water for two days at a time, and presumably the same problem occurred during the crusades and campaigns of 1095–1291.[103] There were certainly many occasions when it was better to dismount to fight (as at Agincourt in 1415, when the ground was too muddy to use cavalry effectively) and if a knight's horse was killed under him he might well have to fight on foot whether he liked or not. Yet, despite its drawbacks, the horse gave the medieval noble status; it was the symbol of his superior position in society. An army of mounted knights, in armour and with their banners flying, was, as

Froissart declared, a beautiful sight.[104] The ceremonies and festivities of the nobility in the later Middle Ages were centred on the figure of the mounted warrior: the tournament, the banquets based on Arthurian legend. The horse was a means of displaying nobility – even more so when it was armoured, or covered with magnificent coloured trappings. The medieval nobleman was hardly going to give up his horse and go on foot like the rest of society. He might dismount temporarily for tactical reasons, but when the battle was over he would get back on his horse again.

* * *

Armour underwent dramatic changes during our period; from the plates sewn on to leather of the Roman army, to scales sewn on to leather and chain mail, to cloth-covered armour (designed to withstand lance thrusts) and finally to plate. With each change, the cost increased – with the exception of cloth-covered armour, which was within the reach of the humble infantryman. Armour originally included a shield, but with the advent of plate armour the shield was no longer necessary, although the infantryman might use a small shield on his arm, a buckler. The wearing of armour was regarded by those in the centre of Catholic Europe as an indication of wealth, and of a civilised society, in the Roman tradition. Gerald of Wales's insistence in his 'History and Topography of Ireland', written in the 1180s, that the Irish did not wear armour formed part of his thesis that the Irish were barbarous and corrupt, and that King Henry II of England had God's support in conquering and civilising them.[105] Again, the Frisians, another group on the outside of European chivalric society, did not conform to the European standard in armour, generally lacking a helmet.[106]

The Roman soldier since republican times had body armour of metal strips sewn on to leather, and covering his shoulders (the *lorica*). He also had a rounded helmet, which protected the back of the neck and the cheeks, but left the front of the face uncovered (the *cassis* or *galea*). In the late Empire, the metal-strip armour was replaced with chain mail; either of interwoven metal links or of metal scales fixed on to a linen backing. Both of these ideally required an undergarment of leather to prevent chaffing. It has been argued that these new forms of *loricae* were less protective than the old version, but were cheaper. However, they did cover a larger part of the body, because they went half way down the thigh or to the knee, and could be given sleeves to protect the arms. They also allowed for greater manoeuvrability by the wearer.

Metal armour was expensive. Apparently, not all of those who fought in the armies of western Europe in the fifth century to the eighth century wore metal body armour, as it seldom appears in graves with the owner's other personal possessions. However, one could argue that the fact that armour was only rarely buried with its owner does not mean that the owner had no armour, but that this valuable equipment had been passed on to his sons. The Vikings' disdain for body armour was well advertised, and certainly formed part of their ferocious reputation.

Shields were traditionally made from strips of wood, covered in leather. There would be a metal boss in the centre to hold the shield together. It would be carried by a leather strap that went over the arm. Ideally, it should have an adjustable strap, or a longer strap in addition to the short arm strap, so that it could be slung over the back when on the move. The traditional shield, as used by the Roman army and by the Germanic tribes who took over the government of the Western Empire from the fifth century onwards, was a large object which covered most of the body from chin to knee and on which a dead or wounded warrior could be carried from the battlefield. But shields came in different shapes and sizes: there were large rectangular shields, small round shields, convex shields that curved around the body, and elliptical shields. Which sort of shield was used depended on the user: a cavalryman would require a smaller, lighter shield which would not impede the horse, while an infantryman would want something to cover most of the body. The fact that classical Latin had at least five words for 'shield': *scutum, clipeus, parma, pelta, ancile*, indicates not only that there was a variety of shields, but also that they were very important to this military-minded people.

The first definite information about what armour medieval warriors were expected to wear on active service comes from law codes. Between 680 and 687 the Visigothic King Ervig produced a legal code in which he decreed that some of his warriors should wear armour, and most should have shields, suggesting that until this point some had been coming for service without this equipment. Likewise, in 750 King Aistulf of the Lombards laid down that his richest and most powerful nobles would be armed with full armour, including a shield and weapons.[107]

Charlemagne set out in a series of capitularies (laws) of 792–3, 802–3 and 805 various regulations about the armour that his warriors should supply for themselves. All those holding offices or benefices in his kingdom should own a full set of armour, including a shield; a horse and weapons; they should have their own helmets and byrnies (a coat of chain mail or scale armour, although historians disagree over exactly how it was constructed). The capitulary of 805 stated that all those who held more than 12 manses of land should have their own armour and serve as a cavalryman in the army. Failure to comply would mean loss of land and armour. The capitulary of 802–3 also required all infantry to bring a shield.[108]

The visual evidence of the Bayeux tapestry, produced in the late eleventh century, has been much used by historians attempting to establish the details of the armour worn in contemporary mainstream western Europe. The tapestry appears to show the warriors wearing chain-mail shirts, with a mail hood which can be drawn up over the head, and a chin-piece which laced on to the hood and covered the lower face, and which when unlaced fell down across the upper chest as a square of mail. The edges of the mail are bound with leather, or possibly cloth. Some of the warriors are wearing chain-mail leggings; but most wear cloth (or leather) around the lower legs, some held up by cross-lacing and some with no visible means of support. The mail shirts are slit front and rear to enable the wearer to walk easily and to ride a horse, and reach to just below the knee. They have sleeves, which reach three-quarters of the way down the arm, but there are no coverings for the hands. Warriors also wear a conical helmet over the hood of the mail shirt, with a nose-piece to protect the nose. They carry a long, kite-shaped shield on their left arm, a long sword on the left hip (apparently worn under the mail shirt, with the hilt poking through a purpose-made slit in the mail), and a lance carried in the right hand. Some of the shields are decorated with various patterns, presumably to aid recognition of the warrior on the battlefield. A few of the Saxons' shields are oval or round rather than kite-shaped. There is insufficient space here to go into discussion of the manufacture of these items of armour, which has been discussed by others elsewhere.[109]

There is much the pictures do not tell us: for instance, what was worn under the mail shirt (we assume a padded leather or cloth undergarment) or how the mail leggings (later called *chausses*) were held up: later evidence indicates that they were laced up the back; they may also have been attached with straps to a belt at the waist, as were the cloth *chausses* worn by men in everyday life. It is possible that the square of mail on the chest of the mail shirt is not the unlaced chin-piece but special reinforcement. However, we know that the chain-mail chin-piece appeared soon afterwards as part of the mail hood or *coif*; it was called a 'ventilator', the *ventaille*, and was laced to the coif, protecting the lower face and neck. Many a fictional epic or romance of the twelfth century onwards reaches its climax as the defeated knight's *ventaille* is unlaced and he is told that he must declare himself defeated (*outré*) or die.

From the twelfth century onwards, with increased economic growth and rapid technological advance in metal working, the complexity and strength of armour increased rapidly. Armour could be double- or triple-mesh chain mail; hand-coverings were introduced to protect the hands, and foot-coverings added to the *chausses*. The body could be totally covered in mail armour. Even the face was virtually covered with mail, and as helmets became more all-covering – the full-face *healme* ('helm') appeared in the early thirteenth century – it became impossible to recognise a knight in his armour, a fact which was exploited to its limits (and *ad nauseam*) by the fiction writers of the day. Inside the full-faced helmet, even the knight's voice was distorted. How, then, could a warrior be recognised? The answer was through the decoration on the surcoat and the shield.

The surcoat first appears in illustrations of the second half of the twelfth century, in white. It was effectively a long sleeveless shirt, slit back and front to allow for movement. Originally it simply kept the sun off the mail shirt, helping to keep the wearer cool in sunny climates. But by the late twelfth century it was being used to display the owners' distinctive symbols.

From at least the early twelfth century, and possibly earlier if the shields in the Bayeux Tapestry are a guide, warriors were putting symbols on their shields to help them to be recognised on the battlefield and on the tournament field. Initially these symbols were not hereditary, but there was an obvious advantage for all the members of one family, who would be fighting together and who would want to be able to recognise each other, to have the same or very similar symbols on their shields. If they carried a banner on the battlefield, the symbol would also be on the banner. These symbols were also appearing on their personal seals by the 1140s, and when warriors began to wear surcoats they also appeared there. Their wives also placed their husband's and their own family's symbols on their seals, and on their clothes.[110]

We may wonder where these symbols came from. Some symbols have stories attached; others, such as a snarling lion or an eagle or a dragon, have an obvious military significance. We may only speculate how far the initial designs were adopted on the spur of the moment, and who originally produced a symbol and said: 'Wear that; then I'll be able to spot you on the battlefield.' In that wives were frequently depicted in literature and in visual arts arming their husbands for battle, and in that one of the purposes of the tournament was to win a warrior a good reputation for his military prowess in the eyes of the women of his class, it is possible that the women had as much influence over the adoption of military symbols as the men. Again, it would have been the women of the household who were responsible for producing the design on the surcoat and on the banner, for needlework was a woman's skill.

The armour of the thirteenth century, for all its all-covering nature, was still not complete protection. While it is true that the nobility were seldom killed on the battlefield, chain mail was not an effective protection against a lance thrust or a stabbing sword; it only protected against slashes. The full-face helmet protected the face and was a fine vehicle for display – all sorts of symbols could be mounted on the top – but allowed for little visibility by the wearer and was rather heavy. Infantry did not use the full-faced helmet, but a *chape de fer*, a steel cap, or kettle hat. This was a conical helmet with a wide brim to protect the back of the neck and the face. In the fourteenth century, the bascinet or basinet was developed, a close-fitting conical helmet that covered most of the face except eyes, nose and mouth and might have a moveable visor to protect those areas; this was much used by infantry, and also by cavalry.[111]

Plate armour first appeared in the late thirteenth century, as small pieces to protect vulnerable parts of the body: the shoulders, the knees and the elbows. One form of plate armour was the cloth-covered plate armour known as the 'coat of plates' or *brigantine*. This had strips of metal placed horizontally across the body, encased in padded cloth, to form a jacket. The brigantine was relatively cheap and allowed for great mobility, while protecting the body. In kettle hat and brigantine, the infantry were secure against most things that the cavalry could throw at them. The outer cloth covering could be decorated with the symbols of the infantryman's employer, or left plain. It could also be shaped to act like a corset, emphasising the manly curves of the wearer; the noble knight and writer Geoffrey de Charny complained that such garments restricted knights' movements in battle and had led to some being killed.[112]

The nobility often wore simply a brigantine. However, from the mid-fourteenth century solid breastplates of steel also began to appear on battlefields. These covered the upper torso: chest, back and sides. The waist and hips were protected by hoops of metal riveted to cloth, on the same sort of principle as Roman republican armour. This itself was soon superseded by a sort of skirt of metal hoops to cover the waist and hips. The breast-and-back plate was worn by infantry soldiers as well as by cavalry.[113]

Complete coats of plate were in general use by the early fifteenth century. Those wearing these did not cover the beauty of the burnished white metal with surcoats. Nor did they need to carry a shield; the armour itself was sufficient. It was possible to add a lance-rest to the right side of the chest, and a chin-and-neck protector could also be added. Chain-mail foot and hand protection had been replaced by overlapping plates fashioned to form *sabatons* (shoes) or gauntlets; the *chausses* were replaced by greaves made of plate. The helmet, which in the thirteenth century had tended to being flat topped, became curved again (deflecting blows more effectively). The moveable visor was developed in the early fourteenth century, so that the front of the helmet could be opened sideways or upwards to allow the warrior to cool off a little.[114]

Plate armour was heavy and took a long time to put on, but because it was carefully shaped to fit the body and distributed its weight evenly around the body it may have been easier to move in than chain mail.[115] Because no surcoat was worn, the helmet and the banner (if the owner had one) were the only means of showing the wearer's identity. In the sixteenth century a method of gilding armour was developed, so that armour itself could be decorated. It had long been possible to varnish armour, to prevent it becoming rusty as soon as it rained; now it was possible to cover armour with the wearer's own heraldic design.[116]

* * *

Other forms of military equipment were also used on the battlefield. For example, banners were a type of standard, a symbol of a military leader that was displayed on the battlefield as a rallying point. The Roman army had famously had eagles as the standards for legions, and dragon-standards for the cohorts.[117] A banner often had religious significance: Christian armies frequently had a cross on their banner, or the image of a local saint. The medieval standard is well described by the author-compiler of the *Itinerarium peregrinorum et gesta regis Ricardi*, a complete account of the Third Crusade:

> It is a very long beam like a ship's mast placed on very solid planks on top of four wheels, held together by joints. It is covered with iron and appears invulnerable to sword, axe or fire. From the very top flutters the king's flag, which is commonly called 'the banner'. It is the custom to assign a force of elite knights to protect this implement, especially in the field of battle, so that it may not be broken down by hostile attack or knocked down by some injury; because if it happened to be knocked down by some accident then the army would be thrown into confusion and scattered because it would not see any rallying point. ... the infirm and wounded are brought here to be cared for and even those who happen to be killed in battle are brought here if they were renowned or illustrious men. So it stands, strongly constructed 'to rally the peoples' [Isaiah ch. 11 v. 10]. Because it stands, it is called a Standard. It is sensible to have it placed on wheels because it can be drawn forward as the enemy falls back or drawn back as they attack, according to the state of the battle.[118]

The banner, in this case Richard I's banner with two lions *passant regardant*, formed part of the standard; it was the symbol fluttering from the top of the pole. But the whole equipage, pole, banner and wheeled cart, together made up the standard. In Italy, such standards formed a focus for civic pride: mounted on richly decorated carts, drawn by oxen and with a large bodyguard of infantry. The first *carroccio* of this sort was set up at Milan in 1039; by the late twelfth century other cities such as Parma, Cremona, Bologna, Florence and Pavia had adopted the custom.[119]

Standards did not need to be so complex; Richard's was designed for an army on the march, so that if it were attacked, the whole army, stretched out in a long column over many miles, had some opportunity of seeing where the standard was. In a battlefield situation the standard would normally be the commander's banner on a long pole, carried by a leading warrior (or, in certain circumstances such as a crusade, a cleric). That warrior must hold the banner upright at all times, which would impede his ability to fight; so a bodyguard was required. The enemy would be anxious to capture the banner or to knock it to the ground, for when the banner vanished, the army was reckoned to be defeated and its troops would retreat from the field.[120]

How many banners could there be on the field? In theory, every knight *banneret* had his own banner with his own warriors who would follow it into battle. Sir John Chandos was made a knight banneret in 1360, but did not display his banner in battle until 1367, when he asked the express permission of his commander, Edward the Black Prince. On the other hand, one Sir Guy de Blois who was made a squire in Prussia in 1367 displayed his banner in the field at once.[121] In practice, on a battlefield one banner should be supreme, the banner of the commander-in-chief; that was the banner that all should follow. Other banners displayed could be a sign of rebellion.[122] But at tournaments and other festival occasions, every warrior of sufficient rank to have his own banner displayed it with pride.

Banners could also be used for signalling to the troops, either before battle began or during battle. Vegetius's description of military signals remained true throughout the Middle Ages: the 'voiced', the 'semi-voiced' and the 'mute' (Book 3, Chapter 5). The 'voiced' signal was the password for the night watch, or the battle cry: just as Froissart's pages ring with the French battle cry of 'Montjoie, Saint Denys!' while the English reply 'Saint George! Guyenne!'[123] 'Semi-voiced' signals were the audible signals given by trumpets, horns or bugles. By sounding, these could give the signal to advance or to fall back. For example, at the battle of Arsūf on 7 September 1191 the signal to attack the Muslims was given by six trumpets being blown at three different places in the crusader army: two at the front of the army, two in the middle and two at the rear. 'This was so that the Christians' signal could be distinguished from the Saracens', for the Muslims were also blowing trumpets, sounding horns and banging drums, not only in order to give signals but also to terrify their enemy. As it happened, however, two of the Christian knights charged too soon, and the rest followed without waiting for the trumpets to blow.[124]

As for the 'mute' signals, Vegetius described the standard bearer advancing where the general commanded, holding up the standard so that all could see and follow. Alternatively, the general could give directions by gesturing with a whip or clothing.[125] Banners could also be used to give visual signals without the bearer having to advance. At its crudest, the descent of the banner meant that the army should withdraw. The unfurling of a banner indicated open war had begun.[126] The *Prophecies de Merlin*, written in French by a Venetian in the 1270s, describes banners of different colours being used to give signals on a battlefield; one colour is raised for one section of the army to advance, a different colour for a different section of the army.[127] The detail given in this 'fictional' source indicates that this was actual Venetian practice at the time of writing, although it is difficult to find examples of such usage in the 'historical' sources. To take an example of slightly different usage from outside Christendom: during the siege of Acre in 1189–91, the Muslims inside the city raised a flag as a call for aid from the Muslim army encamped beyond the besieging Christian army.[128] Flags could be used for sending signals outside the context of battle: in fourteenth- and fifteenth-century France, villagers keeping a look out from the church tower for approaching armies could ring the bells to warn of danger, but if the use of the bells for such a secular purpose was not allowed, they would raise a flag instead.[129] Another form of mute signalling was smoke signals; the besieged Muslims of Acre in 1189–91 used smoke signals to call for help from their compatriots encamped beyond the crusader army, as well as beating on drums.[130]

* * *

During the period covered by this study, some warriors supplied their own arms and armour for battle, although the weapons of professional warriors in permanent employment (for example, in a royal entourage) would normally be supplied to them by their employer, and by the late fifteenth century soldiers in standing armies would expect their arms to be supplied and losses made good. Yet even if the troops supplied their own equipment, a military commander would have to ensure that they had the means of equipping themselves, sometimes to the extent of banning exports of arms; and organise inspections to ensure that the warriors were properly equipped and ready for war.[131] The commander should also ensure that they knew how to use this equipment. It is to this that we must now turn.

5

The practice of land warfare

It is a commonplace among historians of medieval warfare that battle was rarely engaged – as Vegetius had stated, battle should be avoided as far as possible because it involved too many risks and its result was final. It was often better to draw out a campaign and to harass the enemy by burning crops and besieging buildings, rather than commit everything to a few hours of direct engagement. This chapter, therefore, will consider various ways in which warfare was waged, and not simply battles. The discussion will follow the logical course of a campaign, from initial training to the final peace.

*   *   *

Vegetius and all those who followed him agreed that after the army had been recruited it must be trained. Partly, this was a matter of keeping warriors occupied so that they could not get into trouble or start fighting among themselves – a constant concern in armies, where many physically fit males who have been brought up to be aggressive are gathered together in close confinement for many days, often in conditions of great tension. One example of what could go wrong was related by the chronicler and eyewitness Jean le Bel. The English army was assembled at York in 1327 for a campaign against the Scots. Lord Jean of Hainault, uncle of Philippa of Hainault, queen of England, had joined the English with a company of knights and squires. While the army was garrisoned at York, the English archers and the squires of Hainault got into a fight over a game of dice which turned into a serious riot, with the English firing arrows at the Hainaulters. Jean le Bel himself was unable to get into his lodgings and had to take refuge elsewhere. The Hainaulters went in fear of their lives for three weeks, until the campaign got underway.[1]

Training also ensured that soldiers were fit, and that they became accustomed to working together and to obeying commands, thus improving discipline on the field as well as confidence and morale in battle. Vegetius had written that recruits should be trained to march in step, to jump and vault (so that they could cross ditches), and to swim. Every morning they should practise fighting with wicker shields and wooden swords, aiming blows at a wooden post as if at an opponent; they should throw practice-javelins and practise with the bow, the sling and darts. They should prac-tise marching carrying a heavy weight, and be drilled in battle manoeuvres and tactics. They should practise leaping on to a wooden horse from both sides, while holding drawn sword and lance.[2] This was so that if cavalry-men were thrown in battle or their horse was killed under them, they could mount again quickly. In Vegetius's day, before the adoption of the stirrup, this skill was essential; but the ability to mount swiftly continued to be essential for cavalry until recent times, and medieval epics and romances give as one of the characteristics of the doughty knight that he could leap into the saddle without using the stirrup.[3] Modern children who learn to vault on to and over wooden horses at school have little idea that they are learning to mount a horse in a battlefield situation!

There is a problem, however, in establishing what training was actually given to armies during the medieval period. Vegetius's instructions on train-ing were repeated by the medieval writers who translated and adapted his work, but it is not clear how far this systematic training was actually followed. Sometimes the additions of medieval writers are suggestive of actual practice: Bachrach has argued that Hrabanus Maurus's descriptions of recruits practising blows with a club against six-foot wooden posts placed upright in the ground must reflect contemporary ninth-century prac-tice.[4] But other evidence does not mention training: for example, Christine de Pisan subtly adapted Vegetius's instructions to mean that nobles should train their children, reducing training within the army to a minimum.[5] Most modern historians have concluded that training was too expensive and too time-consuming for medieval commanders to invest in.[6] John France notes that William the Bastard's army 'spent much of the summer of 1066 exercising together at Dives, and this may in part account for the control that its commander was able to exert at Hastings'. But he found no other examples.[7] The regulations for the military religious order of the Temple include references to knights practising their arms; but they do not lay down instructions for training, as if the form and procedure for train-ing was not something for the order to dictate.[8] Not until the 1473 ordi-nance of Charles the Bold did a commander lay down a regular training regime to be followed by the troops: 'which seems to have been wholly new', as Vaughan comments. Nevertheless, despite this new training on the classical model, Charles the Bold's army was defeated in the field.[9]

We could argue that it should not have been necessary to train warriors. Whereas the late Roman army was a professional army, recruited from the pacific peasantry and trained for a lifetime's career in war, medieval armies were supposed to be made up of people who were already trained in war. The peasants were expected to bring their own weapons to Charlemagne's army (assuming, therefore, that they knew how to use them); the settlers on the Castilian frontier with the Moors were expected to act as cavalry and footsoldiers in expeditions against the Moors and to defend their towns (so presumably they already knew how to fight); the knights who joined the armies of the Hundred Years War were warriors by right of their birth and their station in society (so should have learnt how to fight in childhood). As there were 'schools of arms' in existence by the thirteenth century, set up by masters of arms to train individuals, individuals could have learnt martial skills before coming to the army.[10]

On the one hand it is true that medieval fictional literature often implies that it was not necessary to train in arms to be a warrior, and that the true-born member of the warrior class could simply don armour, take up arms, mount a horse and ride out to engage the enemy. Hence Rainouart, brother of Guiborc, lady of Orange, although brought up as a servant and a scullion at the court of Louis the Pious, becomes a fully fledged and skilful knight the moment that he is knighted.[11] Again, the bullied noblewoman in *Berengier au lonc cul*, determining to teach her common-born boastful husband a lesson, dons arms, mounts a horse and rides to attack him although – presumably – she has never handled a lance before in her life. At the sight of this fine knight (as he thinks), the husband surrenders without a blow and does homage.[12]

Nevertheless, on the other hand it seems unlikely that the confident knightly stance and handling of the lance could be learned so easily, otherwise knighthood would not have been held in such esteem. The writers of these particular stories were not trying to tell us that knighthood was easy; they were making the socio-political point that only those born to knighthood could learn it. Berengier's husband, a common-born man, finds knighthood very difficult. As medieval literature, both 'fictional' and 'factual', also insists that a warrior should be active and keep up the exercise of arms (the *miles strenuous*),[13] it would be reasonable to assume that real warriors were also expected to practise.

What is more, even trained warriors need to learn how to fight together. Even if it were not necessary to start from scratch, they should learn battle manoeuvres and tactics: for instance, how to fight in close formation. This could be learned by experience in campaign, but until the experience was learned the army would be operating inefficiently.

Yet little information survives on how warriors learned to fight. Some illustrations survive from the later Middle Ages showing children, lance in hand, practising attacking targets on foot, or mounted on a pull-along 'horse' on wheels, dragged by their companions.[14] There is some information in contemporary biographies. Cuvelier, biographer of Bertrand du Guesclin, constable of France (d. 1380), described him as a very violent, difficult child, the despair of his parents: Bertrand organised his friends into having 'tourneys' in which they fought each other and knocked each other down, and regularly went home with his clothes torn and covered in blood from superficial wounds. He also wrestled with the local peasants and was rebuked by his aunt for indulging in such common pursuits. Only in his late teens did he acquire a horse and begin 'doing the rounds' of the local tournaments.[15] Bertrand's training was apparently left entirely to his own whims; his parents played no role in it although his maternal uncle gave him a little support. The biography of Jean le Maigre, called 'Boucicaut', marshal of France and governor of Genoa (d. 1421), describes how, as a child in the second half of the fourteenth century, he played games suitable for a future commander: he and his brother Geoffrey gathered together the children of his age and they played at attacking or defending a small hill, one group against the others. They also played at battles: making bascinets out of their hats, riding on sticks and armed with strips of bark. They played children's games, such as *barres* (a form of 'tag') and *croc madame* (perhaps a game of 'trip-you-up'), and leaping, throwing darts, hurling the stone and such like.[16] The description of the hero's wondrous childhood that presaged his later valiant deeds of war was a commonplace of epic literature, but there was nothing unusual about such games, which children still play. As these games were also good training for a military career, it is likely that these accounts are describing the sort of military games that these heroes, and other warriors of the period, really did play in childhood.

Boucicaut's biographer says nothing of whether his parents also hired teachers in arms for him. Instead, he depicts his subject spending long hours in training when he had left home and entered the royal service. Although the biographer was clearly presenting Boucicaut as an idealised figure and an example for others to emulate, it is worth setting out these exercises here as they may give us some impression of the sort of exercises an active warrior of the late medieval period could have performed. Boucicaut is presented jumping on to his war-horse while fully armed, without using the stirrup, and running or walking long distances on foot to give himself stamina and to accustom himself to hard work. We are told that he spent long periods striking with his fist or with a hammer, to build up his arm muscles and toughen his hands, doing somersaults in full armour (except for the helmet), and that he wore a mail shirt when he was dancing. He leapt up on to a horse's shoulders, in front of a man already on the horse, simply grasping the man's sleeve with one hand; he grasped a war-horse by the ear, placing his other hand on its saddle, and leapt right over it; he climbed up the narrow gap between two walls using arms and legs only, without any other aid, going up as high as a tower; dressed in a mail shirt, he climbed up a tall ladder placed against a wall without using his feet, using his hands only, and then took off the mail coat with one hand while hanging on to the ladder with the other. These exercises, the biographer tells us, were devised by Boucicaut himself to build up his stamina and enable him to perform more effectively in battle and siege situations. The implication is that he went far beyond the efforts of most warriors of his day, but that other warriors could be far more effective in military affairs if they followed his example.[17] Again, Boucicaut's training was entirely on his own initiative.

A biographer of the Chevalier Bayart, in the early sixteenth century, noted that when the Chevalier was not out fighting he would engage in some martial exercise with his troops: wrestling, leaping, throwing, thereby keeping his own men fit. This was indeed a form of training – but, again, Bayart's biographer saw it as exceptional, an indication of his master's exceptional qualities as a commander. He was certainly exaggerating his hero's qualities, but the fact he laid stress on such martial exercises suggests that they were unusual.[18]

The romance *Perceforest* apparently described the experience of most young nobles at the period when it was written in the 1330s and 1340s. 'In tourneying with our horses and in suffering the knightly deeds of doughty knights we become knights ourselves.'[19] This picture was endorsed by the contemporary noble knight Geoffrey de Charny, who did not expect young men-at-arms to encounter any organised system of training. The best way to learn the art of warfare, he wrote, was to listen to men of experience talking about warfare, and to see warriors with their weapons and armour. The first exercise that they would encounter (presumably at home, or in the household of their lord) was the joust, which they would practise; and then they would go to tournaments.[20] Presumably these informal jousts included the sort of informal knock-abouts, the *bohort*, or *béhourd*, in padded garments and with light weapons, which medieval romances often depict the young knights organising on the open area in front of a fortress, and which were mentioned occasionally in the chronicles (usually only when someone important had been killed).[21]

The tournament was essentially practice for war mixed with pageantry and entertainment; a 'martial game'.[22] The first record of this activity dates from the late eleventh century, when Geoffrey of Malaterra wrote of the wars of Robert Guiscard and his brother Roger, Norman conquerors of southern Italy and Sicily. He described a tourney at a siege in 1062, when the young warriors from the opposing sides jousted in order to win honour and glory. In the early thirteenth century, Péan Gatineau, a canon of the abbey of St Martin of Tours, wrote that Geoffrey de Preuilly, a noble warrior who had been killed in 1066 at Angers, had invented tournaments. However, evidence from charters and from other chronicles indicates that tournaments first became popular in the last decade of the eleventh century and the early decades of the twelfth century. By 1130, the tournament was so well established as a warrior activity that the Church Council at Clermont banned it, and declared that anyone killed in a tournament could not receive Church burial.[23]

The twelfth-century tournament could be an *ad hoc* knockabout, as under the walls of a besieged city, but it could also be a carefully organised event involving warriors from a wide geographical area. Early tournaments took place in the open countryside and could range over miles of land, with contestants taking refuge in farmhouses and using them as fortresses to fight off opponents. Rather than combats between individuals on horse or foot, the emphasis was on combats between 'armies', on horseback, fighting with the couched lance; the intention was to practise and show off battle skills rather than individual finesse. These tournaments were bitterly fought, and deaths were not unusual (as noted by the Council of Clermont); feuds could be pursued, and long-held rivalries fought. As in real war, contestants adopted martial tactics, for instance hanging back until the other combatants were tired and then riding in and sweeping the field. Prisoners were taken and held for ransom, and booty was taken. Tournaments could offer a serious threat to law and order, and a strong ruler would not want them in his country: Kings Henry I and Henry II of England banned them.[24] Yet a tournament was not intended to be a deadly exercise. It could appear to be like war, but it was essentially for practice and to win honour and glory for those taking part.

If the early tournament could be a rough and ready affair, by the early thirteenth century tournaments were becoming more organised and ritualised. Formal and elaborate tournaments were arranged to celebrate a special occasion: the accession of a monarch, a royal marriage, the knighting of the royal heir or a special festival at which the king wore his crown. Yet despite the pageantry and formality surrounding these later tournaments, they nevertheless had serious military value. The battle *en masse*, the *melée*, taught men-at-arms how to fight together and to support each other in the lines of battle. As a lord would attend tournaments with the same band of warriors who would accompany him to battle, these events became valuable training for the pressures of battle. So from the early fourteenth century, in the indentures for service issued by lords in England, one of the services required of the indentured knight was to attend his lord at tournaments. If a lord did not attend a certain tournament, his knights could join other retinues, just as they would in battle.[25] However, the tactics required for the tournament field were not always those required for the battlefield. At the battle of Worringen in 1288, between the duke of Brabant and the archbishop of Cologne and his allies, the cavalry on the archbishop's side advanced in a thin, broad line, which would give maximum impact in a tournament situation but was perilous in battle where a close-knit, narrow formation would have more impact. Both sides realised the error and the broadly spaced knights tried to regroup, only resulting in complete confusion in their ranks.[26] Nevertheless, if tournament tactics did not always work in the field, the fighting practice was valuable. King Richard I of England lifted the ban on tournaments in England in August 1194 because he wanted English knights to be able to practise their arms so that they would be more effective warriors if he went on crusade again, or if he went to war against another enemy.[27]

Geoffrey de Charny assumed that, having 'done the tournaments' as we might now say, the young man-at-arms would go to war. He envisaged his enthusiastic young warrior making enquiries as to where the most honourable war was to be found at that time, and then going to join it.[28] Whatever other wars were in progress, the most honourable form of warfare was to fight for Christendom, and therefore the young man-at-arms looking for glory would go to the crusading fronts of Europe.[29]

Froissart recounts under 1346 how when the English captured the Norman town of Caen, the constable, the chamberlain of France and other knights and squires were trapped on the city gate in fear of the Welsh and Irish footsoldiers, whom they expected would butcher them without mercy. Then they saw Sir Thomas of Holland approaching; they recognised him because they had been companions and had seen each other in Granada, Prussia, in the East and in several other places where good knights meet: in short, on the crusading fields of Christendom. They hailed him from the top of the gate and asked for his help; he came and rescued them, and they surrendered to him.[30] For these knights, the crusade was almost the equivalent of the later 'Grand Tour'.

In the field of war, Charny wrote, the young men-at-arms should take note of all that was going on. They would discover by observation and experience how to organise a raid on the enemy, how to organise cavalry and infantry, and how to defend or attack towns and castles (he gave a few details, but made no attempt to lay down any guidelines). They should travel around and experience sieges and battles in many different areas, seeking to increase their skill and to win honour and glory.[31] Charny had no time for theory, or for any form of systematic training: all was down to the individual. Such a warrior would be prized by any commander fortunate enough to employ him; presumably this warrior would also bring with him a body of loyal, experienced companions on horse and on foot. Charny himself ascribed the highest value to great lords who had seen this sort of experience, for, first, such a lord had no need to seek honour and glory, and yet did so; and, second, he could have far more influence than could a man-at-arms from a lesser background, and could encourage other warriors to strive to excel in imitation of his deeds.

Certainly, this form of self-taught noble warrior, knights such as Boucicaut and Bertrand du Guesclin, were excellent military commanders and achieved marvels in war, but they were essentially free agents. Like the members of the warbands and the royal and seigneurial entourages mentioned in Chapters 1 and 2 above, their personal sense of loyalty tied them to their king, but they also fought on their own account, as Guesclin himself did during the Anglo-French war. The self-taught warrior, trained and tested outside the control of the king or the common benefit, could be less a force for law and order and the protection of the 'common good' and more a disruptive element in society.[32]

Before the introduction of the tournament, what training was there for the cavalry? Hunting on horseback was a form of training, at least in horsemanship and in building stamina. There is some indication that the sort of military practice on horseback that was in use in Vegetius's day survived into the medieval period. According to the chronicler Nithard, when Louis the German and Charles the Bald made an alliance in 842, games of horsemanship were held. These involved two teams who charged each other and took it in turns to wheel and withdraw. No blows were actually exchanged; this was more a display of manoeuvres, the sort of skills that were essential for a cavalry unit. Nithard noted that such displays were often held for purposes of training.[33] It is possible that these were a descendant of the sort of manoeuvres that Vegetius had recommended for military training. The fact that such training is not mentioned by other writers does not mean that it did not happen; chroniclers would not normally mention routine activities.

In Italy, festivals of horsemanship continued throughout the Middle Ages. Those taking part carried spears and rode horses through various manoeuvres. It has been suggested that these were a continuation of classical displays of horsemanship.[34] In the same way, civic horse races were probably a continuation of classical tradition, and were originally designed as part of cavalry training. Such continuing traditions hint that organised training of cavalry continued throughout the Middle Ages. But, outside the traditions of the Italian cities, specific evidence for such training is hard to find. It appears that cavalry training, at least by the twelfth century, was *ad hoc* and individual, neither systematic nor organised on a group basis.

The tournament was not designed as training for the footsoldiers, although – even more than the cavalry – their lives on a battlefield could depend on keeping close formation and working together. While the skills of using a bow and wielding a club (for instance) could be learned in everyday life and tested at fairs and at local competitions, the infantry, even more than the cavalry, needed to be drilled to work together.

The famous parliament at Westminster in 1337 forbade all games throughout England except practising with the bow.[35] This did not amount to systematic training, although it did encourage it. English longbowmen were certainly disciplined, and impressed the Dutch at Brouwershaven in January 1426 – but, nevertheless, they lost the battle against heavy cavalry.[36]

The infantry of the cities of Italy, the Low Countries and Germany from the twelfth century onwards was strictly organised by district or guild, with officers set over each division. The individuals liable for military service would be responsible for supplying their own weapons and horses, if applicable, so were also presumably responsible for their own training. While townspeople did take part in tournaments in some areas, such as

Pavia and Florence, and Munich and Magdeburg,[37] this was not training for infantry. Presumably the town constables and captains who were responsible for commanding the divisions were also responsible for ensuring that those eligible for service trained. It appears that the archers trained together, but for those armed with other weapons this was not possible because of cost. Instead, they received some practice in war by taking part in small expeditions during time of peace. Verbruggen pointed out that they were united by civic pride, carried their own banner as a focus for their group loyalty, and wore a uniform to give them a sense of group cohesion and loyalty.[38]

Strong discipline could assist in keeping a group together even if they were not accustomed to working together in war. Knightly associations drew up their own procedures. 'Brothers in arms' would agree to support each other in war and share booty.[39] The statutes attached to the religious rule of the military religious order of the Temple set out the officials of the order and their respective responsibilities and give instructions on how to act while on the march, how to set up camp, what equipment each warrior was allowed to have, how to charge in battle and what to do if the retreat was sounded.[40] Later, secular, orders of knighthood had regulations governing knightly conduct: orders such as the order of the Band, founded by King Alfonso XI of Castile in around 1330; and the order of the Star, founded by King John II of France in 1351.[41] Both the religious and secular chivalric orders laid down standards of behaviour, but were unlikely to affect the overall strategy in war because their members were relatively few. So the Templars, for instance, would charge all together into the thick of the enemy with excellent discipline, but unless the rest of the Christian forces followed them they would be cut to pieces – which happened rather frequently.[42]

More significant for our purposes are regulations governing an entire army. The communal armies of the Low Countries were governed by custom and regulation: at Valenciennes a charter of 1114 laid down that the members of the communal army had to follow their banners, and no one should march in front of the banner or lag behind.[43] In 1420 John Žižka organised the radical Hussite Christians who had set up their base on 'Mount Tabor' (originally the hill of Hradiště, in south Bohemia) into a well-disciplined and highly effective army. Apart from making use of traditional peasant arms such as flails and pikes, and the offensive use of wagons on which guns were mounted, Žižka laid down the command structure of the army. Four captains were appointed, whom the whole community obeyed. In 1423 the organisation of the army was formalised with written statutes, which emphasised obedience and order above all: they set out arrangements for marching and camping, and for the division of booty, and laid down the punishments for breaches of discipline. Those under army discipline included women as well as men. The statutes also set out the personnel within the army: lords, captains, knights, squires, townspeople, craftspeople and peasants. They were underpinned by strong religious piety and the absolute assurance that God was on their side. The so-called 'Hussite battle song' makes mention of all ranks:

> Therefore archers and lancers
> Of knightly rank
> Pikesmen and flailsmen
> Of the common people,
> Do all keep in mind the generous Lord ...

> You must remember the password
> As it was given to you.
> Always obey your captains.
> Each shall help and protect the other.
> Each shall look for and stay with his own battalion.

> You baggage boys and grooms,
> Keep it in mind
> That you forfeit not your lives
> By theft or robbery,
> And let yourselves never be tempted by spoil ... [44]

The organisation of the Taborite army was a significant factor in its victories over the crusades sent against the Hussites over the next decade, although apparently the only formal training consisted of launching attacks on the Catholics. Singing on the march was in itself a form of training; it helped keep discipline while on the move, raised morale and (if within hearing) could intimidate the enemy.[45]

In short, despite hints that classical training in cavalry manoeuvres had survived in some aspects throughout the Middle Ages, especially in horse racing in Italian towns, there is little specific evidence of systematic formalised training of warriors in the Middle Ages. A few groups of crack troops, such as the order of the Temple and the Taborites, had regulations that ensured that they would operate as a disciplined and united fighting force on the field. Town armies had regulations to ensure discipline and noble men-at-arms learnt the basics of war on the tournament field. But the main means of learning war was to experience it. This was why the professional mercenary armies were often so much more effective on the battlefield than semi-professional levies. Their vast experience on the battlefield made them better warriors than their opponents.

* * *

The army must usually march to reach the place of conflict, and unless this was simply an overnight raid or sallying out of a fortress to engage an enemy at the gates, it needed to ensure supplies of food, water and equipment. The question then arose: should the commander allow the army to forage to feed itself, or should it have its own supplies without relying on the country through which it was passing? Foraging could be risky, and it was not unusual for foragers to be ambushed and killed.[46] In 572 the Saxons travelled through Gaul pillaging as they went, until they were stopped by Count Eunius Mummolus of Auxerre, who forced them to pay with gold for all they had taken.[47] During the First Crusade, foraging by some of the crusading armies passing through eastern Europe brought down the ire of the locals upon them; at Belgrade the authorities refused to allow Walter 'Sans Avoir' and his army admittance to buy food and supplies, presumably because the city could not supply so many. There was violence and 60 of the party were killed.[48]

In addition, while foraging for food from the enemy was part and parcel of war – taking resources from the enemy for oneself – foraging for food from one's own side is bad strategy: it arouses local hostility and may lead to the locals attacking the army which is supposed to be protecting it. The introduction of wholly paid armies in England and France in the early fourteenth century should have reduced the problem of pillaging to a certain degree, but soldiers expected to be able to take booty.[49] The problem of pillaging soldiers was particularly acute in France during the Hundred Years War, with soldiers claiming allegiance to either side taking property from non-combatants, either as part of the price for 'protecting' them, or as the booty of war. The problem grew worse when soldiers were not paid, so that non-combatants complained that soldiers who claimed to be their allies were doing them more harm than those who were their enemies. After his victories in Normandy, King Henry V of England tried to ensure that relations between his troops and the local inhabitants remained good; his soldiers had to remain in their garrisons and were not allowed to go out plundering. If anything was taken, it should be paid for, and any complaints should be brought before civilian officials.[50] Half a century later, Duke Charles the Bold of Burgundy tried to stamp out pillaging by paying his troops, but was not entirely successful.[51]

If the army were not to survive by foraging or buying food, it had to supply itself in some other manner: either by carrying its own food or by ensuring supply lines so that food could reach it from its base. Long supply lines, especially those overseas, always presented a logistical problem. Ideally, the army should carry its own food, but this would involve an enormous baggage train, for it was not only necessary to carry dry produce such as grain but also meat, which should travel on its own feet until required.[52] Hence the army of the First Crusade, after the loss of horses from drought and lack of fodder, was able to use oxen as mounts and goats and sheep as beasts of burden as it travelled through Asia Minor – the goats and sheep might have been collected by the army on the road, but could equally well have been brought along as a source of food. Water was more of a problem, for it is heavy and bulky to carry, and becomes foul if not properly stored. Water supplies found *en route* may be contaminated, and the inexperienced traveller does not know how to select or find a sound water source. The anonymous author of the *Gesta Francorum*, describing the first crusaders' travels through Asia Minor, states that they carried skins full of water through the dry areas.[53] During the Third Crusade, water supplies were a major concern as the Christian army moved south from Acre in the early autumn when many of the riverbeds were dry and the water ran some distance underground. It was necessary to dig down in the riverbeds to find water. The main reason that Richard I of England, commander-in-chief of the crusade, refused to advance against Jerusalem was that he could not guarantee water supplies for his army; he was also very concerned about securing his supply lines from the coast. In the same way, the main reason that the army of the kingdom of Jerusalem was defeated by Saladin at Hattin in July 1187, leading to the Third Crusade, was the Christian army's problems in finding a sufficient water supply on the road to Tiberias.[54] Horses in particular need generous supplies of water, although the horses used in warfare in the Latin East had presumably been trained to require less.[55]

The army of the Third Crusade carried its own food in its march inland towards Jerusalem in December–January 1191–2. The weather was extremely wet, so that armour rusted and clothes fell to pieces, while biscuit – the 'twice-baked' bread which had formed a basic part of military rations since classical times – went soggy and crumbled away, and bacon simply rotted.[56] Hence even a well-supplied army could find itself without adequate supplies due to adverse conditions.

Sea transport could be a means of supplying an army on the march. During the Third Crusade, Richard I of England used his ships to protect and supply the crusading army as it marched down the coast.[57] Control of the sea gave a commander a major logistical advantage, used (for example) by King Edward I of England in his invasion and conquest of the kingdom of Gwynedd in 1276–7 and 1282–3. It is notable that Edward made a point of ensuring that his new castles in Gwynedd could be easily supplied from the sea.[58] However, sea transport was always at the mercy of the weather and enemy action, even more so than transport by land. In 1372 the English fleet, bringing reinforcements and money for the English forces and their allies in France, was attacked by the Castilian fleet off La Rochelle; the English fleet was destroyed and the ship carrying the soldiers' wages was sunk.[59]

Armies usually moved during the summer, during the drier weather when the ground was less muddy – and preferably after the grain harvest was in, so that food was available. Alternatively, in areas where the ground froze in winter (such as Livonia), winter transport might be preferable to travel over marshy ground in summer.[60] Some members of the army walked, some rode horses; some who would fight on foot rode horses until they reached the place of battle, while others who would fight on horseback rode a saddle-horse while their war-horse travelled light in order to be fresh on arrival. What slowed down an army's movements was not the infantry so much as the baggage (for the army could only move as quickly as its slowest component) and the sort of country over which they would be transporting that baggage. Speed of movement varied: Bachrach has estimated that the armies of Pepin III, marching to Aquitaine in 760, covered 30 kilometres a day (around 18.5 miles) – but he sees this as rapid movement for an army. In contrast, in 1191 Richard I of England spent 16 days, from 26 August to 10 September, in covering the 115 kilometres from Acre to Jaffa – an average of just over seven kilometres a day, or around four and a half miles. Richard's army was moving in hostile terrain, over difficult roads – the coast road was so overgrown that the army was forced to take the inland road for the second half of the journey. The infantry were carrying all their own equipment and supplies, and the weather was so hot that if they tried to make longer daily stages, footsoldiers collapsed and died with the heat and lack of water. The army was also being continually harassed by Saladin's army. Conversely, Pepin had been travelling in his own land, in more equable climatic conditions.[61]

The state of the roads – and whether there were any roads – was, obviously, a crucial factor in the speed of march. In the earlier Middle Ages, where Roman roads survived, armies could travel more quickly. From the eleventh century, rulers began to repair and build roads and bridges, which enabled more rapid travel. The commander of the army might have to arrange transportation over a river, by constructing a bridge or arranging for boats to ferry the army across.[62]

Whenever the army was travelling, food, water, equipment and other baggage had to be carried. The poor soldiers might carry their own, but there is a limit to how much individual soldiers can carry. (Vegetius had envisaged the soldiers of the late Roman army carrying the equivalent of just over 43 modern pounds weight, just over 19.5 kilograms.[63] A modern backpacker will know that this allows a change of clothing, bedding and a modern lightweight tent, and a day's food and water – not much more.) The army on the move clearly needed the facilities for carrying more than this, and so baggage wagons and baggage animals were needed.

In 585 Gundovald used both camels and horses to carry his gold and silver, which was to pay his supporters; these were left behind in Gundovald's rapid retreat into Comminges.[64] Gundovald was an exceptional case, for he had support from the Byzantine emperor. For those without such patronage horses were generally used to carry baggage (the *sommier* or packhorse, or even the *roncin*, the rouncey or nag, but not the high-quality riding horse or palfrey and definitely not the war-horse or destrier), or variations thereon such as the mule or donkey. The use of goats and sheep to carry baggage in cases of extreme need has just been mentioned. King Guntram's army that went to deal with Gundovald in 585 used wagons.[65] In 806 Charlemagne wrote to Abbot Fulrad of

St Quentin with details of that year's mobilisation, instructing him in what equipment his troops should bring: he assumed that the abbot's force would be using carts to carry their armour, weapons, other implements and food. They were to bring food for three months, weapons and clothing for six months, and should forage for nothing except grass, firewood and water.[66] Jean Froissart describes the baggage wagons of Edward III's great army in 1359, each drawn by four horses. The army was divided into three, each with its own vanguard, rearguard and baggage in the centre, each travelling separately.[67] Jean le Bel explains that, when he and the Hainaulters who formed part of the English army were going to attack the Scots in summer 1327, the king gave instructions for each person to supply their own carts and everything they needed for a stay in the field (i.e., in tents) plus their cooking equipment.

> So each person began to provide for themselves according to their means and their rank, and bought tents and carts and little horses to pull them as is the custom in that country, and they found on sale plenty of pots, boilers, cauldrons and the other necessities which those in the army needed.[68]

The army then set out north, the king and his barons waiting for two days to pick up stragglers, and travelled north to Durham and then into Northumberland. But the journey became such heavy going through the hills and valleys, marshes and stony countryside that the wagonners and their horses were left behind, as were the packhorses. The army ended up camping in the open air with nothing to drink but river water and without their food or equipment, exhausted by the heat, and shortly afterwards soaked to the skin by the rain. The king and the nobles sent messengers on little horses into Newcastle-upon-Tyne to buy bread and wine, with the king's assurance that payment would be promptly made. The messengers returned with some supplies, and accompanied by people from the town who had come to sell food and wine to the army at vastly inflated prices – 'badly-baked bread in panniers on little horses and mules, poor wine in big barrels and other supplies'. Food was so short that the army fought over the merchants, and all the time it did nothing but rain, so that the horses' harness rotted on their backs and the horses developed sores. If a horse cast a shoe there was no means of getting it reshod, and no shelter for them or for the soldiers. The only fuel was green grass – and all the time there was no sign of the Scots, whom they had come to find.

This particular expedition was a good example of the logistical problems of supplying an army in hostile terrain without ensuring one's supply lines before setting out, while also facing a highly mobile and adaptable enemy who has no interest in coming to battle. Eventually, without having engaged the enemy, the English retreated to Durham, where they recovered their baggage carts and tents.[69]

An army on the march was particularly vulnerable to attack. By necessity strung out as a relatively narrow column, typically with the baggage in the centre for safety, it could be attacked from front, rear or flank, and if it was attacked the extremities of the army would have difficulties in coming to the assistance of the endangered section. Classical writers had emphasised the importance of arranging the army on the march so that it could quickly redeploy to meet an attack.[70] Such redeployment presupposed the discipline and drilling in manoeuvres for which the Roman army is famous but for which, as has been seen, there is little unequivocal evidence in medieval armies. Some historians have argued that medieval armies could and did redeploy effectively, but medieval descriptions of medieval battles seldom allow us positively to identify a redeployment to battle formation while on the march.[71] Einhard admitted in his biography of Charlemagne that when Charlemagne's army was attacked in the Pyrennees at Roncesvalles in 778, it was marching in a long column; the Basques attacked the rearguard and the rear of the baggage train. The vanguard, unaware of what had happened, went on ahead. By the time that the extent of the disaster was known, the Basques, lightly armed and familiar with the mountainous terrain, had vanished into the hills.[72] Charlemagne's army apparently had no reliable means of signalling from rear to front and vice versa (although according to legend, the commander of the rearguard, Charlemagne's nephew Roland, refused to blow his horn to summon aid because he believed he would be dishonoured if he called for reinforcements).[73]

Travelling to the Holy Land during the Third Crusade, the Emperor Frederick Barbarossa (d. 1190) arranged his army in three sections, the van under his son Duke Frederick of Swabia (d. 1191), the baggage and the rear under his own command. When the rearguard was attacked as they passed through the narrow defiles and mountains of Asia Minor (3 May 1190), 'the dreadful news reached the duke's ears' and he rushed back on horseback, followed by his troops, to rescue his father; but the writer does not tell us how the information was brought to him. During an assault on the rearguard as the army of the Third Crusade marched south from Acre towards Jaffa on 25 August 1191, King Richard (in the van) was informed of the attack by one John fitz Luke who galloped ahead to inform him; the king went back with a detachment of his troops to assist the rear. When the rear was attacked at Arsūf on 7 September 1191, the master of the Hospitallers rode forward to inform King Richard and to ask for aid, which the king refused as he thought the rear was capable of looking after itself, and he did not wish to stop the advance.[74] Apparently, these armies had no means of sending information from one end of the army to the other, except by direct word of mouth. In the battle at Arsūf horns were used to give the signal for an attack, yet it seems that these were not used to call for help. However, once the decision was taken by the commanders of the rearguard to move over from defence to attack, the forces of the rearguard reformed into battle lines and charged the enemy (although two of the leading knights did charge before the signal was given). Clearly, there was the potential for redeployment while on the march, even if it was somewhat *ad hoc* and disorganised.

Another example of redeployment while on the march occurred in 1476 near Prise Gaulaux (near Grandson in what is now western Switzerland). The Burgundian army under Duke Charles the Bold, moving north-east after the capture of Grandson, caught sight of a large body of allied infantry troops from Schwyz, Thun, Bern and Zürich advancing towards them on higher ground. The duke redeployed his forces from a marching formation in three divisions into a single body in battle formation. The allied vanguard moved down the hill to the attack and the Burgundians drew back and tried to encircle the enemy, and then launched attacks, including a cavalry charge. However, the allied infantry held firm and continued to advance. The Burgundians then panicked, apparently because the duke had given instructions for a strategic withdrawal (to draw the enemy further on to the plain) and thought that they were being given instructions to retreat. So they ran away, leaving the allies in control of the field.[75]

* * *

War could be conducted in a variety of ways. Raiding or ravaging was one; it weakened the enemy by destroying supplies of crops and livestock and demoralising the people of the country.[76] By the thirteenth century, rulers waging war on each other would place severe trade restrictions upon merchants trading with the 'enemy nation', including arresting and holding merchants from the other side and impounding ships carrying their goods. The inconvenience and loss of trade hit both sides and did nothing to make the war popular with the ruler's subjects, but it could form a useful source of income for the ruler in the form of confiscated goods. Duke Charles the Bold of Burgundy used such measures during his war with France in 1475–6.[77]

War could also involve sieges of fortresses and pitched battle. The nature of war depended on the aims of the commanders. For example, raiders seldom committed themselves to sieges, as the nature of their warfare was to come and go quickly. If they stopped to besiege a fortress, the enemy would have time to form a relief force and attack them. Only commanders seeking more weighty aims and able to commit troops, time and supplies to war would commit themselves to a long-term siege.

The purpose of a siege was to capture a defended point, be it a fortress, a town, or a defended hilltop. The besiegers hoped to win booty (money, moveables and prisoners) and/or to gain control of the defended point. On a frontier where most of the population either lived in fortresses or retreated to them when the enemy appeared, the besiegers were unlikely to hold on to the defended point when they had captured it. They were well aware that strong relief forces would arrive shortly and recover the point; and their primary aim was not to gain territory so much as to harass the enemy and enrich themselves. So they would capture, destroy, loot and take prisoners and/or slaves and withdraw. Hence, for instance, in the south Welsh March, where 'Norman' castles fell regularly to Welsh raiders, the Welsh raiding party might hold the castle for a period, but often simply sacked the castle and left it to be reoccupied by the owning family. The history of the castle of Llansteffan or Llanstephan, on high ground overlooking the west bank of the River Twyi estuary, reflects various strategies from conquest to temporary raiding. It was captured by Maredudd ap Gruffudd in 1146; a relief force was repelled, and the Normans did not recapture it until 1158. In 1189 it fell to Prince Rhys of Deheubarth (south-west Wales; d. 1197), but was back in the hands of its owner, William de Camville, by 1192. It fell to Llywelyn ap Iorwerth of Gwynedd in 1215, but in 1223 William Marshal the younger (d. 1231) recovered authority over the area. In 1257 it was captured again, but was soon back in the hands of the Camvilles.[78] In some cases these castles fell so quickly that one wonders whether the defenders abandoned them in the face of a strong raiding force, or whether there was treachery within the garrison – who were probably drawn from or related to the local Welsh.

Even a conqueror might prefer to avoid sieges. In theory, a commander in the process of conquering an area of territory could not afford to leave fortresses or other defensible positions in the hands of the enemy, as the enemy forces could regroup within these defences and launch counter-attacks. Against this consideration was the problem that sieges took time and could tie up forces for many weeks, slowing down the campaign. If the conquering forces were bound to serve only for a set period, by the time a siege was over they might be due to return home. Again, if the conquering army stopped to besiege a fortress, it would be an easy target for its enemy; while it was on the move, it was more difficult to engage. The final and devastating defeat of the expansionist and ambitious Duke Charles the Bold of Burgundy at Nancy in January 1477 was at the hands of the force that had come to relieve the city, which the duke had been besieging since October the previous year.[79]

So an invader might decide to avoid fortresses and concentrate on devastating the country, perhaps leaving a small force to surround and neutralise fortresses. If the countryside were devastated sufficiently, then the inhabitants of the fortress would be unable to hold out, as they would lose their source of provisions; eventually, they would be so weakened that they could be besieged and captured easily. Such a strategy relied on there being no obvious relief force to come to their rescue. This was the policy adopted by Sultan Saladin against the crusader states in 1187–9: Saladin relied on securing quick surrenders, and if a fortress held out against him or appeared impregnable – such as Tortosa or Marqab – he simply passed it by.[80] Having secured the rest of the country, he would be able to return at a later date to deal with the remaining few fortresses. Again, Sultan Baybars adopted a strategic policy against 'Frankish' fortresses in the county of Tripoli in 1270–1. The Hospitallers' castle of Crac des Chevaliers, apparently impregnable, could be more easily captured in March–April 1271 because the area in which it stood had been effectively under the sultan's control since the previous year.[81]

It was possible to save a good deal of time by taking the defenders of a fortress or city by surprise. Jean Froissart related how, in 1339, the Hainault knight Walter de Manny and a group of companions attempted to capture Mortagne by surprise, hoping that the castellan would not have heard that King Edward III had declared war on King Philip VI of France (d. 1350). They dressed up as women carrying baskets, and fooled the porter on the town gate into thinking that they were local women coming to the market. Inside the town, however, they were unable to capture the castle as the castellan was already aware of the war and had put the castle into a state of defence. They withdrew after setting fire to a few houses. Later they were able to capture Thun l'Evêque by surprise, rushing into the town when the gates were opened in the morning to allow the animals out to graze.[82] At around the same time, according to Cuvelier, the young Bertrand du Guesclin succeeded in capturing the 'English' castle of Fougeré in Brittany by disguising himself and his force of 60 men as workmen and as women.[83] The similarity of these accounts indicates that either this was a standard tale to demonstrate the ingenuity of the young warrior-hero, or that this sort of trick was used rather frequently.

If the strongpoint was warned that an attack was likely to be made and had time to put itself into a state of defence, then a siege would be necessary to capture it.[84] Sieges had certain conventions which dated from classical times. On arrival at the strongpoint, the commander of the besieging force should call upon the inhabitants to surrender. If they did so, it was usual to allow them to depart on their own terms, with their property. If they decided to stand a siege, but later decided to treat for peace, they would be lucky if they were allowed to leave with life and limb – they would probably have to leave all their property behind. In this case, the non-combatants might be allowed to depart while the fighting men were taken prisoner. If the fortress fell by storm, all inside it could expect no mercy; they could be killed or taken prisoner, and their property looted.[85] This was the besieging army's 'reward' for their patience and courage during the siege, revenge for their costs and losses, and to encourage the next fortress to surrender quickly.

The commander of the fortress about to go under siege must weigh up the risks and decide whether to surrender or to defend the fortress. If it were possible to send a message to a relative, ally or the ruler of the area to bring aid, and that aid would come within a reasonable period, then the besieged commander should elect to defend the fortress. To surrender under these circumstances would appear to the commander's peers to be treacherous and cowardly. If sufficient forces and supplies were available to defend the fortress, then the fortress should be defended. But if the commander of the fortress could not be certain of being relieved, and could not be certain of having the resources to defend the fortress, it was acceptable to surrender it. While some commentators claimed that the defending commander should fight to the death, it was also agreed that in such circumstances it could be better to save lives and retain one's forces to fight another day.[86] Alternatively, if the enemy's main aim was loot, it was possible to pay the enemy to go away.[87]

If the commander of the fortress declared an intention to defend his fortress, the attacking commander might decide not to waste time and forces on an attack, but move on. Otherwise, the fortress should be blockaded so that all entries and exits were cut off (which in practice was not always possible), and the attacking army would sit down to starve the fortress out. The attackers would also launch attacks using siege machinery, as described in the previous chapter, attempting to take the fortress by storm. Unless the fortress was sited on solid rock, the attackers would attempt to dig tunnels under the walls, weakening the foundations so that the walls would crumble and fall, allowing access into the fortress. If the fortress stood on water – by a river, lake or sea – then it was necessary to blockade both by land and water, and to attack by land and water. Attack should be concentrated on the weak points in the defences: that is, the entrances, any point not covered by fire from the walls or towers, and any point where the walls were low or were overlooked from outside by higher ground.

While the defenders were obviously in a difficult position, their situation was not hopeless. They were fighting on their 'home ground'. Until the development of the counterweight trebuchet, they were not facing any machine which could do the fortress serious damage. Unless their ruler had already been defeated, they stood a good chance of being relieved. Provided that their commander had laid in good supplies of food and weapons and they had a guaranteed supply of fresh water, they should be able to hold out for many months. They had proper housing within the fortress. In contrast, their opponents were far from home and had only temporary housing, and if the weather was very hot or very cold they suffered accordingly. The besiegers had to forage for their food, unless their commander had taken care to establish efficient supply lines, and they might have problems finding a reliable source of fresh water. They were unlikely to have proper sanitation in the camp; disease often broke out among besiegers. They were in danger of being attacked by a relief force, and by those inside the city. The Venerable Bede recounted in his *Historia Ecclesiastica*, completed in 731, how King Osric of Deira (southern Northumbria, covering roughly the area which is now Yorkshire) was killed in 634 when he was besieging King Cadwallon of the Britons and his army in a strong city: Cadwallon and his army sallied out, took Osric by surprise, killed him and defeated his army.[88]

However, not all besieged fortresses were in such a good situation. If the attacking force was well supplied and no relief came, the besieged might face a siege lasting over a year. Food would then become short. In such circumstances the defending commander might decide to evict non-combatants from the fortress: men too old to fight, and women and children. Although these persons could help in defending the town by hurling missiles from the walls, they were not so useful in hand-to-hand fighting. Yet, in evicting the non-combatants, the commander would be evicting the parents, wives and children of the defenders, and therefore seriously undermining the morale of his troops. In addition, evicting the non-combatants and leaving them to the mercy of the enemy would earn the condemnation of outsiders, such as the ruler of the area, possibly even now hurrying to the scene to relieve the fortress. If part of the purpose of holding the fortress was to defend the people of the area – for instance, as the Hospitallers defended Christian Rhodes against the Muslim Ottoman Turks in 1480 – then to evict the non-combatants was to negate the very purpose of the fortress. To evict the non-combatants from the besieged town was very much an act of last resort. The enemy force, itself probably short of food by this time, was unlikely to allow the non-combatants to enter its camp and would leave them to die between the lines, thus undermining the morale of the defenders still further. However, the enemy commander might decide to take them in and take care of them. This in itself could encourage the defenders to surrender, believing that they too would find mercy from the attackers.

Taking in the non-combatants might also gain valuable information for the attacking commander. In the early sixth century Gundobad of Burgundy besieged his brother Godigisel in his city of Vienne. As the defenders grew short of food, Godigisel expelled the non-combatants from the city, including the engineer who was in charge of the aqueduct. The engineer went to Gundobad and showed him how he could break into Vienne through the water gate and take the enemy in the rear. Vienne fell, Godigisel was killed, and Gundobad became king of the whole of Burgundy.[89]

For a siege was not only a matter of physical force but also of diplomacy. Some fortresses that fell to siege did fall by storm or starvation, but many others fell through negotiation, either between the commanders or between the attacking commander and individuals within the city. In 585, when all military efforts by King Guntram's army to capture the town of Comminges had failed, the leading supporters of Gundovald were persuaded by the besiegers to abandon him and surrender the city in return for promises that their lives would be spared. These promises were not kept; the traitors were killed, and the town was sacked.[90] In 1372 the fortress of La Rochelle, held for the English, fell to the French through trickery. The commander, who could not read, was falsely informed by his advisors that a letter that had been brought to him was from King Edward III of England informing him that he was coming to inspect the town and that the commander should come out to greet him. The letter was from King Edward III, but was an old letter on a different subject; when the commander came out of the castle with his forces, he was ambushed and the fortress was taken.[91] Alternatively, the whole garrison might decide that it was not in their interests to hold out any longer. In 1342 the burghers of Dinan in Brittany killed the commander of their city because he refused to surrender to Louis of Spain (the subordinate of Charles of Blois, claimant to the county of Brittany). In 1345 the garrison of the castle of Montségur imprisoned their commander, who refused to surrender to the attacking English; they then allowed the English to enter.[92] If the fortress fell by treachery, those who betrayed it might be spared; but they might equally well be killed, on the basis that persons who betray their comrades once will probably betray again.

By whatever method the fortress was acquired, the commander of the besieging force must decide what to do with it. First, there was booty to be dealt with. If the fortress fell by storm, the troops were usually allowed to plunder freely. However, the commander might command them to gather all plunder and prisoners together to be divided up; a portion to the commander, a portion to the army. This method ensured that all involved in the capture received a fair share of the proceeds, but could be difficult to enforce. In the early 480s King Clovis of the Franks was ravaging the country around Soissons, which he had just captured. All the booty was taken to Soissons for division: the king took a share, and his warriors took their shares. Clovis asked his troops, as a special favour, if he could take a certain ewer in addition to his normal share, as he had been asked to restore it to the church from which it was taken. Some agreed, but one objected, and wanted to divide the ewer up, splitting it with his axe. Clovis took the ewer and returned it to its original owners. 'At the end of that year', Gregory of Tours explains, 'he ordered the entire army to assemble on the parade ground, so that he could examine the state of their equipment.' Coming to the man who had objected, he rebuked him for the poor state of his weapons, and then split his head with his axe, as the man had split the ewer.[93] This account is interesting not only for the insight it gives into how the first Christian Merovingian king divided up the booty – apparently by custom and consent – but also for the mention of an annual military parade at which the troops were reviewed by the king.

What Gregory does not tell us is the extent of Clovis's share. Documentary evidence for the customs that controlled the division of booty is sparse for the early Middle Ages. By the late eleventh century Spanish monarchs usually claimed a fifth of their subjects' booty. Welsh law allocated the king a third.[94] The division of the rest of the booty could be overseen by the king to prevent disputes. King Richard I of England was praised for his fair dealing with booty during the Third Crusade, ensuring that both those who went on an expedition and those who stayed behind to guard the baggage received their share.[95] But there was still scope for dispute. After the capture of the city of Jerusalem by the First Crusade, on 15 July 1099, the troops ransacked the city, but some of the inhabitants of the city took refuge on the roof of the Aqsa mosque. The Christian leader Tancred wanted them kept alive (perhaps he was hoping for ransoms) but on the following day some of the soldiers went up on the roof and killed the refugees, to Tancred's fury.[96]

One of the problems with allowing the troops to plunder was that when they broke rank they could be ambushed and killed by the enemy; on the other hand to attempt to stop them would lead to discontent and possible loss of control. The troops regarded plunder as their due after the dangers of war; it was also a vital source of money, as well as food and equipment. Chronicles and 'fictional' writing abounded with moralising tales warning against seeking plunder while forgetting to keep a good look out for ambush.[97]

The poor and non-combatants were usually killed by a plundering army, unless they could be put to work in some way; but the wealthy could be held for ransom. By the mid-fourteenth century the taking of ransoms for nobles was largely governed by custom. Prisoners could be exchanged for prisoners of similar value taken by the other side, ransomed for an agreed sum, released on the security of a promise to pay in the future (possibly with the additional security of a hostage, such as the prisoner's son), or could remain as prisoners if they could not pay or if their captor did not want to release them. Jean Dunbabin's recent study indicates that noble prisoners were sometimes well looked after, but sometimes badly treated on the basis that they would then be more anxious to ransom themselves. Nobles were not always put in chains, but those of lesser status were usually chained. Their captor might insist that they paid for their own upkeep in prison. Dunbabin noted that ladies of noble rank were usually treated well.[98] Some groups did not pay ransoms: the Templars did not, and in the early sixteenth century the Chevalier Bayart discovered that the Germans did not. It was said of those who would not pay ransoms that they gave only 'a belt and a dagger' or 'a pike and a dagger' as their ransoms; simple signs of warriorhood, as if they would die rather than pay a ransom.[99]

The lives of wealthy prisoners were usually respected, but not always. In 746, after defeating the Alemanni, Carloman executed his prisoners on the grounds that they had broken earlier oaths to keep the peace. At Acre in 1191 Richard I of England executed around 3000 Muslim prisoners because, he said, Saladin had not kept to the terms of their peace treaty; this action was criticised in Europe as barbarous. In 1373 at Derval in France, the prisoners on both sides were executed when the opposing commanders could not agree on surrender terms; but everyone who heard about this was shocked. At Agincourt in 1415 Henry V of England ordered the English to kill their prisoners. According to the French chronicler Enguerran Monstrelet, writing over 20 years after events, this step was taken 'so that they would not be able to assist their compatriots'.[100]

Having dealt with booty and prisoners, the commander must decide whether to sack it and proceed, leaving it a ruin, or garrison it, thus tying up troops who might be needed in the field. If a relief force was on the way, it might be best to get out of the area quickly; alternatively, if he intended to hold the fortress, he must stay and defeat the relief force in battle.

Historians now generally agree that by the mid-fourteenth century, formal battles were relatively rare, as commanders tried to avoid battle. There were exceptions: Clifford J. Rogers has recently argued that King Edward III of England actively sought battle, provoking his enemy into attacking him so as to retain the advantage of his strong defensive forces.[101] It has also been pointed out that in the period 1450–1530 there were 'an exceptional number of pitched battles', but historians differ on why this occurred. Malcolm Vale pointed to 'Charles the Bold's failure to make good use of artillery in battle, retarding for a little its devastating effects upon cavalry in the field'; Andrew Ayton and J. L. Price observed that this was the period when 'the use of the new artillery rendered most fortifications in Europe obsolete', so that sieges were very quick, and the real competition was on the battlefield; while Maurice Keen has noted 'the attraction of quick results' in the face of 'the enormous and spiralling cost of large-scale warfare', which made commanders anxious to bring a conflict to a quick and decisive conclusion.[102] However, all agree that after 1530 the emphasis was once again on sieges rather than pitched battle.[103]

Vegetius, as mentioned above, had advised against battle because it carried so many risks, and his translators and adapters in the Middle Ages all agreed with him. For modern historians one of the biggest problems presented by battles is to establish what actually happened. Because those who took part in the battle rarely had the opportunity to get a general overview of events, eyewitness accounts of battles are often misleading and contradictory. Non-eyewitness accounts are often extremely brief, or else are an adaptation of a classical battle account, with names changed as appropriate. It is, then, no surprise that modern historians have difficulty in reaching a consensus over the events in any particular battle.

Vegetius emphasised that any commander intending to commit troops to battle must ensure adequate knowledge of the enemy and their plans – in other words, use spies.[104] These are seldom mentioned by chroniclers, although contemporary writers record, for instance, that Richard I of England employed Muslim spies during the Third Crusade, while Ramón Muntaner describes how, after the murder of Roger de Flor in 1305, he himself recruited four poor Greeks to spy on the movements of the Byzantine forces on behalf of the Catalan Company.[105] Vegetius also noted that the commander should be very careful where he chose to meet the enemy. He should plan to take them by surprise, if possible, in an ambush. This was essential if he were outnumbered. At Murten in June 1476 Duke Charles the Bold of Burgundy, already heavily outnumbered, was taken by surprise by the allied Swiss and Lotharingian forces; he was so unprepared for battle that he had not even reached the battle line before his troops were effectively defeated.[106] Such events could be due to lack of intelligence information, or misuse of this information.

If the commander were well informed and confident that he could meet the enemy in open field, he should (according to Vegetius) draw his troops up carefully in lines on a carefully chosen site. If using cavalry, he should choose smooth, open country; if infantry, broken ground, so that the enemy could not use their cavalry effectively. It would be wise to have the sun and the wind at their backs, in the faces of the enemy.[107] With this in mind, it is interesting that at the battle of Crécy in 1346 the French king, Philip VI, engaged King Edward III of England in battle even though (according to Jean Froissart) the French were positioned so that they had the rain and wind in their faces. It appears that Edward had chosen his battlefield with care and prepared it beforehand, and Philip VI engaged him without realising his poor position.[108]

Vegetius had made much of pre-battle planning, the drawing up of troops on the field, and pre-battle speeches to arouse courage and morale in the troops. For those recording actual events, the first two made poor stories and were often left out; and as the chroniclers were seldom present for the battle, they had to imagine the pre-battle speech. However, careful work by modern historians indicates that medieval commanders who won battles had generally planned the battle carefully beforehand, as had Edward III at Crécy: for instance, physically preparing the field by digging trenches, arranging infantry and cavalry with care, and deciding in which order divisions of the army should engage.[109] Gregory of Tours describes the Thuringians preparing the field to meet the Frankish cavalry in 531: they dug ditches and covered them with turves and grass, so that the Franks charged straight into them. The Franks, however, realised the trick after the first few losses, changed their tactics and defeated the Thuringians. In around 572 Count Mummolus engaged the Longobards, or Lombards, in battle near Embrun; he built ramparts of trees to surround them before launching his attack.[110] At Courtrai in 1302 the Flemings dug ditches as part of their pre-battle preparations; at Mons-en-Pévèle in 1304 they arranged their lines to take advantage of the ditches which were already present and arranged their carts and wagons behind their lines as a sort of fortress into which they could retreat if necessary.[111] At Kephissos (or Cephissos) in 1311 the Catalan Company prepared the battlefield by damming the river Kephissos, so that the plain became a quagmire and the cavalry of Walter V de Brienne, duke of Athens, were trapped in the mud. The Catalans then slaughtered them.[112] At Loudon

Hill in 1307 and at Bannockburn in 1314 the Scots dug ditches and pits on the battlefield to disrupt the cavalry charge of the English knights.[113]

Even when two armies faced each other in the field, there was the question of whether or not to engage. The longer the two sides waited (especially in the heat or the cold) the less they were able to fight; they grew increasingly tense, and hunger and thirst set in. So there could be advantage in delay – provided one's own troops were suffering less than the enemy. The side which eventually opened proceedings had the advantage in initiative, but was taking the risk of defeat; the side which held off longest risked nothing, but lost the initiative. A commander might decide at last to draw off rather than fight – although such an apparent retreat was bad for morale, and if the enemy then attacked, the army would be more likely to be defeated.

If battle was eventually engaged, the commander-in-chief might well not actually engage battle in person, but wait behind the lines overseeing the battle and giving orders, as Bachrach has described Charles Martel doing in the first half of the eighth century.[114] It was regarded as risky for the commander to fight in person, for the death or capture of the commander would be a disaster for the army: as in the case of King John II of France, captured by the English at Poitiers in 1356. Nevertheless, the commander who led from the front, as Richard I of England did, was a great morale-booster for the troops. Richard's advisers attempted to persuade him not to risk his life on the battlefield, but he retorted that if he did not he could not expect his men to do so.[115]

In extreme circumstances the commander-in-chief did not appear on the field at all, or could be sent away for safety, as in the case of Queen Philippa of England in 1347. As David Bruce, king of Scotland, led his forces in a raid on the north of England, she assembled an army at Newcastle upon Tyne. She addressed the whole army, urging them to defend the 'king's good and honour', and appointed three bishops and four knights to take charge of the war. She was then escorted safely back to Newcastle, and her army engaged the Scots at Neville's Cross. Jean Froissart, her secretary, insisted that the victory that followed was hers, even though she had not been physically present.[116]

The tactics used in each battle would depend on how each army was made up, and the weapons in use. Vegetius had laid out seven ways in which battle could be joined (Book 3, Chapter 20): suggesting different arrangements of cavalry and infantry, which part of the army should attack first, and how to make best use of the terrain. He also specified where different sorts of troops should be deployed and recommended that there should be a reserve at the rear, which could move about and support the other forces.[117] Vegetius's suggestions about where to deploy, for example, the light infantry (behind the more experienced heavy infantry) appear to be simply common sense, and clearly a reserve was useful if there were sufficient forces. Froissart records that Sir Hugh de Caverley fulfilled the role of reserve for the English at the battle of Auray in October 1364: Hugh did not engage his forces completely, but took his battalion wherever it was needed. When the battle was won, Hugh's role was greatly praised.[118] However, examination of actual medieval battles suggests that Vegetius's battle plans generally remained theoretical models rather than being used in practice.

Because of the problems of ascertaining exactly what happened in a battle this study must be restricted to battles which have been reconstructed by modern historians. Three battles have been selected, which are well separated chronologically and have been reconstructed in sufficient detail to allow some conclusions to be drawn, while not being among the most studied of medieval battles: Poitiers in 732, Carcano in 1160 and Neuss in 1475.

At the battle of Poitiers on 25 October 732, the army of Charles Martel engaged the forces of Abd ar Rachman al-Ghafiqi, governor of Spain. Bernard Bachrach has reconstructed the battle in detail. The Muslim army had advanced north from Spain and apparently intended to proceed from Poitiers to Tours. Charles had marched to meet them, and the two armies had manoeuvred around each other for the previous seven days. Finally, Abd ar Rachman took the initiative in attack. Both armies were large: Bachrach concludes that Charles had the advantage in forces, while Abd ar Rachman had the advantage in weapons and armour. Charles drew up his forces on foot in a dense phalanx. The archers of the Muslim army, some mounted and some on foot, fired on the Franks from a safe distance. The Muslim army, which consisted of cavalry and infantry, then charged the Franks and engaged in hand-to-hand combat. The Franks' ranks remained unmoving before the enemy's attack, 'like a wall' or 'like a glacier from the frozen north', according to the anonymous Spanish chronicler of the battle. The Muslim commander was killed in the battle. Eventually, the Muslims broke ranks and fled – but the Franks did not pursue them. The Franks then withdrew to their fortified encampment, Charles planning to attack the Muslims' camp on the following day.[119]

This was apparently a classic battle against a defensive force with a strong position. The initial firing by the archers was intended to break up the defensive lines, but failed to do so. Likewise, the final retreat could have drawn the Franks out from their defensive position, allowing any Muslim reserve force to ambush them; but, again, the Franks maintained discipline and did not break rank or pursue the enemy. The chronicler did not record what artillery, if any, the Franks were using; he concentrated on the Muslim forces. This reconstruction of the battle indicates that Charles did not use cavalry at all, so that the battle is rather different from those envisaged by Vegetius – but its use of disciplined defence tactics would have won his approval.

The battle of Carcano has been reconstructed by John France.[120] It took place in the context of the north Italian campaigns of the Emperor

Frederick Barbarossa, on 9 August 1160, and was fought between the emperor and the city of Milan, which sought to remain independent from the emperor's authority. The Milanese had besieged the castle of Carcano; if they captured it, they would greatly strengthen their position and that of their allies against the enemy, and could damage communications between the emperor and Germany. The Milanese army consisted mainly of infantry, but there were also some cavalry. The city of Brescia had also sent 200 knights to the army, making perhaps 500 or 600 knights in all. There may also have been troops from the local area. France estimates that the Milanese army was between 5000 and 6000 strong.

Frederick summoned a large army, much of which did not arrive until after the battle was over. He had some troops from Germany, and forces from Italian cities that supported him: Pavia, Novara, Vercelli and Como, and local forces. France estimates a total of 2500 to 3000 troops, including 400 cavalry. Frederick travelled quickly to Carcano, and took up a position on lower ground, with the enemy on the ridge above. His position would have prevented the Milanese besieging army from receiving supplies from Milan.

Frederick then moved out of the camp with most of his force, climbing the ridge to meet the enemy. Meanwhile, the Milanese attacked the imperial camp, and defeated the small infantry force that had been left to defend it. The emperor, seeing what had happened, counter-attacked and drove the Milanese out of the camp. While he and part of his army was so engaged, the cavalry of his Italian allies continued to advance to higher ground. But the Brescian and Milanese cavalry attacked them unexpectedly, scattering and pursuing them. Heavy rain put an end to hostilities. The emperor withdrew from the field; but his allied cavalry eventually returned to camp. While the Milanese were left in possession of the field (and were therefore the victors), they had suffered the heaviest casualties.

The battle illustrates how the terrain could give one side the advantage – in this case the Milanese – and how quick thinking and an ability to seize the initiative could be decisive – in this case by attacking the emperor in the rear and ambushing his cavalry. In engaging before his forces were fully assembled and in attacking a force which had the advantage in terrain, Frederick was certainly not following Vegetius's theoretical guidelines. But although the Milanese defeated Frederick, they did not destroy him, and he was able to conquer their city in March 1162.

The battle of Neuss of 23 May 1475 has been reconstructed by Richard Vaughan.[121] For this battle we have a very detailed description of the arrangement of the rival armies, produced by one of the two commanders, Duke Charles the Bold of Burgundy. The battle was fought between the duke of Burgundy and the forces of the emperor, Frederick III of Habsburg (reigned 1440–93), and was indecisive.

According to Duke Charles, he divided his forces into two 'battles', the usual term for the major divisions of the army in this period. Each was a miniature army, containing both cavalry and infantry, drawn up in lines as set out by Vegetius. In the first 'battle', commanded by Philip de Croy, count of Chimay, there were men-at-arms (i.e., cavalry of knightly and non-knightly rank) on the two wings, while the infantry of pikemen and archers together – one pikeman to four archers – was drawn up in ranks in the centre. The duke does not mention handgunners, although in fact both sides also employed them. There was a reserve force on each wing. The second 'battle' had men-at-arms on each wing, then a body of archers on the right and left of the centre, and the chamberlains and gentlemen of the bedchamber in the centre. Behind were three bodies of reserve troops. There were also additional troops not included in these squadrons.

Charles had been besieging the town of Neuss since August 1474, and the emperor had come to relieve the siege. On being informed of the approach of the relief force, Charles left sufficient troops to continue the siege and moved the rest of his army to the river that was between him and the emperor's army. He gave orders regarding the deployment of his troops, but was annoyed by the length of time taken to deploy. The army then forded the river. The imperial forces' artillery (i.e., heavy guns) fired at the Burgundian army as it approached, and the Burgundians replied in kind. Charles drew up his forces to have the advantage from the sun and the wind, and so as to attack the emperor's camp at its weakest point. The Burgundian artillery (handgunners as well as archers) advanced and fired into the emperor's camp. Then Charles gave the signal for the advance. Trumpets sounded, and shouting their battle cries the troops advanced.

The right wing attacked a hillock where the Germans were placed, and captured it. The enemy counter-attacked; the wing drew back; the reserve came up and reinforced the wing, repulsing the enemy. As the Germans pressed on the right wing, the commanders of the wing sent word to the duke that they needed help, and he sent them some archers from the second 'battle' and part of the reserve of the second battle. The cavalry of the reserve moved more quickly than the archers and engaged the enemy first; but without archers, they could not withstand the German artillery and were forced to fall back. The duke's account portrayed this as a genuine retreat, but the account of Johanne Petro Panigarola, the Milanese ambassador at the Burgundian court, indicates that it was a feigned retreat designed to draw the enemy out of their camp. The Germans then counter-attacked with cavalry and infantry, and drove the right wing back to the second battle, which also retreated as far as Duke Charles's own guard, 'which stood firm'. The duke then intervened in person and led an additional squadron to the assistance of the wing, personally rallying the scattered troops. The German forces were driven back and fled. A report was then brought to the duke that his left wing and reserve had driven the enemy back into their camp. The duke decided to move against the Germans' baggage train, but at that point the light failed and the Burgundians were forced to retreat.

This battle was certainly fought in compliance with Vegetian guidelines, but despite Charles's careful planning, he was unable to dislodge the Germans from their camp. He attempted to use cavalry and infantry tactically, but was frustrated by the slowness of his troops in manoeuvring, and the fact that the cavalry moved too fast for the archers to keep up and engage the enemy at the same time. Given Charles's great interest in classical warfare, he probably was attempting to follow the example of Roman generals and hence his manoeuvres and tactics were more complex than those of many commanders of his day. Although his ordinances of 1473 indicate that his army was drilled so as to be able to execute complex manoeuvres, these did not necessarily translate into effective action in the battlefield.

What these battles demonstrate is that the decisive factors in obtaining victory were disciplined troops and good leadership, quick thinking and the ability to make the most of an advantage, and an awareness of what one's forces could be expected to achieve. Complex manoeuvres and the size of the army were less important.

* * *

When battle had been engaged, only the commander-in-chief and the commander's immediate entourage would have any clear idea how it was progressing, and even this depended on the commander having chosen a position giving a good view of the whole field. As battles could spread out over a wide area, it could be very difficult to know what was going on all over the field and to act in time to prevent a problem developing into a disaster. An experienced commander should be ready for the unexpected, but there were many occasions when this was not the case. When King Clovis of the Franks went to attack Gundobad of Burgundy in around 500, he had persuaded Gundobad's brother Godigisel to support him. Gundobad, unaware of his brother's treachery, asked him for aid and Godigisel promised him that he was coming with his army to join him. Godigisel did join Gundobad – but when battle was joined, Godigisel changed sides. Gundobad fled, and was forced to resort to trickery and diplomacy to win a humiliating peace treaty from Clovis.[122] It was not unusual for allies to desert during the course of a battle, if they thought that the battle was going badly for their side. For example, at a battle on the River Winwaed in 655, between Oswy of Northumbria and Penda of Mercia, Oswy's nephew Æthelwald sided with Penda and guided him through the country, then abandoned Penda when the battle began.[123] At Nicopolis in 1396 some of the eastern European allies of King Sigismund of Hungary retreated.[124] In both cases, the abandoned commander suffered a heavy defeat.

The feigned retreat was apparently much used as a means of persuading the opponents to break their battle lines and/or to lead them into an ambush. Although historians are not in agreement as to whether the

Normans' retreat at Hastings in 1066 was feigned, the effect was the same – drawing the Saxons out of their strong position and enabling them to be surrounded and cut down.[125] At Tagliacozzo in 1268 the Germans had won the battle, but when they broke rank to pillage they were ambushed by the forces of Charles I of Anjou and defeated.[126]

It was quite possible for part of the army to flee while another part remained on the field and defeated the opposition, but the end of a battle usually came when one side threw down their weapons and ran away, leaving the other in possession of the field. The side in possession of the field would generally camp there, symbolising their victory. However, the victory could be more apparent than real. Both the Muslim Il-Ghazi ibn-Artuk of Mardin (d. 1122) and the Christian King Baldwin II of Jerusalem (d. 1131) claimed victory at Tell Danith in the principality of Antioch in August 1119. Neither remained in control of the field, but whereas Il-Ghazi retreated to Aleppo, King Baldwin returned to the battlefield the following day and claimed it.[127] Both Flemings and French claimed victory at Mons-en-Pévèle in 1304; the French were still on the field and the Flemings retreated, but both sides had suffered heavy losses, and the Flemings claimed that they withdrew only because they had run out of food.[128]

Vegetius had advised that a commander should ensure that the enemy could retreat if necessary, for if they could not do so they would be more inclined to fight to the end, with heavier losses for both sides. A commander should also ensure a line of retreat in case of defeat. It might be possible for the retreating army to regroup and attack again; possibly to ambush the now over-confident enemy as they pursued.[129] This is exactly what befell the Normans after the battle of Hastings in 1066; although the ambushes laid by the retreating Saxons did not reverse the result of the battle.[130]

After the battle, bodies were stripped of armour, and the victorious side buried their own dead. The defeated side might be given permission to take away their dead, as William of Normandy allowed the English to bury their dead after Hastings. But he refused to allow the body of his defeated rival, King Harold of England, to be handed over to Harold's mother Gytha for burial.[131] After the battle on the plain of Arsūf in September 1191, the crusaders returned with an armed force to find the body of the noble knight James of Avesnes, and brought it back to Arsūf for burial; the fact that Muslims did not interfere with them emphasises that this conflict was a crusader victory.[132] Although death in battle was seen as glorious and the fitting end for a warrior, it was also the occasion for enormous grief. The death of James of Avesnes was marked with mourning by the whole crusading army, with groans and sighs, weeping and wailing. The biographer of Boucicaut described the grief of the ladies of France after the death of their menfolk at Nicopolis in 1396: 'it was pathetic to hear their laments and complaints. Many have not yet ceased to mourn, for all the time that has passed, and I believe that they never will cease.'[133] While such descriptions of grief were conventional, they reflect a deep dichotomy in the warrior ethic: on the one hand war was a means of winning glory and honour, on the other it brought terrible sorrow to those involved in it.

The war could end when one side withdrew to their own territory, with the surrender of one side and acceptance of the other's authority, or with a peace treaty as if between equals. Sometimes the defeated side would pay the victor to go away: forcing an enemy to make a treaty or to pay tribute was in itself a sign of victory.[134] So Clovis's campaign against Gundobad of Burgundy in the early sixth century ended with Gundobad agreeing to pay tribute;[135] the Saxon Widukind surrendered to Charlemagne in 784 and received baptism as Charlemagne's godson;[136] the Emperor Frederick Barbarossa's wars against the cities of northern Italy and the papacy ended with the Peace of Venice in 1177 and the Peace of Constance of 1183, in which captured territory was restored and oaths of fidelity were taken.[137] Such treaties did not last forever, but they marked the end of hostilities for the time being. Treaties were strengthened by the exchange of hostages – the children and relatives of the defeated party – and the giving of oaths. If the fear of dishonour did not force the parties to an oath to respect their promises, they could be coerced by the threat that if they broke their oaths their loved ones who were held hostage would be killed.[138] The hostages' lot was unenviable, for their families might well decide to go to war again despite the risk to the hostages' lives. The hostages would be executed if their captor decided that their families had broken their oaths or the treaty as a whole, or if their captor decided to renew the war for any other reason. The execution of hostages could itself be a cause of war: in 531 King Theuderic of the Franks attacked the Thuringians because (he said) the latter had horribly murdered the hostages the Franks had given them after the last peace treaty.[139]

In fact, peace could never be assured. Although Wace and his twelfth-century listeners might declare that peace is better than war and benefits the country, the fact that young men could best win social prestige through taking part in war, that governments reinforced their authority through war, and that war brought economic gains meant that, throughout the medieval period, somewhere in Europe a war of some sort was in progress.

6

Naval warfare

The sea played various roles in warfare during the medieval period. It could simply be the geographical area over which warriors must travel before engaging in military action. Ships could be used as a base for attacking coastal fortifications. Some warfare was actually fought at sea, between warriors standing on the decks of ships: this warfare was naval in its situation, but otherwise was similar to land warfare. Once the ships had grappled each other and been drawn together, the battle was fought with bows, javelins and swords as it was on land; the ship acted simply as the method of transportation. However, by the thirteenth century it is possible from the surviving sources to identify tactics or methods of fighting which were specific to naval warfare, and which set warfare at sea apart from warfare on land.

Naval warfare was affected, far more than warfare on land, by geophysical phenomena: such as the wind, the tide and sea currents. It was also affected by the sort of ships in use, their potential for speed, their seaworthiness and their capacity. The design of shipping used in military situations changed considerably during the medieval period. As in the raising of armies, the organisation of fleets was controlled by the emperor at the beginning of the period, became the responsibility of individuals during the period, and was becoming again the responsibility of governments (such as the king, or the ruling council of an Italian city state) by the end of the period. Much 'war at sea' was what we would now call piracy, carried on with a commercial purpose: to win booty and capture slaves. Some was defensive, to crush pirates. But there were also campaigns fought largely at sea, such as those fought between the leading Italian maritime states, Genoa and Venice, and the War of the Sicilian Vespers, 1282–1302. No nation could be said to have achieved 'control of the sea' during the Middle Ages, as it was never possible to keep track of where a ship-borne enemy might be in order to attack and eliminate it. Those peoples who engaged in piracy and coastal raiding could achieve effective control of the sea by disrupting shipping, but this was anarchy rather than rulership: no one ruler could claim to control all shipping.

This chapter will consider the development of ship design, engagements at sea and specifically naval battle tactics, and, finally, how naval forces were raised and organised.

* * *

Ships were built on two basic models. The first design was the clinker-built type, in which the hull was constructed from overlapping planks fastened together; crossbeams were added at a later stage of construction, inside the basic hull shape. This construction had been used in classical times and was used by the Germanic tribes by the fourth century BC. The second design was the 'carvel type', or 'frame built', assembled around an internal frame, with the planks forming the hull placed edge to edge. The method of constructing an interior frame first and then building the hull around it seems to have begun in the Mediterranean in the seventh century AD and to have been well established by the twelfth century; the earliest examples in northern Europe date from the late thirteenth century.[1] The frame-first construction technique allowed larger ships to be built, and also allowed ships to be built more quickly.

Ships could be powered by oars (or paddles) or by sails, or both. It is worth noting that for most of the Middle Ages most rowed ships were rowed by free oarsmen, not slaves. There were two basic methods of rigging the sails. The classical method was the square sail, which caught the wind when it was behind the stern of the vessel, and could be manoeuvred to catch a wind coming at other angles. But it was not so adaptable to diverse wind conditions as the lateen sail, in which a right-angled triangular sail was rigged on an inclined yardarm, so that the leading point was towards the prow and the right-angle of the triangle was tied to the stern of the ship ('fore and aft' rigging). This sail could make use of most wind directions. The date of the adoption of the lateen sail in Europe has been much debated; it was certainly in use from the ninth century, and possibly from the fifth. In the later Middle Ages, large ships had both square and lateen sails.[2]

In classical times, ships were steered with twin steering oars at the stern. In northern Europe, ships were steered with a single side rudder. In the thirteenth century, side rudders were replaced by stern rudders. Gillian Hutchinson explains the change as a result of other developments in ship design: as ships grew larger, it was more difficult for shipwrights to balance the ship correctly for a side rudder, and as ships grew higher, side rudders could not be made long enough to reach from the deck to the water level, for the side rudder must be constructed from a single piece of timber. She argues that the side rudder was actually more efficient than the stern rudder, but simply could not be adapted to meet the requirements of ship design.[3]

The typical ship of the second half of our period, say after 1000, was rather different from the classical ship. The classical ships sailed relatively low in the water by modern standards, with a long profile and a square sail; the later medieval ship sailed high in the water, with rounded lines, and a square sail or square and lateen sails. These are generalisations, but give a general idea of the changes in design. The classical ship could also be powered by oars; but although many warships of the medieval period were long and low and powered by oars, the larger ships stood too high out of the water to be rowed.

The classical Roman warship was the *liburna*, a large ship with a high fighting platform, propelled by oars. It had a ram at the front, designed to hole enemy ships beneath the waterline and sink them. It needed a large crew of rowers and was slow and difficult to manoeuvre. In the late Roman Empire a new type of warship was developed. It was propelled by oars, but perhaps only a third as many as the *liburna*, and had a sail, possibly a lateen sail. It was long, narrow and had a very shallow draught. Its narrowness, light weight and small draught made it very fast in comparison to the *liburna*. The 'scouting skiffs' that Vegetius describes assisting the large warships in his day were probably representatives of this modern, light warship. John Haywood suggests that this new design of ship was based on Germanic warship design of the same period.[4]

The Byzantines developed the *liburna* to produce a new heavy warship, the dromond, which was oar-propelled with a lateen sail. It made little use of the ram, but was sometimes fitted with war machines for hurling Greek fire. The Arabs developed their own warships from the seventh century: these were apparently large, heavy and slow, but Barbara Kreutz has argued that this was because they sailed in all weathers and had to be stable in heavy seas. They were sail-propelled. Kreutz argued that Muslim ship design provided the basis for the *tarida*, a round-hulled, lateen-rigged ship much used by Christians and Muslims in the Mediterranean by the twelfth century.[5]

Arguably the most famous ships of the medieval period were those of the Vikings. Their ships were essentially transport vessels rather than warships, in that they carried warriors across the sea rather than being intended for warfare at sea, but they could be lashed together to form a fighting platform for sea battle. The Vikings had many different sorts of vessels, the most famous being the *drakaar* or 'dragon ship'. This was a long, relatively slender, low vessel with a shallow draught, propelled by both oars and sails. Its relative slenderness in relation to its length and its shallow draught made it fast and manoeuvrable, and it could travel up rivers. These vessels could carry horses, so that once they were beached the warriors could mount and ride across the countryside raiding. The vessels could also be transported across land on rollers, then put back into the water at a suitable point to continue on their journey. In this way the Vikings were able to cross the Russian countryside, hauling their ships overland between rivers and across watersheds.

Although early ships like the one excavated at Gokstad in 1880, dating from the late ninth century, had a crew of 30 to 40 men, later ships were apparently bigger.[6] The ships could travel alone, but often moved in fleets. The size of these fleets has been a subject of great debate among historians: some were small groups of six or seven vessels, but contemporaries also wrote of ships as far as the eye could see. Modern historians now tend to regard these fleets as consisting of hundreds rather than thousands of vessels.[7]

For ships after 1000, historians and archaeologists identify a few basic types: the hulk, the cog, the carrack and the galley. Pictorial evidence shows the hulk as a crescent-shaped sailing ship, its prow and stern high out of the water. It is similar to the Mediterranean 'round ship', which had a rounded profile, and normally had two masts with lateen sails and steering oars. The cog appears as a vessel with high sides, with a straight stern and prow and a flat keel, and a single mast with a square sail. With its high sides, it had more space for cargo than the rounded hulk. The cog was apparently not known in the Mediterranean until the late twelfth century. In the North Sea both these types of ship were clinker-built and were propelled by sails, although smaller vessels could be propelled by oars. In the Mediterranean they were frame-built. The carrack or *coche* was a Mediterranean development from the earlier 'round ship' with characteristics of the cog added. It was a large ship, frame-built, with a round hull and a two-, later three-masted rig.[8] The galley was a long, low ship, propelled primarily by oars but also with sails for use when the wind was suitable. There were different types, for use in war or for trade, and galleys were built to different lengths, varying, for instance, from the Genoese long galley of 1383, which was 124 feet (38 metres) long, 14 feet (4.25 metres) in the beam and with a depth of five feet nine inches (1.75 metres), to the Florentine great galley of the fifteenth century, 143 feet nine inches (43.8 metres) long, 19 feet two inches (5.8 metres) in the beam and nine feet six inches (2.9 metres) deep.[9] Warships had a long, pointed prow, with a 'spur' on the end with which to ram and hole enemy ships. This prow was different in operation from the prow of the classical warship, which had been at water level and holed ships below the water line; the medieval galley rammed at deck level. As Susan Rose has pointed out, the Viking longship was of this basic 'galley' type;[10] the ships that King Richard I of England took to the east as warships, known as 'sneckas', were also ships of this type.[11] ·

There were many other named types of ship, but they can generally be identified as belonging to one of these four basic types. As Susan Rose has underlined, there was no structural difference in this period between warships and merchant vessels: the same design of ship performed both functions. In the Mediterranean the galley was the design used as a warship, while in the North Sea the cog was developed as a warship.[12] But any sort of ship could be used in war, for ships were needed to carry warriors, supplies and horses. In June 1099 the arrival of six Genoese ships at Jaffa, carrying wood and engineers, was decisive in enabling the army of the First Crusade to storm and capture Jerusalem.[13] In a fleet carrying an army overseas, the galleys could be arranged to protect the other vessels: this was the arrangement of King Richard's fleet (*classis*) as he left Sicily for the Holy Land in April 1191.[14]

The transportation of armies over long distances by sea raised various problems, not least of which was to ensure an adequate supply of drinkable water. John Pryor has pointed out that it would require many hours for a twelfth-century ship to take on enough water for its crew for even five days; and the weight of that water would add considerably to the weight of the ship, not to mention the space required to store it.[15] The water then had to be kept sweet and sterile until it was drunk. Food could not easily be kept during long voyages, except in a preserved form – the twice-baked bread or 'biscuit' and bacon which were also usual army provisions. But even these preserved foods deteriorated after a long period, or in damp conditions. It was therefore necessary for the ships to go into shore regularly to buy or steal food. The ships were constructed of wood, which does not last for long periods in the sea unless it is regularly removed from the water and treated to kill shipworm (which bores through the hull, eventually holing the ship), rot and other destructive forms of life.

Navigation techniques were developing throughout the period: the Vikings set up tall stone crosses as sailing marks; in other parts of Europe, church steeples, mountain tops or ancient standing stones could play the same role. Fires could be lit to guide ships: in Britain and Ireland it was generally the responsibility of the Church to keep these burning. The Vikings knew how to navigate across wide stretches of water, but in northern climes it was often impossible to navigate by the sun or stars because the sky was overcast. The magnetic compass, discovered in China, reached Europe in the twelfth century; the English monk Alexander Neckham explained excitedly that it could indicate the position of the Pole Star when the sun and stars were obscured by cloud. The earliest surviving sea chart, produced in the maritime city of Pisa, dates from around 1275, and shows the Mediterranean coast in detail.[16]

* * *

For the whole of our period, a major use of ships in military activity was to transport warriors on raiding expeditions. It was this sort of raiding which the *scaphae exploratoriae* or scouting skiffs and the Danube patrol boats mentioned by Vegetius were presumably intended to prevent.[17] As it was difficult to predict when a raiding party might descend on the coast, in this sort of warfare the attacker had the advantage over the defender. With swift vessels it was possible to land, ravage and escape with booty and prisoners before the enemy had time to collect an army and launch a counter-attack.[18] In answer to early raiding by Germanic tribes on the coasts of Britain and Gaul, the Roman authorities built a chain of fortifications on both sides of the channel. In the fourth century these were put under the authority of one official, the *comes litoris Saxonici*: the 'count of the Saxon shore'. These forts were built to withstand a siege, with massive fortifications on which artillery could be mounted, indicating that they were expecting more than a simple hit-and-run raid. The forts also had their own naval detachments and a military garrison. John Haywood has argued that the intention was to detect raiders as they approached and to intercept them at sea as they returned from their raid. He also suggested that the Roman authorities may have employed former Germanic raiders and their ships in order to fight off other raiders.[19] This would certainly have matched their policy on land.

Systems of sea-borne defence against raiders continued into the medieval period. Gregory of Tours recounts how, around 520, the Danes under their King Chlochilaich raided the Gaulish coast, coming ashore and devastating a region, then returning to their ships with booty and prisoners. They put to sea, but King Theuderic sent his son Theudebert with an army. The Danish king was killed, the fleet was defeated in a naval battle, and the booty and prisoners were recovered.[20]

Clearly, this battle was a major military event, as it is mentioned in a number of later sources, including *Beowulf*, where we are told that the king's name was actually Hygelac. Regrettably, none of the sources tell us anything about the naval battle; even *Beowulf*, in which warriors travelling by ship are a commonplace, concentrates on the battle on the land.[21] The speed and effectiveness of the Frankish response indicates that the Frankish kings did have a system of defence for their coastline and were able to react quickly to sea-borne raids. Although historians have not agreed over where Theudebert got his fleet, he clearly had a fleet at his disposal. For a king without a navy, it was possible to hire one – in 760 the Byzantine imperial fleet worked alongside the Lombards against Pepin III of Gaul.[22]

From the late eighth century Charlemagne organised naval forces to protect his domains in the Mediterranean and in the north. A fleet was built to defend the mouth of the Rhône, to prevent Muslim pirates from sailing up the river to raid. Forts were constructed along the southern French and western Italian coasts. He apparently also had a fleet stationed on the Spanish coast to attack Muslim pirates if they appeared. Not only did these fleets attack pirates as they came to harry the coast; they also sailed out to look for pirates and destroy them. Haywood notes that 'the Franks were remarkably successful in bringing the pirates to battle', for, as has been noted before, it was very difficult for a defender to actually catch naval raiders at sea. In a series of naval engagements between 807 and 813 the Franks defeated the pirates and recovered booty and prisoners. In 813 the Muslim pirates also suffered the loss of a fleet of 100 ships in a storm. While raiding continued, it was contained – unlike the situation in the north.[23]

On the north coast of Gaul, the raiders were Vikings. Here there were more navigable rivers, enabling the raiders to penetrate deep inland in their shallow ships. As in the south, as raids became a problem at the beginning of the ninth century, Charlemagne ordered the construction of a fleet and in 810 he stationed fleets on all the navigable rivers on the north and west coasts of his domains. He constructed forts at ports and at the mouths of rivers and a string of beacons along the coast so that warnings of attack could be quickly conveyed. A fleet was stationed at Boulogne to control the entry to the 'English Channel'. In short, his defences resembled those of the late Roman 'Saxon shore'.[24]

However, Charlemagne was not successful in containing Viking raids. Haywood has pointed out that, unlike his Roman predecessors, he only controlled the southern shore of the 'English Channel', and was less able to control what shipping went through it.[25] The Vikings established bases in Scotland, Ireland and the Isles that enabled them to raid more widely than the Germanic tribes had done. In addition, Charlemagne did not have a standing army; when a raid came, an army had to be raised to meet it, and that took time – by which time the raiders had moved on. Under Charlemagne's son Louis the Pious the problem grew greater; the rebellion of Louis's sons in 830 meant that the emperor could not enforce his commands, and in addition the Vikings were raiding in increasing force. Louis was able to keep them at bay to some extent through diplomacy. For instance, he was able to bring pressure to bear on King Horic of Denmark in 836 and 838 to arrest and execute pirate leaders who had raided Louis's realms.[26]

Later in the ninth century, defence became more localised. The breakdown of co-ordinated defence systems was partly a result of the wars between Louis's sons, but also a recognition that a kingdom-wide defence system, centrally organised, could not react quickly enough to raiders. Authority had to be delegated to the official on the spot, to raise troops and organise ships. Some responses were still organised by the ruler. Charles the Bald's defensive bridges on the Seine have already been considered in Chapter 3, and these could hold up the Vikings' ships, even if they did not always prevent them from continuing up the river. In the Seine the Vikings had to contend with a high tidal range and the winding course of the river, and avoid beaching on the sandbanks; but nevertheless fleets of hundreds of vessels sailed up the river in 845, 861 and 885, without running aground or becoming entangled with each other. In the Loire, they had to get around shifting sandbars and deal with the fact that the current runs at very different speeds in different parts of the river. In 862 12 ships ran aground on the sand and were captured by Robert the Strong, count of Anjou, who was responsible for local defence. Nevertheless, fleets successfully sailed up the Loire in 864 and 869.[27] Overall, this localised defence did not seem to work as well as a centrally organised system had done. Haywood notes that by the time of King Charles the Fat (resigned 887) the Franks were looking back nostalgically on Charlemagne's organisation, and suggests that Notker the Stammerer's stories about Charlemagne's war against the Northmen were intended to encourage Charles the Fat to engage the enemy in the same way.[28]

Across the Channel, in Wessex, King Alfred of Wessex in 896 built a fleet to intercept and combat the Vikings' ships. His ships were basically like the Viking 'longships', but they were almost twice as long as the Vikings' ships, with 60 or more oars.[29] As Patrick Wormald has pointed out, Alfred was not the first English ruler to have a military fleet; in the seventh century King Edwin of Northumbria must have had one.[30] The *Anglo-Saxon Chronicle* indicates that Alfred had ships before he built his new fleet, for his ships fought the Viking ships in 875, 882 and 885. The *Chronicle* states that Alfred made his ships bigger than the Viking ships so that they would be swifter, steadier and higher. Presumably they would be faster with more oars, while their higher sides made them better able to cope in heavy seas. In their first engagement Alfred's ships attempted a tactical manoeuvre, blocking the Viking ships into an estuary; but while they prevented some of the Viking ships from escaping, the rest got away because Alfred's ships ran aground. There followed a battle on the sand until the tide came in, whereupon the remaining Vikings managed to float their remaining ships and escape.[31] Alfred also used the Frankish tactics of blocking rivers: in 895 he blocked the River Lea so that the Vikings encamped on the river could not escape. The Vikings abandoned their ships and fled overland, and the Londoners took their ships.[32]

In the twelfth century the Danish coastlines were themselves subject to raids by pirates from the north-east German coast, the Wends – who were still largely pagan. In 1151 or 1152 a certain Wetheman set up a guild at Roskilde to defend the area against Wendish piracy. The Danish chronicler Saxo Grammaticus calls this guild a *piratica*, which in this context apparently means a naval expeditionary force. The guild was rather similar to the military confraternities and military religious orders that were founded in southern France and in the Iberian Peninsula and the crusader states of the East at the same period. It had military aspects: all members were equal, and booty was divided equally, whatever their social status. But it also had religious aspects: before setting off on their expedition against the pirates, the members confessed their sins to a priest and took communion as if they were on their deathbed. The expedition counted as penance for their sins. It was organised like a pilgrimage, taking a minimum of food, with only their weapons as luggage, sleeping at the oars. The guild was supported by the local townspeople, who gave financial support in return for a share of the booty, and agreed that the guild could take anyone's ship without permission in return for an eighth of the booty.

Saxo informs us that this guild won many victories, even when heavily outnumbered, without loss of blood. He regarded the war against the Wends as a just war, for the Wends preyed upon the Danes without just cause. Modern historians have questioned his depiction of this military activity, for the Danes also raided the Wends, taking tribute, cattle and slaves.[33]

The geography of the region – many islands, with long and winding coastlines, and a flat landscape – meant that it was impossible to close the coast to attackers. The best that could be achieved was to block seaward access to harbours and rivers with stones and poles driven into the seabed, so that any ship that tried to enter would be stuck on the underwater barricade.[34] In response to a similar danger from pirates and raiders, elsewhere in Christendom some ports had a chain strung across the harbour mouth, which could be raised to keep out hostile shipping.[35] In contrast, during the wars between the Italian city-states in the later Middle Ages, the ports were blocked by enemy action: ships were sunk at the entrance to an enemy harbour, thereby ruining the rival city's trade.[36]

During the Hundred Years War, French fleets raided English coastal towns, most famously attacking Southampton one Sunday morning in 1338. In response, coastal defences were put into operation. Walls were built to defend vulnerable towns, including provision for artillery: at Southampton gunloops were incorporated into the walls in the 1380s, and cannon were mounted on the new Catchcold Tower, built in the early 1400s. Gunloops were also incorporated when the main gate of Carisbroke Castle, Isle of Wight, was rebuilt in the 1380s. John R. Kenyon has pointed out that these defences were essentially a continuation of earlier defences with arrowslits for defensive fire, but the designs had been brought up to date to allow cannon to be used.[37]

In the later Middle Ages, the mercantile wars between the Italian city-states, especially Venice and Genoa, and the towns of the Hanseatic League in northern Germany and the Baltic, included incidents of the ships' crews of one side attacking and boarding the vessels of the other side and seizing their cargoes. This was more piracy than battle, although it formed part of the process of war. This sort of raiding put commercial pressure on the enemy and could restrict an enemy's ability to wage war and encourage them to seek terms. Venice and Genoa were also involved in some larger scale battles where one side captured the other's vessels and took their goods as plunder; but, as Rose notes, these battles had no long-lasting effect in the progress of the war.[38]

Raids could eventually become invasion, just as the Germanic raids of the late Roman period had eventually become permanent settlements. Likewise, some of the Viking raids of the ninth to eleventh centuries became permanent settlements, in Ireland, in the English Danelaw and in Normandy in France, where the Norsemen under Rollo were deliberately settled in 911 by Charles *Simplex* ('the Simple' or 'Straightforward':

d. 929) in order to gain Rollo's assistance against other raiders.[39] In 1066 Duke William of Normandy launched an invasion of England: the army was carried by ship across the English Channel. Earlier in the same year a ship-borne invasion fleet had also arrived in northern England from Norway, led by King Haraldr Harthráthi (Harald Hardrada, d. 1066) of Norway and Tostig, earl of Northumbria. King Harold of England met both armies on land; the Norwegians were defeated at Stamford Bridge (Lincolnshire), but the Norman army was victorious at Hastings (Sussex). In around 1046 Robert Guiscard, a minor noble from Normandy, brought a band of warriors to Italy. He established himself at a castle at S. Marco Argentano in Calabria, southern Italy, from which he launched raids on the surrounding area. From the 1060s he launched raids on Sicily (held by the Arabs, who had conquered it from the Byzantines in the ninth century), and in a series of expeditions involving land and sea action he conquered it. He then went on to launch naval raids against Byzantine territory such as Durazzo (now Durrës in north-west Greece) and captured the islands of Malta and Gozo.[40] Clearly, although Guiscard was a raider, he was not simply out for short-term gain; he also wanted to acquire territory permanently.

During the 1120s King Roger II of Sicily (d. 1154) sent ships to aid Rafi', governor of Gabes in North Africa, against his overlord, 'Ali, emir of Mahdiyyah. The result was a war between Roger and 'Ali, which was carried on as a series of coastal raids. Roger reoccupied Malta and allied with Ramón Berenguer III (d. 1131), count of Barcelona (who himself was at war with Muslims, by land and sea). In 1135 Roger's fleet attacked and captured the island of Jerba (or Djerba) off the North African coast, which was a haunt of pirates. Mahdiyyah became effectively a tributary of Roger II. Roger's sea-borne army went on to capture a broad sweep of territory along the North African coast, 'from Tripoli to the borders of Tunis'. In these campaigns, Roger II seems to have initially set out to stop sea-borne piracy against his own territories, and then moved on to conquest.[41]

While both Roger II and his Muslim adversaries had sea power, neither had control of the seas. They were not the only powers operating ships in the area: others included the Byzantines and the Italian trading cities, including Amalfi, Pisa, Genoa and Venice. For example, Mahdiyyah had been captured and sacked in 1087 by a combined Pisan-Genoese fleet, with financial backing from Countess Matilda of Tuscany, overlord of Pisa, and the support of Pope Victor III.[42] Likewise, the sea-borne warfare of the military religious order of the Hospital, based at Rhodes from around 1309, was founded on raiding coastal Muslim settlements.[43]

Like land-based raiding, the short-term aim of aggressive raiding was to win booty and prisoners, while the long-term aim was to weaken the enemy so that it could be conquered. However, this long-term aim proved impractical against mainland targets, which could be easily reinforced from the land. While it was possible to capture and hold Malta, for instance, the Norman rulers of Sicily were unable to hold on to their African conquests, which were finally lost in 1160. In the eastern Mediterranean, the Hospitallers were to find that by allying with Muslim rulers and playing them off against each other they could achieve as much or more than they could by raiding. Trading agreements with the Muslims meant that their goods could now be obtained legally rather than by violence and avoided disruption to trade. Duke Philip the Good of Burgundy sent his fleet to the East in 1441 to harass Muslim settlements in order to distract the attention of the Mamluks and Ottomans from Christian targets such as Rhodes or Constantinople. Yet this fleet's activities against the Turks disrupted Genoese trade, and led to open conflict between Burgundians and Genoese in the Black Sea.[44] Marshal Boucicaut's raids on the Syrian-Palestinian coastline in 1403 only served to anger the friendly rulers of the coastal towns and infuriate the Venetians, whose representatives in these towns suffered badly in the raids. Boucicaut's reply to Venice's formal complaint was that he had found himself in Cyprus with an army, and he did not want to lose the opportunity of attacking the sultan of Egypt's property.[45] It was a response with which generations of raiders would have had sympathy, although the Venetians were not impressed.

At the other end of Europe, the situation around the Irish Sea was different, although with similar effect. There was no aspect of holy war here; sea raids were a part of normal life, a means of winning wealth and honour and establishing authority. Here, all parties (Irish, Scots, Vikings, Welsh, English and, after 1066, the Normans) had sea power, and all used it to prey on their neighbours; but as they were equally matched, the raiding had little long-term impact at a 'national level'. It had considerable impact at a local level, however. For example, few villages were situated on the Glamorganshire coast in south Wales in medieval times – they were built further inland, to avoid the attention of pirates.

Wind direction and sea currents gave no one group advantage, and the large tidal ranges and often stormy conditions added to the adventure of raiding.[46] Campaigns were carried on equally by land and sea. In the late eleventh century Gruffudd ap Cynan (d. 1137), intent on winning Gwynedd from the Normans, waged war on land from bases in the mountains, and then went to the Isle of Man and, in alliance with the king of Man, launched naval raids on Anglesey and Gwynedd. The Norman earls of the area, Hugh of Chester and Hugh of Shrewsbury, then launched naval raids on Anglesey in retaliation, but were defeated in a sea battle (1098). With these victories behind him, Gruffudd was able to establish himself finally in Gwynedd because King Henry I of England needed a reliable ally to control the region, and selected Gruffudd as the most suitable candidate.[47] Gruffudd's panegyrist, setting out a glorious ancestry for the king of Gwynedd, declared that his ancestors had built and owned castles, commanded royal fleets and showed prowess as warriors and saints.[48] By emphasising the importance of fleets, he demonstrated that sea power was an essential part of authority in the countries bordering the Irish Sea.

While raiding – piratical or as part of a larger campaign of attrition – was the major form of naval military activity in the medieval period, there were some battles at sea. In areas where the sea was the easiest transportation surface, either because the land had no usable roads or because it was too broken up by water, sea-borne combat was as common as combat on land. The deck of a ship could provide a better surface for a fight than a marsh or a steep hillside. The Scandinavians were involved in sea-borne conflict relatively frequently, compared to Europeans elsewhere. The fleet that was being attacked often tied their ships together, for mutual protection and to provide a better fighting platform. It was also normal for smaller ships to carry relief troops, which could be brought up to the main battle platform to relieve those who were tired. The more famous battles include those at Hafrsfjord in around 872, Svolder or Svoldr in 1000, Aarhus in 1044, Nisaa in 1062 and the Gotha River in 1159.[49]

At Aarhus, King Magnús of Norway and Denmark and his forces fought Earl Svein (or Swein or Swend), a claimant to the throne of Denmark. Svein's ships were lashed together; King Magnús attacked. The battle raged at the bows of the lashed ships. Those at the bows used spears to reach their opponents; those further back threw javelins. Some threw stones; some used bows. At first King Magnús stood behind a shield rampart formed by his own retinue, but as the battle raged he leapt over the rampart and charged into the bows of the enemy's ships, giving a great shout to encourage his men. Led by the king, his army gradually overran their enemy's ships, finally clearing Svein's ship – either killing the enemy or taking them prisoner. Those who wished to avoid the dishonour of imprisonment or death leapt into the sea. Svein and much of his army fled.[50]

Apart from the fact that the defeated warriors had to swim for it, this appears to have been very much like a battle on land. Other battles at sea during our period may reinforce this impression. For example, the sea battle between Magnús berfœttr, king of Norway ('Magnus Barefoot') and the forces of Hugh of Montgomery, earl of Shrewsbury, off Anglesey in 1098 was described by contemporary Norse poets as an exchange of arrow-fire and hand-to-hand fighting with swords and spears. With their formulaic battle descriptions, these poems could have been describing a battle on land.[51] Taking a later example, in a battle between the French invading forces (bringing reinforcements to the Lord Louis) under Eustace the Monk and the English defending forces under Philip d'Albini off Sandwich on 24 August 1217, the battle began much as it would on land, with the artillery firing off. First, the English crossbowmen fired a dense volley, and then the English bombarded the French with quick lime, fired from a cog that was much higher out of the water than Eustace's flagship. The English then came alongside and threw their grappling irons on to the

French ships, holding the ships together and allowing them to board. Hand-to-hand fighting ensued. Eustace had a trebuchet on board, but could not use it because the ship was not steady in the water. Eustace was captured and beheaded. Some of the French ships escaped, but most of the reinforcements were taken and Louis was forced to treat for peace.[52]

This battle did show the English making some use of the particular opportunities battle at sea offered. They began by sailing past the French fleet (much to the amusement of the French) and then turned and sailed back with the wind behind them. They therefore had the wind with them for their bombardment, which could not have worked if they had been firing into the wind. For the most part, however, the battle was much as it would have been on land. If the thought of using a trebuchet on board ship seems too alarming to contemplate, it must be remembered that Vegetius had expected ships to have mangonels and catapults on deck – the same artillery as the Roman army used on land.[53] It is, however, interesting to note that the author of the later *Roman de Fulk fitz Warin*, writing just before 1314, imagined that the main object of the English in this battle was to ram and sink the French, rather than capturing and killing them.[54] This matches some contemporary descriptions of sea battle during the Third Crusade and elsewhere, although modern historians regard the main object of naval warfare at this period to have been capturing ships rather than sinking them.[55]

Again, at the battle of Sluis in 1340 (when King Edward III of England, with his invasion fleet, met the French fleet off the Flemish coast) the battle proceeded very much as it would have done on land. Edward placed his strongest ships in the front line. He provided a strong guard for the ladies, and sent them out of the front line. He placed archers in the front rank and placed two ships of archers between each ship of men-at-arms. He manoeuvred his fleet carefully so that the sun would not be in his warriors' eyes as they fought – and when it transpired that this was unavoidable, he withdrew for a time until the sun had moved. Meanwhile, the French also drew up their lines. They had the great ship *Christofle* that they had captured from the English; it was full of artillery and crossbowmen. They advanced on the English blowing their trumpets; the archers fired. They threw grappling irons to hold the English ships so that they could board. The fighting was hand-to-hand. The Flemish came to relieve the English. The English won the day and the French fled.[56]

In such circumstances, clearly the fleet with the most ships and the most warriors had the advantage. However, in the hands of a skilled naval tactician, who was able to take advantage of the opportunities which naval warfare offered, this need not be the case. Such a general was Roger de Lauria, admiral of Aragon.[57]

At Malta in July 1283, the Bay of Naples in June 1284, Las Hormigas off the coast of Catalonia in September 1285, the Battle of the Counts (off Castellamare in the Bay of Naples) in June 1287, at Cape Orlando in July

1299 and at the island of Ponza in June 1300, Lauria showed a tactical ability which set him above his contemporaries. The setting was the war of the Sicilian Vespers, in which Peter III of Aragon (d. 1285) had supplied assistance to the Sicilians who were in revolt against their king Charles I of Anjou (d. 1285). Lauria and his mother had been exiled from Sicily because of their support for the Hohenstaufen monarchs of Sicily whom Charles had destroyed; his father had died fighting for the Hohenstaufen King Manfred at Benevento in 1266. In April 1283 Lauria was made admiral of Aragon. At Malta he set out to destroy Charles's fleet, with which Charles intended to launch a counter-attack on Sicily. The Aragonese fleet was smaller than Charles's fleet (how much smaller is disputed by modern historians), but Lauria overcame the numerical disadvantage by using superior tactics.

He arrived at the Grand Harbour of Malta just before dawn and drew up his own fleet, cabling his galleys together. This was not quite the same as lashing them as the Vikings used to do, for the galleys still had space to use their oars. However, it held them together and prevented an enemy vessel from passing between them either to attack or to escape. Then he sent a message ashore, challenging the enemy to come out and fight him. Charles's army abandoned its strong defensive position on the beach and sailed out into the deep water of the harbour. Charles's fleet bombarded the Aragonese, who did not reply, apparently waiting for their opponents to run out of ammunition. When the bombardment finally ended, the Aragonese returned the bombardment and closed with their enemy. Charles's fleet could not easily turn or flee past the cabled galleys, but a few escaped. The majority of Charles's forces were killed.

Historians do not agree over why Lauria's tactics were so successful. Pryor suggested that his archers were superior and his warriors were more lightly armed than the heavily armed knights employed by Charles, so able to keep their footing better at sea. Lawrence Mott has not accepted his conclusions and has argued that Charles's forces were unwilling to board the Aragonese fleet because they had 'neither the weapons nor the training to cope with the Catalans'. He also suggests that the Aragonese (or Catalan) vessels were constructed differently from their opponents' vessels, so that they could not easily be boarded; perhaps that they were much taller ships, so that Charles's forces could not easily climb up on to them. The contemporary accounts of the battle are contradictory. What is clear is that Lauria did not fight according to tradition: he did not exploit the advantages of surprise, preferring to engage his opponent in deep water; he did not close with his enemy at once, preferring to remain at long range. However, he won a convincing victory.

In the Bay of Naples in 1284, Lauria again succeeded in coaxing a superior fleet out of its safe haven to engage his smaller force. He did this by ravaging and burning the area around the enemy fleet's haven, so that public outcry would force it to come out and deal with him. When the enemy fleet, commanded by Charles of Anjou's son Charles of Salerno, came out of its haven in Naples, Lauria feigned a retreat to Castellamare. He only turned to fight once he had lured Charles's fleet out into deep water and too far from port to flee back. He had reinforcements in Castellamare, who came out to join him but were not seen by Charles's fleet until it was too late; possibly because they came up behind Lauria, and possibly because Lauria and the reinforcements were between Charles and the sun. Contemporary reports depict Lauria's ships drawn up in tight ranks while Charles's ships were not in a proper battle line. Pryor suggests that Charles had not had time to redeploy his troops – no sooner was he out in deep water than Lauria's fleet turned on his.

Some of Charles's fleet then fled. Lauria's vessels bombarded Charles's ships with arrows and other missiles – one account states that soap was hurled to make the French decks slippery so that the knights could not fight. Charles's ships were all captured; he himself only agreed to surrender when Lauria had his ship holed.[58]

It was, then, possible to fight at sea in a somewhat different manner to how one would fight on land, using the space between the two fleets to advantage, failing to come to grips until one had the upper hand, and using bombardment carefully, while exploiting the wind and sun as one would on land.[59] It is not clear how naval commanders gave instructions to the rest of the fleet in battle. The Byzantines used flags to signal between vessels by day, and western fleets may also have used this system. Western fleets did use lanterns to signal by night – but during the day this would be less effective. Another possible means of giving signals would be by trumpet and horn; this was the practice in the Venetian fleet in 1428, and in the Burgundian fleet by 1470.[60]

The war machines and ammunition used at sea were usually similar to those used in land battle and sieges. It has been noted that heavy artillery such as trebuchets could be mounted on the decks of ships: even siege towers and ladders could be placed on ships to attack coastal fortresses, as used by the Pisans during the siege of Acre in September 1190 (Third Crusade), and by the Hospitallers and the duke of Austria during the siege of Damietta in 1218 (Fifth Crusade).[61] Crossbowmen played an important role in battles from the thirteenth century onwards.[62] But sometimes different sorts of ammunition were used at sea. We have already noted the use of lime and soap to disable enemy personnel. Fire ships were sometimes used in the medieval period: according to the Byzantine historian Procopius, in 455 the Vandals used fire ships during their invasion of Italy, to break up the line of the Roman fleet.[63] In 1184 the Danes, after clearing a Wendish harbour of its protective blockade of stakes and stones prior to launching an attack, set fire to a ship and sailed it into the harbour; but the ship became lodged on a stake that had been overlooked, and burned to the water line without doing any damage to the town.[64] Many medieval descriptions of 'fire ships' in fact refer to ships equipped with machines to hurl Greek fire or other incendiary devices. Such a weapon was particularly devastating at sea, for once a ship was set alight there was no escape for the crew but to leap into the waves. Most records of incendiary devices being used during our period refer to the Byzantines and Muslims rather than the Catholic Europeans who are under discussion here.[65] However, there are a few references to western Christians using Greek fire. The archbishop of Cologne in a naval bombardment of his own city in 1252 had a wooden siege tower set up on a barque to hurl Greek fire into the city; but the barque caught fire instead and was destroyed.[66] The armaments issued to the fleet of Charles I of Anjou, king of Sicily, in the 1270s and 1280s refer to supplying ships with *ampule de igne sulfureo vel greco*, pots of sulfurous or Greek fire, and *roccette ad ignem proiciendum*, rockets for shooting fire (as used by the Byzantines), as well as pots of quick lime.[67]

During the fourteenth century western Christian ships started to make use of new technology. Kelly DeVries has identified the earliest reference to gunpowder weapons on board ships as dating from 1337–8, when an English vessel, the *All Hallow's Cog*, was being refitted. The refit included the installation of 'a certain iron instrument for firing quarrels and lead pellets, with powder, for the defence of the ship'. From this date shipboard guns appear with increasing frequency in records of shipping. They were installed in Burgundian vessels by the 1390s, and were used in the Lombard Wars in Italy in the 1420s and 1430s. They were used on Swedish ships at Stockholm and Visby in the fifteenth century.[68]

These weapons were mounted on deck, as artillery had traditionally been, but by the early fifteenth century they had been given swivel bases, so that they could be aimed, and were mounted in the bow of a galley (complementing the traditional 'spur' or ram for attacking enemy vessels) or the sides of other types of vessel. Unlike traditional artillery pieces, the muzzle of the guns protruded out over the edge of the ship. Kelly DeVries has pointed out that once the guns were fixed in position it would be impossible for the gunner to reach the muzzle of a gun in order to load it; so shipboard gun design was adapted so that guns could be loaded from the rear. Guns also had to be securely fixed to the deck so that they did not roll about in action. An illustration of 1470–80 shows a Dutch ship with gunports, through which the muzzles of the guns protrude.[69] Having these heavy guns on deck made high-sided warships very top-heavy and unstable, and so by the second half of the sixteenth century the guns were being installed below deck, nearer to the waterline. This made working conditions for the gunners unpleasant, but meant that the ship was less likely to capsize.

The early shipboard cannon do not seem to have been very effective at sinking ships, but DeVries argues that, like the traditional machines of war used at sea, their main purpose was as anti-personnel devices. On occasion they could be used against fortifications on land, as in 1445 when a

Burgundian ship bombarded the Turkish fortification at Giurgevo on the Danube until its bombard burst. It was not until the end of the fifteenth century that these weapons began to be used to hole and sink other vessels. At the battle of Zonchio (Navarino on the Ionian Sea) in 1499 one Venetian round ship was sunk by Turkish gunfire. Three Turkish ships were sunk as an indirect result of Venetian gunfire: cannonballs from the Venetian ships ignited the Turkish gunpowder, blowing up their ships.[70]

* * *

After the fall of the Western Roman Empire there was no such thing in western Europe as a standing fleet. As ships were built of timber, they required constant upkeep, and no western European ruler could afford the expense of keeping ships on standby, idle.[71] Where did the ships used by these warriors and raiders come from?

Bachrach has suggested that the ships used by the Carolingians were recruited as required, for instance by commandeering civilian ships. The ships' own sailors would sail them in the performance of their military duties, but the soldiers for the ships would have to be specially trained for naval duties.[72] The famous ships constructed for King Alfred in 896 may have been crewed by Frisians, paid for by the king. He may also have employed Danish sailors. However, the fleet of 885 that defeated the Vikings at the mouth of the River Stour was raised more locally, in Kent.[73] During the following century it is clear that English kings generally employed outsiders and their ships as part of their navy. King Æthelred II (d. 1016) employed various Scandinavian bands, including Pallig, who had been employed to help the king with his ships, and Thorkell the Tall, who with his men was maintained by Æthelred in return for defending England against sea-borne raiders. In order to pay them, Æthelred levied a tax called *heregeld*. His Danish successors also employed ships and their crews in their fleet, paid for by the *heregeld*. The fact that when these crews were paid off they took the ships with them indicates that these were their own ships, not the king's ships. In effect they formed a 'standing fleet' for the defence of the realm, as long as they were employed. When they were no longer employed, they took their ships to earn a living elsewhere.

But the kings also took a levy of their subjects' ships for naval service. Nicholas Hooper has suggested that the *butsecarls* or 'boat-cheorls' who appear in the *Anglo-Saxon Chronicle* and Domesday Book were inhabitants of the maritime towns of Kent and Sussex who owed naval service to the king. In addition, the king could raise a fleet from the realm by ordering that all fit ships should be assembled at London, in order to form a fleet to defend the country – a ship-levy, or *scipfyrd*. This was all very well until there were no ships fit to use in the country; then the king had to order that new ships be built, as was done in 1008. Like the obligation to defend the *burhs*, the obligation to provide a ship was linked to land. Each 310 hides had to supply a warship. There is also evidence in Domesday Book (1086), of ship service being owed by ecclesiastical lords, who had to supply a ship and the men to crew it. However, it also appears that many of those areas that were due to supply a ship negotiated to commute this obligation into a money payment.[74]

The ships that were supplied by area did not pass into royal ownership, but remained in the ownership of the people or person who supplied them. These people were therefore responsible for the expense of maintaining the ship, but could also use the ship to earn money by trade or piracy when it was not required by the king. The crews were also raised through a levy on the land, in the same way as the army was levied, with a term of service of two months. If a campaign went on longer, the ships had to return to port for relief crews. Hooper has noted that this system of raising ships was not in fact very effective; it did not prevent England being successfully taken over three times in the eleventh century, nor did it prevent hostile raids and landings throughout the eleventh century.[75]

The general pattern seen in England in the tenth and eleventh centuries is also seen at other periods and elsewhere. When Richard I of England was preparing for his crusade in 1189, his officials went around the ports of his domains – England, Normandy, Anjou and Aquitaine – commandeering the best ships. The king paid two-thirds of the cost of the ship; the remaining third was borne by the owner, as a contribution towards the crusade. The king also paid the crew's wages. He issued regulations for the sailors of the fleet, including tough disciplinary regulations. According to the contemporary historian Ambroise, Richard gave instructions at Tours for his fleet to sail around the coast into the Mediterranean and meet him at Messina in Sicily; he himself travelled overland across France, sailing from Marseilles to Messina.[76] By the fourteenth century, the administration of the ships in the royal service had developed; the official in charge was the 'clerk of the king's ships', and he paid the crews and was responsible for keeping the ships properly equipped. There was still no royal shipyard, but some kings did maintain a small squadron of ships for their own use rather than for war. Under King Henry V, up to 36 ships were under the care of the clerk of the king's ships, but after his death the ships were sold or left to decay, the government preferring to hire ships as required.[77]

The French kings of this period also relied largely on hiring ships from ship's captains, although Philip IV additionally founded a royal shipyard in the 1290s. It is not clear how significant this yard was in providing ships to the French navy, but the yard at least built the warships which formed the core of the navy, while the rest of the navy was made up of merchants' vessels commandeered as required.[78]

The military religious order of the Hospital of St John, which kept up naval action against the Mamluks and Ottomans in the eastern

Mediterranean from the early fourteenth century, never had more than three or four galleys available for naval campaigns (even in the early modern period it usually had only six or seven galleys of its own). Instead of buying more galleys, the order licensed corsairs to operate against Muslim shipping and the ships of Christian merchants who traded with the Muslims. This *corso*, as it was called, brought the Hospital some income through the licences, without the financial burden of buying and equipping ships. Individual brothers and outsiders bore the cost themselves, and received their payment in the booty they collected. While the Hospitallers' *corso* is definitely known to have operated from the early fifteenth century, it had probably been going on for far longer. This type of *guerre de course* was frequently employed by late medieval rulers as a form of 'low level but officially sanctioned warfare' against rival shipping.[79]

At the same time, however, some rulers were investing heavily in their own ships, built specifically for their own use. The fleet of Charles I of Anjou, king of Sicily, was constructed according to strict guidelines which specified the dimensions, fittings and rigging. Weapons were issued at royal expense for the use of the warriors on these ships, although the oarsmen were expected to provide their own swords. Armaments for the ships were supplied by the king, as were other accessories such as flags, tar and other materials for caulking and waterproofing the ships, filling brads or nails to stud the hulls against ship worm, casks, barrels, axes and so on. John Pryor has suggested that the flags could have been used for signalling between ships by day: this was a Byzantine practice, although not known to have been used elsewhere by western ships at this period. Yet, as Charles of Anjou was using Byzantine 'Greek fire' and Byzantine rockets, perhaps he was also using their signalling systems. Royal documents also laid down how the crews were to be organised, the size of the crew on each ship, salary rates and the provisions for the ships, with the quantity of wheat to go into a set quantity of biscuit. Other provisions were cheese, salt pork, wine and beans or chickpeas. Exactly how the crews were recruited is not known, although the very highest officers were appointed by the king.[80]

The fleets of the Italian city-states were state financed. In 1302 the Venetian government established a state monopoly on shipbuilding. All the ships which sailed out of Venice were built at the state shipyard, the Arsenale, which had its own skilled workforce and associated crafts such as ropemakers and sailmakers. The galleys were hired out to contractors for trading voyages, and the contractors charged merchants for sending their goods on the ships. The state laid down where the ships were to go; they travelled in fleets of three or four ships to specific areas such as Cyprus, Alexandria and Flanders.[81] The Florentines initiated a similar system in the fifteenth century.[82] In Genoa, the merchants owned the galleys and hired them to the state in time of war. In the Iberian Peninsula, the situation was different again. At Barcelona the crown and the city authorities worked together; there was no state shipyard, and when not in use for war the king's warships were hired out to merchants. At Valencia the king and the city authorities co-operated so that the city provided port and dockyard facilities. In time of war, merchants were asked to provide ships for the royal fleet, and the equipping and crewing of these were financed by the city authorities. Shipmasters were granted licences to pursue pirates. The city of Valencia also maintained its own ship for this purpose between 1456 and 1460.[83]

The fleet that Duke Philip the Good of Burgundy sent to the East in 1441 had been constructed at Sluis, Brussels and Antwerp specifically at his order.[84] However, his son, Duke Charles the Bold, hired or commandeered from others the warships for his fleet as he needed them. So, for instance, in 1469 he hired ships from Spanish, Portuguese and Genoese merchants. His fleet was not particularly effective in its operations, which were mainly attempts to stop English raids against the coastline of his territories. Charles issued sailing orders to the commander of his fleet, as he issued marching orders to the commanders of his armies. The ordinances issued in 1470 to the captain of the fleet, Henrik van Borselen, include instructions that passwords should be issued to each ship every night so that the they could recognise each other while at sea. Each ship should sail close to the captain of the fleet's ship, and the password would be shouted across. At night, signals would be given between ships by lanterns placed on the poop of the ships. During the day, signals were given by pennons being flown from the poop, and by the blowing of trumpets. In battle, pillaging was not permitted until the enemy had been completely defeated.[85] All these practices were very similar to practice on land.

* * *

While much of naval warfare resembled war on land, and its main purpose throughout most of Europe was to support land-based war, warfare by sea did have some features that set it apart from war on the land. Perhaps the most striking of these were that throughout the medieval period, the aggressor rather than the defender had the advantage in sea raiding and when battle was engaged, it was likely to be far more decisive than on land. As a writer of the late twelfth century declared, drawing on the work of Vegetius:

> What could be more dangerous than a conflict at sea? What could be more savage? Such various fates await the combatants! – either they are burned to death, or drown in the waves, or die from their wounds.[86]

Conclusion

This survey has considered theoretical approaches to warfare during the period 300–1500, the personnel involved in war – how armies were recruited and who served in them – fortifications and other buildings used in warfare, equipment used by warriors, and how war was fought by land and sea. Overall, it is clear that some aspects of war remain constant. In the period covered by this study, commanders concentrated on raiding and devastation of the enemy's land rather than pitched battles. Throughout the period, there were sieges of strongpoints, although the quality of siege artillery varied. Those who had ships at their disposal used them for both trading and raiding. Throughout the period, armies consisted of warriors on horseback, supported by warriors on foot. Highly mobile raiding bands did not always include the warriors on foot; in areas such as Frisia where the landscape was not easily passable for horses, armies generally lacked warriors on horseback. In areas of rough terrain such as Ireland and the west and north of the British Isles, mounted warriors generally dismounted to fight. Nevertheless, the overall pattern remained.

There were certain standards in warfare. The work of Vegetius, itself an epitome of earlier writings, was the standard textbook of war on land and at sea throughout the medieval period. But there were also expectations of how warriors should behave. In that war was always a means of gaining honour, warriors should behave honourably towards each other – which meant not betraying their comrades and not running away in time of battle. Other expectations changed with time. The standards of the Christian Church – that warfare should be for the common benefit, excess violence should be avoided, and non-combatants should be excluded from war – did have an impact by the late Middle Ages, although often honoured in the breach.

How far did convention rule warfare? Convention was important in establishing what was expected of a commander and of a warrior, but warfare is an essentially practical activity and a military leader who allowed convention to take prior place to practicality would soon be defeated by a more pragmatic opponent. Medieval warfare was not static, and never predictable. An imaginative and resourceful commander could often outflank and out-think a more conventional opponent. However, many conventions in warfare, such as the protection of non-combatants, existed to protect the vulnerable from the dangers of war. The fact that commentators laid increasing emphasis on the need to spare non-combatants, for example, reflected the growing danger of war during the Middle Ages; the more effective war became, the more the need to protect those who could not protect themselves.

At the beginning of our period, some war was still organised by a central authority, the Roman government. During our period war became privatised, although war also continued to be one of the responsibilities of government, for the ability to wage and win wars was an essential part of authority. Rather than untrained men being recruited into a standing army, warriors either made a personal career of war in the entourage of a lord, or were called up to serve as required. They were expected to come to war ready trained and equipped. By the end of the period, rulers had taken back much of the responsibility for waging war. War, apart from that waged by overall rulers of kingdoms, was outlawed; and rulers were once again employing warriors on a long-term basis. As systems of government developed, taxation could be levied and collected, recruitment became more efficient, larger armies could be paid and fed, and armies could be maintained for a longer term. However, warriors were generally employed *en bloc*, under a captain, rather than having personal contracts.

Naval warfare developed to a degree, as commanders such as Roger de Lauria exploited the potential of the sea to win battles through use of superior tactics rather than simply using the ship as a fighting platform; but it would be true to say that at the end of our period battle at sea was still, as Richard Harding has put it: 'a variant of land warfare in the confined conditions of ship-to-ship combat.'[1]

At first glance it is easy to see why historians of the fourteenth to seventeenth centuries talk of 'a military revolution' which changed the face of warfare: a change from emphasis on cavalry to emphasis on well-trained infantry; larger, professional standing armies, recruited and paid by the government; the introduction of gunpowder artillery, which made war more expensive but gave the besieger an advantage in sieges; physical changes to fortresses in order to oppose the new artillery. However, when we look more carefully at the broad sweep of military history through the medieval period, we see that skilled warriors fought on foot throughout the period, that governments always recruited and paid armies, although in various different ways, and that military architecture was constantly developing and changing to meet the threat of new siege machinery such as the counterweight trebuchet. In defining the 'military revolution' we must not simply consider what changed but also measure degrees of change, in order to decide when the crucial phases of the revolution took place – the fourteenth century? – the sixteenth century? – the seventeenth century? The solution to this problem must depend on what we believe to be the most important change in warfare. Historians of the tenth century might argue, for instance, for the introduction of the stone castle as a military revolution; historians of the twelfth might see the growing concentration on the cavalry charge as a revolution. The present author would see the 'military revolution' of the late Middle Ages as less of a revolution, which implies sudden change, and more of an evolution over the period from the early fourteenth century to the late sixteenth, in which warfare became less individualised and more the concern of the 'state'.

It is clear that war affected every part of medieval society. Anyone – children, adult men and women and the elderly, peasants, merchants and religious people – could be called on and expected to play their role in wartime. Towns and cities were protected by walls for defence in time of war; administrative centres were built as fortresses. War spawned its own expertise in engineers who could design fortresses and build heavy artillery. It shaped the self-image of the nobility in every realm in Catholic Europe. Throughout our period, war remained a means of winning wealth and fame, of establishing oneself in society through the honour that came from achieving success in war. The poor could grow rich; the unmarriageable could win spouses. War also absorbed immense wealth, and had an enormous cost in terms of human death and suffering. At this distance it is difficult to say whether the rewards were worth the expense.

The Middle Ages gave to the modern age the concept of the just war, certain standards of conduct in warfare such as the invulnerability of prisoners, and the conviction that in an ideal world there would be no war. It also bequeathed to the modern age immense architectural relics of war, in the form of fortified cities and castles, and a great heroic literature of Beowulf, the Cid, Oliver and Roland, Bertrand du Guesclin and their like. It is certain that, whatever conclusions historians may draw, the romanticised tales of medieval warfare will continue to fascinate generations of humans to come, as they fascinated generations in the medieval period.

Notes

Preface

1. The *Oxford English Dictionary* gives 1616 as the earliest date for the use of the term 'the middle ages' to refer to the period between the fall of the Western Roman Empire and the 'modern day'.
2. R. C. Smail, *Crusading Warfare, 1097–1193* (Cambridge: Cambridge University Press, 1956), p. v; reprinted with introduction by Christopher Marshall (Cambridge: Cambridge University Press, 1995), p. xi.
3. Philippe Contamine, *La Guerre au moyen âge* (Paris: Presses universitaires de France, 1980), translated as *War in the Middle Ages*, trans. Michael Jones (Oxford: Basil Blackwell, 1984), p. xii.
4. See, for instance, Roger Collins, *Early Medieval Europe 300–1000*, 2nd edn (Basingstoke: Macmillan – now Palgrave Macmillan, 1999), p. xx, and see also p. xxiv; Contamine's study began with the fall of the Roman Empire in the West: part 1, chapter 1; Bernard Bachrach has traced continuity of the institutions and military practice of the late Roman Empire in the West through the Carolingian period to the eleventh century: see, in particular, Bernard S. Bachrach, *Fulk Nerra, the Neo-Roman Consul, 987–1040: A Political Biography of the Angevin Count* (Berkeley: University of California Press, 1993), and *Early Carolingian Warfare: Prelude to Empire* (Philadelphia: University of Pennsylvania Press, 2001). For continuity of military equipment and technology from the classical period to the end of the medieval period see Kelly DeVries, *Medieval Military Technology* (Ontario: Broadview, 1992); and see also the work of Paul Chevedden, for example 'Artillery in Late Antiquity: Prelude to the Middle Ages', in *The Medieval City Under Siege*, ed. Ivy A. Corfis and Michael Wolfe (Woodbridge: Boydell, 1995), pp. 131–73. For other aspects of continuity see, for example, Edith Ennen, *The Medieval Woman*, trans. Edmund Jephcott (Oxford: Basil Blackwell, 1984), pp. 2–3; Jacques Le Goff, *Medieval Civilization 400–1500*, trans. Julia Barrow (Oxford: Basil Blackwell, 1988), p. 3; *Women in Medieval Western European Culture*, ed. Linda E. Mitchell (New York and London: Garland, 1999), p. 113; Roger Stalley, *Early Medieval Architecture* (Oxford: Oxford University Press, 1999), pp. 13–15; Jean Dunbabin, *Captivity and*

Imprisonment in Medieval Europe, 1000–1300 (Basingstoke: Palgrave Macmillan, 2002), pp. 18–19.

5. Jean Froissart, *Chronicles*, selected, trans., and ed. Geoffrey Brereton (repr. Harmondsworth: Penguin Books, 1978) is a selection of extracts from J. A. C. Buchon's edition of 1840 with comparisons to the editions of Kervyn de Lettenhove (1867–77) and the edition published by the Société de l'histoire de France (1869–77): see pp. 26–7 of Brereton's translation. In this book I have used the recent edition of Froissart's text published by George Diller, 1991–8, based on the Amiens text, which Diller argues convincingly to be the first version of the text: see Jean Froissart, *Chroniques: Livre 1: le manuscrit d'Amiens, Bibliothèque municipal no. 486*, ed. George T. Diller, 5 vols (Geneva: Droz, 1991–8), vol. 1, pp. ix–xiii, esp. p. xix.

Introduction

1. Bachrach, *Early Carolingian Warfare*, pp. 26–7. On the importance of booty see Timothy Reuter, 'Plunder and Tribute in the Carolingian Empire', *Transactions of the Royal Historical Society*, 5th series, 35 (1985), 75–94.
2. On what follows see Chapter 1, pp. 23–7.
3. For consideration of the concept of holy war see Jonathan Riley-Smith, *What were the Crusades?*, 3rd edn (Basingstoke: Palgrave Macmillan, 2002), p. 7; Hans Eberhard Meyer, *The Crusades*, trans. John Gillingham, 2nd edn (Oxford: Oxford University Press, 1988), pp. 16–17.
4. Pierre Riché, *The Carolingians: A Family who Forged Europe*, trans. Michael Idomir Allen (Philadelphia: University of Pennsylvania Press, 1993), p. 88; *Gesta Francorum et aliorum Hierosolimitanorum*, ed. and trans. Rosalind Hill (London and Edinburgh: Thomas Nelson and Sons, 1962), p. 90.
5. For raiding see, for example, Gregory of Tours, *The History of the Franks*, trans. Lewis Thorpe (Harmondsworth: Penguin, 1974), Bk 3 chs 11–13, pp. 171–3; Bk 8 ch. 30, p. 459, ch. 42, p. 473; Bk 9 ch. 18, pp. 500–1. Hereafter cited as 'Gregory of Tours'.
6. John Gillingham, 'The Beginnings of English Imperialism', *Journal of Historical Sociology*, 5 (1992), 392–409; idem, 'The English Invasion of Ireland', in *Representing Ireland: Literature and the Origins of Conflict, 1534–1660*, ed. B. Bradshaw, A. Hadfield and W. Maley (Cambridge: Cambridge University Press, 1993), pp. 24–42; idem, 'Foundations of a Disunited Kingdom', in *Uniting the Kingdom? The Making of British History*, ed. Alexander Grant and Keith J. Stringer (London: Routledge, 1995), pp. 48–64.
7. Reuter, 'Plunder and Tribute', 92–4.
8. Example cited by Angus MacKay, 'Religion, Culture and Ideology on the Late Medieval Castilian-Granadan Frontier', in *Medieval Frontier Societies*, ed. Robert Bartlett and Angus MacKay (Oxford: Oxford University Press, 1989), pp. 217–43: here p. 228 and note 44.
9. On what follows see Eric Christiansen, *The Northern Crusades*, 2nd edn (Harmondsworth: Penguin, 1997), pp. 167–76; Maurice Keen, *Chivalry*

(New Haven and London: Yale University Press, 1984), pp. 172–4; Norman Housley, *The Later Crusades: From Lyons to Alcazar, 1274–1580* (Oxford: Oxford University Press, 1992), pp. 398–401; Norman Housley, *Documents on the Later Crusades, 1274–1580* (Basingstoke: Macmillan – now Palgrave Macmillan, 1996), pp, 109, 112 note 5.

10. Christiansen, *Northern Crusades*, p. 167.

11. Ibid., p. 171.

12. Anne Curry, *The Hundred Years War* (Basingstoke: Macmillan – now Palgrave Macmillan, 1993), pp. 62–4.

13. The surname 'the Bastard' reflected the fact that his mother had not been married to his father.

14. J. F. Verbruggen, *The Art of Warfare in Western Europe During the Middle Ages* (Woodbridge: Boydell, 1999); John Gillingham, 'Richard I and the Science of War', in *War and Government in the Middle Ages: Essays in Honour of J. O. Prestwich*, ed. John Gillingham and J. C. Holt (Woodbridge: Boydell, 1984), pp. 78–91, and in *Anglo-Norman Warfare: Studies in Late Anglo-Saxon and Anglo-Norman Military Organization and Warfare*, ed. Matthew Strickland (Woodbridge: Boydell, 1992), pp. 194–207; Matthew Bennett, 'The Development of Battle Tactics in the Hundred Years War', in *Arms, Armies and Fortifications in the Hundred Years War*, ed. Anne Curry and Michael Hughes (Woodbridge: Boydell, 1994), pp. 1–20; Matthew Strickland, 'Securing the North: Invasion and the Strategy of Defence in Twelfth-Century Anglo-Scottish Warfare', in *Anglo-Norman Warfare*, ed. Matthew Strickland (Woodbridge: Boydell, 1992), pp. 208–29; Bachrach, *Early Carolingian Warfare*, pp. 46–50, 207, 217–27.

15. On the dissolution of the Roman Empire in the West see Collins, *Early Medieval Europe*, pp. 96–115.

16. For examples, see, for instance, *Itinerarium peregrinorum et gesta regis Ricardi*, ed. William Stubbs, vol. 1 of *Chronicles and Memorials of the Reign of Richard I*, Rolls Series 38 (London: Longman, 1864), Bk 1 ch. 2, pp. 7–8; Bk 4 ch. 20, pp. 275–6; for a translation see *Chronicle of the Third Crusade*, trans. Helen Nicholson (Aldershot: Ashgate, 1997), pp. 25–6, 258. For convenience future references will be to my translation only, but giving book and chapter numbers so that readers may refer back to the Latin original. Ambroise, *Estoire de la guerre sainte: histoire en vers de la troisième croisade*, ed. Gaston Paris (Paris: Imprimerie nationale, 1897), lines 6632–734. See also, for example, Matthew Paris, *Chronica majora*, ed. H. R. Luard, 7 vols, Rolls Series 57 (London: Longman, 1872–83), vol. 4, pp. 25–6; vol. 5, pp. 152–3; and the reactions of overwhelming grief after the defeat of the crusading army at Nicopolis in 1396, trans. Housley, *Documents*, pp. 106–7.

17. For examples of the non-combatants suffering in warfare or conflict, regarded as an atrocity and yet as unavoidable, see *Raoul de Cambrai, chanson de geste*, ed. Paul Meyer and A. Longnon (Paris: Librairie de Firmin Didot, 1882), lines 1462–1594; *Jourdain de Blaye (Jordains de Blaivies), chanson de geste*, ed. Peter F. Demblowski (Chicago and London: University of Chicago Press, 1969), lines 532–711.

18. *La Chanson de Roland*, ed. F. Whitehead (Oxford: Blackwell, 1942), lines 969, 989, 1064, 1090, 1734, 1927, and see also for 'dulce France', 'sweet

France', lines 16, 109, 116, 360, etc.; and see *The Song of Roland*, trans. Glyn Burgess (Harmondsworth: Penguin, 1990), p. 25; Thomas Elmham, *Liber Metricus de Henrico Quinto*, in Anne Curry, *The Battle of Agincourt: Sources and Interpretations* (Woodbridge: Boydell, 2000), p. 46. On this question see, for example, *Concepts of national identity in the Middle Ages*, ed. Simon Forde, Lesley Johnson and Alan V. Murray (Leeds: University of Leeds, School of English, 1995); *Medieval Europeans*, ed. Alfred P. Smyth (Basingstoke: Macmillan – now Palgrave Macmillan, 1998).

19. Collins, *Early Medieval Europe*, pp. 167, 169.

20. On the writing of history in the Middle Ages see, for example, Antonia Gransden, *Historical writing in England*, 2 vols (London: Routledge, 1974; Ithaca, NY: Cornell University Press, 1982). For the influences upon chroniclers and the distortions in their work see, for example, Antonia Gransden, 'Propaganda in English Medieval Historiography', *Journal of Medieval History*, 1:4 (1975), 363–81; and see notes 21–5 below.

21. For example, on Archbishop William of Tyre's account of the battle of Montgisard in 1177 see Peter W. Edbury and John Rowe, *William of Tyre: Historian of the Latin East* (Cambridge: Cambridge University Press, 1988), p. 77 and note 74; Helen Nicholson, 'Before William of Tyre: European Reports of the Military Orders' Deeds in the East, 150–1185', in *The Military Orders*, vol. 2, *Welfare and Warfare*, ed. Helen Nicholson (Aldershot: Ashgate, 1998), pp. 111–18: here pp. 117–18 and note 24.

22. See, for instance, M. K. Lawson, *The Battle of Hastings, 1066* (Stroud: Tempus, 2002), pp. 98–103.

23. This problem is set out clearly by Verbruggen, *Art of Warfare*, pp. 10–11.

24. Nancy F. Partner, *Serious Entertainments: The Writing of History in Twelfth-Century England* (Chicago and London: University of Chicago Press, 1977).

25. To take two well-known examples, the 'history' of Archbishop William of Tyre and the chronicle of Matthew Paris have inspired some searching criticism in recent years. See, for instance, on William of Tyre, D. W. T. C. Vessey, 'William of Tyre and the Art of Historiography', *Mediaeval Studies*, 35 (1973), 433–55; R. H. C. Davis, 'William of Tyre', in *Relations between East and West in the Middle Ages*, ed. Derek Baker (Edinburgh: Edinburgh University Press, 1987), pp. 64–76; Edbury and Rowe, *William of Tyre*, esp. pp. 167–74; on Matthew Paris see Richard Vaughan, *Matthew Paris* (Cambridge: Cambridge University Press, 1958), esp. pp. 131–6, 261–5; Marie Luise Bulst-Thiele, 'Zur Geschichte der Ritterorden und des Konigreichs Jerusalem in 13. Jahrhundert bis zur Schlacht bei La Forbie am 17. Okt 1244', *Deutsches Archiv für Erforschung des Mittelalters*, 22 (1966), 197–226. In a similar vein see Harriet M. Hansen, 'The Peasants' Revolt of 1381 and the Chronicles', *Journal of Medieval History*, 6 (1980), 395–415.

26. Froissart, *Chronicles*, trans. Brereton, pp. 17–24; *Froissart Across the Genres*, ed. Donald Maddox and Sara Sturm-Maddox (Gainesville: University of Florida Press, 1998), esp. pp. 2 and 11, note 4. In recent historiography Froissart is cited as a generally reliable historian: see, for example, *The Peasants' Revolt of 1381*, ed. R. B. Dobson, 2nd edn (London: Macmillan, 1983), pp. xxxi–iv, 6–7; and the articles in *Arms, Armies and*

Fortifications in the Hundred Years War, ed. Anne Curry and Michael Hughes (Woodbridge: Boydell, 1994), pp. 7, 10, 13, 15, 103, 108, 117, 121, 125, 187.

27. Verbruggen, *Art of Warfare*, pp. 13–14, 54, 64–7, 70–1, 88, 90–5, 105–6.

28. For example Wolfram von Eschenbach's *Parzival*, written between 1200 and 1210, survives in 86 manuscripts, 44 of which date from the thirteenth century: Bernd Schirok, *Parzivalrezeption im Mittelalter* (Darmstadt: Wissenschaftliche Buchgesellschaft, 1982), p. 57; the vulgate *Lancelot* survives in 'around a hundred' manuscripts: *Lancelot*, ed. Alexandre Micha, 9 vols (Geneva: Droz, 1978–83), vol. 1, p. ix; the vulgate prose *Tristan* survives in over 80 manuscripts and fragments: *Le roman de Tristan en prose*, ed. Philippe Ménard et al., 9 vols (Geneva: Droz, 1987–97), vol. 1, p. 8. On the impact of medieval 'fictional' literature on medieval society and the problems of assessing it as a historical source see also Helen Nicholson, *Love, War and the Grail: Templars, Hospitallers and Teutonic Knights in Medieval Epic and Romance, 1150–1500* (Leiden: Brill, 2001), pp. 8–16; and on Arthurian impact on castles in particular see Richard K. Morris, 'The Architecture of Arthurian Enthusiasm: Castle Symbolism in the Reigns of Edward I and his Successors', in *Armies, Chivalry and Warfare in Medieval Britain and France: Proceedings of the 1995 Harlaxton Symposium*, ed. Matthew Strickland (Stamford, Lincs: Paul Watkins, 1998), pp. 63–81.

29. *Gyron le Courtoys, c.1501*, introduction by C. E. Pickford (London: Scolar, 1977), fol. 1c.

30. Keen, *Chivalry*, pp. 5, 103, 107, 51–2.

31. Ibid., pp. 103–13.

32. Ibid., pp. 113–19; Nicholson, *Love, War and the Grail*, pp. 191–9. On this problem see also Dennis H. Green, *Medieval Listening and Reading: The Primary Reception of German Literature, 800–1300* (Cambridge: Cambridge University Press, 1994), pp. 237–69; Dennis H. Green, *The Beginnings of Medieval Romance: Fact and Fiction, 1150–1220* (Cambridge: Cambridge University Press, 2002).

33. See, for example, *Le chevalier à l'épée*, lines 39–44, in *Two Old French Gauvain Romances*, ed. R. C. Johnston and D. D. R. Owen (Edinburgh: Scottish Academic Press, 1972); *Les Merveilles de Rigomer von Jehan*, ed. Wendelin Foerster, vol. 1, Gesellschaft für romanische Literatur vol. 19 (Dresden: Max Niemayer, 1908), lines 15644–67.

34. See, for instance, the different figures given by Kelly DeVries, *Medieval Military Technology* (Ontario: Broadview, 1992), p. 47; Andrew Ayton, 'Arms, Armour and Horses', in *Medieval Warfare: A History*, ed. Maurice Keen (Oxford: Oxford University Press, 1999), pp. 186–208. here p. 191.

35. See Chapter 2, pp. 56–7, and Chapter 4, pp. 104–5.

36. See, for example, the excellent detailed studies of Carroll Gilmor, 'Naval Logistics of the Cross-Channel Operation, 1066', *Anglo-Norman Studies: Proceedings of the Battle Conference*, 7 (1984), 105–31; idem, 'The Logistics of Fortified Bridge Building on the Seine under Charles the Bald', *Anglo-Norman Studies*, 11 (1988), 87–106; idem, 'War on the Rivers: Viking Numbers and Mobility on the Seine and Loire, 841–886', *Viator*, 19 (1988), 79–109; and of John Pryor, for example: John Pryor, 'The

Transportation of Horses by Sea During the Era of the Crusades: Eighth Century to 1285 A.D.', *Mariner's Mirror*, 68 (1982), 9–27, 103–25; reprinted in his *Commerce, Shipping and Naval Warfare in the Medieval Mediterranean* (London: Variorum, 1987), no. V; *idem*, '"Water, water, everywhere, Nor any drop to drink." Water Supplies for the Fleets of the First Crusade', in *Dei gesta per Francos: études sur les croisades dédiées à Jean Richard; Crusade Studies in Honour of Jean Richard*, ed. Michel Balard, Benjamin Z. Kedar and Jonathan Riley-Smith (Aldershot: Ashgate, 2001), pp. 21–8.

37.   John F. Benton, ' "*Nostre Franceis n'unt talent de fuïr*": The Song of Roland and the Enculturation of a Warrior Class', in his *Culture, Power and Personality in Medieval France*, ed. Thomas N. Bisson (London Hambledon Press, 1991), pp. 147–65, and see esp. pp. 150–1 for consideration of the 'heroic blow'; Edward Steidle, '*Meilz valt mesure*: Oliver, the Norman Chroniclers and the Model Commander', *Romance Philology*, 45 (1991), 251–68. Hrabanus Maurus is quoted by Bachrach, *Early Carolingian Warfare*, p. 89. For a discussion which takes the descriptions of knightly blows more seriously see Michael Prestwich, '*Miles in armis strenuus*: The Knight at War', *Transactions of the Royal Historical Society*, 6th series, 5 (1995), 201–20, esp. 207, 212–13. On military training or lack of it see below, Chapter 5, pp. 113–22.

38.   For example, Smail, *Crusading Warfare*, pp. 1–21, etc.; Verbruggen, *Art of Warfare*, pp. 1–5; Bernard S. Bachrach, 'Medieval Siege Warfare: A Reconnaissance', *Journal of Military History*, 58 (1994), 119–33; Charles Coulson, 'Cultural Realities and Reappraisals in English Castle-Study', *Journal of Medieval History*, 22 (1996), 171–208; Anne Curry, 'Medieval Warfare: England and her Continental Neighbours, Eleventh to the Fourteenth Centuries', *Journal of Medieval History*, 24 (1998), 81–102; John France, 'Recent Writing on Medieval Warfare: From the Fall of Rome to *c.*1300', *Journal of Military History*, 65 (2001), 441–73.

1   The theory of warfare

1.   For a recent translation of Vegetius's work see *Vegetius: Epitome of Military Science*, trans. with notes and intro. by N. P. Milner, 2nd edn (Liverpool: Liverpool University Press, 1996), especially the introduction, pp. xiii–xli. What follows is based on this edition and on Milner's introduction. The work is hereafter cited as Vegetius, *De re militari*. For the date see also W. Goffart, 'The Date and Purpose of Vegetius' *De Re Militari*', *Traditio*, 33 (1977), 64–100; P. Richardot, 'Dating the "De Re Militari" by Vegetius', *Latomus*, 57 (1998), 136–47. Richardot suggests a dating of 386–8 (p. 147). See also Michael M. D. Reeve, 'The Transmission of Vegetius's *Epitoma rei militaris*', *Aevum – Rassegna di Scienze Storiche Linguistiche e Filologiche*, 74 (2000), 243–354.

2.   Vegetius, *Epitome*, trans. Milner, pp. xiii–xiv; Charles R. Shrader, 'The Influence of Vegetius' *De re militari*', *Military Affairs*, 45:4 (December 1981), 167–72; Bernard S. Bachrach, 'The Practical Use of Vegetius' "De

re militari" during the Early Middle Ages', *Historian*, 47 (1985), 239–55, reprinted in his *Warfare and Military Organisation in Pre-Crusade Europe* (Aldershot: Ashgate, 2002), no. I; Christopher Allmand, 'The Fifteenth-Century English Versions of Vegetius' *De Re Militari*', in *Armies, Chivalry and Warfare*, ed. Strickland, pp. 30–45.

3. Alexander Murray, *Reason and Society in the Middle Ages* (Oxford: Oxford University Press, 1978), pp. 129, 447 note 69. See also Charles R. Schrader, 'A Handlist of Extant Manuscripts Containing the *De re militari* of Flavius Vegetius Renatus', *Scriptorium*, 33 (1979), 280–305, listing 243 medieval and post-medieval manuscripts and part manuscripts of Vegetius's work, plus 81 translations.

4. For instance, the late twelfth-century composer of an account of the siege of Acre, 1189–91, used Vegetius's descriptions of naval warfare in his description of a naval battle: Hans E. Mayer, *Das Itinerarium peregrinorum: eine zeitgenössische englische Chronik zum dritten Kreuzzug in ursprünglicher Gestalt*, Monumenta Germaniae Historica Schriften (Stuttgart: A. Hiersemann, 1962), p. 322 note 2, p. 323 notes 1–2. See also Shrader, 'Influence of Vegetius'; Allmand, 'Fifteenth-Century English Versions'; and see below.

5. Timothy Reuter, 'Carolingian and Ottonian Warfare', in *Medieval Warfare*, ed. Keen, pp. 13–35: here p. 19.

6   Bachrach, *Early Carolingian Warfare*, pp. 86–8.

7   Bernard S. Bachrach, 'The Angevin Economy, 960–1060: Ancient or Feudal?', *Studies in Medieval and Renaissance History*, 10 (1988), 3–53: here 33.

8. For a later instance where French geography made Vegetius's advice obvious good sense see, for instance, Clifford J. Rogers, 'The Age of the Hundred Years War', in *Medieval Warfare*, ed. Keen, pp. 136–60: here pp. 146–7.

9. Jim Bradbury, *The Medieval Siege* (Woodbridge: Boydell, 1992), pp. 85–6; Murray, *Reason and Society*, pp. 127–8, 446 note 58.

10. Gillingham, 'Richard I and the Science of War', in *Anglo-Norman Warfare*, ed. Strickland, pp. 198, 203–4, 207.

11. Murray, *Reason and Society*, pp. 128–9, 446–7 notes 66, 68.

12. M. T. Clanchy, *From Memory to Written Record, England 1066–1307*, 2nd edn (Oxford and Cambridge, MA: Blackwell, 1993), p. 226.

13. Ibid.

14. Procopius of Caesarea, *History of the Wars*, trans. H. B. Dewing, Loeb Classical Library, 6 vols (London: William Heinemann, 1919), vol. 3, pp. 17–19; Bk 5: *The Gothic War*, ii. 12–15.

15. *Les deux rédactions en vers du Moniage Guillaume, chansons du geste du XII siècle*, ed. Wilhelm Cloetta, Société des anciens textes français, 2 vols (Paris: Firmin Didot, 1906–11), vol. 1, p. 6 lines 130–3. Historically, William was Duke William of Toulouse (d. 812).

16. *The Book of Chivalry of Geoffroi de Charny: Text, Context and Translation*, ed. and trans. Richard W. Kaeuper and Elspeth Kennedy (Philadelphia: University of Pennsylvania Press, 1996), pp. 14–16, 18–23, 48–64; Maurice Keen, 'Chivalry, Nobility and the Man-at-Arms', in *War, Literature and Politics in the Late Middle Ages*, ed. C. T. Allmand

(Liverpool: Liverpool University Press, 1976), pp. 32–45, here pp. 36–8; Elspeth Kennedy, 'Theory and Practice: The Portrayal of Chivalry in the Prose *Lancelot*, Geoffrey de Charny, and Froissart', in *Froissart Across the Genres*, ed. Maddox and Sturm-Maddox, pp. 179—94.

17. Charny, *Book of Chivalry*, pp. 102–5.

18. Murray, *Reason and Society*, p. 129.

19. Jaroslav Folda, *Crusader Manuscript Illumination at Saint-Jean d'Acre, 1275–1291* (Princeton, : Princeton University Press, 1976), pp. 16–17, and the sources cited in note 68; Michael Prestwich, *Edward I* (London: Methuen, 1988), p. 123.

20. Prestwich, *Edward I*, pp. 228–9.

21. *Li livres du gouvernement des rois: a XIIIth century French version of Egidio Colonna's Treatise De regimine principum, now first published from the Kerr ms.*, trans. Samuel Paul Molenaer (New York: Columbia University Press, 1899; repr. New York: AMS Press, 1966), pp. xv–xix, xxvi–viii; for specific reference to Vegetius's work in the French translation see p. 376 line 5, p. 379 line 17, p. 383 line 17, p. 384 lines 17, 37, p. 385 line 28, p. 388 line 20, p. 396 line 17, p. 414 line 20, p. 418 line 25; Murray, *Reason and Society*, p. 129. Egidio's book *De regimine principum* is sometimes confused with another, shorter work of the same title, consisting of four books. The first book and part of the second were possibly composed by Thomas Aquinas (*c*.1225–1274); the rest was composed around 1300 by Ptolemy of Lucca (*c*.1236–1327). The final two chapters make extensive use of Vegetius. The work survives in many manuscripts, indicating that it circulated widely, and it apparently had considerable impact on later political writers – but this does not mean that it influenced warriors. See *Li livres du gouvernement des rois*, p. xx; and *On the Government of Rulers: De Regimine Principum, by Ptolemy of Lucca with portions attributed to Thomas Aquinas*, trans. James M. Blythe (Philadelphia: University of Pennsylvania Press, 1997), pp. vii–ix, 1–8, 51, 104, 105, 111, 139, 190, 210, 231 and note 90, 235, 244, 245, 246–7, 277–8, 283–4, 285–6, 287–8, also 45–9 on influence.

22. *L'art de chevalerie: traduction de 'du re militari' de Végèce par Jean de Meun, publié avec une étude sur cette traduction et sur Li Abrejance de l'ordre de chevalerie de Jean Priorat*, ed. Ulysse Robert, Société des anciens textes français (Paris: Firmin Didot, 1897), p. viii.

23. *Li Abrejance de l'ordre de chevalerie: mis en vers de la traduction de Végèce de Jean le Meun par Jean Priorat de Besançon*, ed. Ulysse Robert, Société des anciens textes français (Paris: Firmin Didot, 1897); *L'art de chevalerie*, pp. iii, viii, x–xii.

24. *Knyghthoode and Bataile: A XVth Century Verse Paraphrase of Flavius Vegetius Renatus' Treatise 'De Re Militari'*, ed. R. Dyboski and Z. M. Arend, Early English Text Society, original series, 201 (Oxford: Oxford University Press, 1935), pp. xxii, xxvi and note 3, xxxiv note 3; *Dialogus inter Militem et Clericum: Richard fitzRalph's Sermon: 'Defensio Curatorum' and Methodius: 'Þe Bygynnyng of þe World and þe Ende of Worldes'*, [translated] by John Trevisa, Vicar of Berkeley, ed. Aaron Jenkins Parry, Early English Text Society, original series, 167 (London: Oxford University Press, 1925), pp. xciv–vii.

25. Allmand, 'Fifteenth-Century English Versions', p. 44.
26. *The Book of Fayttes of Armes and of Chyvalrye translated and printed by William Caxton from the French original by Christine de Pisan*, ed. A. T. P. Byles, Early English Text Society, original series, 189 (London: Oxford University Press, 1932), pp. xi–xvi, xxxi–vi, 291. There is no modern edition of Christine's French text. The original French version survives in several manuscripts; I have used British Library MS Harley 4605. When I had completed the study of Christine's book for this work a translation appeared based on a different manuscript, Brussels Bibl. Roy. MS 10476, which was possibly produced for Duke John the Fearless of Burgundy: Christine de Pizan, *The Book of Deeds of Arms and of Chivalry*, trans. Sumner Willard, ed. Charity Cannon Willard (Philadelphia: Pennsylvania State University Press, 1999). Willard suggests that John the Fearless was the original patron of the work: p. 5–6. I will give references to all three versions of the text here.
27. This is at present most conveniently consulted in its translation: G. W. Coopland, *The Tree of Battles of Honoré Bonet* (Liverpool: Liverpool University Press, 1949). On Bouvet see N. A. R. Wright, 'The *Tree of Battles* of Honoré Bouvet and the Laws of War', in *War, Literature and Politics*, ed. Allmand, pp. 12–31; and Keen, 'Chivalry, Nobility, and the Man-at-Arms', pp. 34–5.
28. *Book of Fayttes of Armes*, ed. Byles, pp. xxvi–li. For Christine's use of Vegetius see also Charity Cannon Willard, 'Pilfering Vegetius? Christine de Pisan's *Faits d'Armes et de Chevalerie*, in *Women, the World and the Worldly: Selected Proceedings of the St Hilda's Conference, 1993*, vol. 2, ed. Lesley Smith and Jane H. M. Taylor (Cambridge: D. S. Brewer, 1995), pp. 31–5: here 33, 35–6.
29. Sydney Anglo, *The Martial Arts of Renaissance Europe* (New Haven and London: Yale University Press, 2000), pp. 12, 122, 125, 128–9.
30. See Introduction, p. 12.
31. Charny, *Book of Chivalry*, pp. 102–5; Richard Barber and Juliet Barker, *Tournaments: Chivalry and Pageants in the Middle Ages* (Woodbridge: Boydell, 1989), pp. 95–6.
32. Anglo, *Martial Arts*, pp. 33–4.
33. Ibid., pp. 125–8.
34. See, for example, Hans Talhoffer, *Medieval Combat: A Fifteenth-Century Illustrated Manual of Swordfighting and Close-Quarter Combat*, trans. and ed. Mark Rector (London and Philadelphia: Greenhill Books and Stackpole Books, 2000), esp. p. 9. See also Anglo, *Martial Arts*, pp. 21–7.
35. For example, see Anglo, *Martial Arts*, p. 150, on the poleaxe.
36. Barber and Barker, *Tournaments*, pp. 103, 197–201; Anglo, *Martial Arts*, pp. 230–3, 256–8.
37. Alan Forey, 'The Military Orders in the Crusading Proposals of the Late Thirteenth and Early Fourteenth Centuries', *Traditio*, 36 (1980), 317–45, and in his *Military Orders and Crusades* (Aldershot: Ashgate, 1994), VIII; Antony Leopold, *How to Recover the Holy Land: The Crusade Proposals of the Late Thirteenth and Early Fourteenth Centuries* (Aldershot: Ashgate, 2000); Silvia Schein, *Fideles Crucis: The Papacy, the West, and the Recovery of the Holy Land* (Oxford: Oxford University Press, 1991);

Verbruggen, *Art of Warfare*, pp. 288–307. See also, for example, Ramon Muntaner's advice to King James II of Aragon regarding the expedition to Sardinia, 1322: Ramon Muntaner, *Crònica*, ed. Marina Gustà (Barcelona: Edicions 62, 1979), ch. 272, translated as: *The Chronicle of Muntaner*, trans. Lady Goodenough, 2 vols, Hakluyt Society, 2nd series vols 47, 50 (1920, 1921), vol. 2, pp. 652–9: hereafter cited as 'Ramon Muntaner'.

38.   Both groups forbade killing: *Heresies of the High Middle Ages*, trans. Walter L. Wakefield and Austin P. Evans (New York: Columbia University Press, 1969, 1991), pp. 52, 241. See also James of Vitry, 'Sermones', in *Analecta novissima spicilegii solesmensis: altera continuatio 2, Tusculana*, ed. J. B. Pitra (Paris: Roger et Chernowitz, 1888), Sermon 38, p. 419.

39.   *Picatrix: The Latin Version of the Ghāyat Al-Hakīm*, ed. David Pingree (London: Warburg Institute, 1986), p. 115, lines 1–20, Bk 3, ch. 7, section 11. On the date of the Spanish translation, see David Pingree, 'Between the *Ghāya* and *Picatrix* I: the Spanish Version', *Journal of the Warburg and Courtauld Institutes*, 44 (1981), 27–56, here 27. On the sources of the work see *idem*, 'Some of the Sources of the *Ghāyat Al-Hakīm*', *Journal of the Warburg and Courtauld Institutes*, 43 (1980), 1–15. I have selected a quotation from this text to illustrate this point partly because the text will be unfamiliar to most readers, and partly because – unlike most writers against war in medieval Europe – it is not a heavily Christianised text, but presents a religious-neutral point of view.

40.   Bertrand de Born, quoted by Verbruggen, *Art of Warfare*, p. 37.

41.   Honoré Bouvet, *Tree of Battles*, Bk 1 ch. 1, p. 81.

42.   *Picatrix*, pp. xv–xxiii. A useful although now dated introduction to the text and its influence is provided by Frances A. Yates, *Giordano Bruno and the Hermetic Tradition* (London: Routledge, 1964), pp. 49–56. For further information on the context see, for example, Alejandro García Avilés, 'Two Astromagical Manuscripts of Alfonso X', *Journal of the Warburg and Courtauld Institutes*, 59 (1996), 14–23; Frank Klaassen, 'English Manuscripts of Magic, 1399–1500: A Preliminary Survey', in *Conjuring Spirits: Texts and Traditions of Medieval Ritual Magic*, ed. Claire Fanger (Stroud: Sutton, 1998), pp. 3–31: here pp. 14–15. The Latin translation of *Picatrix* was apparently made in the early fourteenth century: A. d'Agostino, 'Frammento Ambrosiano del *Picatrix*', *Studi Medievali*, 3rd series 20:1 (1997), 255–60: here 257.

43.   For example, Matt. 5 v. 9, 6 v. 39, 26 v. 52.

44.   Tertullian, 'De idolatria', xix, translated in *Ante Nicene Fathers: The Writings of the Fathers down to A.D. 325*, ed. Alexander Roberts and James Donaldson, rev. edn. A. Cleveland Coxe, 10 vols (Peabody, MA: Hendrickson Publishers, 1994), vol. 3, p. 73.

45.   See, for instance, the case of the centurion Marcellus in 298 at Tangier: *Roman Civilisation: Sourcebook II: The Empire*, ed. Naphtali Lewis and Meyer Reinhold (New York: Harper & Row, 1966), pp. 595–6.

46.   See, for instance, from the first half of the fourth century (*c.*330–48): Hegemonius, *Acta Archelai (The Acts of Archelaus)*, trans. Mark Vermes, intro. Samuel N. C. Lieu, Manichaean Studies IV (Turnhout: Brepols, 2001), p. 36, I. 6.

47. *Augustine: Political Writings*, trans. M. W. Tkacz and D. Kries, intro. E. L. Fortin (Indianapolis: Hackett, 1994), pp. 219–20, 221–9.

48. See Jean Flori, *Idéologie du glaive: préhistoire de la chevalerie* (Geneva: Droz, 1983), p. 41.

49. Ibid., pp. 52–7.

50. Ibid., pp. 59–61. See also Georges Duby, *The Three Orders : Feudal Society Imagined*, trans. Arthur Goldhammer; with a foreword by Thomas N. Bisson (Chicago: University of Chicago Press, 1980). Originally published as: *Les trois ordres, ou L'imaginaire du féodalisme* (Paris: Gallimard, 1978).

51. Odo of Cluny, 'Vita sancti Geraldi Auriliacensis comitis', *Patrologia Latina*, ed. J. P. Migne, 217 vols and 4 vols of indexes (Paris: Migne, 1844–64), vol. 133, cols 639–702. See also Flori, *Idéologie du glaive*, pp. 109–11. For a translation of Odo's 'Life' of Gerald of Aurillac, see: *St. Odo of Cluny: being the Life of St. Odo of Cluny by John of Salerno, and the Life of St. Gerald of Aurillac by St. Odo*, trans. and ed. Gerard Sitwell (New York: Sheed and Ward, 1958).

52. H. E. J. Cowdrey, 'The Peace and Truce of God in the Eleventh Century', *Past and Present*, 46 (1970), 42–67, esp. 43–4. See also, for instance, Marcus Bull, *Knightly Piety and the Lay Response to the First Crusade: The Limousin and Gascony, c.970–1130* (Oxford: Oxford University Press, 1993), 21–69. For the peace in Lotharingia see Alan V. Murray, *The Crusader Kingdom of Jerusalem: A Dynastic History 1099–1125* (Oxford: Prosopographica et Genealogica, 2000), pp. 25–6.

53. Frederick H. Russell, *The Just War in the Middle Ages* (Cambridge: Cambridge University Press, 1975); Maurice Keen, *The Laws of War in the Late Middle Ages* (London: Routledge, 1965), pp. 63–73.

54. Keen, *Laws of War*; Maurice Keen, 'The Jurisdiction and Origins of the Constable's Court', in *War and Government*, ed. Gillingham and Holt, pp. 159–69; reprinted in his *Nobles, Knights and Men-at-Arms in the Middle Ages* (London: Hambleton Press, 1996), pp. 135–48; Maurice Keen, 'Treason Trials Under the Law of Arms', *Transactions of the Royal Historical Society*, 5 series, 12 (1962), 85–103; reprinted in his *Nobles, Knights and Men-at-Arms*, pp. 149–66.

55. John Gilchrist, 'The Papacy and War Against "the Saracens", 795–1216', in *International History Review*, 10 (1988), 174–97.

56. Ian Robinson, 'Pope Gregory VII and the Soldiers of Christ', *History*, 58 (1973), 169–92: esp. 180. See also H. E. J. Cowdrey, 'Pope Gregory VII and the Bearing of Arms', in *Montjoie: Studies in Crusade History in Honour of Hans Eberhard Mayer*, ed. Benjamin Z. Kedar, Jonathan Riley-Smith and Rudolf Hiestand (Aldershot: Variorum, 1997), pp. 21–35.

57. Guibert of Nogent, *The Deeds of God through the Franks: Gesta Dei per Francos*, trans. Robert Levine (Woodbridge: Boydell, 1997), p. 28 (amended).

58. Jonathan Riley-Smith, *The First Crusade and the Idea of Crusading* (London: Athlone Press, 1986), p. 29.

59. See now Christopher Walter, *The Warrior Saints in Byzantine Art and Tradition* (Aldershot: Ashgate, 2003).

60. John of Salisbury, *Policraticus*, ed. Clement C. I. Webb, 2 vols (Oxford: Clarendon Press, 1909), Bk 7 ch. 21, vol. 2, p. 193 lines 4–5, p. 198 lines 17–18. The Hospitallers began as a hospitaller order, but began to take on military responsibilities in the 1120s and 1130s: Helen Nicholson, *The Knights Hospitaller* (Woodbridge: Boydell, 2001), pp. 9–13.

61. John of Salisbury, *Policraticus*, Bk 6 ch. 9, vol. 2, p. 23 line 22, p. 24 line 24.

62. Ibid., Bk 6 ch. 8, vol. 2, p. 23 lines 18–19.

63. Jean Flori, *L'Essor de la chevalerie, Xie-XIIe siècles* (Geneva: Droz, 1986), pp. 249–52.

64. Flori, *L'Essor de la chevalerie*, pp. 257–63.

65. See the analysis of his work by Nicholas Wright, *Knights and Peasants: The Hundred Years War in the French Countryside* (Woodbridge: Boydell, 1998), pp. 6, 17, 29, 46, 50, 56, 58, 60, 68, 82, 89, 93–4, 95, 96–7.

66. *La Chanson de Roland*, ed. F. Whitehead (Oxford: Blackwell, 1942), lines 1877–82.

67. William Compaine Calin, *The Old French Epic of Revolt: Raoul de Cambrai, Renaud de Montauban, Gormond et Isembard* (Geneva: Droz, 1962).

68. Scholars generally agree that it was composed after 1210; the latest date for composition is less clear. For one suggestion see Alexandre Micha, *Essais sur le cycle Lancelot-Graal* (Geneva: Droz, 1987), p. 12. He suggests a date for the whole Vulgate Cycle of 1225–30 or possibly 1215–35.

69. For Brun's later career see, for example, *Gyron le Courtoys*, fols 227v–257v, here spelt 'Brehus'; for the date (1235–40) see Roger Lathuillère, *Guiron le Courtois. Étude de la tradition manuscrite et analyse critique* (Geneva: Droz, 1966), pp. 31–4. For his role in the *Prophecies de Merlin*, written in the 1270s, see Richard Trachsler, 'Brehus sans Pitié: portrait-robot du criminel arthurien', in *La violence dans le monde médiéval* (Aix-en-Provence: Cuerma, 1994), pp. 527–42.

70. Keen, *Laws of War*, pp. 73–81.

71. *Beowulf*, trans. Michael Alexander (Harmondsworth: Penguin Books, 1973), p. 53. See also now *Beowulf: A Verse Translation*, trans. Seamus Heaney, ed. Daniel Donoghue (New York: W. W. Norton, 2002), pp. 3–78: here lines 64–72.

72. *Beowulf*, trans. Alexander, pp. 64, 71; trans. Heaney, lines 407–24, 631–8.

73. *Beowulf*, trans. Alexander, pp. 72, 96; trans. Heaney, lines 677–87, 1443.

74. *Beowulf*, trans. Alexander, pp. 78–9, 83–4; trans. Heaney, lines 873–914, 1019–52.

75. *Beowulf*, trans. Alexander, pp. 70, 84–6, 87–8, 91–3, 111–12, 150–1; trans. Heaney, lines 612–41, 1070–8, 1115–18, 1169–89, 1215–32, 1276–1340, 1928–54, 3150–3.

76. *Beowulf*, trans. Alexander, pp. 102, 133–6, 141–2; trans. Heaney, lines 1626–43, 2596–711, 2845–91.

77. *Beowulf*, trans. Alexander, pp. 100, 102, 103, 105–7, 139; trans. Heaney, lines 1553–6, 1609–11, 1627, 1656–8, 1724–84, 2794–801. On this theme see also Graham D. Caie, 'Christ as Warrior in Old English Poetry', in *War and Peace in the Middle Ages*, ed. Brian Patrick McGuire (Copenhagen: C. A. Reitzel, 1987), pp. 13–28.

78. *Chanson de Roland*, lines 1008–16.

79. Ibid., lines 1047–8.

80. Ibid., lines 2258–396.

81. See Steidle, '*Meilz valt mesure*', 251–68.

82. Jean Bodel, *La Chanson des Saisnes*, ed. Annette Brasseur (Geneva: Droz, 1989), lines 5914–45, 5956–75, 6105–10.

83. For the 'order' of knighthood see, for example, *Moniage Guillaume*, vol. 1, 2nd redaction, lines 509–29.

84. *Le Roman de Brut de Wace*, ed. Ivor Arnold, vol. 2, Société des anciens textes français (Paris: Firmin Didot, 1940).

85. *L'Histoire de Guillaume le Maréchal*, ed. Paul Meyer, 3 vols, Société de l'histoire de France (Paris: Renouard, 1891–1901), lines 1884–8 (for example), 3485–520, 18598–604, 18702–6, 19085–106, 3332–64, 4319–430, 6677–864, 7312–18, 8753–72, 3477–80, and (for example) 14512–16.

86. For some of these references and others see Nicholson, *Love, War and the Grail*, p. 206; *Gyron le Courtoys, c.1501*, fol. 284v. For a summary of *Guiron* see Lathuillère, *Guiron le Courtois*.

87. Keen, *Chivalry*, pp. 239, 252.

88. Wright, *Knights and Peasants*, pp. 41–4, etc. On this see also Keen, *Laws of War*, pp. 1–3.

89. See Keen, *Chivalry*, pp. 33–4; but see also Flori, *L'Essor de la chevalerie*, pp. 329–30, indicating that chivalric ideals actually originated in the Empire.

90. Verbruggen, *Art of Warfare*, pp. 190–203; Kelly DeVries, *Infantry Warfare in the Early Fourteenth Century: Discipline, Tactics and Technology* (Woodbridge: Boydell, 1996), pp. 32–48. DeVries considers this to be a French victory.

91. Froissart, *Chroniques: manuscrit d'Amiens, Bibliothèque municipal no. 486*, ed. George T. Diller, 5 vols (Geneva: Droz, 1991–98), vol. 3, pp. 17–26, chs 510–14. Diller argues that this represents the first version of Froissart's chronicle: vol. 1, pp. ix–xxiii, esp. p. xix. Jean Froissart, *Chroniques. Dernière rédaction du premier livre. Édition du manuscrit de Rome, Reg. lat. 869*, ed. George T. Diller (Geneva: Droz, 1972), pp. 717–43, chs 221–9. For a modern analysis of the battle see DeVries, *Infantry Warfare*, pp. 155–75, esp. 166–7, 169–71; Bennett, 'Development of Battle Tactics', p. 10.

92. Bennett, 'Development of Battle Tactics', pp. 10–11.

93. Froissart, *Chroniques: manuscrit d'Amiens*, vol. 3, p. 106, ch. 557.

94. Ibid., pp. 107–19, chs 557–62; Bennett, 'Development of Battle Tactics', pp. 12–13.

95. Froissart, *Chroniques: manuscrit d'Amiens*: Cocherel: vol. 3, pp. 301–15, chs 659–66: here p. 308, ch. 662 lines 92–4; Pontvallain: vol. 4, pp. 115–17, ch. 811: here p. 116, ch. 811 lines 59–62.

96. From the chronicles of Enguerran de Monstrelet, Jean le Fèvre and Jean de Waurin, in Curry, *Battle of Agincourt*, here pp. 161–2. See also for analysis Bennett, 'Development of Battle Tactics', pp. 16–17.

97. See Rogers, 'The Age of the Hundred Years War', p. 142; Bennett, 'Development of Battle Tactics', pp. 4–5.

98. See also Bennett, 'Development of Battle Tactics', pp. 10–18; he shows that the French commanders were attempting to adapt their tactics and were sometimes successful, but that keeping discipline among their troops was a problem.

99. Frederick G. Heymann, *John Žižka and the Hussite Revolution* (Princeton: Princeton University Press, 1955), pp. 291–302.

100. Ibid., pp. 305, 450–2.

2   Military personnel

1.   Gregory of Tours, Bk 7 chs 24–6, 28, 35, 38, 42, pp. 406–7, 409, 418–19, 423, 426.

2.   *Chronicle of James I King of Aragon*, trans. John Forster (London: Chapman and Hall, 1883; repr. Farnborough: Greg International, 1968; repr. New York: AMS, 1983), chs 153–5, pp. 253–6. A new translation, *The Book of Deeds of James I of Aragon: A Translation of the Medieval Catalan 'Libre dels Fets'*, has been prepared by Damian J. Smith and Helena Buffrey and is due to be published by Ashgate in 2003.

3.   *European Crossbows: A Survey by Josef Alm*, trans. H. Bartlett Wells, ed. G. M. Wilson (Leeds: Royal Armouries Museum, 1994), p. 6; Gregory of Tours, Bk 5 ch. 20, Bk 5 ch. 48, Bk 10 ch. 16, pp. 285, 315, 574; see also, for the use of the bow by the Franks, Bernard S. Bachrach, 'Procopius, Agathias and the Frankish Military', *Speculum*, 45 (1970), 435–41: here 438 and note 12.

4.   On this see, for instance, Bernard S. Bachrach, 'Military Organization in Aquitaine under the Early Carolingians', *Speculum*, 49 (1974), 1–33; Bachrach, *Early Carolingian Warfare*, pp. 52, 208–12.

5.   For what follows see A. H. M. Jones, *The Later Roman Empire, 284–602*, 2 vols (Oxford: Oxford University Press, 1964), pp. 614–18; Vegetius, *De re militari*, Bk 1 chs 2–8, pp. 3–9.

6.   See Andrew Ayton, *Knights and Warhorses: Military Service and the English Aristocracy Under Edward III* (Woodbridge: Boydell, 1994), p. 150 and note 66, citing Richard Agar Newhall, *Muster and Review: a Problem of English military Administration 1420–1440* (Cambridge, MA.: Harvard University Press, 1940), pp. 53–4; and Christopher Allmand, *The Hundred Years War: England and France at War, c.1300–c.1450* (Cambridge: Cambridge University Press, 1988), pp. 114–15.

7.   Jones, *Later Roman Empire*, pp. 607–11, 619–23.

8.   Ibid., pp. 611–12, 618–19.

9.   Ibid., p. 612.

10. Janet Nelson, *Charles the Bald* (London: Longman, 1992), pp. 151, 187–8, 193, 204–6, 208, 213.

11. *Ottonian Germany: The Chronicon of Thietmar of Merseburg*, ed. and trans. David A. Warner (Manchester: Manchester University Press, 2001), Bk 2 ch. 7, p. 96.

12. See Angus Mackay, *Spain in the Middle Ages: From Frontier to Empire, 1000–1500* (Basingstoke: Macmillan, 1977), pp. 18–19.

13. Richard I: T. Stapleton, *Magnus Rotulus Scaccarii Normanniae* (London: Society of Antiquaries, 1842), vol. 1, p. 221. I am grateful to Dr Vincent Moss for drawing this reference to my attention. Hungary: Malcolm Barber, *The Two Cities: Medieval Europe, 1050–1320* (London: Routledge, 1992), p. 379.

14. Lucera: John France, *Western Warfare in the Age of the Crusades, 1000–1300* (London: UCL Press, 1999), p. 129; Benevento: ibid., pp. 179–80. On Italy see also Giovanni Amatuccio, 'Saracen Archers in Southern Italy', an online article written for the De Re Militari Society at: http://www.deremilitari.org/Saracen%20archers.htm

15. Ramon Muntaner, ch. 228.

16. Sven Ekdahl, *Die Schlacht von Tannenberg 1410: Quellenkritische Untersuchungen*, 1: *Einführung und Quellenlage* (Berlin: Duncker and Humblot, 1982), pp. 196-7.

17. Vegetius, *De re militari*, Bk 1 ch. 7, p. 8 note 4; Ammianus Marcellinus, *Res Gestae*, in *Ammiani Marcellini rerum gestarum libri qui supersunt*, trans. J. C. Rolfe, 3 vols, Loeb Classical Library 300, 315, 331 (London: William Heinemann, 1971), Bk 19 ch. 11.7, vol. 1, pp. 528–9, and Bk 31 ch. 4.4–6, vol. 3, pp. 402–5.

18. For this see Bachrach, *Early Carolingian Warfare*, pp. 52–4.

19. This theory is described by François Louis Ganshof, *Feudalism*, trans. Philip Grierson, 3rd edn (London: Longmans, 1964). Originally published as *Qu'est-ce que la féodalité?* 4th edn (Brussels: Presses universitaires de Bruxelles, 1968).

20. Susan Reynolds, *Fiefs and Vassals: The Medieval Evidence Reinterpreted* (Oxford: Oxford University Press, 1994).

21. Ibid., pp. 46–7.

22. Ibid., pp. 48–74.

23. Ibid., p. 379.

24. Bachrach, 'Military Organization in Aquitaine', 20; Roger Collins, *Charlemagne* (Basingstoke: Macmillan – now Palgrave Macmillan, 1998), pp. 126–7.

25. Bachrach, 'Military Organization in Aquitaine', 29, 31. Although Bachrach is discussing Aquitaine here, he implies that these capitularies applied to the whole of Charlemagne's domains.

26. See also Stephen S. Evans, *The Lords of Battle: Image and Reality of the 'Comitatus' in Dark-Age Britain* (Woodbridge: Boydell, 1997).

27. Peter Coss, *The Knight in Medieval England, 1000–1400* (Stroud: Alan Sutton, 1993), p. 102.

28. Alan Forey, 'The Military Orders and the Spanish Reconquest in the Twelfth and Thirteenth Centuries', *Traditio*, 40 (1984), 197–234, reprinted in his *Military Orders and Crusades*, no. V: here p. 230.

29. Richard Vaughan, *Charles the Bold: The Last Valois Duke of Burgundy* (London: Longman, 1973), pp. 219–20.

30. Daniel Waley, *The Italian City-Republics*, 3rd edn (London: Longman, 1988), pp. 53–4; on mercenaries, see pp. 97–9, 101.

31. Manuel González Jiménez, 'Frontier and Settlement in the Kingdom of Castile (1085–1350)', in *Medieval Frontier Societies*, ed. Bartlett and Mackay, pp. 49–74: here pp. 57–8.

32. William Chester Jordan, *Louis IX and the Challenge of the Crusade: A Study in Rulership* (Princeton: Princeton University Press, 1979), pp. 65–6.

33. Coss, *Knight in Medieval England*, pp. 102–3; 'Private Indentures for Life Service in Peace and War, 1278–1476', ed. Michael Jones and Simon Walker, in *Camden Miscellany XXXII*, Camden Society, 5th Series, 3 (1994), pp. 1–190: here pp. 10–11, 14–15; Andrew Ayton, 'English Armies in the Fourteenth Century', in *Arms, Armies and Fortifications*, ed. Curry and Hughes (Woodbridge: Boydell, 1994), pp. 21–38: here pp. 25–6; Michael Prestwich, 'Cavalry Service in Early Fourteenth Century England' in *War and Government*, ed. Gillingham and Holt, pp. 147–58: here pp. 147–8. For a survey of the recruitment of armies in fourteenth- and fifteenth-century England, France and Italy see Contamine, *War in the Middle Ages*, pp. 150–65.

34. Coss, *Knight in Medieval England*, pp. 104–7; Ayton, 'English Armies in the Fourteenth Century', pp. 21–38.

35. Anne Curry, 'English Armies in the Fifteenth Century', in *Arms, Armies and Fortifications*, ed. Curry and Hughes, pp. 39–68.

36. Stephen D. B. Brown, 'Military Service and Monetary Reward in the Eleventh and Twelfth Centuries', *History*, 74 (1989), 20–38; France, *Western Warfare*, pp. 60–2, 70–6.

37. Froissart, *Chroniques. Dernière rédaction*, p. 449, ch. 125 lines 18–20.

38. Burton Annals in *Annales monastici*, ed. Henry R. Luard, 5 vols, Rolls Series 36 (London: Longman, 1864–1869), vol. 1, p. 494.

39. J. C. Holt, *Magna Carta*, 2nd edn (Cambridge, Cambridge University Press, 1992), p. 464–5 clause 51.

40. Ramon Muntaner, chs 200–43: see esp. chs 201, 225, 227, 230, 233 for the company's composition and equipment. For the later history of the company see, for instance, Kenneth M. Setton, *Catalan Domination of Athens, 1311–1388* (Cambridge, MA: The Medieval Academy of America, 1948; rev. edn London: Variorum, 1975); R. Ignatius Burns, 'The Catalan Company and the European Powers, 1305–1311', *Speculum*, 29 (1954), 751–71; Housley, *The Later Crusades*, pp. 161–5, 169–71, and 477 for further reading. For earlier mercenary groups and leaders see Contamine, *War in the Middle Ages*, pp. 244–7.

41. Kenneth Fowler, *Medieval Mercenaries, vol. 1: The Great Companies* (Oxford: Blackwell, 2001). On Innocent VI's crusade see pp. 34–5; on Pontvallain and the end of the Companies see pp. 294–301.

42. Maurice Keen, 'The Changing Scene: Guns, Gunpowder, and Permanent Armies', in *Medieval Warfare*, ed. Keen, pp. 272–91: here 283–4. On the re-emergence of permanent armies see Contamine, *War in the Middle Ages*, pp. 165–72.

43. Vaughan, *Charles the Bold*, pp. 16–18.

44. Ibid., pp. 211–13.

45. Ibid., p. 213.

46. Maurice Keen, 'The Changing Scene: Guns, Gunpowder, and Permanent Armies', in *Medieval Warfare*, ed. Keen, pp. 281–7. Thomas F. Arnold, 'War in Sixteenth-Century Europe: Revolution and Renaissance', in *European Warfare, 1453–1815*, ed. Jeremy Black (Basingstoke: Macmillan – now Palgrave Macmillan, 1999), pp. 23–44: here pp. 25–9, citing Clifford

Rogers, 'The Military Revolutions of the Hundred Years War', reprinted in *The Military Revolution Debate*, ed. Clifford J. Rogers (Boulder, CO.: Westview Press, 1995), pp. 55–94; Geoffrey Parker, 'The "Military Revolution, 1560–1660" – a Myth', reprinted in *The Military Revolution Debate*, ed. Rogers, pp. 37–54; and Geoffrey Parker, *The Military Revolution: Military Innovation and the Rise of the West, 1500–1800* (Cambridge: Cambridge University Press, 1988 and 1996).

47. Ramon Muntaner, ch. 194.

48. Bachrach, *Early Carolingian Warfare*, pp. 58, 331 note 21.

49. Evans, *Lords of Battle*, pp. 27–32; France, *Western Warfare*, pp. 3, 6, 128–30: here 129–30.

50. Vaughan, *Charles the Bold*, pp. 391, 397, 427–8.

51. Clifford J. Rogers, 'The Age of the Hundred Years War', in *Medieval Warfare*, ed. Keen, pp. 136–60: here p. 160; Keen, 'The Changing Scene', pp. 272, 280. By the end of the sixteenth century armies were very much larger: see Andrew Ayton and J. L. Price, 'Introduction: The Military Revolution from a Medieval Perspective', in *The Medieval Military Revolution: State, Society and Military Change in Medieval and Early Modern Europe*, ed. Andrew Ayton and J. L. Price (London and New York: Tauris Academic Studies, 1995), pp. 1–22: here p. 3, citing 'the estimated 200,000 men supported by Spain in the 1590s'.

52. Michael Prestwich, *War, Politics and Finance Under Edward I* (London: Faber and Faber, 1972), pp. 58, 99; S. D. Church, 'The Earliest English Muster Roll, 18/19 December 1215', *Historical Research*, 67 (1994), 1–17.

53. Georges Duby, *La société aux xi et xii siècles dans la region mâconnaise* (Paris: A. Colin, 1953).

54. Georges Duby, 'Lineage, Nobility and Knighthood: The Mâconnais in the Twelfth Century – a Revision', in *The Chivalrous Society*, trans. Cynthia Postan (London: Edward Arnold, 1977), pp. 59–80, and *passim*; Coss, *Knight in Medieval England*, pp. 5–7; Jiménez, 'Frontier and Settlement', pp. 57–8; Michael Harney, 'Siege in Medieval Hispanic Epic and Romance', in *The Medieval City Under Siege*, ed. Ivy A. Cortis and Michael Wolfe (Woodbridge: Boydell, 1995), pp. 177–90: here p. 182. For Italy see Waley, *Italian City-Republics*, p. 120.

55. See, for example, Keen, *Chivalry*, pp. 23–7; Coss, *Knight in Medieval England*, pp. 7–8; France, *Western Warfare*, p. 56.

56. See, for example, Coss, *Knight in Medieval England*, p. 46; France, *Western Warfare*, p. 57; and see Keen, *Chivalry*, pp. 45–9.

57. See, for example, Coss, *Knight in Medieval England*, pp. 30–46.

58. See, for example, Keen, *Chivalry*, pp. 30–4; Coss, *Knight in Medieval England*, pp. 47–60.

59. Coss, *Knight in Medieval England*, pp. 60–2, 67–71.

60. Béroul, *Le roman de Tristan: poème du XIIe siècle*, ed. Ernest Muret, 4th edn revised by L. M. Defourques (Paris: H. Champion, 1982), lines 965–1039, 1235–1302, 1668–1746, 2479–88, 3577–3614, 3985–4072. Governal is Tristan's *maistres* (teacher) and also his *escuiers* (squire).

61. *La Règle du Temple*, ed. Henri de Curzon, Société de l'histoire de France (Paris: Reynouard, 1886), sections 157, 161, 171–2; translated as *The Rule of the Templars: The French Text of the Rule of the Order of the Knights*

Templar, trans. J. M. Upton-Ward (Woodbridge: Boydell, 1992), pp. 58, 59, 61.

62. Carlos de Ayala Martínez, 'The *Sergents* of the Military Order of Santiago', in *The Military Orders*, vol. 2: *Welfare and Warfare*, ed. Nicholson, pp. 225–33: here pp. 228, 229.

63. Coss, *Knight in Medieval England*, p. 128.

64. Froissart, *Chroniques. Dernière rédaction*, p. 439, ch. 122 lines 29–32.

65. For some examples of mass knightings for military needs see Waley, *Italian City-Republics*, p. 26 (twelfth and early thirteenth century); and Froissart, *Chroniques: manuscrit d'Amiens*, vol. 4, p. 7, ch. 754 lines 55–7 (1369).

66. Heymann, *John Žižka*, pp. 219, 305.

67. Gerald of Wales, *Expugnatio Hibernica: The Conquest of Ireland*, ed. and trans. A. B. Scott and F.-X. Martin (Dublin: Royal Irish Academy, 1978), p. 248 lines 44–8.

68. France, *Western Warfare*, p. 219–20.

69. Ayton, 'English Armies in the Fourteenth Century', p. 33; Froissart, *Chroniques: manuscrit d'Amiens*, vol. 2, p. 248, ch. 404.

70. Matthew Strickland, 'Military Technology and Conquest: The Anomaly of Anglo-Saxon England', *Anglo-Norman Studies*, 19 (1996), pp. 353–82: here pp. 359–69, 382; Matthew Bennett, 'The Myth of the Military Supremacy of Knightly Cavalry', in *Armies, Chivalry and Warfare*, ed. Strickland, pp. 304–16; Donnchadh ó Corráin, 'Prehistoric and Early Christian Ireland', in *The Oxford History of Ireland*, ed. R. F. Foster (Oxford: Oxford University Press, 1989), pp. 1–43: here p. 41; John V. Kelleher, 'The Battle of Móin Mhór, 1151', *Celtica*, 20 (1988), 11–27: here 27, for a reference to horsemen leaving the battlefield with the kings.

71. Verbruggen, *Art of Warfare*, pp. 174–5; Froissart, *Chroniques: manuscrit d'Amiens*, vol. 1, pp. 220–1, ch. 171.

72. Stephen Morillo, 'The "Age of Cavalry" Revisited', in *The Circle of War in the Middle Ages*, ed. Donald J. Kagay and L. J. Andrew Villalon (Woodbridge: Boydell, 1999), pp. 45–58: here pp. 53–4.

73. Quoted by France, *Western Warfare*, p. 68.

74. Verbruggen, *Art of Warfare*, pp. 162–3.

75. Ambroise, *Estoire*, lines 11396–652; *Chronicle of the Third Crusade*, Bk 6 chs 22–3, pp. 361–8.

76. See, for example, Rogers, 'Age of the Hundred Years War', pp. 142–5; DeVries, *Infantry Warfare*; Verbruggen, *Art of Warfare*, pp. 111–203.

77. Keen, 'The Changing Scene', pp. 287–90; Ayton and Price, 'Introduction: The Military Revolution', esp. pp. 1–17; Arnold, 'War in Sixteenth-Century Europe', pp. 23–29, citing, for example, Jeremy Black, *A Military Revolution? Military Change and European Society, 1550–1800* (Basingstoke: Macmillan – now Palgrave Macmillan, 1991); Parker, 'The "Military Revolution, 1560–1660" – a Myth', and Parker, *The Military Revolution*; Michael Roberts, 'The Military Revolution, 1560–1660', reprinted in *The Military Revolution Debate*, ed. Rogers, pp. 13–35; Clifford J. Rogers, 'The Military Revolutions of the Hundred Years War', reprinted in *The Military Revolution Debate*, ed. Rogers, pp. 95–116.

78. Susan Edgington, 'Medical Knowledge in the Crusading Armies: The Evidence of Albert of Aachen', in *The Military Orders: Fighting for the*

Faith and Caring for the Sick, ed. Malcolm Barber (Aldershot: Variorum, 1994), pp. 320–6.

79. Vegetius, *De re militari*, Bk. 2 ch. 11, p. 43. On Carolingian engineers see Bachrach, *Early Carolingian Warfare*, pp. 212, 233.

80. Translated by Housley, *Documents*, pp. 39–40. For other examples from the twelfth and thirteenth century see France, *Western Warfare*, p. 125.

81. Christine de Pisan, *Book of Fayttes*, Bk 2 ch. 30, pp. 160–1; see also, for the original French, BL Harley MS 4605, fols 60v–61r; *Book of Deeds*, trans. Willard, Bk 2 ch. 31, pp. 123–4.

82. *Histoire des ducs de Normandie et des rois d'Angleterre*, ed. Francisque Michel, Société de l'histoire de France, no. 18 (Paris: Jules Renouard, 1840; repr. New York: Johnson Reprint, 1965), p. 163.

83. *Chronicle of the Third Crusade*, Bk 3 ch. 11, p. 213; Ambroise, *Estoire*, lines 4909–26 (slightly different account).

84. *The Old French Crusade Cycle, vol. 8: The Jérusalem Continuations: The London-Turin Version*, ed. Peter R. Grillo (Tuscaloosa: University of Alabama Press, 1994), lines 7086–90.

85. Gerhard W. Kramer, *The Firework Book: Gunpowder in Medieval Germany*, trans. Klaus Leibnitz (London: Arms and Armour Society, 2001), pp. 21, 26.

86. Both women and men were involved in arms manufacture, from making wire for mail to string-making for bows or attaching the fletchings to arrows: see, for instance, Agnes Hecche of York, daughter of an armourer, who was trained in mailwork: P. J. P. Goldberg, *Women, Work and Life Cycle in a Medieval Economy: Women in York and Yorkshire c.1300–1520* (Oxford: Oxford University Press, 1992), p. 128. Goldberg identified in the poll tax records for 1379 and 1381 for Oxford and York a total of three households headed by a woman where the occupation was 'armaments' (ibid., pp. 91–2) – the two at York were fletchers and the one at Oxford was a stringer (p. 96).

87. Wright, *Knights and Peasants*, pp. 80–116.

88. Honoré Bouvet, *The Tree of Battles*, Bk 4 ch. 70, p. 168. For medieval clerical attitudes to women fighting see James M. Blythe, 'Women in the Military: Scholastic Arguments and Medieval Images of Female Warriors', *History of Political Thought*, 22 (2001), pp. 242–69.

89. Carolyne Larrington, *Women and Writing in Medieval Europe: A Sourcebook* (London and New York: Routledge, 1995), p. 158. On women in warfare see, for instance, my 'Women on the Third Crusade', *Journal of Medieval History*, 23 (1997), 335–49, and the other works cited therein, esp. Megan McLaughlin, 'The Woman Warrior: Gender, Warfare and Society in Medieval Europe', *Women's Studies – an Interdisciplinary Journal*, 17 (1990), 193–209; see also now *Gendering the Crusades*, ed. Susan Edgington and Sarah Lambert (Cardiff: University of Wales Press, 2001), which includes an extensive bibliography on women's involvement in warfare in the medieval period. On noble women's involvement in warfare see also Jean A. Truax, 'Anglo-Norman Women at War: Valiant Soldiers, Prudent Strategists or Charismatic Leaders?', in *The Circle of War*, ed. Kagay and Villalon, pp. 111–25.

90. On classical precedent see, for instance, Michael R. Evans, '"Unfit to Bear Arms": The Gendering of Arms and Armour in Accounts of Women on

Crusade', in *Gendering the Crusades*, ed. Edgington and Lambert, pp. 45–58: here pp. 49–51.

91.   *Eneas: roman du XIIe siècle*, ed. J.-J. Salverda de Grave, 2 vols (Paris: Édouard Champion, 1925–9), vol. 2, lines 7177–224; translated as *Eneas: A Twelfth-Century French Romance*, trans. John A. Yunck (New York and London: Columbia University Press), pp. 196–7.

92.   See, for example, Maligne in *Le Roman de Laurin, fils de Marques le senéchal*, ed. Lewis Thorpe (Cambridge: W. Heffer, 1995), pp. 290–3, 300–2, 361–2; Silence in Heldris de Cornualle, *Silence: A Thirteenth-Century French Romance*, ed. and trans. Sarah Roche-Mahdi (East Lanzing: Michigan University Press, 1992); and the anonymous noblewoman in *Les Prophesies de Merlin*, ed. Anne Berthelot (Cologny-Geneva: Fondation Martin Bodmer, 1992), pp. 147–8.

93.   *Libellus de expugnatione terrae sanctae per Saladinum*, in Ralph of Coggeshall, *Chronicon Anglicanum*, ed. J. Stevenson, Rolls Series 66 (London: Longman, 1875), pp. 220, 228; *Chronique d'Ernoul de de Bernard le trésorier*, ed. L. de Mas Latrie, Société de l'histoire de France (Paris: Renouard, 1871), pp. 157–9, 174; *La continuation de Guillaume de Tyr (1184–1197)*, ed. Margaret Ruth Morgan (Paris: Paul Geuthner, 1982), sections 29, 30, 32, 44; translated in Peter W. Edbury, *The Conquest of Jerusalem and the Third Crusade* (Aldershot: Scolar, 1996), pp. 36–7, 38, 48.

94.   Kelly DeVries, 'A Woman as Leader of Men: Joan of Arc's Military Career', in *Fresh Verdicts on Joan of Arc*, ed. Bonnie Wheeler and Charles T. Wood (New York and London: Garland, 1996), pp. 3–18; Deborah Fraioli, 'Why Joan of Arc Never Became an Amazon', in ibid., pp. 189–204; Deborah A. Fraioli, *Joan of Arc: The Early Debate* (Woodbridge, Suffolk and Rochester, NY: Boydell, 1999).

95.   Bachrach, *Early Carolingian Warfare*, p. 59.

96.   H. J. Cowdrey, *Pope Gregory VII, 1073–1085* (Oxford: Oxford University Press, 1998), pp. 296–307.

97.   Christine de Pisan, *The Treasure of the City of Ladies, or the Book of the Three Virtues*, trans. Sarah Lawson (Harmondsworth: Penguin, 1985), part 2 ch. 9, p. 129.

98.   Frank Stenton, *Anglo-Saxon England*, 3rd edn (Oxford: Oxford University Press, 1971), pp. 324–9, 333, 335, 529; *The Anglo-Saxon Chronicle: A Revised Translation*, ed. Dorothy Whitelock with David C. Douglas and Susie I. Tucker (London: Eyre and Spottiswode, 1965), pp. 62–7.

99.   *Chronique de Jean le Bel*, ed. Jules Viard and Eugène Déprez, Société de l'histoire de France (Paris: Renouard, 1904, repr. Paris: Slatkine/ H. Champion, 1977), vol. 1, ch. 47, pp. 271–8, Froissart, *Chroniques: manuscrit d'Amiens*, vol. 2, pp. 157–8, ch. 351; pp. 198–210, chs 374–80; pp. 213–14, ch. 382.

100. Froissart, *Chroniques: manuscrit d'Amiens*, vol. 3, p. 54, ch. 531 lines 20–24.

101. The French word is *amie*, meaning 'beloved' or 'girlfriend'. These women were clearly on a relatively equal footing with their menfolk; they were not, for example, slaves. As will be seen in the story of Margaret the Englishwoman, the two parties were regarded as having obligations to each

other. Hence I have used the modern term 'partner', which seems the nearest modern equivalent to the relationship.

102. Froissart, *Chroniques. Dernière rédaction*, pp. 892–3, ch. 721.

103. Antoine de la Salle, *Jehan de Saintré*, ed. J. Misrahi and Charles A. Knudson (Geneva: Droz, 1967), p. ix.

104. For instance, at the battle of Dorylaeum, 1 July 1098, during the First Crusade: *Gesta Francorum et aliorum Hierosolimitanorum: The Deeds of the Franks and the Other Pilgrims to Jerusalem*, ed. Rosalind Hill (London: Nelson, 1962), Bk 3 ch. 9, p. 19; and at a battle outside Damietta on 29 August 1219, during the Fifth Crusade: 'Fragmentum de captione Damiatae', in *Quinti belli sacri scriptores minores*, ed. Reinbold Röhricht, Société de l'Orient Latin, 162 (Geneva: J.-G. Fick, 1879), p. 187.

105. *Gesta Francorum*, Bk 3 ch. 9, p. 19.

106. On this see, for instance, Goldberg, *Women, Work and Lifecycle*, p. 135; and the references in my 'Women in Templar and Hospitaller Commanderies', in *La commanderie, institution des orders militaries dans l'Occident medieval*, ed. Anthony Luttrell and Léon Pressouyre (Paris: CTHS, 2002), pp. 125–34: here p. 132 and note 23.

107. Christine de Pisan, *Book of Fayttes*, Bk 2 ch. 37, p. 176, lines 10–12; see also the original French in BL Harley ms 4605, fol. 66v; *Book of Deeds*, trans. Willard, Bk 2 ch. 39, p. 136.

108. For this service the vernacular chronicler Ambroise labelled them 'good as apes', the comparison with apes always being an insult during the medieval period: Ambroise, *Estoire*, line 5698. On ape imagery in medieval art and literature see, for example, Kenneth Varty, *Renart the Fox: A Study of the Fox in Medieval English Art* (Leicester: Leicester University Press, 1967), pp. 60–7. In modern British society women who pick lice off their dependants are generally known as mothers, and if Ambroise had said that his women were 'as good as mothers', he would not have caused nearly so much resentment among modern commentators.

109. See, for instance, women firing a stonethrower during the Albigensian Crusade (1281), translated in Janet Shirley, *Song of the Cathar Wars: A History of the Albigensian Crusade* (Aldershot: Ashgate, 1996), p. 172; the women of the Catalan company defending Gallipoli (1305), in Ramon Muntaner, ch. 227; women defending Montalban (1366), in Froissart, *Chroniques: manuscrit d'Amiens*, vol. 3, p. 389, ch. 702 lines 55–60.

110. Vaughan, *Charles the Bold*, p. 209. Charles apparently reckoned that one prostitute was as good as another, and did not expect the men to fight over the common women, nor the women over the men. In addition, he was apparently unaware of the risk of spreading venereal disease among the troops – although the sexual transmission of disease was becoming known at this time. See Claude Quétel, *History of Syphilis*, trans. Judith Braddock and Brian Pike (London: Polity Press/Basil Blackwell, 1990), pp. 11–12. I am indebted for this reference to Rachel Bowen, doctoral student at Cardiff University. For one version of the medieval story of army prostitutes fighting between themselves over the men see *The Avowing of Arthur*, lines 909–72, in *Middle English Metrical Romances*, ed. Walter Hoyt French and Charles Brockway Hale (New York: Russell and Russell, 1930), pp. 607–46.

111.　John Gillingham, *Richard I* (New Haven and London: Yale University Press, 1999), pp. 40, 41, 49–50. Richard was born in September 1157. Geoffrey de Charny envisaged a youth receiving his first military experience at the age of 15: 'Le Livre Messire Geoffroi de Charny', ed. Arthur Piaget, *Romania*, 26 (1897), 394–411: here 409, lines 712–4.

112.　Nicholas Orme, *Medieval Children* (New Haven and London: Yale University Press, 2001), p. 327: this was the age at which noble boys could inherit land, 'allegedly because their military duties needed more strength and understanding'. See also Shulasmith Shahar, *Childhood in the Middle Ages*, trans. Chaya Galai (London and New York: Routledge, 1990), p. 28.

113.　Honoré Bouvet, *Tree of Battles*, Bk 4 ch. 94, pp. 184–5.

114.　Wright, *Knights and Peasants*, pp. 46, 72, 81.

115.　Gregory of Tours, Bk 7 chs 37, 42: pp. 421, 426.

116.　Bachrach, *Early Carolingian Warfare*, pp. 28–9.

117.　Ibid., p. 61.

118.　Ibid., pp. 151–7.

119.　Anna Comnena, *Alexiad*, Bk 10 ch. 8; trans. as *The Alexiad of Anna Comnena*, trans. E. R. A. Sewter (Harmondsworth: Penguin, 1969), pp. 317–18.

120.　Ambroise, *Estoire*, lines 1607–617; *Chronicle of the Third Crusade*, Bk. 2 ch. 33, p. 186.

121.　Anglo, *Martial Arts*, p. 22.

122.　The humour of *Les enfances Vivien*, ed. Magali Rouguier (Geneva: Droz, 1997), is based on this premise.

123.　*La continuation de Guillaume de Tyr (1184–1197)*, ed. Margaret Ruth Morgan (Paris: Paul Geuthner, 1982), ch. 33, pp. 45–6. See also the translation by Peter W. Edbury, in *The Conquest of Jerusalem and the Third Crusade: Sources in Translation* (Aldershot: Scolar, 1996), p. 39.

124.　Waley, *Italian City-Republics*, pp. 27–9.

125.　Coss, *Knight in Medieval England*, pp. 125–6.

3　Military buildings

1.　For a nineteenth-century representation of such a tree fort see the plate facing p. 372 in *The Oxford Illustrated History of the Crusades*, ed. Jonathan Riley-Smith (Oxford: Oxford University Press, 1995).

2.　Wright, *Knights and Peasants*, pp. 104–14.

3.　Ibid., pp. 101–2; *La très joyeuse, plaisante et récréative histoire du gentil seigneur de Bayart, composée par le loyal serviteur*, ed. J. Roman, Société de l'histoire de France (Paris: Renouard, 1878), pp. 206–8.

4.　*Willelmi Tyrensis archiepiscopi Chronicon*, ed. R. B. C. Huygens, 2 vols, Corpus Christianorum continuatio medievalis 63, 63A (Turnholt: Brepols, 1986), Bk 19 ch. 11, p. 879: hereafter cited as 'William of Tyre'. For a translation see Archbishop William of Tyre, *A History of Deeds Done Beyond the Sea*, trans. Emily Babcock and A. C. Krey, 2 vols (New York: Columbia University Press, 1941; repr. Octagon Books, 1976), vol. 2, p. 495.

5.　DeVries, *Medieval Military Technology*, pp. 188–9.

6. Richard Avent, *Cestyll Tywysogion Gwynedd: Castles of the Princes of Gwynedd* (Cardiff: HMSO, 1983), pp. 7–9. Anglo-Norman examples include Morlais Castle (north of Merthyr Tydfil, built by Gilbert de Clare, 'the Red', in the 1280s) or Carreg Cennen in Carmarthenshire, both apparently built on the sites of Iron Age hill forts. Carreg Cennen may have replaced a Welsh castle on the site: J. M. Lewis, *Carreg Cennen Castle* (Cardiff: Cadw: Welsh Historic Monuments, no date), pp. 5–7. Morlais has a huge cistern to hold drinking water, and could stand a long siege; but Carreg Cennen does not.

7. John Larner, *Italy in the Age of Dante and Petrarch, 1216–1380* (London: Longman, 1980), p. 89; Waley, *Italian City-Republics*, pp. 122–30.

8. David Nicholas, *Growth of the Medieval City from Late Antiquity to the Early Fourteenth Century* (London and New York: Longman, 1977), pp. 121–2, 192, 197, 247; William Anderson, *Castles of Europe, from Charlemagne to the Renaissance* (London: Elek, 1970), p. 154.

9. Wright, *Knights and Peasants*, pp. 6, 82, 89, 97, 102, 104.

10. Froissart, *Chroniques: manuscrit d'Amiens*, vol. 4, pp. 37–45, chs 769–73.

11. For examples in addition to those given here see, for instance, Ramsey Abbey, converted to a castle by Geoffrey de Mandeville during the 1140s: *Gesta Stephani*, ed. and trans. K. R. Potter, with new introduction and notes by R. H. C. Davis (Oxford: Oxford University Press, 1976), ch. 83, p. 164; and the monastery of Mount Tabor in the Latin Kingdom of Jerusalem, which was fortified and in which the monks and people of the villages around found refuge when Saladin raided the area and from which they defended themselves, forcing him to withdraw: Denys Pringle, *The Churches of the Crusader Kingdom of Jerusalem: A Corpus*, vol. 2, L–Z (excluding Tyre) (Cambridge: Cambridge University Press, 1998), pp. 66–7, citing William of Tyre, Bk 22 ch. 27 (26), p. 1052.

12. Quoted by Anderson, *Castles of Europe*, p. 69.

13. Jacques Miquel, *Sites Templiers et Hospitaliers du Larzac et commanderies du Rouergue* (Millau: Éditions du Beffroi, 1989), pp. 17–21, 32–3, 44–7.

14. *The National Monuments of Ireland in the Charge of the Commissioners of Public Works in Ireland* (Dublin: Bord Failte Eireann, 1964), nos 120, 215, pp. 20, 39.

15. See Anderson, *Castles of Europe*, p. 154, and fig. 188, p. 158 fig. 193. For castles built by bishops on frontiers see also Werner Meyer, 'Grenzbildung und Burgenbau', in *Château Gaillard: Études de Castellologie médiéval, XVII: Actes du Colloque International tenu à Abergavenney, Wales (Royaume-Uni), 29 août–3 septembre 1994* (Caen: University of Caen, 1996), pp. 135–44: here pp. 135–7.

16. Gregory of Tours, Bk 7 ch. 35, p. 419; *The Continuations of the Old French Perceval of Chretien de Troyes*, vol. II: *The First Continuation, Redaction of Mss E M Q U*, ed. William Roach and Robert H. Ivy (Philadelphia: American Philosophical Society, 1950, repr. 1965), lines 5548–54; Ambroise, *Estoire*, lines 4253–6, 4283–93; *Chronicle of the Third Crusade*, Bk 1 chs 69, 71, 73, pp. 129, 130, 131.

17. Vegetius, *De re militari*, Bk 1 chs 21–5, pp. 23–5; C. M. Gilliver, *The Roman Art of War* (Stroud: Tempus, 1999), pp. 20, 77–8.

18. Vegetius, *De re militari*, Bk 4 chs 1–30, pp. 121–39.

19. See Nicholas, *Growth of the Medieval City*, pp. 10–14 on the 'walled city as an urban type'; see also DeVries, *Medieval Military Technology*, pp. 181–3.

20. For a description of Constantinople see Richard Tomlinson, *From Mycenae to Constantinople: The Evolution of the Ancient City* (London and New York: Routledge, 1992), pp. 212–23.

21. Ammianus Marcellinus, Bk 18 ch. 9.1–2; vol. 1, pp. 464–5.

22. DeVries, *Medieval Military Technology*, pp. 181–7.

23. Nicholas, *Growth of the Medieval City*, p. 113; Anderson, *Castles of Europe*, p. 72 fig. 73.

24. Gregory of Tours, Bk 2 ch. 37, p. 154.

25. See, for example, James C. Tracy, 'To Wall or not to Wall: Evidence from Medieval Germany', in *City Walls: The Urban Enceinte in Global Perspective*, ed. James C. Tracy (Cambridge: Cambridge University Press, 2001), pp. 71–87; Kathryn L. Reyerson, 'Medieval Walled Space: Urban Development v. Defense', in ibid., pp. 88–116.

26. Gregory of Tours, Bk 3 ch. 19, pp. 182–3 (Dijon); Bk 2 ch. 21, p. 133 (walls of Clermont Ferrand); Bk 3 ch. 8, p. 169 (walking on the city walls at Zülpich); Bk 3 ch. 13, pp. 172–3 (Chastel-Marlhac); Bk 7 chs 34, 37–8, pp. 417, 420–2, 423 (siege of Comminges); Bk 8 ch. 29, p. 458 (gates of Soissons and the gatekeeper); Bk 8 ch. 30, p. 459 (siege of Carcassonne); Ammianus Marcellinus, Bk 18 ch. 8.13, pp. 462–3, Bk 19 ch. 7.7, pp. 504–7.

27. The historiography is summarised by DeVries, *Medieval Military Technology*, pp. 174–8.

28. Ibid., p. 176.

29. Ibid., p. 175.

30. Benjamin Isaac, *The Limits of Empire: The Roman Army in the East*, rev. edn (Oxford: Oxford University Press, 1992), pp. 372–418: here pp. 416–17.

31. Everett L. Wheeler, 'Methological Limits and the Mirage of Roman Strategy', *The Journal of Military History*, 57 (1993), 7–41, 217–40.

32. Patrick Wormald, 'Offa's Dyke', in *The Anglo-Saxons*, ed. James Campbell (London: Penguin, 1982, 1991), pp. 120–1.

33. Wormald, 'Offa's Dyke', p. 121; Bachrach, *Early Carolingian Warfare*, p. 35.

34. Wormald, 'Offa's Dyke', p. 121; Anderson, *Castles of Europe*, p. 22.

35. Christiansen, *Northern Crusades*, 2nd edn, p. 28; Anderson, *Castles of Europe*, p. 24; Gerhard Mildenburger, *Germanische Burgen* (Munster, Westfalia: Aschendoffsche Verlagsbuchhandlung, 1978): the appendices contain plans of pre-Roman ringworks and those built during the Roman period, and maps showing their location and distribution.

36. *Heinrici Chronicon Livoniae*, 2nd edn, ed. Leonid Arbusow and Albert Bauer, *Monumenta Germaniae Historica Scriptores rerum Germanicarum in usum scholarum* (Hanover: Hahnsche Buchhandlung, 1955), pp. 108–9; trans. as *The Chronicle of Henry of Livonia*, trans. James A. Brundage (Madison: University of Wisconsin Press, 1961), pp. 127–8.

37. Øystein Ekroll, 'Norwegian Medieval Castles: Building on the Edge of Europe', in *Château Gaillard: Études de Castellologie médiéval, XVIII: Actes du Colloque International tenu à Gilleleje (Danemark), 24–30 août 1996* (Caen: University of Caen, 1998), pp. 65–73: here p. 65.

38. On the hall see also Evans, *Lords of Battle*, pp. 88–105 and his citations.

39. The debate is summarised by DeVries, *Medieval Military Technology*, pp. 190–2. See now also Bachrach, *Early Carolingian Warfare*, p. 31. For military works built to attack fortresses during this period (e.g. Pepin/Pippin III against Bourges) see ibid., p. 212.

40. Roger Collins, *Charlemagne* (Basingstoke: Macmillan – now Palgrave Macmillan, 1998), pp. 66–8.

41. DeVries, *Medieval Military Technology*, p. 91: summarising Gabriel Fournier, *Le château dans la France médiévale* (Paris: Aubier Montaigne, 1978), pp. 36–8; and Rosamund McKitterick, *The Frankish Kingdoms under the Carolingians, 751–987* (London: Longman, 1983), p. 51: See also Riché, *The Carolingians*, pp. 128–9, 132–3; Collins, *Charlemagne*, pp. 53, 161 (fortresses in conquered Saxony).

42. Robert M. Van Heeringen, 'The Construction of Frankish Circular Fortresses in the Province of Zeeland (SW Netherlands) at the End of the Ninth Century', in *Château Gaillard: XVIII* (1998), pp. 241–9: here p. 243.

43. H. B. Clarke, 'The Vikings', in *Medieval Warfare*, ed. Keen, pp. 36–58: here p. 37.

44. Nelson, *Charles the Bald*, pp. 205–6, 213; DeVries, *Medieval Military Technology*, pp. 199–200.

45. Gilmour, 'The Logistics of Fortified Bridge Building', 87–106; Brian Dearden, 'Charles the Bald's Fortified Bridge at Pîtres: Recent Archaeological Investigations', in *Anglo-Norman Studies*, 11 (1988), pp. 107–12.

46. Van Heeringen, 'Construction of Frankish Circular Fortresses', p. 245.

47. Patrick Wormald, 'The Burhs', in *The Anglo-Saxons*, ed. Campbell, pp. 152–3.

48. Wormald, 'The Burhs', p. 153; Timothy Reuter, 'Carolingian and Ottonian Warfare', in *Medieval Warfare*, ed. Keen, pp. 13–35: here pp. 22–3; Richard L. C. Jones, 'Fortifications and Sieges in Western Europe, *c.*800–1450', in ibid., pp. 163–85: here p. 167; Anderson, *Castles of Europe*, p. 40.

49. H. B. Clarke, 'The Vikings', in *Medieval Warfare*, ed. Keen, pp. 36–58: here pp. 49–52.

50. DeVries, *Medieval Military Technology*, pp. 202–3; France, *Western Warfare*, pp. 82–3.

51. David R. Cook, 'The Norman Military Revolution in England', *Proceedings of the Battle Conference on Anglo-Norman Studies*, 1 (1978), 94–102, 214–6; DeVries, *Medieval Military Technology*, pp. 204–8.

52. Jones, 'Fortifications and Sieges', pp. 169–70; Ekroll, 'Norwegian Medieval Castles', p. 66.

53. Van Heeringen, 'Construction of Frankish Circular Fortresses', p. 248.

54. Thomas F. Glick, *From Muslim Fortress to Christian Castle: Social and Cultural Change in Medieval Spain* (Manchester and New York: Manchester University Press, 1995), pp. 106–12; DeVries, *Medieval Military Technology*, pp. 216–17.

55. The debate is summarised by DeVries, *Medieval Military Technology*, pp. 214–15.

56. William of Tyre, Bk 21 ch. 25 (26), lines 20–34, p. 997.

57. T. C. Bauer, 'Batenburg Castle (The Netherlands)', *Château Gaillard: Études de Castellologie médiéval, XVI: Actes du Colloque International tenu à Luxembourg, 23–29 août 1992* (Caen: University of Caen, 1994), pp. 21–32: here pp. 22–3.

58. For this view see, for instance, Cook, 'Norman Military Revolution in England', pp. 94–7.

59. Smail, *Crusading Warfare*, pp. 230–44.

60. *Oppidis atque castris: Einhardi Vita Karoli, 9*, in *Monumenta Germaniae Historica Scriptores*, vol. 2, ed. George H. Pertz (Hanover, 1829: repr. Stuttgart: Anton Hiersemann, 1976), p. 447 lines 37–8. See also the translation in Einhard, *The Life of Charlemagne*, trans. Lewis Thorpe (Harmondsworth: Penguin, 1969, 1970; repr. London: Folio Society, 1970), p. 40.

61. *The Continuations of the Old French Perceval of Chretien de Troyes*, ed. William Roach, vol II part 2: Lucien Foulet, *Glossary of the First Continuation* (Philadelphia: American Philosophical Society, 1955), p. 40; see also, for instance, *Le Livre d'Artus*, in *The Vulgate Version of the Arthurian Romances, edited from Manuscripts in the British Museum*, ed. H. Oskar Sommer, 8 vols (Washington: Carnegie Institution of Washington, 1908–16), vol. 7, p. 94 lines 24–30, 48: Lord Gawain arrives at a *chastel* and is admitted by the porter. Passing through the gate, he is in the *vile* (town). He and his squire Eliezer find lodging in a butcher's barn and then go to visit the lady in *la sale*, the Hall. For representations of fortified cities in Old French 'fictional' literature see Wolfgang G. Van Emden, 'Medieval French Representations of City and Other Walls', in *City Walls*, ed. Tracy, pp. 530–72. Verbruggen and Bachrach have discussed the problem of definition: see, for example, Bernard Bachrach, 'Early Medieval Fortifications in the "West" of France: A Revised Technical Vocabulary', in *Technology and Culture*, 16 (1975), 531–69; reprinted in his *Warfare and Military Organisation*, no. VI.

62. For example, Smail, *Crusading Warfare*, 2nd edn, pp. 60–2, 204–6. Smail argued that the defensive function of the crusaders' castles in the crusader states had been exaggerated. See also, for example, Kristian Molin, *Unknown Crusader Castles* (New York and London: Hambleton, 2001), pp. 64–78, 236–42.

63. For the administrative and 'outward-going' functions of the castle which required it to be open to passers-by rather than closed see the previous note and Molin, *Unknown Crusader Castles*, pp. 271–98.

64. Lewis, *Carreg Cennen Castle*, pp. 2–3.

65. Nicholson, *Knights Hospitaller*, p. 40; Mar Villalbí, Toni Forcadell Vericat and Pere Lluís Artiguea Conesa, 'El castell d'Amposta. Nota preliminar', *Quaderns d'Història Tarrconense*, 13 (1994), 185–98.

66. Murray, *Crusader Kingdom of Jerusalem*, p. 48; Anderson, *Castles of Europe*, p. 154.

67. Ekroll, 'Norwegian Medieval Castles', pp. 66–9.

68. Jean Gimpel, *The Medieval Machine: The Industrial Revolution of the Middle Ages*, 2nd edn (Aldershot: Wildwood House, 1988), pp. 114–46; A. J. Taylor, 'Master James of St George', *English Historical Review*, 65 (1950), 433–57.

69. Avent, *Castles of the Princes of Gwynedd*, pp. 17, 20; Richard Avent, 'Castles of the Welsh Princes', in *Château Gaillard: Études de Castellologie médiéval, XVI: Actes du Colloque International tenu à Luxembourg, 23–29 août 1992* (Caen: University of Caen, 1994), pp. 11–20: here pp. 15–16.

70. DeVries, *Medieval Military Technology*, pp. 236–7; Stephen Johnson, *Conisbrough Castle* (London: HMSO, 1984); R. Allen Brown, *Orford Castle* (London: HMSO, 1982).

71. DeVries, *Medieval Military Technology*, p. 237, for the size of Pembroke round tower; regrettably I did not note the height of Ewyas Lacy castle tower when I visited it. Lise Hull estimates the height as 35 feet (10.6 metres), at: http://www.castlewales.com/longtown.html .

72. Pierre Héliot, 'Le château de Coucy', *Archeologia*, 46 (May 1972), 50–55; Jean Mesqui, 'Les programmes résidentiels du château de Coucy du XIIIe au XVI siècle', *Congrès archéologique de France*, 148 part 1 (1990–4), 207–47; DeVries, *Medieval Military Technology*, p. 238.

73. M. W. Thompson, *Pickering Castle* (London: HMSO, 1984), pp. 4, 6–7, 19.

74. David Abulafia, *Frederick II: A Medieval Emperor* (Harmondsworth: Allen Lane, 1988), pp. 270, 280, 285, 287–8; Wulf Schirmer, *Castel del Munte: Forschungsergebnisse der Jahre 1990 bis 1996* (Mainz: Von Zabern, 2000).

75. On the question of influence on castle-building in the crusader states see Smail, *Crusading Warfare*, pp. 230–44. See also Paul E. Chevedden, 'Fortifications and the Development of Defensive Planning During the Crusader Period', in *The Circle of War*, ed. Kagay and Villalon, pp. 33–43; Hugh Kennedy, *Crusader Castles* (Cambridge: Cambridge University Press, 1994), pp. 57, 61; Ronnie Ellenblum, 'Frankish and Muslim Siege Warfare and the Construction of Frankish Concentric Castles', in *Dei gesta per Francos*, ed. Balard, Kedar and Riley-Smith, pp. 187–98; Joan Fuguet I Sans, 'Els Castells Templers de Gardeny i Miravet i seu paper innovador en la poliocètica i l'arquitectura catalanes del segle XII', *Acta historica et archæologica Mediævalia*, 13 (1992), 353–74; *idem*, 'De Miravet (1153) a Peníscola (1294): novedad y persistencia de un modelo de fortaleza Templaria en la provincia Catalano-Aragonesa de la Orden', in *Acri 1291. La fine della presenza degli ordini militari in Terra Sancta e i nuovi orientamenti nel XIV secolo*, ed. Francesco Tommasi (Perugia: Quattroeme, 1996), pp. 43–67; Jones, 'Fortifications and Sieges', p. 179. See also France, *Western Warfare*, pp. 93–4.

76. For Båhus see Ekroll, 'Norwegian Medieval Castles', p. 70.

77. Anderson, *Castles of Europe*, p. 205.

78. Ibid., pp. 158–9.

79. Kari Uotila, 'The Collapse of Defence in Finnish Castles Around 1500', in *Château Gaillard: Études de Castellologie médiéval, XIX: Actes du Colloque International tenu à Graz (Autriche) 22–29 août 1998* (Caen: University of Caen, 2000), pp. 297–303: here pp. 299, 300.

80. See on all this Morris, 'Architecture of Arthurian Enthusiasm': on Caernarfon castle see pp. 65, 71–2, citing Arnold Taylor, 'The King's Works in Wales, 1277–1330', in *The History of the King's Works*, I: *The Middle Ages* (London: HMSO, 1963), pp. 293–408: here 369–71. See also Arnold Taylor, *Caernarfon Castle and Town Walls* (Cardiff: Cadw, 1986), pp. 3, 39; Emden, 'Medieval French Representations', pp. 559, 561; citing Michael

Prestwich in *Castles: A History and Guide*, ed. R. Allen Brown with Michael Prestwich and Charles Coulson (New York: Greenwich House, 1982), pp. 53–4.

81. Philip Dixon, 'Design in Castle-Building: the Controlling of Access to the Lord', in *Château Gaillard, XVIII* (1998), pp. 47–57: here p. 50.

82. Jones, 'Fortifications and Sieges', pp. 180–1; Anderson, *Castles of Europe*, p. 283; Elias Kollias, *The Medieval City of Rhodes and the Palace of the Grand Master*, 2nd edn (Athens: Ministry of Culture, 1998), pp. 73–89.

83. Keen, 'The Changing Scene', pp. 278–9; Arnold, 'War in Sixteenth-Century Europe', pp. 25–6, citing Parker, 'The "Military Revolution, 1560–1660"', and Parker, *The Military Revolution*; Ayton and Price, 'Introduction: The Military Revolution', pp. 3, 6–7.

84. George Hill, *A History of Cyprus*, vol. 3: *The Frankish Period, 1432–1571* (Cambridge: Cambridge University Press, 1948), p. 847.

85. Hans L. Janssen, Tarquinius J. Hoekstra and Ben Olde Meirink, 'Fortification of Castles in the Northern Netherlands During the Gelre-Habsburg Conflict (1492–1543)', in *Château Gaillard, XIX* (2000), pp. 123–47: here pp. 125–8.

86. Anderson, *Castles of Europe*, pp. 209, 211.

87. See, for example, Simon Pepper, 'Siege Law, Siege Ritual, and the Symbolism of City Walls in Renaissance Europe', in *City Walls*, ed. Tracy, pp. 573–604; citing C. J. Duffy, *Siege Warfare*. vol. 1: *The Fortress in the Early Modern World 1494–1660* (London: Routledge, 1979); *idem*, vol. 2: *The Fortress in the Age of Vauban and Frederick the Great, 1660–1789* (London: Routledge, 1985).

4   Military equipment

1. Christine de Pisan, *Book of Fayttes*, Bk 2 ch. 20, p. 154: BL Harley 4605, fol. 58r; *Book of Deeds*, trans. Willard, Bk 2 ch. 21, p. 118. On this section of her work see also Contamine, *War in the Middle Ages*, pp. 141–2.

2. *Book of Fayttes*, Bk 2 chs 20–32, pp. 154–62; BL Harley 4605, fols 58r–61v; *Book of Deeds*, trans. Willard, Bk 2 chs 21–33, pp. 118–25.

3. Stones were generally smoothed to a spherical shape before being used as missiles, in order to ensure that they flew straight. Examples of medieval stones hurled from stone-throwing machines may be seen at, for example, the castle of Arsūf in Israel and at Caerphilly Castle in south Wales.

4. BL Harley 4605, fol. 60r: 'vi^m de plomb'. The unit is given as pounds in Willard's translation.

5. On the role of cannon in the 'military revolution' see Keen, 'The Changing Scene', pp. 273–80; Arnold, 'War in Sixteenth-Century Europe', pp. 25–8.

6. Heymann, *John Žižka*, pp. 100–1, 295–6; Gilliver, *Roman Art of War*, p. 108 plate 45, pp. 28, 96, 100, 110.

7 Reproduced, for example, in Heymann, *John Žižka*, plate 3, facing page 178; *Oxford Illustrated History of the Crusades*, ed. Riley-Smith, p. 283.

8. Vegetius, *De re militari*, Bk 1 chs 12–18, pp. 12–18.

9. Ibid., Bk 4 chs 13–22, pp. 127–34. On Roman siege machinery in general see Gilliver, *Roman Art of War*, pp. 134–47; Paul E. Chevedden, 'Artillery in Late Antiquity: Prelude to the Middle Ages', in *The Medieval City Under Siege*, ed. Ivy A. Corfis and Michael Wolfe (Woodbridge: Boydell, 1995), pp. 131–73; DeVries, *Medieval Military Technology*, pp. 127–32. On mobile field artillery see Vegetius, *De re militari*, Bk 3 ch. 24, p. 114; Gilliver, *Roman Art of War*, p. 108 plate 45, pp. 28, 96, 100, 110; Chevedden, 'Artillery', pp. 141–2.

10. Bachrach, *Early Carolingian Warfare*, pp. 109, 324 note 162, p. 326 note 173.

11. Gregory of Tours, Bk 7 ch. 37, pp. 420–1.

12. Chevedden, 'Artillery', pp. 163–4.

13. DeVries, *Medieval Military Technology*, p. 134. See also Bachrach, *Early Carolingian Warfare*, pp. 114–15, 328–9 note 206; Paul E. Chevedden, 'The Invention of the Counterweight Trebuchet: A Study in Cultural Diffusion', *Dumbarton Oaks Papers*, 54 (2000), 71–116. Reproduced by the De Re Militari Society at http://www.deremilitari.org/articles.htm.

14. Bachrach, *Early Carolingian Warfare*, p. 326 note 182.

15. Ibid., pp. 108, 114, 239.

16. Ibid., pp. 57, 109–10.

17. Ibid., pp. 109, 111, 326 notes 171, 172, 184. On Paul the Deacon see Collins, *Charlemagne*, pp. 8, 119. The technical English term is for a *petraria* is 'petrary', but as this is an obsolete word I prefer to use the term 'stonethrower'.

18. Bachrach, *Early Carolingian Warfare*, p. 329 note 212, and p. 330 note 215. On the *Annales* see Collins, *Charlemagne*, p. 4.

19. Carroll M. Gillmor, 'The Introduction of the Traction Trebuchet into the Latin West', *Viator*, 12 (1981), 1–8: here 6 and note 22; Bachrach, *Early Carolingian Warfare*, p. 329 note 211. On all this debate see Bradbury, *Medieval Siege*, pp. 250–70; and Chevedden, 'Invention of the Counterweight Trebuchet'.

20. Ibid., p. 136; Gillmor, 'Introduction of the Traction Trebuchet', 2–3, 6–7.

21. Gillmor, 'Introduction of the Traction Trebuchet', 5 note 18; Chevedden, 'Artillery', p. 163. Again, the brief reference in various later texts to 'new and choice types of machines' (*machinamenta*) being used against the Northmen at the siege of Angers in 873 does not prove that stone-throwing siege machines were in regular use at this period, because this reference gives no indication of what sort of machines were being used: see Gillmor, 'Introduction of the Traction Trebuchet', 6 and note 21.

22. *Itinerarium peregrinorum*, ed. Stubbs, Bk 6 ch. 13, p. 401: *Interioribus quidem furent petrariae, sed minus periti fuerant ad utendum*; trans. in *Chronicle of the Third Crusade*, p. 350: 'Those inside the city certainly had stonethrowers but they were not skilled enough to use them.' See also the sad tale told by France, *Western Warfare*, pp. 124–5.

23. Gillmor, 'Introduction of the Traction Trebuchet', 6 and note 23.

24. Ibid., 2; DeVries, *Medieval Military Technology*, p. 137; *De expugnatione Lyxbonensi: The Conquest of Lisbon, Edited from the Unique Manuscript in Corpus Christi College, Cambridge, with a Translation into English*, ed. and trans. Charles Wendell David (New York: Columbia University Press,

1936), pp. 134/5 and note 3, pp. 136/7, and see also 142/3, 162/3. See now the new edition *De expugnatione Lyxbonensi: The Conquest of Lisbon*, ed. and trans. Charles Wendell David, with a new foreword and bibliography by Jonathan P. Phillips (New York: Columbia University Press, 2001), same pagination: and p. xxi on the author.

25. *De expugnatione Lyxbonensi*, trans. C. W. David, pp. 134/5, 142/3–146/7, 158/9–164/5. A *funda* was a leather sling; a *fundabulum* was a war machine which hurled stones; an *arcus balearis* was a type of *ballista*, which could fire darts or quarrels.

26. These arguments are considered by Chevedden, 'The Invention of the Counterweight Trebuchet', 81–6.

27. *Gesta Francorum*, Bk 2 ch. 7, Bk 10 ch. 37, pp. 14, 90.

28. Ralph of Caen, *Gesta Tancredi in expeditione Hierosolymitana*, ch. 96, in *Recueil des historiens des croisades: Historiens occidentaux*, 5 vols (Paris: Imprimerie royale, 1841–95) (hereafter cited as *RHC Occ*), vol. 3, p. 694.

29. The account by Guibert, abbot of Nogent, who was not on the crusade, refers to the *balistis ac fundis* with which the Christians fired the heads of their defeated Turkish enemies back into the Turkish-held city of Nicaea. While this may not be what actually happened, it suggests that he expected the Christian forces to be using hurling machines: *Guitberti abbatis Sanctae Mariae Novigenti: Historia quae inscribitur Dei Gesta per Francos*, ed. R. B. C. Huygens, Corpus Christianorum continuatio mediaevalis, 127a (Turnholt: Brepols, 1996), Bk 3.6, p. 146 line 291, and see lines 297–8; and see also Bk 7.36, p. 334 line 1771: *balearis instrumenta*. For a translation, see *The Deeds of God Through the Franks*, trans. Levine, here p. 62. The terms Guibert uses here implies catapults operated by tension or traction. Albert of Aachen, writing in the early twelfth century but a secondhand source, refers to the crusaders using *arcus balearii*. This was the correct classical term and meant a type of *ballista*, which fired darts: Albert of Aachen, *Historia*, in *RHC Occ*, vol. 4, Bk 2 ch. 33, p. 324, Bk 6 ch. 9, p. 471, Bk 6 ch. 16, p. 475. For the Latin see Charles Du Fresne Du Cange, *Glossarium mediae et infimae latinitatis*, with supplements by D. P. Carpentier, and additional material ed. G. A. L. Henschel (Paris: Firmin Didot, 1840–50), vol. A–B, pp. 549–50; Chevedden, 'Artillery', p. 141. A later reworking of Peter of Tudebode's chronicle, the *Historia peregrinorum*, refers to Robert, count of Normandy, using *fundae baleariae*, but here they are clearly hurling stones. However, as this is a later source, it probably reflects contemporary stonethrowers when the reworker was writing, not during the crusade: 'Tudebodus Imitatus et continuatus', *Historia peregrinorum*, ch. 121, in *RHC Occ*, vol. 3, p. 221.

30. Ambroise, *Estoire*, lines 4941–7; *Chronicle of the Third Crusade*, Bk 3 ch. 11, p. 213.

31. Ambroise, *Estoire*, lines 3529–60, 4743–800; *Chronicle of the Third Crusade*, Bk 1 ch. 47, pp. 103, 208–9.

32. Modern historians generally use the term 'trebuchet' to refer to all stonethrowing artillery in use during the Middle Ages: see, for instance, the important study by Donald R. Hill, 'Trebuchets', *Viator*, 4 (1973), 99–116 (and there are some useful diagrams on 115–16). Although there is insufficient space here to set out my reasons in full, I would argue that the

term 'trebuchet' should only be used for the counterweight trebuchet. The origins of the term 'trebuchet' have been much debated. Recently, Paul Chevedden has concluded that the original term was Latin and meant a three-armed device: Chevedden, 'Invention of the Counterweight Trebuchet', 98–102. I have great respect for Chevedden's scholarship and generally I agree with his conclusions. However, as it is generally agreed that the counterweight trebuchet first appeared in the eastern Mediterranean area (although the date is disputed) and as the western Europeans in the eastern Mediterranean area, the so-called 'Palestinian Franks' of the crusader states, spoke French, it seems to me more likely that the original western European term for the counterweight trebuchet was French and that the Latin word was coined from the French, not the other way around. For instance, the *Robert Dictionnaire de la langue française* derives the word from the old French and Frankish words *tres* (meaning 'au delà') and *bûk* (meaning 'tronc du corps'), the compound word meaning 'to fall'- a reference to the machine's action: *Le Robert Dictionnaire de la langue française*, 2nd edn, vol. 9 (Paris: Robert, 1992), p. 465. According to the *Robert*, the earliest appearance of the word is in the *Chanson de Roland*.

33. 'Fragmentum de captione Damiatae', in *Quinti belli sacri scriptores minores*, p. 181.
34. Ibid., pp. 177–8.
35. DeVries, *Medieval Military Technology*, p. 137; Chevedden, 'The Invention of the Counterweight Trebuchet', 71–3.
36. *History of the Albigensian Crusade: Peter of les Vaux de Cernay's Historia Albigensis*, trans. W. A. Sibly and M. D. Sibly (Woodbridge: Boydell, 1998), p. 277 [612] and note, and p. 276 [610] and note 125.
37. *Histoire des ducs de Normandie*, pp. 178, 188, 192, 195.
38. DeVries, *Medieval Military Technology*, p. 138; Cheveden, 'Invention of the Counterweight Trebuchet', 86–7.
39. Cheveden, 'Invention of the Counterweight Trebuchet', 760–86.
40. Jones, 'Fortifications and Sieges', pp. 174–5; Chevedden, 'Invention of the Counterweight Trebuchet', 72.
41. Froissart, *Chroniques: manuscrit d'Amiens*, vol. 4, p. 78, ch. 789 line 50: *enghiens*, rather than *kanons*.
42. DeVries, *Medieval Military Technology*, p. 140.
43. Theresa Vann, 'Guillaume Caoursin's *Descriptio obsidione Rhodiae* and the Archives of the Knights of Malta', in *The Crusades and the Military Orders: Expanding the Frontiers of Medieval Latin Christianity*, ed. Zsolt Hunyadi and József Laszolovszky (Budapest: Central European University, 2001), pp. 109–20. In her original conference paper, Prof. Vann said more on this subject than is published here.
44. For the 'cat' see *De expugnatione Lyxbonensi*, p. 160/1 (here it is a 'Welsh cat', clearly a special variety of the animal); *Histoire des ducs de Normandie*, p. 178; Bahā al-Dīn ibn Shaddād, *The Life of Saladin*, trans. C. W. Wilson and C. R. Conder (London: Palestine Pilgrims Text Society, 1897), p. 214, and see now the new translation by D. S. Richards, *The Rare and Excellent History of Saladin* (Aldershot: Ashgate, 2001), p. 129; Ambroise, *Estoire*, lines 4815–6; *Chronicle of the Third Crusade*, Bk 3

ch. 8, p. 210; Froissart, *Chroniques: manuscrit d'Amiens*, vol. 2, p. 146, ch. 344 lines 25–6; for the 'sow', see *Chronicle of the Third Crusade*, Bk 1 ch. 59, p. 115 and note 242; *Itinerarium peregrinorum*, ed. Stubbs, p. 456, under 'sus'.

45. Ambroise, *Estoire*, lines 4781–6; *Chronicle of the Third Crusade*, Bk 3 ch. 7, p. 209, cf. Ambroise, *Estoire*, 3401–32; *Chronicle of the Third Crusade*, Bk 1 ch. 36, pp. 90–1.

46. Ambroise, *Estoire*, lines 937–40, 970–2, 1087–90; *Chronicle of the Third Crusade*, Bk 3 chs 20, 24, Bk 3 ch. 4; pp. 167, 171, 204.

47. Bachrach, *Early Carolingian Warfare*, pp. 109, 111, 326 note 184.

48. Jones, 'Fortifications and Sieges', p. 174; Bradbury, *Medieval Siege*, pp. 85–6, 159–60; Michael Toch, 'The Medieval German City under Siege', in *The Medieval City Under Siege*, ed. Corfis and Wolfe, pp. 34–48: here pp. 41–2; Froissart, *Chroniques: manuscrit d'Amiens*, vol. 3, p. 90.

49. France, *Western Warfare*, pp. 115–16.

50. On Greek fire and this problem see DeVries, *Medieval Military Technology*, pp. 140–2.

51. DeVries, *Medieval Military Technology*, pp. 143–5, and picture on p. 144. On guns and gunpowder see also, for example, Bradbury, *Medieval Siege*, pp. 282–95; Contamine, *War in the Middle Ages*, pp. 139–50.

52. Contamine, *War in the Middle Ages*, p. 140; see also Bradbury, *Medieval Siege*, p. 284.

53. Froissart, *Chroniques: manuscrit d'Amiens*, vol. 2, p. 10, ch. 257 line 13, p. 45, ch. 278 line 23.

54. Ibid., vol. 3, p. 90, ch. 548 line 43.

55. Ibid., vol. 4, p. 379, ch. 942 lines 51–66. See also DeVries, *Medieval Military Technology*, pp. 145–6.

56. Kramer, *The Firework Book*, pp. 11–12.

57. Robert D. Smith and Ruth Rhynas Brown, *Bombards: Mons Meg and her Sisters* (London: Royal Armouries, 1989).

58. Contamine, *War in the Middle Ages*, p. 200; Contamine did not mention the defeat at Nancy in 1477, so presumably did not judge that Charles had a clear superiority in artillery at that battle. See also Vaughan, *Charles the Bold*, pp. 222–3 on Charles's guns.

59. On the potential brittleness of cast iron see R. A. Higgins, *Properties of Engineering Materials* (London: Hodder and Stoughton, 1977), pp. 216–22. For the use of cast iron shot in this period see Contamine, *War in the Middle Ages*, p. 145. DeVries mentions engineers referring to exploding cannonballs (*Medieval Military Technology*, p. 158); perhaps these were cast iron balls that exploded by accident.

60. Bradbury, *Medieval Siege*, p. 291; DeVries, *Medieval Military Technology*, p. 158.

61. DeVries, *Medieval Military Technology*, pp. 148–9. Christine de Pisan does not mention handguns.

62. *Histoire du gentil seigneur de Bayart*, pp. 281, 318, 335, 412–21. For a more modern although 'popular' account see Samuel Shellabarger, *The Chevalier Bayard: A Study in Fading Chivalry* (London: Skeffington & Son, no date: 1928), pp. 209–13, 232, 242, 342–7. On the impact of handguns on warfare see also Bert S. Hall, 'The Changing Face of Siege Warfare:

Technology and Tactics in Transition', in *Medieval City Under Siege*, ed. Corfis and Wolfe, pp. 257–75

63. DeVries, *Medieval Military Technology*, pp. 152–4.

64. Smith and Brown, *Bombards: Mons Meg and her Sisters*, p. 66.

65. Bachrach, *Early Carolingian Warfare*, p. 112; Chevedden, 'Artillery', pp. 143–9; *European Crossbows: A Survey by Josef Alm*, trans. H. Bartlett Wells, ed. G. M. Wilson (Leeds: Royal Armouries Museum, 1994), pp. 6–7; Jim Bradbury, *The Medieval Archer* (Woodbridge: Boydell, 1985), pp. 8–10.

66. Chevedden, 'Artillery', p. 146; Bradbury, *Medieval Archer*, pp. 8–10, 26–7, 146–50.

67. Ambroise, *Estoire*, lines 4815–35, 4927–42; *Chronicle of the Third Crusade*, Bk 3 chs 8, 12, pp. 210, 213.

68. Bradbury, *Medieval Archer*, pp. 148–9; Alm, *European Crossbows*, pp. 34–6, 39–40.

69. Alm, *European Crossbows*, pp. 55–6, 64, 69–79.

70. DeVries, *Medieval Military Technology*, pp. 35–6.

71. France, *Western Warfare*, pp. 219–20. On their bows see Bradbury, *Medieval Archer*, pp. 12–14.

72. DeVries, *Medieval Military Technology*, p. 37; Bradbury, *Medieval Archer*, pp. 12, 14–15, 33–8, 75.

73. Bradbury, *Medieval Archer*, pp. 14–15, 71–5.

74. Sven Ekdahl, 'Horses and Crossbows: Two Important Warfare Advantages of the Teutonic Order in Prussia', in *The Military Orders*, vol. 2, ed. Nicholson, pp. 119–51: here p. 151.

75. See, for example, *Meliadus de Leonnoys, 1532*, introduction by C. E. Pickford (London: Scolar Press, 1980), fol. 26r: an archer shoots le Morhault without his being able to fight back.

76. Bachrach, *Early Carolingian Warfare*, pp. 102–3.

77. *The Bayeux Tapestry and the Norman Invasion*, ed. Lewis Thorpe (London: Folio Society, 1973), plate 60.

78. DeVries, Medieval Military Technology, pp. 25–8; France, Western Warfare, p. 23. For a giant using a mace see *Le Livre d'Artus*, p. 314 line 14–p. 315 line 24; *The Alliterative Morte Arthure : A Critical Edition*, ed. Valerie Krishna preface by Rossell Hope Robbins (New York: B. Franklin, 1976), lines 1105–32.

79. Bachrach, *Early Carolingian Warfare*, pp. 84–5.

80. *The Bayeux Tapestry*, plates 66, 69, 75, 78; France, *Western Warfare*, p. 23; Ambroise, *Estoire*, line 4657–63; *Chronicle of the Third Crusade*, Bk 3 ch. 5, p. 206.

81. Gerald of Wales, *The History and Topography of Ireland*, trans. John J. O'Meara (Harmondsworth: Penguin, 1982), Bk 3 chs 93, 100, pp. 101, 107.

82. Froissart, *Chroniques: manuscrit d'Amiens*, vol. 3, p. 347, ch. 684 lines 41–3.

83. Anglo, *Martial Arts*, pp. 148–71; DeVries, *Medieval Military Technology*, pp. 18, 30, 32; citing Charles H. Ashdown, *Armour and Weapons in the Middle Ages* (London: Holland Press, 1925), pp. 131–2; David C. Nicolle, *Arms and Armour of the Crusading Era, 1050–1350* (White Plains: Kraus

International, 1988 repr. London: Greenhill Books and Mechanicsburg, PA: Stackpole Books, 1999), *passim*; R. Ewart Oakeshott, *European Weapons and Armour: From the Renaissance to the Industrial Revolution* (London: Lutterworth Press, 1980), pp. 49–51, 72–4.

84. Anglo, *Martial Arts*, pp. 150, 152–9.
85. DeVries, *Medieval Military Technology*, pp. 30–2; citing Ashdown, *Armour and Weapons*, pp. 125–35; Oakeshott, *European Weapons and Armour*, pp. 51–6; Verbruggen, *Art of Warfare*, pp. 169–70; Nicolle, *Arms and Armour*, no. 974; see also France, *Western Warfare*, p. 23.
86. Johannes A. Mol, 'Frisian Fighters and the Crusade', in *Crusades*, 1 (2003), 89–110.
87. *Chronicle of the Third Crusade*, Bk 6 ch. 4, p. 341. Ash was regarded as the best wood for a lance, although other hardwoods could be used: Bachrach, *Early Carolingian Warfare*, pp. 93, 318 note 79. In the well-known noble romance *Perceforest*, written in the 1330s or early 1340s, the knights cut a branch of a *fresne* (ash tree) to use as an *ad hoc* lance: *Quatrième Partie du Roman de Perceforest*, ed. Gilles Roussineau (Geneva: Droz, 1986), vol. 2, p. 843 lines 312–15.
88. DeVries, *Medieval Military Technology*, p. 13, quoting Rosemary Ascherl, 'The Technology of Chivalry in Reality and Romance', in *The Study of Chivalry*, ed. H. Chickering and T. H. Seiler (Kalamazoo: Medieval Institute, 1989), p. 271.
89. Froissart, *Chroniques: manuscrit d'Amiens*, vol. 3, p. 185, ch. 596 lines 58–60.
90. Roger of Howden, *Gesta regis Henrici secundi*, ed. William Stubbs, Rolls Series 49, 2 vols (London: Longman, 1867), vol. 2, pp. 155–6; *idem*, *Chronica*, ed. William Stubbs, Rolls Series 51, 4 vols (London: Longman, 1868–71), vol. 3, pp. 93–4; Ambroise, *Estoire*, line 6026; *Chronicle of the Third Crusade*, Bk. 4 ch. 14, p. 243.
91. Bachrach, *Early Carolingian Warfare*, pp. 98–9.
92. DeVries, *Medieval Military Technology*, pp. 10–12; see also Bachrach, *Early Carolingian Warfare*, pp. 93–5.
93. See, for instance, Matthew Strickland, 'Military Technology and Conquest', pp. 361–6.
94. The debate is summarised by DeVries, *Medieval Military Technology*, pp. 13–14, 95–110. See also John France, *Victory in the East: A Military History of the First Crusade* (Cambridge, Cambridge University Press, 1994), pp. 70–1, 372.
95. For fighting with the sword on horseback see Anglo, *Martial Arts*, pp. 253–8.
96. Gilliver, *Roman Art of War*, p. 116, quoting Polybius, 2.33. 1–16.
97. Bachrach, *Early Carolingian Warfare*, p. 90.
98. See, for example, *Chanson de Roland*, lines 2344–8; Mario Roques, 'Ronsasvals: poème épique provençal', *Romania*, 58 (1932), 1–189, line 1592; André Moisan, *Répertoire des nons propres de personnes et de lieux cités dans les chansons de geste françaises et les oeuvres étrangères dérivées*, 2 tomes in 5 vols (Geneva: Droz, 1986), tome 1, vol. 1, p. 442, Galans 3.
99. There is very extensive literature on the development of the sword; for a summary see DeVries, *Medieval Military Technology*, pp. 20–5. See also,

for instance, Contamine, *War in the Middle Ages*, 177–8; France, *Western Warfare*, pp. 22–3. On the question of cut and thrust see DeVries, *Medieval Military Technology*, pp. 24–5, citing Ada Bruhn de Hoffmeyer, 'From Mediaeval Sword to Renaissance Rapier', *Gladius*, 2 (1963), 18–25; and R. Ewart Oakeshott, *The Sword in the Age of Chivalry* (New York: Frederick A. Praeger, 1964), pp. 56–79. See also Anglo, *Martial Arts*, p. 109.

100. *Saladin: Suite et fin du deuxième cycle de croisade*, ed. Larry S. Crist (Geneva: Droz, 1972), p. 129 lines 10–11, p. 130 line 25.

101. *The Medieval Horse and its Equipment: c.1150–c.1450*, ed. John Clark, Medieval Finds from Excavations in London 5 (London: HMSO, 1995), pp. 22–5. See also Ann Hyland, *The Medieval Warhorse: From Byzantium to the Crusades* (Stroud: Sutton, 1994), pp. 145–6; Ann Hyland, *The Warhorse: 1250–1600* (Stroud: Sutton Publishing, 1998), p. 10; France, *Western Warfare*, pp. 23–4, argues that horses were taller than this by the thirteenth century, but his arguments fly in the face of the evidence of horse armour. On the Gringalet see, for instance, *Le Livre d'Artus*, p. 41 lines 36–8, pp. 66 line 35–p. 67 line 14; see also *Trioedd Ynys Prydein: The Welsh Triads*, ed. Rachel Bromwich (Cardiff: University of Wales Press, 1961), pp. civ–vi; on Bayart see *Renaut de Montauban, édition critique du manuscrit Douce,* ed. Jacques Thomas (Geneva: Droz, 1989), lines 884–8.

102. Pryor, 'Transportation of Horses by Sea'.

103. Vivian Gilbert, *The Romance of the Last Crusade: With Allenby to Jerusalem* (New York and London: D. Appleton and Company, 1928), pp. 80–1. Despite the title, this is a serious firsthand account of the Palestine campaign.

104. Froissart, *Chroniques: manuscrit d'Amiens*, vol. 3, p. 100, ch. 554 lines 16–17.

105. Gerald of Wales, *History and Topography of Ireland*, Bk 3 ch. 93, p. 101.

106. Mol, 'Frisian Fighters'.

107. On all of this see DeVries, *Medieval Military Technology*, pp. 56–8.

108. Ibid., pp. 59–62.

109. See DeVries, *Medieval Military Technology*, pp. 63–6, for discussion of all these points and some of the debates. See also France, *Western Warfare*, pp. 16–22, 30–3.

110. Peter Coss, *The Lady in Medieval England, 1000–1500* (Stroud: Sutton, 1998), pp. 38–48.

111. DeVries, *Medieval Military Technology*, p. 89.

112. Charny, *Book of Chivalry*, section 42, lines 175–93; pp. 188/9–190/1. For other contemporary descriptions of armour and the problems of their interpretation see Anglo, *Martial Arts*, pp. 202–11; and Frédérick Lachaud, 'Armour and Military Dress in Thirteenth- and Early Fourteenth-Century England', in *Armies, Chivalry and Warfare*, ed. Strickland, pp. 344–69. On the brigantine see DeVries, *Medieval Military Technology*, pp. 75–6, 85–7.

113. DeVries, *Medieval Military Technology*, pp. 76–7, 85.

114. Ibid., pp. 79–85.

115. Ibid., p. 84.

116. See, for example, Kilian Anheuser, 'Fire-Gilding on European Plate Armour of the 16th Century – Recipes, Objects and Experiments', *Bulletin of the Metals Museum*, 28 (1997), 27–40.

117. Vegetius, *De re militari*, Bk 1 ch. 20, and p. 20 note 2, Bk 2 ch. 6, p. 35, ch. 7, pp. 37–8 and note 1, Bk 2 ch. 13, p. 44.

118. Taken from *Chronicle of the Third Crusade*, Bk 4 ch. 10, p. 237.

119. Waley, *Italian City-Republics*, p. 101.

120. Vegetius, *De re militari*, Bk 1 ch. 20, p. 20; *La Règle du Temple*, sections 164–8, 241, 611, 640; Matthew Bennett, '*La Règle du Temple* as a Military Manual, or How to Deliver a Cavalry Charge', in *Studies in Medieval History presented to R. Allen Brown*, ed. Christopher Harper Bill et al. (Woodbridge: Boydell, 1989), repr. in *The Rule of the Templars*, trans. Upton-Ward, pp. 175–88: here pp. 186-7; Verbruggen, *Art of Warfare*, pp. 89-91. See also the young hero Guibert in *Le siège de Barbastre: chanson de geste du XIIe siècle*, ed. J. L. Perrier (Paris: H. Champion, 1926), lines 5363-90, carrying the banner in battle while he fights against Muslims; he is unhorsed and has to be rescued by his brothers.

121. See Sir John Chandos's banner in Froissart, *Chroniques: manuscrit d'Amiens*, vol. 3, p. 425, ch. 722; *Life of the Black Prince by the herald of Sir John Chandos. Edited from the manuscript in Worcester College with linguistic and historical notes*, ed. Mildred K. Pope and Eleanor C. Lodge (Oxford: Clarendon Press, 1910), lines 3121–56, and note on p. 213. For Guy de Blois see Froissart, *Chroniques: manuscrit d'Amiens*, vol. 3, p. 445, ch. 733 lines 2–4.

122. Keen, 'Treason Trials', in his *Nobles, Knights and Men-at-Arms*, pp. 156–7.

123. For example, Froissart, *Chroniques. Livre 1: le manuscrit d'Amiens*, vol. 2, p. 37, ch. 273 line 34, p. 328, ch. 456 line 25; vol. 4, p. 238, ch. 875 line 90; see also vol. 3, p. 261, ch. 637 line 31, for a French commander fighting 'for God and St George'.

124. *Chronicle of the Third Crusade*, Bk 4 ch. 19, p. 252; Ambroise, *Estoire*, lines 6409–18. The quotation is from the *Chronicle*.

125. Vegetius, *De re militari*, Bk 3 ch. 5, p. 72.

126. Keen, 'Treason Trials', in his *Nobles, Knights and Men-at-Arms*, pp. 157–8.

127. *Prophesies de Merlin*, ed. Berthelot, pp. 253, 255, 256.

128. Ambroise, *Estoire*, lines 4857–9; *Chronicle of the Third Crusade*, Bk 3 ch. 9, p. 211.

129. Wright, *Knights and Peasants*, pp. 102–3.

130. Ambroise, *Estoire*, lines 4648–54; *Chronicle of the Third Crusade*, Bk 3 ch. 5, p. 205.

131 Contamine, *War in the Middle Ages*, pp. 188–90.

5   The practice of land warfare

1. *Chronique de Jean Le Bel*, vol. 1, pp. 42–7, ch. 8.
2. Vegetius, *De re militari*, Bk 1 chs 9–19, pp. 10–19.

3. *La Mule sans frein*, in *Two Old French Gauvain Romances*, ed. Johnston and Owen, lines 350–1 (contrast the non-hero at lines 114–15); *L'âtre périlleux: roman de la Table ronde*, ed. Brian Woledge (Paris: H. Champion, 1936), lines 369–71; *Livre d'Artus*, p. 323 line 31.

4. Bachrach, *Early Carolingian Warfare*, p. 88.

5. Christine de Pisan, *Book of Fayttes*, Bk 1 chs 9–11, pp. 28–38; BL Harley MS 4605, fols 13v–17v; *Book of Deeds*, trans. Willard, Bk 1 chs 9–11, pp. 29–37.

6. For example, Verbruggen, *Art of Warfare*, p. 174: 'Real systematic training of their formations was non-existant for lack of money'. See also Anglo, *Martial Arts*, p. 28.

7. France, *Western Warfare*, p. 70.

8. *Règle du Temple*, sections 95, 128, 315.

9. Vaughan, *Charles the Bold*, pp. 209–10.

10. Anglo, *Martial Arts*, pp. 7–12, 18–20.

11. *Aliscans: chanson de geste, publiée d'après le manuscrit de la Bibliothèque de l'Arsenal et à l'aide de cinq autres manuscrits*, ed. F. Guessard and A. de Montaiglon (Paris: A. Franck, 1870, repr. 1966), lines 8036, 8077–92. There is now a new edition: *Aliscans*, ed. Claude Régnier (Paris: H. Champion, 1990).

12. In *Nouveau recueil complet des fabliaux*, ed. Willem Noomen and Nicolas van den Boogaard, vol. 4 (Assen/Maastricht: Van Gorcum, 1988), pp. 247–77.

13. Prestwich, '*Miles in armis strenuous*'; for an example of the phrase in action see, for example, *Itinerarium peregrinorum*, ed. Stubbs, Bk 1 ch. 7, p. 190 (*virs ... strenuous*), translated as *Chronicle of the Third Crusade*, p. 36. The attitude is most poignantly set out in Chrétien de Troyes, *Érec et Énide*, ed. Mario Roques (Paris: H. Champion, 1952), lines 2430–504, where all the problems that arise for the young couple come because Erec fears that his wife Enid thinks he is an idle knight; see also Chrétien de Troyes, *Yvain (le Chevalier au lion)*, the critical text of Wendelin Foerster with introduction, notes and glossary by T. B. W. Reid (Manchester: Manchester University Press, 1942), lines 2484–578, where Yvain allows himself to be tempted away from his young wife Laudine by his cousin Gawain in order to go tourneying, because Yvain fears that he will be criticised for idleness.

14. Reproduced, for example, in Barber and Barker, *Tournaments*, p. 208; and see the description of King Duarte's book on horsemanship, ibid., pp. 103, 197–201.

15. *La chanson de Bertrand du Guesclin de Cuvelier*, ed. Jean-Claude Faucon, vol. 1 (Paris: Éditions universitaires du sud, 1990), lines 206–597. For the debate over the social status of wrestling, see Anglo, *Martial Arts*, pp. 23, 173–6.

16. *Le Livre des Fais du Bon Messire Jehan le Maingre, dit Bouciquaut, mareschal de France et gouverneur de Jennes*, ed. Denis Lalande (Geneva: Droz, 1985), ch. 4, pp. 16–17, 499 (on 'barres'), 504 (on 'croq madame'). For a recent assessment of this as an historical source see Norman Housley, *The Crusaders* (Stroud: Tempus, 2002), pp. 139–43.

17. *Livre des Fais*, ch. 7, pp. 24–6.

18. *Histoire du gentil seigneur de Bayart*, p. 100; Shellabarger, *The Chevalier Bayard*, pp. 4–21.
19. 'Tout en turnant de noz chevaulx et en souffrant les chevaleries des preux chevaliers deviendrons nous chevaliers': *Perceforest: deuxième partie*, ed. Gilles Roussineau, vol. 1 (Geneva: Droz, 1999), p. 397 para. 726.
20. Charny, *Book of Chivalry*, pp. 100–1.
21. Barber and Barker, *Tournaments*, pp. 164–5, and 29, 30, 32, 153; see also, for example, *Lancelot*, vol. 1, pp. 90–4, section VI, 3–10.
22. Barber and Barker, *Tournaments*, p. 14.
23. Ibid., pp. 15–17.
24. Ibid., p. 19.
25. Coss, *Knight in Medieval England*, pp. 117–19.
26. Verbruggen, *Art of Warfare*, p. 267.
27. Ralph of Diss, *Ymagines historiarum* from *The Historical Works of Master Ralph of Diceto*, ed. William Stubbs, Rolls Series 68 (London, 1876), vol. 2, p. 120. For some of the consequences in England see Jocelin of Brakelond, *Chronicle of the Abbey of Bury St Edmunds*, trans. Diana Greenway and Jane Sayers (Oxford: Oxford University Press, 1989), p. 50.
28. Charny, *Book of Chivalry*, p. 102.
29. 'Livre Messire Geoffroi de Charny', pp. 403–4 lines 329–47.
30. Froissart, *Chroniques: manuscrit d'Amiens*, vol. 2, p. 384, ch. 494 lines 39–61. Jean le Bel told this story first, but did not mention the East or the fact that 'good knights meet' in these locations; Jean le Bel, *Chronique*, vol. 2, p. 82, ch. 71.
31. Charny, *Book of Chivalry*, pp. 102–4.
32. The contradiction is neatly summed up by Keen, *Chivalry*, pp. 231–2.
33. Barber and Barker, *Tournaments*, p. 13, citing *Carolingian Chronicles: Royal Frankish Annals and Nithard's Histories*, trans. Bernhard Walter Scholz, with Barbara Rogers (Ann Arbor: University of Michigan Press, 1970), p. 164; Bachrach, *Early Carolingian Warfare*, pp. 125–30.
34. Barber and Barker, *Tournaments*, p. 77.
35. Froissart, *Chroniques: manuscrit d'Amiens*, vol. 1, pp. 220–1, ch. 171.
36. Richard Vaughan, *Philip the Good: The Apogee of Burgundy* (London: Longman, 1970), pp. 43–4.
37. Barber and Barker, *Tournaments*, pp. 56, 60, 86, 88.
38. Verbruggen, *Art of Warfare*, pp. 144–59, 172–5.
39. Maurice Keen, 'Brotherhood in Arms', in *History*, 47 (1964), 1–17; repr. in his *Nobles, Knights and Men-at-Arms*, pp. 43–62.
40. *Règle du Temple*, sections 77–197; Bennett, '*La Règle du Temple* as a Military Manual', pp. 175–88.
41. On these orders see Keen, *Chivalry*, pp. 179–99.
42. On this see my *The Knights Templar: A New History* (Stroud: Sutton, 2001), pp. 66–9, 75–6.
43. Verbruggen, *Art of War*, p. 175.
44. Heymann, *John Žižka*, pp. 96–101, 492–8, esp. pp. 497–8.
45. See, for example, Bachrach, *Early Carolingian Warfare*, p. 96.
46. Gregory of Tours, Bk 7 ch. 35, p. 419; Ambroise, *Estoire*, lines 7235–52; *Chronicle of the Third Crusade*, Bk 4 ch. 30, p. 269. The Merovingian and Carolingian kings banned foraging: Bachrach, *Early Carolingian Warfare*,

pp. 216–17. Bachrach traces the prohibition back to Roman imperial military regulations.

47. Gregory of Tours, Bk 4 ch. 42, p. 238.
48. France, *Victory in the East*, pp. 90–3.
49. Ayton, 'English Armies in the Fourteenth Century', in *Arms, Armies and Fortifications*, ed. Curry and Hughes, pp. 21–38: here pp. 23–5.
50. Wright, *Knights and Peasants*, pp. 35–6, 38–9.
51. Vaughan, *Charles the Bold*, p. 176.
52. For some studies of kings organising the supplying of their armies see, for example, Bernard S. Bachrach, 'Logistics in Pre–Crusade Europe', in *Feeding Mars: Logistics in Western Warfare from the Middle Ages to the Present*, ed. J. A. Lynn (Boulder, Co: Westview Press, 1993), pp. 57–78: here pp. 70–1; reprinted in his *Warfare and Military Organisation*, no. V; Michael Prestwich, 'Military Logistics: The Case of 1322', in *Armies, Chivalry and Warfare*, ed. Strickland, pp. 276–88.
53. *Gesta Francorum*, Bk 4 ch. 10, p. 23.
54. Ambroise, *Estoire*, lines 6034–8, 10160–70, 10605–23; *Chronicle of the Third Crusade*, Bk 4 ch. 14, p. 243, Bk 6 chs 1, 7, pp. 335, 344; Denys Pringle, 'The Spring of the Cresson in Crusading History', *Dei gesta per Francos*, ed. Balard, Kedar and Riley-Smith, pp. 231–40; *La continuation de Guillaume de Tyr*, sections 40–1; translation in *Conquest of Jerusalem*, ed. Edbury, p. 45.
55. See above, Chapter 4, p. 104.
56. Ambroise, *Estoire*, lines 7639–45; *Chronicle of the Third Crusade*, Bk 4 ch. 34, p. 278.
57. Ambroise, *Estoire*, lines 5545–66; *Chronicle of the Third Crusade*, Bk 4 ch. 5, p. 232.
58. Ifor Rowlands, 'The Edwardian Conquest and its Military Consolidation', in *Edward I and Wales*, ed. Trevor Herbert and Gareth Elwyn Jones (Cardiff: University of Wales Press, 1988), pp. 41–72: here pp. 43–5, 47–8.
59. Froissart, *Chroniques: manuscrit d'Amiens*, vol. 4, pp. 171–5, chs 844–6. For a modern analysis see Susan Rose, *Medieval Naval Warfare, 1000–1500* (London: Routledge, 2002), pp. 67–8.
60. Christiansen, *Northern Crusades*, pp. 170–1.
61. Bachrach, *Early Carolingian Warfare*, p. 222; Ambroise, *Estoire*, lines 5731–6935; *Chronicle of the Third Crusade*, Bk 4 chs 10–24, pp. 236–62.
62. Bachrach, *Early Carolingian Warfare*, p. 137; France, *Western Warfare*, p. 36.
63 Vegetius, *De re militari*, Bk 1 ch. 19, and note 4 on p. 18 of Milner's translation.
64. Gregory of Tours, Bk 7 ch. 35, p. 418. Camels in the south of France seem inherently unlikely – perhaps they are part of Gregory's literary depiction of Gundovald.
65. Ibid.
66. Riché, *Carolingians*, p. 89.
67. Froissart, *Chroniques: manuscrit d'Amiens*, vol. 3, p. 231, ch. 620.
68. Jean le Bel, *Chronique*, vol. 1, p. 48, ch. 9. For a list of equipment for a campaign in Scotland in 1306–7, including tents, armour, cooking equipment, carts and horses, see Lachaud, 'Armour and Military Dress', pp. 367–9.

69. Jean le Bel, *Chronique*, vol 1, pp. 48–77, chs 9–13. For further observations on the problem of carrying an army's essential equipment see, for example, Robert Hardy, 'The Longbow', in *Arms, Armies and Fortifications*, ed. Curry and Hughes, pp. 161–81: here pp. 169–70.

70. Gilliver, *Roman Art of War*, pp. 51–5.

71. Bachrach, *Early Carolingian Warfare*, p. 97, argues that Hrabanus Maurus's comments on redeployment reflect actual practice and are not simply repeating Vegetius's work. He also argues that in 553 at Rimini the Frankish foragers successfully redeployed to a defensive formation against the Byzantines: pp. 180–2. R. C. Smail (*Crusading Warfare*, pp. 173–4) argued that during the First Crusade the crusaders used a redeploying manoeuvre during the battle of Antioch, 28 June 1098; this is disputed by France, *Victory in the East*, pp. 284, 291.

72. Einhard, *Life of Charlemagne*, p. 40.

73. *La Chanson de Roland*, lines 1049–109.

74. Ambroise, *Estoire*, lines 5759–808, 6368–91; *Chronicle of the Third Crusade*, Bk 1 chs 22–3, pp. 60–1, Bk 4 chs 10, 19, pp. 238, 251–2.

75. Vaughan, *Charles the Bold*, pp. 374–6.

76. See, for example, the introduction above, pp. 3–4; Ayton and Price, 'Introduction: The Military Revolution', pp. 7–8, and the citations in note 29 on p. 19; and the effects of 'the harrying of the north' described in J. J. N. Palmer, 'The Conqueror's Footprints in Domesday Book', in *Medieval Military Revolution*, ed. Ayton and Price, pp. 23–39; and see also his 'War and Domesday Waste' in *Armies, Chivalry and Warfare*, ed. Strickland, pp. 256–75.

77. Vaughan, *Charles the Bold*, p. 405.

78. Peter H. Humphries, *Llansteffan Castle* (Cardiff: Cadw, 1988, 1996); see also John R. Kenyon, 'Fluctuating Frontiers: Normanno-Welsh Castle Warfare *c.*1075 to 1240', in *Château Gaillard: XVII* (1996), pp. 119–26.

79. Vaughan, *Charles the Bold*, pp. 419–32.

80. 'Imâd al-Dîn al-Isfahânî, *Conquête de la Syrie et de la Palestine par Saladin (al-Fath al-qwsî l-fath al qudsî)*, trans. Henri Massé (Paris: Paul Geuthner, 1972), pp. 124–5.

81. Kennedy, *Crusader Castles*, pp. 148, 149.

82. Froissart, *Chroniques. Dernière rédaction*, pp. 303–5, ch. 78.

83. *Chanson de Bertrand du Guesclin*, ed. Faucon, lines 921–1163.

84. Much work has been done on medieval sieges in recent years. For what follows see, for instance, Bradbury, *The Medieval Siege*; and *The Medieval City Under Siege*, ed. Corfis and Wolfe.

85. See, for instance, Froissart, *Chroniques: manuscrit d'Amiens*, vol. 2, p. 146, ch. 344.

86. For examples of these two views see: *The Chivalric Vision of Alfonso de Cartagena: Study and Edition of the Doctrinal de los caualleros*, ed. Noel Fallows (Newark, DE: Juan de la Cuesta, 1995), pp. 224–5, part 5; Judi Upton-Ward, 'The Surrender of Gaston and the Rule of the Templars', in *The Military Orders: Fighting for the Faith*, ed. Barber, pp. 179–88.

87. See, for example, Nicholson, *Knights Templar*, p. 66.

88. Bede, *Historia Ecclesiastica*, Bk 3 ch. 1, translated as Bede, *The History of the English Church and People*, trans. Leo Sherley-Price (Harmondsworth: Penguin, 1955, 1968), p. 141.

89. Gregory of Tours, Bk 2 ch. 33, pp. 147–8.

90. Ibid., Bk 7 ch. 38, pp. 421–4.

91. Froissart, *Chroniques: manuscrit d'Amiens*, vol. 4, pp. 206–9, ch. 861.

92. Ibid., vol. 2, p. 222, ch. 387 lines 37–43, p. 335, ch. 461.

93. Gregory of Tours, Bk 2 ch. 27, pp. 139–40.

94. William G. Zajac, 'Captured Property on the First Crusade', in *The First Crusade: Origins and Impact*, ed. Jonathan Phillips (Manchester: Manchester University Press, 1997), pp. 153–80: here p. 157.

95. *Chronicle of the Third Crusade*, Bk 6 ch. 6, pp. 343–4; Ambroise, *Estoire*, lines 10579–86 (less praising of Richard).

96. *Gesta Francorum*, Bk 10 ch. 38, p. 92; France, *Victory in the East*, pp. 353–6.

97. For example, Ambroise, *Estoire*, lines 3481–91; *Chronicle of the Third Crusade*, Bk 1 ch. 40, pp. 95–6.

98. Dunbabin, *Captivity and Imprisonment in Medieval Europe*, pp. 114–24; for some examples of prisoner–exchange and payment of ransoms see, for example, Froissart, *Chroniques: manuscrit d'Amiens*, vol. 2, pp. 306–7, ch. 443; vol. 2, p. 331, ch. 458; vol. 3, pp. 35–6, ch. 520; vol. 4, pp. 118–19, ch. 812 lines 26–36; p. 290, ch. 900 lines 22–3.

99. The evidence for the Templars is summarised by Alan Forey, 'The Military Orders and the Ransoming of Captives From Islam (Twelfth to Early Fourteenth Centuries)', *Traditio*, 40 (1984), 197–234; reprinted in his *Military Orders and Crusades*, no. VI and see Addenda, VI, pp. 263–4, for another example. On Bayart see *Histoire du gentil seigneur de Bayart*, pp. 388–9 and note 1: the editor assumed that the Germans would not pay because they were too poor.

100. Bachrach, *Early Carolingian Warfare*, pp. 40–1; *Chronicle of the Third Crusade*, Bk 4 ch. 4, p. 231 and notes 6 and 7 on contemporary reactions; Froissart, *Chroniques: manuscrit d'Amiens*, vol. 4, pp. 287–8, ch. 898; Curry, *Battle of Agincourt*, p. 163, and see p. 472 for discussion.

101. Clifford J. Rogers, *War Cruel and Sharp: English Strategy Under Edward III, 1327–1360* (Woodbridge: Boydell, 2000), and see the review by J. J. N. Palmer, *History*, 87 (2002), 278–9.

102. Malcolm Vale, *War and Chivalry: Warfare and Aristocratic Culture in England, France and Burgundy at the End of the Middle Ages* (London: Duckworth, 1981), p. 171; Ayton and Price, ' Introduction: The Military Revolution', pp. 3, 7; Keen, 'The Changing Scene', p. 287.

103. Arnold, 'War in Sixteenth-Century Europe', p. 25.

104. Vegetius, *De re militari*, Bk 3 ch. 9. And see Bachrach, *Early Carolingian Warfare*, pp. 202, 204–5; Contamine, *War in the Middle Ages*, p. 226; J. R. Alban and C. T. Allmand, 'Spies and Spying in the Fourteenth Century', in *War, Literature and Politics*, ed. C. T. Allmand, pp. 73–101.

105. Ambroise, *Estoire*, lines 10269–82; *Chronicle of the Third Crusade*, Bk 6 ch. 3, p. 338; Ramon Muntaner, ch. 120.

106. Vaughan, *Charles the Bold*, pp. 392–3. For this period, 'Swiss' is an imprecise term, but convenient short-hand for 'confederate troops from the area now known as Switzerland'.

107. Vegetius, *De re militari*, Bk 3 chs 13–14.

108. Froissart, *Chroniques: manuscrit d'Amiens*, vol. 3, p. 17, ch. 510 lines 27–8; Bennett, 'Development of Battle Tactics', pp. 5, 6–10.

109. See, for example, Verbruggen, *Art of Warfare*, pp. 204–7.

110. Gregory of Tours, Bk 3 ch. 7, p. 168 (there is no date in the text; the date is from Bachrach, *Early Carolingian Warfare*), Bk 4 ch. 42, pp. 236–7.

111. DeVries, *Infantry Warfare*, pp. 13, 22, 36–7, 46.

112. Ramon Muntaner, ch. 240; Setton, *Catalan Domination of Athens*, pp. 9–11.

113. DeVries, *Infantry Warfare*, pp. 53, 56, 72–3

114. Bachrach, *Early Carolingian Warfare*, p. 141.

115. For Richard I see, for example, *Chronicle of the Third Crusade*, Bk 4 ch. 19, p. 257, ch. 28, p. 267, ch. 30, p. 271, Bk 6 ch. 23, pp. 366–8. In the great Arthurian prose romances of the 1230s and later, King Arthur is discouraged by his men from entering the field; he oversees the battle and directs his troops, and himself leads the final *bataille* (battalion) which comes on to the field last, and only if needed. See, for example, *La mort le roi Artu*, ed. Jean Frappier (Geneva: Droz, 1964), pp. 230–1, section 180; *La suite du Roman de Merlin*, ed. Gilles Roussineau, 2 vols (Geneva: Droz, 1996), vol. 1, pp. 105–6, sections 140–1; *Meliadus de Leonnoys*, ch. 94, fol. 32r, ch. 96, fols 36v–37r. Given the popularity of the Arthurian romances among the nobility of western Europe, this caution towards the king leading on the battlefield probably reflected their concerns. On this question see also Verbruggen, *Art of Warfare*, pp. 217–21; Contamine, *War in the Middle Ages*, p. 236 and note 91. In the same vein, Christine de Pisan envisaged the 'good prince' appointing military commanders to deal with military affairs rather than fighting himself: Christine de Pisan, *Le livre du corps de policie*, ed. Robert H. Lucas (Geneva: Droz, 1967), Bk 1 ch. 9, p. 25.

116. Jean le Bel, *Chronique*, vol. 2, pp. 125–31, ch. 76; Froissart, *Chroniques: manuscrit d'Amiens*, vol. 3, p. 39, ch. 522; Froissart, *Chroniques. Dernière rédaction*, pp. 770–92, chs 236–42. See also DeVries, *Infantry Warfare*, pp. 180–1.

117. Vegetius, *De re militari*, Bk 3 chs 14–17.

118. Froissart, *Chroniques: manuscrit d'Amiens*, vol. 3, p. 345, ch. 683, lines 36–43.

119. Bachrach, *Early Carolingian Warfare*, pp. 170–7. The quotations are from p. 170. After some years of debate the date of this battle has been generally agreed as 732.

120. John France, 'The Battle of Carcano: The Event and its Importance', *War in History*, 6 (1999), 245–61.

121. Vaughan, *Charles the Bold*, pp. 198–204. The quotation below is from p. 202.

122. Gregory of Tours, Bk 2 ch. 32, pp. 145–7. For the date see Collins, *Early Medieval Europe*, p. 114.

123. Bede, *History of the English Church*, Bk 3 ch. 24, p. 183. The river is possibly the Went, in Yorkshire.

124. Housley, *Later Crusades*, p. 77.

125. Bernard Bachrach, 'The Feigned Retreat at Hastings', *Mediaeval Studies*, 33 (1971), 344–7; Stephen Morillo, 'Hastings: An Unusual Battle', *Haskins Society Journal*, 2 (1990), 95–103: here 96, 100 note 23, 101 and note 27 for the arguments on both sides; Lawson, *Battle of Hastings*, pp. 198–205.

126. France, *Western Warfare*, p. 182.
127. Walter the Chancellor, *The Antiochene Wars*, trans. Thomas Asbridge and Susan B. Edgington (Aldershot: Ashgate, 1999), pp. 2–3, 155.
128. Verbruggen, *Art of Warfare*, pp. 202–3; DeVries, *Infantry Warfare*, pp. 42–3. DeVries considers this to be a French victory.
129. Vegetius, *De re militari*, Bk 3 ch. 25, pp. 114–15.
130. Orderic Vitalis, *Historia Ecclesiastica*, ed. and translated as *The Ecclesiastical History of Orderic Vitalis*, ed. and trans. Marjorie Chibnall, vol. 2 (Oxford: Oxford University Press, 1969), Bk 3, p. 176, and note 2.
131. Orderic Vitalis, Bk 3, pp. 178, 180.
132. Ambroise, *Estoire*, lines 6631–734; *Chronicle of the Third Crusade*, Bk 4 ch. 21, pp. 258–9.
133. Translated by Housley, *Documents*, no. 34, p. 107.
134. See, for instance, Reuter, 'Plunder and Tribute'.
135. Gregory of Tours, Bk 2 ch. 32, p. 147.
136. Riché, *Carolingians*, p. 105.
137. Barber, *The Two Cities*, pp. 104, 211.
138. On hostages see, for instance, Bradbury, *Medieval Siege*, p. 311.
139. Gregory of Tours, Bk 3 ch. 7, pp. 167–8.

6 Naval warfare

1. On clinker-built ship construction see John Haywood, *Dark Age Naval Power: A Re-Assessment of Frankish and Anglo-Saxon Seafaring Activity* (London and New York: Routledge, 1991), pp. 16–17. I am indebted to Mrs Valerie Rudd for first drawing my attention to Dr Haywood's work on early medieval shipping. For frame-first construction see Barbara M. Kreutz, 'Ships, Shipping and the Implications of Change in the Early Medieval Mediterranean', *Viator*, 7 (1976), 79–109: here 104, 105. See also DeVries, *Medieval Military Technology*, pp. 283–4, 297; Gillian Hutchinson, *Medieval Ships and Shipping* (Leicester: Leicester University Press, 1994), pp. 4–46. For more detail on medieval naval warfare after 1000, see Rose, *Medieval Naval Warfare*.
2. Kreutz, 'Ships', 80–5; Hutchinson, *Medieval Ships*, pp. 59–64. The most familiar modern form of this rigging appears on the dhow.
3. Hutchinson, *Medieval Ships*, p. 50.
4. Haywood, *Dark Age Naval Power*, pp. 46–8; Vegetius, *De re militari*, Bk 4 ch. 37, p. 144.
5. Kreutz, 'Ships', 96–103; Haywood, *Dark Age Naval Power*, p. 117.
6. Clarke, 'Vikings', p. 53; Haywood, *Dark Age Naval Power*, pp. 63–70; Gillmor, 'War on the Rivers', 81.
7. For the debates see, for instance, Gillmor, 'War on the Rivers', 79–109.
8. Hutchinson, *Medieval Ships*, pp. 4–20, 41–4; Haywood, *Dark Age Naval Power*, p. 49; John Pryor, *Geography, Technology and War: Studies in the Maritime History of the Mediterranean, 649–1571* (Cambridge: Cambridge University Press, 1988), pp. 27–86. For later ships see Ian Friel, 'Winds of Change? Ships and the Hundred Years War', in *Arms, Armies and Fortifications*, ed. Curry and Hughes, pp. 183–93.

9. Michael E. Mallett, *The Florentine Galleys in the Fifteenth Century* (Oxford: Clarendon Press, 1967), p. 27.

10. Rose, *Medieval Naval Warfare*, pp. 27–8.

11. Ambroise, *Estoire*, lines 537, 1181, etc.

12. Rose, *Medieval Naval Warfare*, pp. 1, 27, 28.

13. France, *Victory in the East*, pp. 336–7; Pryor, 'The Transportation of Horses'; Pryor, '"Water, water, everywhere, Nor any drop to drink"', pp. 21–8.

14. *Chronicle of the Third Crusade*, Bk 2 ch. 26, p. 274.

15. Pryor, '"Water, water, everywhere"', pp. 21–8.

16. Hutchinson, *Medieval Ships*, pp. 164–82.

17. Vegetius, *De re militari*, Bk 4 chs 37, 46, pp. 144, 151–2.

18. On this see Matthew Bennett, 'Norman Naval Activity in the Mediterranean c.1060–1108', in *Anglo-Norman Studies: The Proceedings of the Battle Conference*, 15 (1992), 41–58: here 56.

19. Haywood, *Dark Age Naval Power*, pp. 34–9.

20. Gregory of Tours, Bk 3 ch. 3, pp. 163–4.

21. Haywood, *Dark Age Naval Power*, pp. 78–85; *Beowulf*, trans. Alexander, pp. 89, 125–6, 129–30; trans. Heaney, lines 1202–14, 2354–68, 2497–506.

22. Peter Llewellyn, *Rome in the Dark Ages*, 2nd edn (London: Constable, 1993), p. 218.

23. Haywood, *Dark Age Naval Power*, pp. 113–16.

24. Ibid., pp. 118–20.

25. Ibid., p. 121.

26. Ibid., p. 129.

27. Gillmor, 'War on the Rivers', 92–101.

28. Haywood, *Dark Age Naval Power*, pp. 135, 207 note 244.

29. Clarke, 'Vikings', p. 53.

30. Patrick Wormald, 'The Ninth Century', in *The Anglo-Saxons*, ed. Campbell, pp. 132–59: here p. 150.

31. *Anglo-Saxon Chronicle*, pp. 48, 50, 51, 57–8.

32. Ibid., p. 57.

33. This guild is discussed in detail by Janus Møller Jensen, 'Denmark and the Holy War: A Redefinition of a Traditional Pattern of Conflict, 1147–1169', in *Scandinavia and Europe, 800–1350: Contact, Conflict and Co-Existence*, ed. J. Adams and K. Holman (Turnhout: Brepols, forthcoming). I am very grateful to Janus Møller Jensen for allowing me to read and cite his unpublished article.

34. Kurt Villads Jensen, 'The Blue Baltic Border of Denmark in the High Middle Ages: Danes, Wends and Saxo Grammaticus', in *Medieval Frontiers: Concepts and Practices*, ed. David Abulafia and Nora Berend (Aldershot: Ashgate, 2002), pp. 173–92: here pp. 183, 184–6, 192.

35. Candia in Crete: Ruthi Gertwagen, 'The Venetian Port of Candia, Crete (1299–1363): Construction and Maintenance', in *Mediterranean Cities: Historical Perspectives*, ed. Irad Malkin and Robert L. Hohlfelder (London: Frank Cass, 1998), pp. 141–58: here p. 152, and note 2. Rhodes town, the Naillac tower: Nicholson, *Knights Hospitaller*, p. 59 (constructed in the early fifteenth century). Tyre: *Continuation de Guillaume de Tyr*, pp. 77–8, section 64; *Conquest of Jerusalem*, ed. Edbury, p. 69. Acre: *Chronicle of the Third Crusade*, p. 117, Bk 1 ch. 60; David Jacoby, 'Crusader Acre in the

Thirteenth Century: Urban Layout and Topography', *Studi Medievali*, 3a serie, 20 (1979), 1–45: here 13–14, reprinted in his *Studies on the Crusader States and on Venetian Expansion* (Northampton: Variorum, 1989), no. V. Constantinople: Jacoby, 'Crusader Acre', 14, note 65. Famagusta in Cyprus: Hill, *History of Cyprus*, vol. 3, p. 857 (description of 1553). Portsmouth: A. D. Saunders, 'Hampshire Coastal Defence Since the Introduction of Artillery with a Description of Fort Wallington', *Archaeological Journal*, 123 (1966), 136–71: here 139 (constructed in the fifteenth century).

36. Mallett, *Florentine Galleys*, p. 13.

37. Michael Hughes, 'The Fourteenth-Century French Raids on Hampshire and the Isle of Wight', in *Arms, Armies and Fortifications*, ed. Curry and Hughes, pp. 121–43; John R. Kenyon, 'Coastal Artillery Fortification in England in the Late Fourteenth and Early Fifteenth Centuries', in ibid., pp. 145–9.

38. Rose, *Medieval Naval Warfare*, pp. 81–97, 105.

39. Jean Dunbabin, *France in the Making, 843–1180* (Oxford, Oxford University Press, 1991), p. 79.

40. Bennett, 'Norman Naval activity in the Mediterranean', 41–8.

41. David Abulafia, 'The Norman Kingdom of Africa and the Norman Expeditions to Majorca and the Muslim Mediterranean', in *Anglo-Norman Studies 7: The Proceedings of the Battle Conference* (1984), 26–49. The quotation is from Ibn al-Athīr, quoted on p. 35.

42. H. E. J. Cowdrey, 'The Mahdia Campaign of 1087', *English Historical Review*, 92 (1977), 1–29.

43. See, for example, Anthony Luttrell, 'The Hospitallers of Rhodes Confront the Turks, 1306–1421', in *Christians, Jews and Other Worlds: Patterns of Conflict and Accommodation*, ed. P. F. Gallagher (Lanham: University Press of America, 1988), pp. 80–116; reprinted in his *The Hospitallers of Rhodes and Their Mediterranean World* (Aldershot: Variorum, 1992), no. II.

44. Vaughan, *Philip the Good*, pp. 270–3.

45. *Livre des Fais*, Bk 2 ch. 31, p. 278 lines 37–9.

46. C. P. Lewis, 'Gruffudd ap Cynan and the Normans', in *Gruffudd ap Cynan: A Collaborative Biography*, ed. K. L. Maund (Woodbridge: Boydell, 1996), pp. 61–77: here pp. 65–6.

47. Lewis, 'Gruffudd ap Cynan', pp. 71–3.

48. K. L. Maund, '"Gruffudd, Grandson of Iago": *Historia Gruffud vab Kenan* and the Construction of Legitimacy', in *Gruffydd ap Cynan*, ed. Maund, pp. 109–16: here p. 110.

49. DeVries, *Medieval Military Technology*, pp. 291, 310 note 19; William Ledyard Rodgers, *Naval Warfare Under Oars, 4th to 16th Centuries: A Study of Strategy, Tactics and Ship Design* (Annapolis: US Naval Institute, 1940, repr. 1967), pp. 79–86; Rose, *Medieval Naval Warfare*, pp. 24–5.

50. Rodgers, *Naval Warfare*, p. 81.

51. Judith Jesch, 'Norse Historical Traditions and the *Historia Gruffud vab Kenan*: Magnús berfœttr and Haraldr Hárfagri', in *Gruffudd ap Cynan*, ed. Maund, pp. 117–47: here pp. 117–19.

52. Rodgers, *Naval Warfare*, pp. 93–5; David A. Carpenter, *The Minority of Henry III* (London: Methuen, 1990), pp. 43–4; Rose, *Medieval Naval Warfare*, pp. 29–31.

53. Vegetius, *De re militari*, Bk 4 ch. 44, pp. 149–50.

54. *Fouke Fitz Warin : roman du XIVe siècle*, ed. Louis Brandin (Paris: H. Champion, 1930), p. 59 lines 4–24, and p. iv for date.

55. Ambroise, *Estoire*, lines 2259–63; *Chronicle of the Third Crusade*, Bk 2 ch. 42, pp. 198–9; 'De ortu Waluuanii, nepoti Arturi', in *The Rise of Gawain, Nephew of Arthur (De ortu Waluuanii nepotis Arturi)*, ed. and trans. Mildred Leake Day (New York and London: Garland Publishing, 1984), p. 64 lines 15–22. The author of the 'De ortu' was probably writing with an eye on Vegetius. For the modern view see Felipe Fernández-Armesto, 'Naval Warfare after the Viking Age, *c.*1100–1500', in *Medieval Warfare*, ed. Keen, pp. 230–52: here p. 238.

56. Froissart, *Chroniques: manuscrit d'Amiens*, vol. 2, pp. 34–9, chs 272–4. For a modern analysis see Rose, *Medieval Naval Warfare*, pp. 64–5.

57. On Roger de Lauria see John H. Pryor, 'The Naval Battles of Roger of Lauria', *Journal of Medieval History*, 9 (1983), 179–216; reprinted in his *Commerce, Shipping and Naval Warfare in the Medieval Mediterranean* (London: Variorum, 1987), VI; Lawrence V. Mott, 'The Battle of Malta, 1283: Prelude to Disaster', in *The Circle of War*, ed. Kagay and Villalon, pp. 145–72; Rose, *Medieval Naval Warfare*, pp. 44–51.

58. Pryor, 'Naval Battles', 189–94.

59. For another example see a battle of spring 1189: *Chronicle of the Third Crusade*, Bk 1 ch. 35, pp. 87–9; Vegetius, *De re militari*, Bk 4 chs 45–6, pp. 150–1. The account of this battle is so like Vegetius's Bk 4, chs 45–46, that it is possible that the writer of the *Itinerarium* simply 'wrote up' this battle based on Vegetius's description.

60. On flag and lantern signals see John H. Pryor, 'The Galleys of Charles I of Anjou, King of Sicily: ca. 1269–84', *Studies in Medieval and Renaissance History*, 14 (1993), 34–103: here 79, 81; on trumpets see Rose, *Medieval Naval Warfare*, p. 127; Vaughan, *Charles the Bold*, p. 229.

61. Ambroise, *Estoire*, lines 3771–822; *Chronicle of the Third Crusade*, Bk 1 ch. 58, pp. 112–13; Oliver, schoolmaster of Cologne, *Historia Damiatina*, in *Die Schriften des Kölner Domscholasters, späteren Bischofs von Paderborn und Kardinalbischofs von S. Sabina*, ed. H. Hoogeveg, Bibliothek des literarischen Vereins in Stuttgart, vol. 202 (Tübingen, 1894), p. 179–80.

62. Rose, *Medieval Naval Warfare*, pp. 125–6.

63. DeVries, *Medieval Military Technology*, p. 287; Kreutz, 'Ships', 83–4, quoting Procopius's 'Vandalic Wars', Bk 3 ch. 6.

64. Jensen, 'Blue Baltic Border of Denmark', p. 183.

65. Douglas Haldane, 'The Fire-Ship of Al-Ṣālih Ayyūb and Muslim Use of "Greek Fire"', in *Circle of War*, ed. Kagny and Villalon, pp. 137–44. For instance, all the references to the use of Greek fire during the Third Crusade, set out in the *Itinerarium peregrinorum* and Ambroise's *Estoire*, relate to Muslim use of the weapon. The Christians never use it. Again, in the fictional 'De ortu Waluuanii', whose naval battle sequence is apparently derived from the *Itinerarium peregrinorum*, it is the pagans and not the Christians who use Greek fire. See, for instance, Helen Nicholson, 'Following the Path of the Lionheart: The *De ortu Walwanii* and the *Itinerarium peregrinorum et gesta regis Ricardi*', *Medium Ævum*, 69 (2000), 21–33: here 26–7.

66. Toch, 'Medieval German City Under Siege', pp. 41–2.

67. Pryor, 'The Galleys of Charles I of Anjou', 78.
68. Kelly DeVries, 'The Effectiveness of Fifteenth-Century Shipboard Artillery', *Mariner's Mirror*, 84 (1998), 389–99: here 389–90, 398 note 23.
69. Ibid., 394–6.
70. Ibid., 393.
71. On shipbuilding in general see Rose, *Medieval Naval Warfare*, pp. 6–23.
72. Bachrach, *Early Carolingian Warfare*, p. 257.
73. Nicholas Hooper, 'Some Observations on the Navy in Late Anglo-Saxon England', in *Anglo-Norman Warfare*, ed. Strickland, pp. 17–27: here pp. 17–18; *Anglo-Saxon Chronicle*, p. 51.
74. Hooper, 'Some Observations', pp. 20–6.
75. Ibid., pp. 26–7.
76. Ambroise, *Estoire*, lines 303–22; *Chronicle of the Third Crusade*, Bk 2 ch. 7, p. 149; Gillingham, *Richard I*, pp. 114, 127.
77. Rose, *Medieval Naval Warfare*, pp. 12–13, 17–18.
78. Ibid., pp. 13–16.
79. The quotation is from Rose, *Medieval Naval Warfare*, p. 42. See Luttrell, 'The Hospitallers of Rhodes Confront the Turks', p. 91; see also Ramon Muntaner, chs 194, 199 for Roger de Flor as a corsair; Pryor, *Geography, Technology and* War, pp. 153–61; Rose, *Medieval Naval Warfare*, pp. 42–3, 72–3, 81–3.
80. Pryor, 'The Galleys of Charles I of Anjou', 77–91: on signals see pp. 79, 81.
81. Mallett, *Florentine Galleys*, pp. 17–18; Rose, *Medieval Naval Warfare*, pp. 7–9.
82. Mallett, *Florentine Galleys*, p. 19.
83. Rose, *Medieval Naval Warfare*, pp. 10–11.
84. Vaughan, *Philip the Good*, p. 270.
85. Vaughan, *Charles the Bold*, pp. 227–8.
86. *Chronicle of the Third Crusade*, Bk 1 ch. 34, p. 88.

Conclusion

1. Richard Harding, 'Naval Warfare, 1453–1815', in *European Warfare, 1453–1815*, ed. Black, pp. 96–117: here p. 98.

Further reading

This list, which is not intended to be comprehensive, concentrates on works in English. It includes major studies and studies not already included in the notes. Other works, especially detailed studies, are set out in the notes to individual chapters. For a more complete bibliography on many aspects of medieval warfare, see the bibliographical surveys listed below.

Bibliographical surveys

Bernard S. Bachrach, 'Medieval Siege Warfare: A Reconnaissance', *Journal of Military History*, 58 (1994), 119–33

Everett U. Crosby, *Medieval Warfare: A Bibliographical Guide* (New York: Garland, 2000)

Anne Curry, 'Medieval Warfare: England and her Continental Neighbours, Eleventh to the Fourteenth Centuries', *Journal of Medieval History*, 24 (1998), 81–102

Kelly DeVries, *A Cumulative Bobliography of Medieval Military History and Technology* (Leiden: Brill, 2002)

John France, 'Recent Writing on Medieval Warfare: From the Fall of Rome to *c*.1300', *Journal of Military History*, 65 (2001), 441–73

General

Single-authored studies

Bernard S. Bachrach, *Warfare and Military Organisation in Pre-Crusade Europe* (Aldershot: Variorum, 2002)

Philippe Contamine, *War in the Middle Ages*, trans. Michael Jones (Oxford: Basil Blackwell, 1984)

John France, *Western Warfare in the Age of the Crusades, 1000–1300* (London: UCL Press, 1999)

Christopher Marshall, *Warfare in the Latin East, 1192–1291* (Cambridge: Cambridge University Press, 1992)

David Nicolle, *Medieval Warfare Source Book: [2] Christian Europe and its Neighbours* (Leicester: Brockhampton Press, 1998)

—— *Medieval Warfare Source Book: [1] Warfare in Western Christendom* (Leicester: Brockhampton Press, 1999)

Michael Prestwich, *Armies and Warfare in the Middle Ages: The English Experience* (New Haven and London: Yale University Press, 1996)

R. C. Smail, *Crusading Warfare, 1097–1193*, 2nd edn with introduction by Christopher Marshall (Cambridge: Cambridge University Press, 1995). The introduction includes a useful bibliographical survey

J. F. Verbruggen, *The Art of Warfare in Western Europe During the Middle Ages from the Eighth Century to 1340*, 2nd edn, trans. Sumner Willard and Mrs R. W. Southern (Woodbridge: Boydell, 1997)

Collections of essays

Anne Curry and Michael Hughes, eds, *Arms, Armies and Fortifications in the Hundred Years War* (Woodbridge: Boydell, 1994)

John Gillingham and J. C. Holt, eds, *War and Government in the Middle Ages: Essays in Honour of J. O. Prestwich* (Cambridge: D. S. Brewer, 1984)

Donald J. Kagay and L. J. Andrew Villalon, eds, *The Circle of War in the Middle Ages: Essays on Medieval Military and Naval History* (Woodbridge: Boydell, 1999)

Maurice Keen, ed., *Medieval Warfare: A History* (Oxford: Oxford University Press, 1999)

Matthew Strickland, ed., *Anglo-Norman Warfare: Studies in Late Anglo-Saxon and Anglo-Norman Military Organisation and Warfare* (Woodbridge: Boydell, 1992)

—— ed., *Armies, Chivalry and Warfare in Medieval Britain and France: Proceedings of the 1995 Harlaxton Symposium* (Stamford, Lincs.: Paul Watkins, 1998)

Journals and series

Anglo-Norman Studies: The Proceedings of the Battle Conference (Woodbridge: Boydell)

Journal of Medieval Military History (Woodbridge: Boydell, for the De re militari Society)

Journal of Military History (Lexington: Virginia Military Inst., Society for Military History)

Medieval Knighthood: Papers from the Strawberry Hill Conferences (Woodbridge: Boydell)

War in History (London: Arnold)

Websites

The De re militari society: www.deremilitari.org

Chapter 1 The theory of warfare

The main primary source remains:

Vegetius, *De re militari*, translated as *Epitome of Military Science*, trans. N. P. Milner, 2nd edn (Liverpool: Liverpool University Press, 1996)

Secondary studies

Jean Flori, *Idéologie du glaive: préhistoire de la chevalerie* (Geneva: Droz, 1983)

—— *L'Essor de la chevalerie, XIe–XIIe siècles* (Geneva: Droz, 1986)

—— *Chevaliers et chevalerie au moyen âge* (Paris: Poche, 1998)

—— *La guerre sainte. La formation de l'idée de croisade dans l'Occident chrétien* (Paris: Aubier, 2001)

Maurice Keen, *The Laws of War in the Late Middle Ages* (London: Routledge, 1965)

—— *Chivalry* (New Haven and London: Yale University Press, 1984)

—— *Nobles, Knights and Men-at-Arms in the Middle Ages* (London: Hambleton Press, 1996)

Peter Noble, 'Military Leadership in the Old French Epic', *Reading Around the Epic: A Festschrift in Honour of Professor Wolfgang van Emden*, ed. Marianne Ailes, Philip E. Bennett and Karen Pratt (London: King's College London, Centre for Late Antique and Medieval Studies, 1998), pp. 171–91

Jonathan Riley-Smith, *The First Crusade and the Idea of Crusading* (London: Athlone, 1986)

Frederick H. Russell, *The Just War in the Middle Ages* (Cambridge: Cambridge University Press, 1975)

Chapter 2   Military personnel

Andrew Ayton, *Knights and Warhorses: Military Service and the English Aristocracy Under Edward III* (Woodbridge: Boydell, 1994)

Jim Bradbury, *The Medieval Archer* (Woodbridge: Boydell, 1985)

Peter Coss, *The Knight in Medieval England, 1000–1400* (Stroud: Alan Sutton, 1993)

Kelly DeVries, *Infantry Warfare in the Early Fourteenth Century: Discipline, Tactics and Technology* (Woodbridge: Boydell, 1996)

—— 'Teenagers at War During the Middle Ages', in *The Premodern Teenager: Youth in Society, 1150–1650*, ed. Konrad Eisenbichler (Toronto: Centre for Renaissance and Reformation Studies, 2002), reprinted at: http://www.deremilitari.org/devries2.htm

Susan Edgington and Sarah Lambert, eds, *Gendering the Crusades* (Cardiff: University of Wales Press, 2001). Also contains a useful bibliography

Stephen S. Evans, *Lords of Battle: Image and Reality of the* Comitatus *in Dark-Age Britain* (Woodbridge: Boydell, 1997)

Kenneth Fowler, *Medieval Mercenaries: Volume 1: The Great Companies* (Oxford: Blackwell, 2001)

Michael E. Mallett, *Mercenaries and their Masters: Warfare in Renaissance Italy* (Totowa, NJ: Rowman and Littlefield, 1974)

Michael Prestwich, *War, Politics and Finance Under Edward I* (London: Faber and Faber, 1972)

Nicholas Wright, *Knights and Peasants in the Hundred Years War in the French Countryside* (Woodbridge: Boydell, 1998)

Chapter 3   Military buildings

Château Gaillard Colloque International: the proceedings of the international Château Gaillard conferences, published annually by the Centre de Recherches Archéologiques Médiévales, Université de Caen

Charles Coulson, 'Cultural Realities and Reappraisals in English Castle-Study', *Journal of Medieval History*, 22 (1996), 171–208

Robert Higham and Philip Barker, *Timber Castles* (London: Batsford, 1992)

David Hill and Alexander R. Rumble, *The Defence of Wessex: The Burghal Hideage and Anglo-Saxon Fortifications* (Manchester: Manchester University Press, 1996)

Hugh Kennedy, *Crusader Castles* (Cambridge: Cambridge University Press, 1994)

Chapter 4   Military equipment

Sydney Anglo, *The Martial Arts of Renaissance Europe* (New Haven and London: Yale University Press, 2000)

Paul E. Chevedden, 'The Invention of the Counterweight Trebuchet: A Study in Cultural Diffusion', *Dumbarton Oaks Papers*, 54 (2000), 71–116

John Clark, ed., *The Medieval Horse and its Equipment, c.1150–c.1450* (London: HMSO, 1995)

Peter Coss and Maurice Keen, eds, *Heraldry, Pageantry and Social Display in Medieval England* (Woodbridge: Boydell, 2002)

Simon Coupland, 'Carolingian Arms and Armor in the Ninth Century', *Viator*, 21 (1990), 29–50

Kelly DeVries, *Medieval Military Technology* (Ontario: Broadview, 1998)

Peter H. Humphries, *Engines of War: Replica Medieval Siege Weapons at Caerphilly Castle*, 2nd edn (Cardiff: Cadw: Welsh Historic Monuments, 1996)

Ann Hyland, *The Medieval Warhorse: From Byzantium to the Crusades* (London: Grange, 1994)

—— *The Warhorse, 1250–1600* (Stroud: Sutton, 1998)

Ewart Oakeshott, *Records of the Medieval Sword* (Woodbridge: Boydell, 1991)

David C. Nicolle, *Arms and Armour of the Crusading era, 1050–1350* (London: Greenhill, 1999)

—— ed., *A Companion to Medieval Arms and Armour* (Woodbridge: Boydell, 2002)

Alan Williams, *The Knight and and the Blast Furnace: A History of Metallurgy of Armour in the Middle Ages and the Early Modern Period* (Leiden: Brill, 2002)

See also the works listed under Chapter 2.

Chapter 5   The practice of land warfare

Bernard S. Bachrach, *Merovingian Military Organisation* (Minneapolis: University of Minnesota Press, 1972)

—— *Early Carolingian Warfare: Prelude to Empire* (Philadelphia: University of Pennsylvania Press, 2001)

Juliet R. V. Barker, *The Tournament in England, 1100–1400* (Woodbridge: Boydell, 1986)

Jim Bradbury, *The Medieval Siege* (Woodbridge: Boydell, 1992)

Ivy A. Corfis and Michael Wolfe, eds, *The Medieval City Under Siege* (Woodbridge: Boydell, 1995)

Anne Curry, *The Hundred Years War* (Basingstoke: Macmillan – now Palgrave Macmillan, 1993)

—— *The Battle of Agincourt: Sources and Interpretations* (Woodbridge: Boydell, 2000)

Clifford J. Rogers, *War Cruel and Sharp: English Strategy under Edward III, 1327–1360* (Woodbridge: Boydell, 2000)

Randall Rogers, *Latin Siege Warfare in the Twelfth Century* (Oxford: Clarendon Press, 1992)

Chapter 6   Naval warfare

Birthe L. Clausen, ed., *Viking Voyages to North America* (Roskilde: The Viking Ship Museum, 1993)

Ole Crumlin-Pedersen, with Christian Hirte, Kenn Jensen and Susan Möller-Wiering, *Viking-Age Ships and Shipbuilding in Hedeby/ Haithabu and Schleswig* (Schleswig: Archäologisches Landesmuseum der Christian-Albrechts-Universität Roskilde: Viking Ship Museum, 1997)

Robert Gardiner and John Morrison, eds, *The Age of the Galley: Mediterranean Oared Vessels since Pre-Classical Times* (Annapolis: Naval Institute Press, 1995)

John Haywood, *Dark Age Naval Power: A Re-Assessment of Frankish and Anglo-Saxon Seafaring Activity* (London and New York: Routledge, 1991)

Gillian Hutchinson, *Medieval Ships and Shipping* (London: Leicester University Press, 1994)

John Pryor, *Commerce, Shipping and Naval Warfare in the Medieval Mediterranean* (London: Variorum, 1987)

—— *Geography, Technology and War: Studies in the Maritime History of the Mediterranean, 649–1571* (Cambridge: Cambridge University Press, 1988)

Susan Rose, *Medieval Naval Warfare, 1000–1500* (London and New York: Routledge, 2002)

Conclusion

Andrew Ayton and J. L. Price, eds, *The Medieval Military Revolution: State, Society and Military Change in Medieval and Early Modern Europe* (London and New York: Tauris Academic Studies, 1995)

Index

Key: archbp = archbishop of; bp = bishop of; c. = count of; d. = duke of; emp. = emperor; k. = king of

Personal names of persons before 1300 are indexed under their first name; those after 1300 are usually indexed under their surname. Saints are indexed under their first name unless cited as objects of veneration, when they are indexed under 'saint'.